Changing Trends in China's Inequality

Changing Trends in China's Inequality

Evidence, Analysis, and Prospects

Edited by

TERRY SICULAR,
SHI LI,
XIMING YUE,
AND
HIROSHI SATO

OXFORD
UNIVERSITY PRESS

Oxford University Press is a department of the University of Oxford. It furthers
the University's objective of excellence in research, scholarship, and education
by publishing worldwide. Oxford is a registered trade mark of Oxford University
Press in the UK and certain other countries.

Published in the United States of America by Oxford University Press
198 Madison Avenue, New York, NY 10016, United States of America.

Library of Congress Cataloging-in-Publication Data
Names: Sicular, Terry, 1955– editor. | Li, Shi, editor. | Yue, Ximing, Sato, Hiroshi editor.
Title: Changing trends in China's inequality : evidence, analysis,
and prospects / edited by Terry Sicular, Shi Li, Ximing Yue and Hiroshi Sato.
Description: 1st Edition. | New York : Oxford University Press, 2020. |
Includes bibliographical references and index.
Identifiers: LCCN 2019034470 (print) | LCCN 2019034471 (ebook) |
ISBN 9780190077938 (hardback) | ISBN 9780190077952 (epub) |
ISBN 9780190077969 (online) | ISBN 9780190077945 (updf)
Subjects: LCSH: China—Economic conditions—2000– |
China—Social policy—21st century. | Equality—China.
Classification: LCC HC427.95 C43273 2019 (print) | LCC HC427.95 (ebook) |
DDC 339.2/20951—dc23
LC record available at https://lccn.loc.gov/2019034470
LC ebook record available at https://lccn.loc.gov/2019034471

1 3 5 7 9 8 6 4 2

Printed by Integrated Books International, United States of America

Contents

Figures

Tables

Preface

This work is the product of the China Household Income Project (CHIP), a long-term collaborative international research project that celebrated its thirtieth anniversary in 2018. The aim of the CHIP and of this work is to provide evidence-based, in-depth analyses of Chinese household incomes, inequality, and related topics. For this purpose, the CHIP has organized a series of large-scale, nationwide household surveys. The first CHIP survey was carried out in 1989 and collected data for 1988. Later rounds of the survey collected data for 1995, 2002, 2007, and 2013.

The chapters in this work are the outcome of mutual cooperation and interaction among members of the CHIP research team. All chapters share in common their use of the CHIP 2013 dataset; most also use earlier rounds of the CHIP survey, especially the the CHIP 2002 and 2007 survey datasets, in order to trace developments over time. The first chapter provides a summary of major findings and background about the survey and measurement issues. Chapter 2 gives an overview of trends in household incomes and inequality in China from 2007 to 2013. These first two chapters establish the basis for and give context to the later chapters. Chapters 3, 4, and 5 look at different facets of distribution among Chinese households from a nationwide perspective: the emergence of a middle class, the distribution of wealth, and the effects of social programs. Chapters 6, 7, and 8 examine inequality and poverty in China's rural and urban sectors. The remaining chapters investigate selected topics in one or the other of the two sectors, including consumption inequality, gender wage inequality, Han-minority income gaps, and the distributional effects of the minimum wage policy. Together, the chapters paint an expansive, detailed picture of the evolution of household income distribution through 2013, a transition year between the end of the Hu Jintao–Wen Jiabao and the start of the Xi Jinping leadership periods. The findings will be of interest to scholars, students, researchers, and policy makers, as well as to interested members of the broader public who wish to understand how Chinese households have fared in the midst of the changing currents in China's economic development and public policies.

This work owes a debt to the researchers who initiated and sustained the CHIP since 1989. In this regard, we acknowledge the special contributions of Keith Griffin, Carl Riskin, and Renwei Zhao, who conceived of and led the early rounds of the project and who trained and inspired the later generations of CHIP researchers. This work builds upon publications based on past rounds of the CHIP survey, especially the following books: *The Distribution of Income in China* (edited by Keith Griffin and Zhao Renwei, St. Martin's Press, 1993); *China's Retreat from Equality: Income Distribution and Economic Transition* (edited by Carl Riskin, Zhao Renwei, and Li Shi, M.E. Sharpe, 2001); *Inequality and Public Policy in China* (edited by Björn A. Gustafsson, Li Shi, and Terry Sicular, Cambridge University Press, 2008); and *Rising Inequality in China: Challenges to a Harmonious Society* (edited by Li Shi, Hiroshi Sato, and Terry Sicular, Cambridge University Press, 2013).

This work and the 2013 CHIP survey on which it is based would not have been possible without substantial funding from the National Natural Science Foundation of China (NSFC Grant No. 71130003/G0311), the Center for International Governance Innovation and Institute for New Economic Thinking (CIGI-INET Grant ID 1306-50307), the Japan Society for the Promotion of Science (JSPS Grant-in-Aid for Scientific Research No. 15H03340 and 24330083), Beijing Normal University, and Beijing Normal University Business School. We thank these organizations for their generous support.

We are especially grateful to the China National Bureau of Statistics (NBS) for its extensive contributions to the 2013 CHIP survey. Former Director Jiantang Ma and former Deputy Director Weimin Zhang, together with other leaders of the NBS, supported and approved of the cooperation on the CHIP survey. The China Economic Analysis and Monitoring Center of the NBS was our direct partner for the survey work, and Center Deputy Director Haifeng Wang and Division Head Ziqing Fan made great efforts throughout the data collection process. The NBS Household Survey Office expended much time and effort, with great care and attention to details, on the survey, providing leadership, expertise, and quality control in many respects, including sample selection, household interviews, and data recording and entry, as well as the questionnaire design, the pre-survey, and the choice of the statistical indicators. Office Director Pingping Wang, Deputy Directors Youjuan Wang and Yi Zhang, and Division Head Wei Wu contributed substantial effort with selfless dedication. In the NBS Office of Household Surveys Yilin Feng, Ran Wang, Jiajia Lian, Jianliang Di, Qian Ma, and others engaged in a large amount of detailed work, often going beyond the call of duty. In addition, the survey would not have been possible without the active cooperation and support of the staff on the household survey teams in each province, city, and county. We gratefully acknowledge the help and support of the many NBS staff and survey workers, from the top down to the ground levels, without whom the survey would not have been possible.

We acknowledge and thank the many faculty and students who contributed to the survey preparation and implementation and the data processing and cleaning. These include faculty members Ximing Yue, Chuliang Luo, Juan Yang, Hui Xu, Haoran He, Zeyun Liu, Minbo Xu, Haiyuan Wan, Yake Wang, Jianguo Wang, and graduate students Xia Gao, Guoqiang Chen, Shanshan Wu, Xiaoxia Liu, Meiting Wang, Meng Cai, Shu Wang, Peng Zhan, Mengbing Zhu, Li Zhang, Liang Xiong, Sui Yang, Xiuna Yang, Yangyang Shen, Chang Yuan, Zihan Nie, Shengfang Zhang, Xiaoren Li, and Zhenjia Yu. We would like to express a special thanks to Xia Gao, who took on a heavy management role and who for the sake of the survey work delayed her thesis defense.

During the process of carrying out the survey, analyzing the data, and writing up the findings, the CHIP team held multiple meetings and workshops. We thank the many colleagues, scholars, and experts who kindly attended these workshops and provided valuable input, including Beijing Normal University Vice Presidents Jianping Ge and Guangju Chen, Dean Desheng Lai, Financial Division Head Yuhong Du, Social Science Division Head Lishuang Fan, National Science Foundation of China Management Division Head Ruoyun Li, Professor Haizheng Li, Professor Wei Zhang, Professor Li Gan, Professor Zhiqiang Liu, and Professor Xiaojun Wang. We also thank the other scholars and researchers who along the way provided support and valuable feedback, including but not limited to Professors Jean Oi, Scott Rozelle, Andrew Walder, and Marty Whyte.

We are grateful to Nancy Hearst, who has carefully edited the chapters and shepherded this book through the publication process. Finally, we thank the many Chinese households that took part in the CHIP survey. This work would not have been possible without their cooperation.

Terry Sicular
Shi Li
Ximing Yue
Hiroshi Sato
May 11, 2019

Contributors and Editors

Sai DING, Professor, Institute of Ethnology and Anthropology, Chinese Academy of Social Sciences

Qin GAO, Professor, School of Social Work, Columbia University

Björn GUSTAFSSON, Professor, Department of Social Work, University of Götenburg; Research Fellow, Institute for the Study of Labor (IZA)

Hisatoshi HOKEN, Professor, School of International Studies, Kwansei Gakuin University

John KNIGHT, Visiting Professor, Department of Economics, Business School, Beijing Normal University; Emeritus Professor of Economics, University of Oxford

Shi LI, Professor, School of Public Affairs, Zhejiang University; Acting Director, China Institute for Income Distribution, Beijing Normal University; Research Fellow, Institute for the Study of Labor (IZA)

Xiaomin LIU, Associate Professor, Institute of Ethnology and Anthropology, Chinese Academy of Social Sciences

Chuliang LUO, Professor, Department of Economics, Business School, Beijing Normal University

Lidan LYU, Associate Professor, Department of Demography, School of Sociology and Population Studies, Renmin University of China

Xinxin MA, Associate Professor, Faculty of Social Sciences, University of Toyama

Hiroshi SATO, Professor, Graduate School of Economics, Hitotsubashi University

Yangyang SHEN, Lecturer, School of Economics and Resource Management, Beijing Normal University; Researcher, China Institute for Income Distribution

Terry SICULAR, Professor, Department of Economics, University of Western Ontario

Jin SONG, Associate Professor, Institute of World Economics and Politics, Chinese Academy of Social Sciences

Lina SONG, Professor, Business School, University of Nottingham

Haiyuan WAN, Associate Professor, Department of Economics, Business School, Beijing Normal University

Yake WANG, Professor, School of Insurance and Economics, University of International Business and Economics

Qingjie XIA, Professor, School of Economics, Peking University

Sui YANG, Assistant Professor, Rural Development Institute, Chinese Academy of Social Sciences

Xiuna YANG, Program Officer, China Development Research Foundation

Ximing YUE, Professor, School of Finance, Renmin University of China

Fuhua ZHAI, Associate Professor, Graduate School of Social Service, Fordham University

Peng ZHAN, Assistant Professor, School of Economics, Nanjing University of Finance & Economics

Abbreviations

CASS	Chinese Academy of Social Sciences
CCP	Chinese Communist Party
CDF	cumulative distribution function
CFPS	China Family Panel Study
CGSS	China General Social Survey
CHFS	China Household Finance Survey
CHIP	China Household Income Project
CHNS	China Health and Nutrition Survey
CIID	China Institute for Income Distribution
CNMWD	Chinese National Minimum Wage Databases
CPI	consumer price index
CRHCPI	Chinese rural poverty household consumption price index
DID	difference in differences
EU	European Union
FDI	foreign direct investment
FGT indexes	Foster-Greer-Thorbecke poverty indexes
GDP	gross domestic product
GE	general entropy
ICP	International Comparison Program
KDE	kernel density estimation
LIS	Luxembourg Income Study
MLD	mean logarithmic deviation
MLSS	Minimum Living Standard Security Scheme
MW	minimum wage
NBS	National Bureau of Statistics
NHFPC	National Health and Family Planning Commission
NLSY	National Longitudinal Study of Youth
NRCMS	New Rural Cooperative Medical System
NRSPS	New Rural Social Pension System
OECD	Organisation for Economic Co-operation and Development
OLS	ordinary least squares
PBC	People's Bank of China
PPI	public pension insurance
PPP	purchasing power parity
PRC	People's Republic of China
QR	quantile regression

RCRE	Research Center of Rural Economy
RMB	*renminbi*
SLC program	sloping land conversion program
SOE	state-owned enterprise
TVE	township and village enterprise
UEBMI	Urban Employee Basic Medical Insurance
URBMI	Urban Resident Basic Medical Insurance

Glossary

dazhuan 大专	vocational post-secondary school
dibao 低保	minimum livelihood guarantee
dinggou renwu 订购任务	compulsory grain purchase quota at below-market prices
duoyu shaoqu fanghuo 多予、少取、放活	"giving more, taking less, and allowing peasants more opportunities"
feigaishui 费改税	tax-for-fee
fupinkuan 扶贫款	poverty alleviation fund
Guojia baqi fupin gongjian jihua (1994–2000) 国家八七扶贫攻坚计划 (1994–2000)	National Eight-Seven Poverty Alleviation Program (1994–2000)
hexie shehui 和谐社会	harmonious society
Hu-Wen xinzheng 胡温新政	Hu-Wen New Policies
huinong 惠农	pro-rural
hukou 户口	household registration system
jiadian xiaxiang 家电下乡	subsidy for electrical appliances

kexue fazhan guan 科学发展观	Scientific Outlook on Development
liang bu chou, san baozhang 两不愁、三保障	achieving no worries about food and clothing, and guarantees for compulsory education, basic medical care, and housing
liangmian yibu 两免一补	"two exemptions and one subsidy"
nongye chanyehua 农业产业化	agro-industrialization
qiche xiaxiang 汽车下乡	subsidy for automobiles
sanwu 三无	"three withouts" (i.e., those without an income, without working ability, or without a legal guardian)
shiqu 市区	city district
shiye danwei 事业单位	public organization
suiji qidian, deng ju chouyang 随机起点，等距抽样	systematic random sampling
wubao 五保	"five guarantees" (i.e., guarantees to provide food, clothing, shelter, medical care, and burial services for rural residents who have no working ability or income source)
wuge yipi 五个一批	"five measurements"
xianyu 县域	county

xiaokang
小康
economically comfortable

yiliao jiuzhu
医疗救助
medical relief fund

yishi yiyi chouzi choulao
一事一议筹资筹劳
one issue, one discussion collection of money and labor services

yiwugong
义务工
unpaid labor contribution

Zhongguo nongcun fupin kaifa gangyao (2001–2010)
中国农村扶贫开发刚要 (2001–2010)
China Rural Poverty Alleviation and Development Outline (2001–2010)

zhongzhuan, jixiao
中专技校
vocational secondary school

Changing Trends in China's Inequality

1

Changing Trends in China's Inequality

Key Issues and Main Findings

Terry Sicular, Shi Li, Ximing Yue, and Hiroshi Sato

1.1 Introduction

In the early 2000s Chinese leaders announced a shift in China's development strategy. During earlier decades, China had emphasized growth of the "productive forces": that is, growth of the gross domestic product (GDP) and its underlying inputs and production processes. As a result, GDP grew rapidly, but the benefits of growth were not distributed equally. Consequently, by the late 1990s income inequality in China was approaching levels found in relatively unequal countries worldwide.

Concerns about rising inequality prompted a reorientation of policies. In 2002–2003, under the new leadership of President Hu Jintao and Premier Wen Jiabao, China launched the Hu-Wen New Policies (*Hu-Wen xinzheng*) and the Scientific Outlook on Development (*kexue fazhan guan*) development strategy, sometimes referred to as the "harmonious society" (*hexie shehui*) programs, which emphasized sustainable and equitable growth. During the following decade, China actively implemented a range of measures, including social welfare programs, social insurance programs, agriculture supports, minimum wage and labor regulations, and poverty interventions to reduce income disparities and to promote shared growth.

According to official statistics, income inequality continued to rise during the next several years, but after peaking in 2008, it began to decline, suggesting that China's harmonious society policy was beginning to yield fruit. The turnaround in inequality raised the possibility that China had reached—or even had already passed—the inflection point in the so-called Kuznets inverted-U curve. The hypothesis behind the Kuznets curve is that inequality rises during the early stages of economic growth, but the emergence of equalizing forces eventually causes inequality to decline.

Terry Sicular, Shi Li, Ximing Yue, and Hiroshi Sato, *Changing Trends in China's Inequality* In: *Changing Trends in China's Inequality*. Edited by: Terry Sicular, Shi Li, Ximing Yue, and Hiroshi Sato, Oxford University Press (2020). © Oxford University Press.
DOI: 10.1093/oso/9780190077938.003.0001

Is the turnaround in China's inequality real? The National Bureau of Statistics (NBS), the government agency that produces official statistics, has not published the details of its calculations and has not made the underlying data available to the public. Furthermore, China's official statistics have been subject to scrutiny and are known to contain biases, raising the question of whether the NBS's estimates of inequality are accurate. If they are accurate, do they represent the beginning of a new, downward trend in inequality or is the decline only temporary? More fundamentally, what would explain the decline in inequality?

This book addresses these questions through in-depth empirical investigations. The analyses in the chapters share the use of household survey data, specifically data from the China Household Income Project (CHIP) surveys, the most recent round of which contains data for 2013. Each chapter uses the CHIP data to examine a different aspect of household income and inequality. Together, the chapters provide a new, detailed picture of trends in Chinese household incomes and inequality through 2013, the end of the Hu-Wen period. They thus provide a baseline for understanding the evolution of incomes and inequality in China during the ensuing Xi Jinping era.

The CHIP surveys are large, nationwide household surveys that since their inception in the 1980s have been a valuable resource for researchers interested in analyzing incomes and inequality in China. Previous rounds of the survey contain data for 1988, 1995, 2002, and 2007. Comprehensive analyses of past rounds can be found in four volumes: *The Distribution of Income in China* (edited by Keith Griffin and Zhao Renwei, 1993); *China's Retreat from Equality: Income Distribution and Economic Transition* (edited by Carl Riskin, Zhao Renwei, and Li Shi, 2001); *Inequality and Public Policy in China* (edited by Björn A. Gustafsson, Li Shi, and Terry Sicular, 2008); and *Rising Inequality in China: Challenges to a Harmonious Society* (edited by Shi Li, Hiroshi Sato, and Terry Sicular, 2013).

Much has changed in China since the 1980s. The economic opportunities for households, as well as the institutional, economic, and policy environments in which households make choices, are very different today from what they were in the past. This book, a sequel to the previous CHIP volumes, analyzes recent trends in income and inequality in the context of such changes.

This first, introductory chapter begins in Section 1.2 with an overview of economic and policy developments relevant to China's inequality and poverty during the period covered by the two most recent CHIP surveys—2007 and 2013. Data and measurement issues are the topic of Sections 1.3 and 1.4, which describe the CHIP survey data and discuss the challenges of accurately measuring household income and inequality. In Section 1.5, we report our estimates, based on the CHIP data, of national income inequality, with comparisons to the official estimates and to estimates based on other independent large-scale household survey datasets that have become available since 2010.

We discuss six cross-cutting findings that emerge from the various chapters in Section 1.6. The first and central finding is that income inequality in China declined during the period of this study. The emergence of a decline, following twenty years of rising inequality, suggests the possibility of a new direction. This finding corroborates the trend reported in the official statistics; however, deeper analysis using the CHIP data raises some questions about the robustness and sustainability of the decline.

Second, the urban/rural income gap, an important facet of inequality in China that was increasing over time, also declined. The analyses in this book provide insights into the factors that contributed to the narrowing of this gap. Third, income gaps between the East, West, and Central regions are no longer a major source of national inequality. Regional income gaps narrowed prior to 2007 and continued to narrow from 2007 to 2013. Consequently, inequality in China is now largely a reflection of inequality within regions.

Fourth, household wealth grew markedly but was distributed unequally. During the period under study, inequality of wealth was a key factor creating upward pressures on national income inequality. Fifth, the rise in household incomes allowed growing numbers of Chinese households to attain levels of income comparable to those of middle-class households in the developed world. By 2013 such households were still in the minority—and were still relatively welloff when they were compared to the rest of the Chinese population—but constituted a substantial share of the population. Sixth, absolute poverty in China continued to decline and by 2013 was quite low. China's war against poverty is not over, however, as stubborn poverty among the remaining poor and rising relative poverty pose continuing challenges.

The chapters in this book contain much substance beyond these six findings and provide details about various aspects of China's changing distributional picture. Topics include an analysis of the factors underlying national trends in income inequality (Chapter 2), China's emerging middle class (Chapter 3), changes in the distribution of wealth (Chapter 4), the effects of social welfare programs (Chapter 5), patterns of income inequality and poverty in rural (Chapters 6 and 7) versus urban (Chapters 8 and 9) China, income gaps between the Han and the ethnic minorities (Chapter 10) and between women and men (Chapter 11), and the distributional effects of the minimum wage (Chapter 12).

1.2 Recent Economic and Policy Developments

In recent years, China has undertaken new policy initiatives and has experienced new economic developments, many of which have had implications for income inequality. In this section, we provide a selective survey of relevant developments. The following chapters will examine aspects of these developments in more depth.

Since 2007 China has undergone several short-term and long-term macroeconomic shifts. The 2008 Global Financial Crisis, a major worldwide economic event, also affected the Chinese economy. Although China's international trade and finance policies insulated the domestic economy from the brunt of the crisis, over the short term China experienced a sharp drop in exports and in inflows of foreign direct investment (FDI). Infrastructure construction under a large government stimulus program moderated the impact of the crisis on China's domestic economy and helped sustain domestic employment, especially for migrant and low-skilled workers. Urban jobs were protected to varying degrees by targeted government policies. For example, in some cities local governments introduced policies to assist "zero-employment families" find work, to provide training programs for the unemployed, to distribute subsidies to enterprises so as to reduce the costs of hiring workers, and to enforce restrictions on firings and layoffs.

Consequently, household employment and earnings weathered the Global Financial Crisis relatively well. During the crisis, urban employment increased so that the number of urban workers rose from 310 million in 2007 to 382 million in 2013, giving an average annual growth rate of 3.5 percent. Furthermore, as shown in the chapters of this book, the wage earnings of urban, rural-to-urban migrant, and rural households were all higher in real terms in 2013 than they were in 2007.

In the wake of the Global Financial Crisis, the path of China's long-term macroeconomic growth shifted to what Chinese leaders refer to as the "New Normal." GDP growth rates slowed to approximately 6 to 7 percent per year, as compared to their earlier double-digit rates. This downshift in macroeconomic growth was accompanied by slower growth in household incomes, especially for urban households (Chapters 2, 6, and 8).

Three decades of rapid economic growth brought major structural changes to the Chinese economy. One such change has been the rise of rural/urban migration and urbanization. Although China's household registration system (*hukou*) still constrains long-term migration and disadvantages rural migrants, the reforms have significantly weakened barriers to labor mobility. Estimates of the scale of migration vary, but by 2013 the population with rural *hukou* living for six months or longer in towns and cities was roughly 140 to 180 million, equivalent to about 10 percent of the national population.

In 2012 China introduced the New Urbanization Program, and in early 2014 it launched the National New Urbanization Plan (2014–2020), which contains a concrete urbanization program involving *hukou* reform, the resettlement of rural communities, and the conversion of rural populations to urban populations so as to achieve the target of an urban population constituting 60 percent of the national population by 2020 (Zhou 2015). The increase in urbanization was already evident during the years covered in this study. According to official statistics, the share of China's urban population rose from 46 percent in 2007 to 54 percent in 2013.[1]

Rising urbanization, together with demographic shifts, has led to marked changes in China's labor supply. Several studies report that China's pool of surplus rural labor has declined (Das and N'Daiye 2013; Cai and Wang 2013; Knight, Deng, and Li 2011; Zhang, Yang, and Wang 2011). Concurrently, the cohorts of young people have become progressively smaller, leading to declining numbers of new entrants to the labor force. Demographers predicted that China's working-age population would reach a turning point in or around 2015 (Lam, Liu, and Schipke 2015; Wang 2011). The official population statistics show that the size of the working-age population (15–64) peaked in 2013 and has since declined.[2] Reports of labor shortages and difficulties in recruiting migrant workers in the cities have become common (e.g., Pomfret and Ruwitch 2014; Rein 2010; Wong 2010; Xinhua 2015). These shifts in labor supply have created upward pressures on wages and may have improved employment opportunities for unskilled and migrant workers.

Education levels in China have been rising, a reflection of government efforts since the late 1990s to expand rural secondary education and university enrollments. The progression rate from junior to senior secondary school rose from 50 percent in 2000 to 81 percent in 2007 and further to 91 percent in 2013.[3] According to UNESCO data, gross enrollment rates in secondary education rose from 61 percent in 2000 to 73 percent in 2007 and further to 96 percent in 2013; tertiary enrollment rates rose from 8 percent in 2000 to 21 percent in 2007 and 30 percent in 2013.[4] This expansion of secondary and tertiary education has helped narrow gaps in education levels (e.g., between women and men). As discussed in later chapters, these changes have had implications for earnings and thus for income and inequality.

During the period under study, China experienced a sharp rise in housing prices. The price increases were related to numerous factors, including urbanization, which drove up urban housing demand and control over the supply of land by different levels of government. Housing price increases have been most extreme in large cities, although reports indicate that they have spread to medium and small cities as well (Chen and Woo 2017).

Rising housing prices have both direct and indirect effects on household incomes and inequality. As explained later in this chapter, the standard definition of household income includes imputed rents from owner-occupied housing. Imputed rents increase as housing prices increase because they are estimated by using data on market rents or the sale price of housing. Changes in housing prices thus directly affect the estimated levels of household income. In addition, because housing is a major component of household wealth, changes in housing prices influence the level and distribution of wealth (see Chapter 4), which in turn affect opportunities for households to earn income.

The previous CHIP book (Li, Sato, and Sicular 2013) discusses changes in China's distributional policies during the period from 2002 to 2007. During those years under the Harmonious Society development strategy, China embarked on an ambitious program to expand coverage of social security and social insurance programs to those who were not previously covered, especially the rural, migrant, and urban informal and unemployed populations. During the period under study here, these efforts continued. Social policies are the focus of Chapter 5, which provides details on the nature of the programs and analysis of their impact on income gaps. Here we provide general background on major developments in these programs after 2007.

In 2009 China adopted the New Rural Pension Scheme, which provided pensions to rural residents who did not have access to urban workers' pension insurance programs. The rural pension scheme expanded rapidly, with coverage increasing from 10 percent of Chinese counties in 2009 to 100 percent in 2012 (Wang 2014). The amount of rural pension payments was low but it increased over time. Though aimed at lower-income households, has the rural pension scheme has not been entirely equitable. Payment levels have differed among provinces and counties, with substantially higher payments in more developed regions. In 2015, for example, rural pension income was 470 yuan per person per month in Beijing and 85 yuan per person per month in the western province of Gansu.[5]

In 2011 China introduced a basic urban pension scheme aimed at urban residents without formal employment who were ineligible for the preexisting employee pension programs. In 2014 the new rural and urban basic pension schemes were merged. Enrollment in the combined rural and urban basic pension programs rose from essentially zero in 2007 to 497.5 million in 2013. As of 2015, enrollment exceeded 500 million people, and pension recipients numbered 148 million.[6] Analyses of the CHIP data reveal evidence of the impact of these pension programs on household income, inequality, and poverty (Chapters 2, 5, 6, and 8).

The government has also expanded health insurance. In 2003 the government launched the New Rural Cooperative Medical System (NRCMS) to reduce the burden of health-care costs on rural households. According to official statistics, the program's coverage increased from 252 million people in 2007 to 487 million people in 2013, with a coverage rate exceeding 95 percent; during the same period, contributions from individuals and governments rose from about 50 yuan per person to over 300 yuan per person (Meng and Xu 2014).[7] In 2007 the government introduced Urban Resident Basic Medical Insurance, a voluntary program providing health insurance to urban residents who did not have formal employment. The program was initially offered in seventy-nine cities, expanded to about one-half of China's cities in 2008, and covered almost all cities in 2009 (Liu and Zhao 2014). Enrollment in the program rose from 43 million people in 2007, its first year, to 296 million people in 2013, and to 377 million people in 2015.[8]

These health insurance programs are financed by a combination of participant contributions and local- and central-government subsidies. Because the participant contributions and the levels of reimbursement vary regionally, the impact of the programs is not uniform. Nevertheless, by increasing the affordability of medical care, these programs have the potential to improve health outcomes and labor productivity, mitigate the economic distress of households facing health problems, and reduce the need for households to save to insure themselves. Through these channels, the programs may have an indirect, positive impact on household income and well-being.

If health insurance reimbursements for medical care are counted as a component of income, these programs will also have a direct impact on measured household income. Prior to 2013, the NBS did not count such reimbursements as income, but this policy changed in 2013. Consequently, part of the growth in household incomes, as shown in the official statistics from 2007 to 2013, reflects the addition of health insurance reimbursements to the official definition of household income. As discussed later, this change and others in the NBS definition of income affect the comparability of NBS household income statistics before and after 2013. For this reason, the CHIP has constructed alternative estimates of household income that treat medical reimbursements and other income components consistently for 2007 and 2013.[9]

A third development in China's social security system has been the implementation of a cash transfer program targeting low-income rural households. The minimum livelihood guarantee, or "*dibao*" program, was first established in cities in 1999, and it was expanded significantly in urban areas in the early 2000s. By 2007, the number of nationwide recipients of the urban *dibao* program was 23 million, but in 2013 there was a modest decline to 21 million. A similar, rural *dibao* program was initiated on a pilot basis in 2004 and it was adopted in nationwide rural areas in 2007. The rural *dibao* program grew rapidly during the period under study, from 36 million recipients in 2007 to 54 million recipients in 2013, an overall increase of 51 percent during a period when the rural population actually decreased by 12 percent. Concurrently, the generosity of the program rose, with rural *dibao* expenditures per recipient increasing from 446 yuan per person per year in 2007 to 1609 yuan per person per year in 2016 (Golan, Sicular, and Umapathi 2017).[10] *Dibao* transfers have consistently been counted as part of household income; therefore, expansion of this program has had both direct and indirect impacts on measured income levels and inequality.

At the same time, the government pursued a "pro-rural" (*huinong*) program to support rural households engaged in agriculture, by means of subsidies for grain production, agricultural inputs, purchase of improved seed varieties, and purchase of agricultural machinery, which together are referred to as the "four subsidies." An additional production subsidy for the conversion of crops to forests on sloped land has been in place since the late 1990s. As discussed in more detail in Chapter 5, the subsidies for grain production, agricultural inputs, and sloped-land conversion take the form of direct cash transfers and are identifiable components of rural household income in the

CHIP 2013 data. In 2013, nearly one-half of the rural households received income from these programs (Chapter 6). The improved seed and machinery subsidies are implicit; that is, they are deducted from the prices based on actual purchases. Although they influence farm income, these amounts are not directly identifiable in the data.

Minimum-wage policies, initially adopted in the 1990s, target the low-wage segment of China's urban labor market. In the early years, minimum-wage levels were low and not strictly enforced. After implementation of the New Labor Contract Law in 2008, enforcement of minimum-wage levels was strengthened. In July 2010 Hainan province and Henan province increased their provincial minimum wages by 30 percent and 33 percent, respectively. In 2011, at least five provinces raised their minimum wages by more than 20 percent, and in 2012–2013 twenty-seven additional provinces also increased their minimum wages (Li, Ye, and Xiong 2014). To some extent, these minimum-wage increases were the result of political competition among local governments in response to the central government's call for a higher wage share in national income. Chapter 12 investigates the consequences of these minimum-wage policies on urban wage distribution (see also Lin and Yun 2016; Li and Ma 2015).

China has pursued an active poverty reduction policy in the rural areas since the 1980s. In the early years, China's rural poverty alleviation strategy sought to develop the local economy. The purpose was to promote economic development in designated poor rural regions and counties, with the idea that low economic development in poor localities was the main cause of poverty. This strategy was successful, with the result that by the 2000s poverty had become more dispersed and a different approach was required. As a result, China's poverty alleviation strategy evolved and began to target smaller areas, e.g., villages instead of counties.

In 2010 the government put forward a new rural strategy for poverty alleviation, outlined in the Poverty Alleviation Program for 2011–2020. Additionally, it increased the rural poverty line to 2300 yuan per person per year, close to the global poverty line of international organizations of US$2 per person per day in purchasing power parity (PPP) terms. As discussed in more detail later in this chapter and in the following chapters, during the period under study absolute poverty in rural China continued to decline. Since then, efforts to combat poverty have continued. For example, at the end of 2013, the government introduced a "precise-targeting" poverty alleviation strategy, which emphasized targeting poor households rather than poor localities. One of the major components of this new strategy is the *dibao* program. Other components include the provision of relief to households with members who have serious illnesses and relocating poor households living in unfavorable environments to better locations.

1.3 The CHIP Data

All the analyses in the following chapters utilize data from the CHIP surveys. The CHIP data are well suited for this purpose. The CHIP surveys are designed to provide detailed household and individual data for research on income distribution and inequality in China, with broad regional coverage.

The CHIP was initiated in the 1980s by researchers at the Chinese Academy of Social Sciences, and in recent years it has been conducted under the auspices of the China Institute for Income Distribution (CIID) at Beijing Normal University. The datasets are available from the CIID.[11] Past rounds of the CHIP survey collected data for 1988, 1995, 2002, and 2007. Descriptions of these rounds can be found in Eichen and Zhang (1993), Li et al. (2008), and Luo et al. (2013). Here we describe the main features of the CHIP surveys, with a focus on CHIP 2013. Individual chapters in this volume discuss additional features related to their respective topics.

The CHIP datasets contain information from two sources. Some variables are provided by the NBS, which collects and collates these variables as part of its annual household survey. Importantly, the NBS variables include household income and expenditures as well as their components. Another set of variables is collected from survey questionnaires designed by the CHIP research team and administered to the households in face-to-face interviews by trained NBS survey workers. The CHIP questionnaires ask for additional information relevant to analyses of income and inequality. Because the circumstances of urban, rural, and rural-to-urban migrant households are not entirely the same, the questionnaires for these three groups are somewhat different. Together, the variables transferred to the CHIP by the NBS and those collected by using the CHIP questionnaires provide rich information about the sample households and their members, including household income and its components; household expenditures and its components; gender, age, education, employment, and *hukou* registration of household members; ownership and values of housing and other assets; participation in social programs and insurance, and so on.

The CHIP survey sample is a subset of the NBS's annual household income and expenditure survey sample. In 2013 the NBS used a nationally integrated sampling frame and stratified random sampling to select its sample. The NBS survey's target sampling unit was the household, and in 2013 it covered 160,000 households in 1,650 county-level administrative units (city districts [*shiqu*] and counties [*xianyu*]) spanning all of China's provinces and provincial-level administrative units. The NBS sample is representative at the provincial and national levels. Prior to 2013 the NBS used separate sample frames for its urban and rural household surveys. Explanation of the NBS household survey framework and methodology can be found in its publications.[12]

The CHIP samples are subsets of the NBS household income and expenditure survey samples. The CHIP provinces are chosen intentionally to span China's three distinct geographic regions—East, Central, and West—so that the survey is representative nationally and for each region. To facilitate analysis of changes over time using the CHIP datasets from 2007 and 2013, most of the provinces in the 2013 survey overlap with those in the 2007 survey. All provinces covered in the 2013 survey except Xinjiang are present in the 2007 survey; all but three of the provinces covered in the 2007 survey (rural Hebei, urban Shanghai, and Fujian) are present in the 2013 survey.

Within each province, the CHIP selected administrative units—city districts and counties—from those in the larger NBS sample by using systematic random sampling (*suiji qidian, deng ju chouyang*). The relative numbers of city districts and counties in each province are based on the shares of the urban versus the rural population within the province, as reported in China's 2010 census.[13] All NBS sample households in the selected administrative units are included in the CHIP 2013 sample.

The full CHIP 2013 sample contains about 20,000 households residing in 233 county-level administrative units in fifteen provinces. With weights, the sample should be representative at the national, regional, and provincial levels. The composition of the CHIP 2013 sample by province and region is shown in Table 1.1.

Households in the CHIP 2013 survey are classified as urban, rural, or migrant on the basis of the criteria shown in Table 1.2, according to which they were administered the relevant questionnaire. Household membership is based on the time spent living within the household. Individuals who resided within the household for over six months of the year were counted as household members.[14]

Table 1.1. CHIP 2013 household sample: Composition by province and region

Province	Region (1 = East; 2 = Central; 3 = West)	Number of administrative units (city districts and counties)	Number of sample households
Beijing	East	7	1145
Guangdong	East	16	1534
Jiangsu	East	21	1485
Liaoning	East	19	1108
Shandong	East	18	1196
Anhui	Central	18	1526
Henan	Central	22	1614
Hubei	Central	16	1289
Hunan	Central	16	1267
Shanxi	Central	16	1276
Chongqing	West	8	988
Gansu	West	11	1006
Sichuan	West	19	1351
Yunnan	West	11	1105
Xinjiang	West	16	1058
Total	All Regions	234	18,948

Notes:

1.) The number of sample households shown in the last column is the number of households for which data were collected by means of the independent CHIP questionnaire (except for Xinjiang, where the CHIP questionnaire could not be administered; however, the NBS provided additional data for Xinjiang from its survey of 1058 households). The number of sample households for which the NBS provided data to the CHIP is similar to these numbers.

2.) The NBS variables are available for all the sample provinces. The CHIP variables are available for fourteen of the sample provinces (but not for Xinjiang).

Some unanticipated challenges arose during the survey. First, although Xinjiang was selected as one of the CHIP sample provinces, the CHIP survey questionnaire could not be administered to the sample households in Xinjiang. To offset this problem, the NBS provided the CHIP with extra information about the Xinjiang sample households from its annual survey. Consequently, the information for the Xinjiang households in the 2013 dataset is not entirely the same as that for the households in the other provinces. For this reason, some chapters in this book do not include Xinjiang in their analyses.

Table 1.2. Classification of urban, rural, and migrant households in the CHIP 2013 survey

Questionnaire administered	Criteria	
	English	Chinese
Urban	Head of household has a non-agricultural *hukou*; place of residence can be either the same or not the same as the place of the *hukou* registration.	户主有非农业户口（包括改为居民户口时的户口性质是非农业户口），包括本地非农业户口(包括改为居民户口时的户口性质是非农业户口）和外地非农业户口(包括改为居民户口时的户口性质是非农业户口）。
Rural	Head of household has an agricultural *hukou*, and the place of residence and the place of the *hukou* registration are the same.	指户主有农业户口(包括改为居民户口时的户口性质是农业户口)而且户口所在地是现住的乡镇（街道）内。
Migrant	Head of household has an agricultural *hukou*, and the place of residence and the place of the *hukou* registration are different.	指户主有农业户口(包括改为居民户口时的户口性质是农业户口)而且户口所在地是现住的乡镇（街道）外。

Note: At the beginning of the survey interview, the enumerator asked the household head for information about his/her *hukou* registration and location of residence. On the basis of this information, the enumerator determined which questionnaire to use, as explained in this table. In locations that had already carried out the *hukou* reform, which eliminates the agricultural versus non-agricultural distinction, the choice of questionnaire was decided on the basis of whether the household head had an agricultural or a non-agricultural *hukou* at the time of the *hukou* reform.

Second, the new, integrated NBS sampling method was designed to better capture rural-to-urban migrant households, but the number of migrant households in the CHIP sample is still smaller than expected. Migrant households in CHIP 2013 account for less than 4 percent of the sample (Table 1.3). The official population statistics, however, report the rural-to-urban migrant population to be about 15 percent of the national population.

In view of the underrepresentation of migrant households in the CHIP 2013 sample and also because the composition of the CHIP sample is not entirely proportional to the composition of the population among regions/provinces and between rural and urban areas as reported in official national population statistics, the CHIP team developed regional/provincial

Table 1.3. Composition of the CHIP sample among urban, rural, and migrant households

	Number of households	% of sample
Urban	7174	38.0
Rural	10,973	58.1
Migrant	726	3.9
Total	18,873	100.0

Source: CHIP 2013 survey, unweighted.

and rural-to-urban migrant sampling weights based on the official population census and inter-census sample surveys. Use of weights is important for analyses that incorporate data spanning regions and sectors and that use data from past rounds of the CHIP surveys to track trends over time.[15] Most chapters in this book employ weights in their analyses.

1.4 Measurement of Income

The NBS publishes well-regarded income statistics that are often cited. It constructs these statistics by using household-level income data from its annual household surveys according to its definition of household income. The income data are collected systematically by using real-time diaries and following well-established practices.

Over time the NBS has taken steps to update and improve its measurement of household income. In 2013, along with implementation of its integrated household survey sampling design, the NBS adopted a new definition of disposable household income per capita. The new income definition, like the one it replaced, is comprehensive and covers both cash and in-kind income (including wage earnings and salaries), net income from household operations (including agricultural and non-agricultural businesses), net income from properties and assets, and transfers, minus taxes. Nevertheless, because of the change in definition, from 2013 onward the NBS estimates of income and its components are not fully consistent with those for the earlier years, a factor that may affect income comparisons across time.

A major aim of the CHIP research has been to use the detailed, household-level information in its surveys to evaluate the official NBS estimates of household incomes and to provide alternative, improved estimates. In view of the 2013 change in the NBS income definition, the CHIP team inspected the details of the new versus the old NBS income definitions. The team then used CHIP data to construct largely consistent, adjusted estimates of NBS household income per capita for 2007 and 2013. Furthermore, an error was found in the NBS calculation of imputed rents on owner-occupied housing. The NBS includes this estimate of imputed rents in its 2013 definition of income but not in its 2007 definition of income. Therefore, the CHIP team subtracted the NBS estimates of imputed rent from the NBS 2013 income.

Except for the exclusion of the NBS's estimate of imputed rents, the CHIP adjustments to NBS income largely follow the 2013 income definition.[16] Hereafter, we refer to the original, unadjusted NBS income variable as "NBS income" and the adjusted, consistent NBS income variable as "adjusted NBS income." Further details about construction of the adjusted NBS income variable are provided in Chapter 2.

As discussed in previous CHIP research publications, an ongoing problem with the NBS household income statistics is that the NBS definition of household income is not fully consistent with standard international practices. Over time, with China's economic changes and statistical improvements, the NBS income measurement has come closer to international practices. The major remaining differences are treatment of imputed rents on owner-occupied housing and implicit subsidies for accommodations rented at below-market rents. Imputed rents were not included in NBS income prior to 2013; in 2013 imputed rents were included in NBS income, but only for urban households, and they were calculated incorrectly. Implicit subsidies on subsidized rental housing were not included in NBS income either in 2013 or in earlier years.

International studies typically recommend including imputed rents on owner-occupied housing as a component of household income (Canberra Group 2001; Smeeding and Weinberg 2001; European Commission 2003). Inclusion of imputed rents is required to ensure comparable treatment of households that live in owned versus rented housing. This necessity can be seen by considering a simple example. Suppose two households are identical except that one holds its savings in a bank account and rents its accommodation, and the other owns its accommodation and holds its savings in the form of equity in its housing. The interest that the first household earns on its bank savings is counted as part of its income. The second household does not earn interest on the equity in its housing. To make the income of the two households consistent, the return on the second household's housing equity should be counted as part of its income. Imputed rents on owner-occupied housing are the estimated returns on such housing equity.

Several methods are commonly used to estimate imputed rents on owner-occupied housing (Sato, Sicular, and Yue 2013; Frick, Goebel, and Grabka 2006). The rental-equivalence approach sets the imputed rent equal to the rent that the owner-occupied housing would earn if it were rented out on the market. The opportunity-cost approach sets the imputed rent equal to the return that the household would earn if its housing equity were invested in a long-term, relatively stable investment. Each of these approaches has both strengths and weaknesses. The CHIP team used the rental-equivalence approach for urban (including migrant) homeowner households and used the opportunity-cost approach for rural homeowner households. Estimates of market rents and market prices of housing were self-reported by the households.[17]

With respect to implicit rental subsidies on below-market rental housing, the usual approach is to subtract the rent that was actually paid by the household from an estimate of the market rent for the household's accommodation (Frick, Goebel, and Grabka 2006). Following standard practices, the CHIP team used the 2007 and 2013 data for urban rental households to estimate a multivariate hedonic regression of rents (self-reported) as a function of the housing characteristics and of the neighborhood of residence. The results of this regression were then used to predict the market rent for each urban rental household. The amounts of the predicted rent were then compared to the rent payments reported by the households. In cases in which the reported rents were less than the predicted rents, the household was considered to have received an implicit rental subsidy. The amount from the housing rent subsidy was set equal to the difference between the predicted and the reported rents.

Using these estimates of imputed rents for owner-occupied housing and of implicit subsidies on urban rental housing, the CHIP constructed an alternative measure of household income, hereafter referred to as "CHIP income." CHIP income is equal to the adjusted NBS income plus the CHIP estimates of imputed rents and implicit urban rental housing subsidies. By 2007 and 2013 the amount from urban housing rental subsidies was on average small (less than 1 percent of urban incomes in both years), so most of the difference between the CHIP income and the adjusted NBS income is due to imputed rents on owner-occupied housing.

Which income definition—NBS income, adjusted NBS income, or CHIP income—is best? We prefer CHIP income because it is consistent over time and closest to international income measurement standards. Nevertheless, a choice among the three income definitions is a matter of judgment and will depend on the research question and the purpose of the analysis. Chapter 2 discusses in some detail these three income calculations and reports estimates of income inequality for each of them.

Most of the analyses in this book examine inequality of income per capita: that is, household income divided by the number of household members. This approach treats all household members as identical in terms of their utility and needs. Although this treatment is standard in the litera-ture, some researchers have pointed out that income per capita ignores intra-household inequality as well as household economies of scale. An alternative approach is to adjust household size by using equivalent scales, which assign different weights to different household members (e.g., higher weights for adults as opposed to children, or for the first as opposed to additional house-hold members). In light of these considerations, some chapters in this book employ equivalence scales.

1.5 Estimates of China's Income Inequality: CHIP, NBS, and Others

In recent years survey research in China has expanded and the number of published estimates of China's national Gini coefficient has grown. Differences among these estimates have led to lively debates about the true level of inequality. Official estimates of China's national Gini coef-ficient have been available since 2013, at which time the NBS released estimates going back to 2003. Previously, the NBS published separate Gini coefficients for urban and rural income inequality but did not publish a Gini coefficient for national income inequality. Some observers have spec-ulated that the absence of an official estimate of the national Gini coef-ficient was because of the politically sensitive nature in China of rising income inequality.

The official estimates of China's national Gini coefficient are shown in Figure 1.1. The official Gini rose from 0.479 in 2003 to 0.491 in 2008. After 2008 it declined, falling below 0.47 in 2014 and thereafter fluctuating be-tween 0.46 and 0.47.

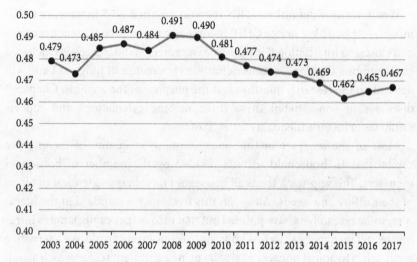

Fig. 1.1 Official estimates of China's national Gini coefficient, 2003–2017

Sources: 2003–2015 are from Department of Household Surveys, National Bureau of Statistics (2016, p. 407). The information for 2016 is from a press conference on China's economic situation by NBS Director Ning Jizhe, January 20, 2017. See http://finance.china.com.cn/news/gnjj/20170120/4077373.shtml. Accessed July 17, 2017.

How do the CHIP estimates compare to the official estimates? Previous CHIP studies report estimates of China's Gini coefficient that, like the NBS estimates, increased through 2007. The CHIP estimates (calculated by using the CHIP income definition) rose from a low of 0.38 in 1988 to 0.45 in 1995, 0.46 in 2002, and 0.49 in 2007 (Griffin and Zhao 1993, p. 50; Riskin, Zhao, and Li 2001; Gustafsson, Li, and Sicular 2008, p. 19; Li, Sato, and Sicular 2013, p. 31).

Do the CHIP estimates for 2013 corroborate the decline in inequality after 2008? Figure 1.2 shows the CHIP estimates for 2007 and 2013 alongside the NBS estimates for the same years. The CHIP estimates calculated by using the NBS income definition are close to the NBS estimates. This result is not surprising, given that they use the NBS income variable and the CHIP sample is a subsample of the NBS household survey sample. Adjustments to NBS income to make the variable consistent over time slightly increase inequality in 2007 and noticeably decrease inequality in 2013, the latter reflecting the subtraction of the NBS estimates of imputed rents on owner-occupied housing. The inequality of CHIP income, which includes imputed rents and implicit housing subsidies, is again higher in 2007 and slightly lower in 2013.

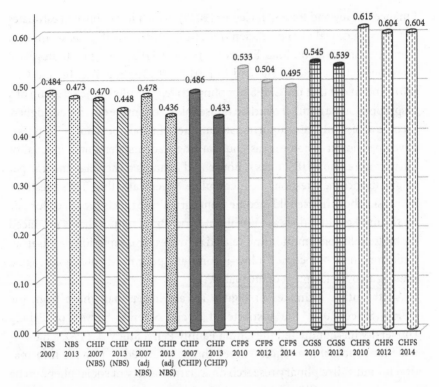

Fig. 1.2 Alternative estimates of China's national Gini coefficient

Notes: NBS refers to the NBS estimates based on its household income and expenditure survey; CHIP (NBS) refers to the CHIP estimates using the CHIP survey data and NBS income; CHIP (adj NBS) uses the CHIP survey data and adjusted NBS income; and CHIP (CHIP) uses the CHIP survey data and CHIP income. CFPS refers to estimates based on the China Family Panel Study survey, CGSS refers to estimates based on the China General Social Survey, and CHFS refers to estimates based on the China Household Finance Survey. See the text and Chapter 2 for more details about the NBS, adjusted NBS, and CHIP income definitions.

Sources: NBS estimates are from Department of Household Surveys, National Bureau of Statistics (2016); CHIP estimates are from Chapter 2; CFPS estimates are from Kanbur, Wang, and Zhang (2017); CGSS estimates are from Xie and Zhou (2014); and CHFS estimates are from Gan (2017).

Importantly, though, all three sets of CHIP estimates show a decline in inequality from 2007 to 2013.

In recent years several other independent, large-scale survey projects that collect nationwide information about household incomes have been launched. Estimates of China's Gini coefficient based on data from these surveys are included in Figure 1.2. The highest estimates are those by the Southwestern University of Finance and Economics, China Household

Finance Survey and Research Center (2012), which has published estimates of China's national Gini coefficient for 2010, 2012, and 2014, based on data from the China Household Finance Survey (CHFS). Several studies have questioned its estimates. Yue and Li (2013a, 2013b) and Yue, Li, and Gao (2013) point out that the CHFS sampling strategy results in the selection of a disproportionate number of urban households from more developed, higher-income areas and a disproportionate number of rural households from less-developed, lower-income areas, thus causing an overstatement of inequality. Furthermore, the CHFS focus is household finances rather than income per se, and its income questions are incomplete. Specifically, the CHFS question-naire asks about household income from agriculture that is produced for sale on the market but it does ask not about agricultural output that is produced for household consumption and related activities. This omission results in an understatement of income for low-income and poor rural households, again causing an overstatement of inequality.

All the other estimates in Figure 1.2 are lower than those from the CFHS. Since 2010, the Institute of Social Science Survey of Peking University has conducted the China Family Panel Study (CFPS), a nation-wide longitudinal household survey that is intended to provide informa-tion for multidisciplinary research on a "large variety of social phenomena in contemporary China" (Xie and Hu 2014, p. 3). Gini estimates based on the CFPS are available for 2010, 2012, and 2014. The China General Social Survey (CGSS) was launched in 2003, and in recent years it has been conducted annually under the auspices of the National Survey Research Center at Renmin University. It is a nationwide repeated cross-section survey intended for general research on social issues. Gini estimates based on the CGSS are available for 2010 and 2012.

CFPS and CGSS estimates for both years are in the range of 0.5, consider-ably lower than those based on the CHFS but higher than those based on the NBS and CHIP, reflecting differences in the samples and income measure-ment. In all cases, however, inequality declines.

Different datasets and different estimates of national inequality of course have different strengths and weaknesses. In our view, for the purpose of ana-lyzing household income and inequality the CHIP has several advantages. First, the CHIP income data are collected in real time by means of diaries and detailed, disaggregated questions. Although the diary method has some drawbacks, it allows for a fuller accounting of income, especially for households with multiple or informal sources of income from farming, self-employment, or household businesses, which are common among rural and migrant households that are generally at the middle and bottom of the income distribution. The income of these types of households tends to be understated by surveys that use the year-end recall method, such as the CFPS, CGSS, and CHFS surveys.

Second, the CHIP surveys were designed for the purpose of measuring household income and inequality. Consequently, they include questions that ask for information specific to these concerns. Using this information, the CHIP researchers have been able to calculate household income in a way that is consistent across time and that follows international income measurement practices and produce estimates by using alternative definitions so as to determine the sensitivity of China's Gini estimates to different approaches (see Chapter 2).

Additional strengths of the CHIP include the following: a.) the data were collected via face-to-face household interviews conducted by professional survey enumerators, with oversight by the CHIP research team; b.) the surveys cover a long span of years in a consistent way; and c.) the sample size is large and has broad regional coverage. Although this approach is not unique to the CHIP, other household surveys do not combine all three of these features.

Of course, no survey data are perfect, including the CHIP data. The fact that the CHIP surveys are cross-sectional rather than longitudinal makes it difficult to identify causality and to investigate questions about income mobility. The content of the CHIP surveys has evolved over time in response to changes in the Chinese economy and the research interests of the CHIP team as well as to changes in survey costs and funding, the political environment, and other considerations. Information in the datasets has also changed, and some rounds of the survey omit information collected in other rounds. Such considerations affected the CHIP 2007 survey, so some chapters in this book present findings based on data from the CHIP 2002 and the CHIP 2013 but not the CHIP 2007.

Because they are drawn from the NBS household survey samples, the CHIP data share the weaknesses of the NBS surveys. In this regard, two major issues in the latest rounds of the CHIP survey are the representativeness of the migrant household sample and the understatement of the incomes of the richest households. Chapter 2 discusses these issues more fully. Later chapters discuss both the weaknesses and strengths of the CHIP survey data specific to the topics of analysis.

1.6 Main Findings

The chapters in this book follow a logical, overall structure. The first set of chapters—Chapters 2 through 5—look at distributional issues in China from a national perspective. Chapter 2 presents the CHIP's central estimates of national income inequality for 2007 and 2013. It analyzes key factors contributing to national inequality, with attention to the changing sources of household income, income gaps between and within regions, and income differences among the urban, rural, and rural-to-urban migrant populations. It also discusses data and measurement issues and presents alternate estimates to explore the robustness of the central estimates. The chapter thus provides background for the chapters that follow.

Chapters 3, 4, and 5 each examine a different facet of China's national income distribution. Chapter 3 looks at the emergence of China's middle class, Chapter 4 looks at the inequality of household wealth, and Chapter 5 looks at the distributional role of social programs for China's urban and rural populations.

In view of the importance of China's rural/urban division to national inequality as well as the unique features of each of these sectors, the following four chapters examine the rural and urban sectors separately. Chapters 6 and 7 examine inequality and poverty in the rural sector; Chapters 8 and 9 focus on the urban sector.

The remaining chapters in the book investigate additional selected topics—income gaps between the Han majority and the ethnic minorities in rural China (Chapter 10), the gender wage gap in urban China (Chapter 11), and the impact of the minimum wage on wage inequality in urban China (Chapter 12).

The chapters share the use of the CHIP data and fit into a broad organizational structure, but they differ in their measurement choices, methodologies, and approaches. For example, some chapters use the CHIP income definition and others use the NBS income definition, some include rural-to-urban migrants in the analysis and others do not, different chapters employ somewhat different inequality and poverty indexes, and so on. In these regards the chapters resemble the diversity of approaches in the broader literature on inequality and poverty. This diversity reflects legitimate differences of opinion about data, methods, and interpretations.

The choices in each chapter of this volume reflect the judgments of the respective authors and yield conclusions that are not always uniform or comparable. Despite these differences, together the chapters give a broadly consistent picture of the major patterns in China's income distribution and yield six main findings.

Finding 1: Income inequality declined from 2007 to 2013, suggesting the possibility of a new trend.

Our base estimates show a distinct decline in national inequality from 2007 to 2013 (see Chapter 2). The decline in the Gini coefficient is in the range of 5 percent to 11 percent, depending on the definition of income. The decline in inequality as measured by using other inequality indexes is larger, ranging from 8 percent to more than 20 percent. The decline is also evident in the official NBS and alternative independent estimates (Figure 1.2).

Further analysis in Chapter 2 raises questions about the robustness of the decline. Adjusting for geographic differences in the cost of living reduces the magnitude of the decline; adjustment for the undercounting of the income of ultra-rich households points to the possibility of an increase in inequality. These adjustments are only suggestive, as they are based on incomplete information and strong assumptions, but they indicate that, at least in part, the decline reflects differential changes in the cost of living among regions and the growing importance (and underrepresentation) of the top tail of the income distribution.

One can also question the statistical significance of the measured decline in inequality. Yang and Yang (2015) use bootstrap methods and the CHIP 2007 data to estimate confidence intervals for the official estimates of the national Gini coefficient from 2008 to 2013. They conclude that some of the annual declines in the Gini during these years are not statistically significant. Furthermore, the presence of disequalizing processes (see Finding 4) and the recent uptick in the official Gini estimates after 2014 (Figure 1.1) raise concerns about whether the decline in national inequality in China from 2007 to 2013 will be sustainable over the long term.

Regardless of these concerns, the decline in the CHIP's base estimates of national inequality is important and noteworthy. This is the first decline in the CHIP's estimates of national inequality since its inception in the late 1980s. Moreover, the decline was accompanied by equalizing shifts in the underlying structure of Chinese household incomes. The analyses in this book find across-the-board reductions in the inequality of most components of household income (Chapter 2) and narrowing income gaps between the urban and rural populations (Finding 2), the East/Central/West regions (Finding 3), rural Han and ethnic minority groups (Chapter 10), and the wage earnings of urban men and women (Chapter 11).

Factors contributing to these equalizing shifts include the large government stimulus program following the 2008 World Financial Crisis and recent demographic shifts that have benefited lower-income earners. Government investments in social welfare programs initiated under Hu Jintao and Wen Jiabao have continued and expanded, with positive distributional consequences (Chapter 5). These and other contributing factors are examined in later chapters.

Finding 2: The urban/rural income gap narrowed.

Past increases in national inequality have been closely associated with the substantial, ongoing widening of the gap between urban and rural incomes. According to CHIP estimates, by 2007 the average urban household income per capita reached 4.0 times that of rural households, an extremely high ratio by international standards.[18] From 2007 to 2013, however, the trend was reversed and the income gap between rural and urban households narrowed markedly to 2.6, a ratio not seen in the CHIP data since the first round of the survey in 1988. This reversal is robust across different income definitions and for adjustments for cost of living differentials (Chapter 2); it is also evident in the official data published by the NBS. The narrowing of the urban/rural gap is an important factor underlying the decline in national inequality from 2007 to 2013.

The decline of the urban/rural gap was the result of faster growth in the per capita income of rural households than in that of urban households (Chapters 2, 6, and 8). From 2007 to 2013 rural incomes rose at an average annual rate exceeding 10 percent (in constant prices), substantially faster than the growth in previous years. The largest contributor to rural income growth was wage income, reflecting the tightening labor market for low-skilled and rural workers after the financial crisis. Rapid growth is also seen in most other sources of rural income, including income from assets, transfers, pensions, and non-agricultural businesses. The only major source of rural income that grew slowly was income from farming. Further analysis of rural incomes can be found in Chapters 2 and 6.

We note that although urban incomes grew more slowly than rural incomes from 2007 to 2013, they nevertheless increased at a reasonable clip—about 5 percent per year in real terms. Wage earnings per urban wage earner grew more rapidly than total income per capita. Slower growth in total income per capita than wage earnings per worker was due to a rising share of urban household members without wage employment, e.g., those who were self-employed or were pensioners. (See Chapter 8.)

Although the urban/rural income gap narrowed, income inequality within urban areas and within rural areas continued to expand. From 2007 to 2013 the Gini coefficient of income inequality within urban areas rose from 0.34 to 0.37 and that within rural areas rose from 0.37 to 0.41 (Chapters 2, 6, and 8).

Finding 3: Income gaps between the East, West, and Central regions shrank and by 2013 were a minor source of national inequality.

During the first decades of the reform period, economic growth in East China outpaced that in the other regions, leading to a widening of regional income differences. Since 2000 the West and Central regions have been catching up with the East. Analyses of the CHIP data for 2002 and 2007 found that the regional income gaps had narrowed (Li, Luo, and Sicular 2013). The chapters in this volume find that this trend continued from 2007 to 2013. Notably, from 2007 to 2013 household incomes in the West basically caught up with those in the Central region, and the East's lead over the other regions continued to shrink. In 2007 the average household income per capita in the East was nearly double that in the Central region and more than double that in the West. In 2013 income in the East was only 50 to 60 percent higher than that in the Central and West regions. After adjustment for regional differences in cost of living, 2013 income in the East was only 20–30 percent higher than that in the other regions. (See Chapter 2.)

This ongoing narrowing of the regional income gaps contributed to the decline in national inequality from 2007 to 2013. By 2013, interregional income gaps contributed less than 10 percent of national inequality (only 4 percent after adjustments for regional differences in the cost of living) (Chapter 2; Li, Luo, and Sicular 2013).[19]

The shrinking regional income gaps reflect several factors. One is the expanding interregional flow of labor, which has contributed to the narrowing of regional wage gaps. Another is the government's regional development policies, including the Western Development Strategy, which was implemented to support economic growth in the West (Li, Sato, and Sicular 2013; Liu, Wang, and Hu 2009). A third factor is the relocation of factories and businesses from higher-wage provinces in the East to lower-wage Central and West provinces. Under these circumstances, in the foreseeable future national inequality will very likely be driven by inequality within, rather than among, the East, Central, and West regions.

Finding 4: Household wealth grew markedly over time and became a key factor contributing to income inequality.

The CHIP 2002 and CHIP 2013 datasets contain detailed information on the components of household wealth, including the value of household holdings of real estate, financial assets, productive assets, and durable consumer goods. As a result, for these two years it is possible to estimate the total value and distribution of household net wealth. Chapter 4, which focuses on wealth inequality, reports that from 2002 to 2013 Chinese household wealth grew at an average annual rate of 17 percent, outpacing growth in household income and GDP. Income derived from wealth also grew rapidly, such that by 2013, on average, asset income accounted for 17 percent of total household income.[20]

Household wealth in China is not distributed equally. Inequality of wealth as measured by the Gini coefficient and calculated with the CHIP data was 0.62 in 2013 (Chapter 4). But the actual level of wealth inequality was likely higher than this, due to an underrepresentation of the wealthiest households in the CHIP sample. Chapter 4, using several different approaches to adjust the estimates for nonresponses and underreporting, reveals that such adjustments yield a Gini coefficient of wealth inequality in the range of 0.63 through 0.72. With or without such adjustments, inequality of wealth remains considerably higher than inequality of income.

The expansion of household wealth in China is a relatively new phenomenon that emerged in the early 2000s, following the privatization of housing and the development of housing and financial markets. Substantial price increases for real estate and other assets in the ensuing years led to rapid increases in the value of household-owned assets, especially in the urban areas (see Chapter 4). Housing ownership remains the single largest component of household wealth. Although housing wealth is not distributed equally, near universal home ownership in China means that virtually all households, both rich and poor, hold wealth.

This expansion of household wealth has had implications for income inequality. CHIP estimates reveal that in 2007 income from assets contributed 11 percent of national income inequality and in 2013 income from assets contributed 19 percent of national income inequality (Chapter 2). Because asset income remained one of the most unequally distributed components of income, this increase occurred even though during this same period income from assets became more equally distributed (Chapter 2). Short-term measures to slow price increases in real-estate markets or to fight corruption may have had a temporary cooling effect on the disequalizing impact of wealth, but without longer-term systematic measures, such as property or inheritance tax policies. These trends in wealth holdings will pose a considerable challenge to future income distribution in China.

Finding 5: The number of households attaining levels of income comparable to those of middle-class households in the developed world grew rapidly and for the first time constituted a substantial share of the population.

Because of rapid macroeconomic growth, between 2007 and 2013 China moved up the ranks in the World Bank's country classifications, from a lower-middle-income country to an upper-middle-income country. Concurrently, a growing proportion of Chinese households joined the ranks of the global middle class. Chapter 3 analyzes trends in China's middle class as defined in relation to international standards: that is, as being neither poor nor rich relative to the median income in the developed world (the European Union). By this definition, China's middle class was equal to only 7 percent of its population in 2007 but it expanded to 19 percent in 2013. Thus, the period under study saw a new development in China—the emergence of a substantial middle class with incomes comparable to those of the middle classes in higher-income countries.

Further analysis reveals that the Chinese middle class is largely an urban phenomenon. In 2013 90 percent of China's middle-class population was urban. One-third of China's urban population was middle class, as compared to only 4 percent of China's rural population (Chapter 3). China's middle class, so defined, remains relatively well off by domestic standards. Consequently, growth of this middle class does not explain the decline in national income inequality from 2007 to 2013, which instead reflects the rapid growth of incomes at the bottom half of China's domestic income distribution (Chapter 2). It is worth noting, moreover, that China's middle class has a relatively high savings rate, which raises doubts about whether the expansion of China's middle class will be an engine for future consumption-driven macroeconomic growth.

Finding 6: The population living in absolute poverty continued to decline and it is now relatively small, but the severity of poverty among those who remain poor and the increase in relative poverty pose future challenges.

In past decades, China made great strides in reducing the number and proportion of people living in absolute poverty. For example, as measured by using the current official poverty line, the incidence of absolute poverty in rural China fell from 76 percent in 1988 to 31 percent in 2002, 19 percent in 2007, and 9 percent in 2013 (Chapter 7). The share of the urban population living in absolute poverty, which was lower than that in the rural areas, shows a similar downward trend (Chapter 8).[21]

Estimates of poverty depend on the choice of the poverty line and the poverty index. The poverty line can be set equal to an absolute level of income (an absolute poverty line) or it can be set relative to the median income (a relative poverty line). The poverty index can measure the proportion of the population living below the poverty line (the poverty rate or the head-count ratio) or it can be a measure of the depth (the poverty gap) or the severity (the squared poverty gap) of poverty.

As discussed in Chapters 7 and 8, poverty declined in terms of the absolute-poverty head count. Estimates of the depth and severity of absolute poverty, however, reveal only minor changes and in some instances they increased. These findings point to the challenges of addressing the stubborn causes of poverty among households that remain poor.

Furthermore, Chapters 7 and 8 report increases in relative poverty from 2007 to 2013. As countries develop and move into upper-middle and high levels of GDP per capita, policy makers turn their attention from absolute to relative poverty.

1.7 Conclusions

The analyses in this book report new and encouraging trends in China's inequality between 2007 and 2013. National income inequality (at least by standard estimates) declined, the urban/rural income gap narrowed substantially, and a significant middle class emerged. This period also saw an ongoing decline of absolute poverty and a further catch-up of Central and West household incomes, as compared to those in the East.

Nevertheless, challenges remain. We find that the decline in inequality is not robust to adjustments for changes in the relative costs of living or for the underrepresentation of incomes at the top tail of the distribution. Furthermore, deeper analysis raises questions about the sustainability of the decline. Growth in, and the unequal distribution of, household wealth has become and is likely to continue to be a disequalizing force. Non-market, nontransparent processes contribute to the accumulation of household wealth, but as yet few mechanisms or policies exist to counteract the rising wealth inequality. Also, stubborn poverty among the remaining poor and rising rates of relative poverty represent new challenges.

The Chinese government has pursued a broad array of policies to address income inequality and poverty. The impact of China's distributional policies has been uneven across programs, regions, and groups, but the analyses in this book indicate that, on balance, such programs have benefited lower-income households and have contributed to the decline in inequality. In light of ongoing disequalizing mechanisms, together with the uptick in official estimates of inequality since 2014 and the slowing macroeconomic growth, continued policy efforts will be needed.

Such policy efforts will be most effective if they are based on careful empirical analysis. The analyses in this book provide a starting point, but they leave many questions unanswered. What factors underlie the recent rapid growth in rural incomes, and is such growth sustainable? How exactly do specific policy programs—e.g., *dibao*, pensions, and taxation—influence incomes? What are the inequality implications of broader macroeconomic trends, such as the slowing GDP growth, migration and urbanization, rising levels of education, and the aging population? Further research and ongoing data-collection efforts, such as those by the CHIP team and other researchers, are needed to answer these questions and to determine whether inequality in China has indeed passed a turning point and will continue to decline in the future.

Notes

1. See Table 2-1, http://www.stats.gov.cn/tjsj/ndsj/2016/indexeh.htm. Accessed June 14, 2017.
2. See Table 2-5, http://www.stats.gov.cn/tjsj/ndsj/2016/indexeh.htm. Accessed June 14, 2017.
3. See Table 21-23, http://www.stats.gov.cn/tjsj/ndsj/2016/indexeh.htm. Accessed June 14, 2017.
4. See http://data.worldbank.org/indicator/SE.SEC.ENRR?locations=CN. Accessed June 14, 2017.
5. For pension income in Gansu, see http://www.10zk.com/news/194566.html. Accessed July 17, 2017. For pension income in Beijing, see http://www.spicezee.com/zhishi/yanglao/103950.html. Accessed July 5, 2017.
6. Statistics on pension program enrollments are from Tables 24-29 and 24-31, http://www.stats.gov.cn/tjsj/ndsj/2016/indexeh.htm. Accessed June 15, 2017.
7. See Table 22-28, http://www.stats.gov.cn/tjsj/ndsj/2014/indexch.htm. Accessed June 15, 2017.

8. See Table 24-29, http://www.stats.gov.cn/tjsj/ndsj/2016/indexeh.htm. Accessed June 16, 2017.

9. The CHIP datasets contain information on medical reimbursements in 2013 but not in 2007, so the alternative CHIP income definitions exclude medical reimbursements in both years.

10. See Tables 22-24 and 2-1, http://www.stats.gov.cn/tjsj/ndsj/2016/indexeh.htm. Accessed June 16, 2017.

11. The datasets and related information are also available at http://www.ciidbnu.org/chip/index.asp. Accessed November 20, 2019.

12. See National Bureau of Statistics (2012, 2014), and http://www.stats.gov.cn/tjsj/ndsj/2014/indexeh.htm. Accessed June 16, 2017.

13. The procedure used to select the CHIP 2013 sample within each province involved several steps. First, the sample size for each province was set roughly in accordance with its population. Second, within each province the shares of urban n_u versus rural n_r sample households—that is, households in city districts (*shiqu*) versus counties (*xianyu*)—was decided on the basis of the shares of urban versus rural populations, as reported in the 2010 population census. Third, separately for the NBS sample city districts (*shiqu*) and counties (*xianyu*) within each province, the average number of NBS sample households per district and county (m_u and m_r respectively) was calculated. Fourth, the number of urban districts (c_u) and counties (c_r) selected from the NBS sample in each province was set equal to the ratio of the preceding numbers ($c_u = n_u/m_u$ and $c_r = n_r/m_r$). Last, by the use of systematic random sampling, within each sample province c_u city districts from the NBS sample city districts, and c_r sample counties from the NBS sample counties were selected.

14. College students living away from home are counted as household members.

15. For a detailed explanation of the weights, see Song, Sicular, and Yue (2013) and Yue and Sicular (2016).

16. For one or two relatively minor items, such as medical insurance reimbursements, the necessary data are not available for 2007 but are available for 2013; for these items, the 2013 income was adjusted to follow the NBS 2007 income definition.

17. The rental-equivalent approach was used for urban households so that the estimates of urban imputed rents were not distorted by the recent rapid increases in the sales price of urban housing (rents tend to be more stable than housing prices). The opportunity-cost approach was used for rural households because rental markets in rural areas are not well developed. In some rural areas where the households did not know the sale value of their housing, they were asked to estimate the cost of replacing their dwellings, information that was then used for the calculation. Note that the CHIP team calculated alternative estimates of incomes and inequality in which the imputed rents for both urban and rural households were calculated by using the opportunity-cost approach. These estimates yielded a somewhat larger urban/rural gap and a higher level of national inequality, but these factors did not alter the trends in inequality over time.

18. The gaps reported here are calculated as the ratio of average per capita income of formal urban households to the average per capita income of rural households.

Including rural-to-urban migrant households in the calculation somewhat reduces the ratio but it does not change the trend over time. See Chapter 2 for estimates that include migrants.
19. Different income definitions and adjustments for differences in the cost of living among regions change the size of the regional income gaps but do not alter the trends. Adjustments for differences in the cost of living reduce the contribution of regional income gaps to national inequality to less than 5 percent. See Chapter 2.
20. Asset income here includes income from imputed rents on owner-occupied housing plus income from other assets. See Chapter 2.
21. Note that the poverty line used for urban China in Chapter 8 is higher than the poverty line used for rural China in Chapter 7. Each chapter explains and justifies its choice of an absolute poverty line.

References

Cai, F. and M. Wang (2013). *Nongcun laodongli zhuanyi xianzhuang yu quzhi* (The current situation and trends in rural labor transfers). Beijing: Zhongguo shehui kexue wenxian chubanshe.

Canberra Group (2001). "Expert Group on Household Income Statistics: Final Report and Recommendations." Ottawa.

Chen, Y. and R. Woo (2017). "Smaller Cities Keep China Home Property Market Hot in April." Reuters, May 17. http://www.reuters.com/article/us-china-economy-homeprices-idUSKCN18E06Y. Accessed July 14, 2017.

Das, M. and P. M. N'Diaye (2013). "Chronicle of a Decline Foretold: Has China Reached the Lewis Turning Point?" IMF Working Paper No. 13/26, International Monetary Fund, Washington, DC.

Department of Household Surveys, National Bureau of Statistics (2016). *China Yearbook of Household Survey 2016.* Beijing: China Statistics Press.

Eichen, M. and M. Zhang (1993). "Annex: The 1988 Household Sample Survey—Data Description and Availability," in K. Griffin and R. Zhao, eds., *The Distribution of Income in China*, 331–346. New York: St. Martin's Press.

European Commission (2003). "Commission Regulation (EC) No 1980/2003 of 21 October 2003 Implementing Regulation (EC) No 1177/2003 of the European Parliament and of the Council Concerning Community Statistics on Income and Living Conditions (EU-SILC) as Regards Definitions and Updated Definitions." Official Journal L 298, 17/11/2003, pp. 0001–0022. https://eur-lex.europa.eu/legal-content/EN/TXT/?uri=CELEX:32003R1980. Accessed December 1, 2018.

Frick, J. R., J. Goebel, and M. M. Grabka (2006). "Assessing the Distributional Impact of 'Imputed Rent' and 'Non-Cash Employee Income' in Micro-Data," in Eurostat, *Comparative EU Statistics on Income and Living Conditions: Issues and Challenges, Proceedings of the EU-SILC Conference, 2007*, 117–134. Helsinki, November 6–8. https://circabc.europa.eu/webdav/CircaBC/ESTAT/eusilc/Library/7_publications/SILC.pdf. Accessed December 1, 2018.

Gan, L. (2017). "Income Inequality an Insufficient Consumption in China." Presentation at the 6th Annual JRCPPF Conference on "Escalating Risks: China's Economy, Society and Financial system," Princeton University, February 16–17. https://jrc.princeton.edu/sites/jrc/files/gan_li_ac_2017.pdf. Accessed July 17, 2017.

Golan, J., T. Sicular, and N. Umapathi (2017). "Unconditional Cash Transfers in China: Who Benefits from the Rural Minimum Living Standard Guarantee (Dibao) Program?" *World Development*, 93(5), 316–336.

Griffin, K. and R. Zhao, eds. (1993). *The Distribution of Income in China*. New York: St. Martin's Press.

Gustafsson, B., S. Li, and T. Sicular, eds. (2008). *Inequality and Public Policy in China*. Cambridge and New York: Cambridge University Press.

Kanbur, R., Y. Wang, and X. Zhang (2017). "The Great Chinese Inequality Turnaround." International Food Policy Research Institute Discussion Paper 01637. http://ebrary.ifpri.org/cdm/ref/collection/p15738coll2/id/131158. Accessed November 30, 2018.

Knight, J., Q. Deng, and S. Li (2011). "The Puzzle of Migrant Labour Shortage and Rural Labour Surplus in China." *China Economic Review*, 22(4), 585–600.

Lam, W. R., X. Liu, and A. Schipke (2015). "China's Labor Market in the 'New Normal.'" IMF Working Paper WP/15/151. International Monetary Fund, Washington DC.

Li, S., C. Luo, and T. Sicular (2013). "Overview: Income Inequality and Poverty in China, 2002–2007," in S. Li, H. Sato, and T. Sicular, eds., *Rising Inequality in China: Challenges to a Harmonious Society*, 44–84. Cambridge and New York: Cambridge University Press.

Li, S., C. Luo, Z. Wei, and X. Yue (2008). "Appendix: The 1995 and 2002 Household Surveys: Sampling Methods and Data Description," in B.A. Gustafsson, S. Li, and T. Sicular, eds., *Inequality and Public Policy in China*, 337–353. Cambridge and New York: Cambridge University Press.

Li, S. and X. Ma (2015). "Impact of Minimum Wage on Gender Wage Gaps in Urban China." *IZA Journal of Labor and Development*, 4(1), 1–22.

Li, S., H. Sato, and T. Sicular, eds. (2013). *Rising Inequality in China: Challenges to a Harmonious Society*. Cambridge and New York: Cambridge University Press.

Li, S., L. Ye, and L. Xiong (2014). "Understanding Impacts of Minimum Wage Policy on Labor Market in China." Presentation at the International Conference on Minimum Wage Policy, Hong Kong University of Science and Technology, September.

Lin, C. and M. S. Yun (2016). "The Effects of the Minimum Wage on Earnings Inequality: Evidence from China," in L. Cappellari, S. W. Polachek, and K. Tatsiramos, eds., *Income Inequality around the World*, Research in Labor Economics 14, 179–212. Bingley, UK: Emerald Group Publishing.

Liu, H. and Z. Zhao (2014). "Does Health Insurance Matter? Evidence from China's Urban Resident Basic Medical Insurance?" *Journal of Comparative Economics*, 42(4), 1007–1020.

Liu, S., Y. Wang, and A. Hu (2009). "Xibu dakaifa chengxiao yu Zhongguo quyu jingji shoulian" (The impact of the Western Development Strategy and regional economic convergence in China). *Jingji yanjiu* (Economic research), no. 9, 94–105.

Luo, C., S. Li, T. Sicular, Q. Deng, and X. Yue (2013). "Appendix I: The 2007 Household Surveys: Sampling Methods and Data Description," in S. Li, H. Sato, and T. Sicular, eds., *Rising Inequality in China: Challenges to a Harmonious Society*, 445–464. Cambridge and New York: Cambridge University Press.

Meng, Q. and K. Xu (2014). "Progress and Challenges of the Rural Cooperative Medical Scheme in China." *Bulletin of the World Health Organization*, 92(6), 447–451.

National Bureau of Statistics (NBS) (2012). *Zhuhu shouzhi yu shenghuo zhuangkuang diaocha fang'an (shixing) 2013 niandu* (China household income and living conditions survey plan [trial] 2013). Beijing: Guojia tongjiju.

National Bureau of Statistics (NBS) (2014). *Zhongguo zhuhu diaocha nianjian 2014* (China yearbook of household survey 2014). Beijing: Zhongguo tongji chubanshe.

Pomfret, J. and J. Ruwitch (2014). "Early Holidays Point to Grim Outlook for China's Small Factories." Reuters, January 14. http://www.reuters.com/article/us-china-migration-idUSBREA0E1K920140115. Accessed July 15, 2017.

Rein, S. (2010). "China's Growing Labor Shortage." *Forbes*, March 15. https://www.forbes.com/2010/03/15/china-labor-shortage-leadership-managing-rein.html. Accessed July 15, 2017.

Riskin, C., R. Zhao, and S. Li, eds. (2001). *China's Retreat from Equality: Income Distribution and Economic Transition*. Armonk, NY: M. E. Sharpe.

Sato, H., T. Sicular, and X. Yue (2013). "Housing Ownership, Incomes and Inequality in China, 2002–2007," in S. Li, H. Sato, and T. Sicular, eds., *Rising Inequality in China: Challenges to a Harmonious Society*, 85–141. Cambridge and New York: Cambridge University Press.

Smeeding, T. M. and D. H. Weinberg (2001). "Toward a Uniform Definition of Household Income." *Review of Income and Wealth*, 47(1), 1–24.

Song, J., T. Sicular, and X. Yue (2013). "Appendix II: The 2002 and 2007 CHIP Surveys; Sampling, Weights, and Combining the Urban, Rural, and Migrant Samples," in S. Li, H. Sato, and T. Sicular, eds., *Rising Inequality in China: Challenges to a Harmonious Society*, 465–485. Cambridge and New York: Cambridge University Press.

Southwestern University of Finance and Economics, China Household Finance Survey and Research Center (2012). *Zhongguo jiating shouru bu pingdeng baogao* (Report on China's household income inequality). Chengdu: Southwestern University of Finance and Economics.

Wang, D. (2014). "China's Pension System Reform." Presentation at the Regional Consultation on Strengthening Income Support for Vulnerable Groups in Asia and the Pacific, UNESCAP Subregional Office for East and North-East Asia, Incheon, Republic of Korea, March 26–27. http://www.unescap.org/sites/default/files/ISS-Meeting_item3-dewen-wang.pdf. Accessed June 17, 2017.

Wang, F. (2011). "The Future of a Demographic Overachiever: Long-Term Implications of the Demographic Transition in China." *Population and Development Review*, 37(S1), 173–190.

Wong, E. (2010). "Labor Shortage Hits China's Manufacturing Hubs." *New York Times*, November 30. http://query.nytimes.com/gst/fullpage.html?res=9905E7D7143CF933A05752C1A9669D8B63&login=email. Accessed July 17, 2017.

Xie, Y. and X. Zhou (2014). "Income Inequality in Today's China." *Proceedings of the National Academy of Science*, 111(19), 6928–6933.

Xinhua (2015). "Factories Turn to Robots amid Labor Woes." *Shanghai Daily*, May 14. http://www.shanghaidaily.com/feature/news-feature/Factories-turn-to-robots-amid-labor-woes/shdaily.shtml. Accessed July 17, 2017.

Yang, Y. and C. Yang (2015). "Zhongguo jini xishu shi fou zhende xiajiangle? Jiyu weiguan shuzhude jini xishu qujian guji" (Did China's income Gini decline? An interval estimation based on Chinese micro data). *Jingji yanjiu* (Economic research), no. 3, 75–86.

Yue, X. and S. Li (2013a). "Women geng yinggai xiangxin shui de jini de xishu?" (Whose Gini coefficient should we believe?). *Wall Street Journal* (Chinese edition), January 24. http://www.cn.wsj.com/gb/20130124/OPN120117.asp. Accessed July 17, 2017.

Yue, X. and S. Li (2013b)."Dui Xi'nan caida jini xishu de zai zhiyi" (Suspicions about the quality of the Gini coefficient numbers of Southwestern University of Finance and Economics). *Wall Street Journal* (Chinese edition), February 5. http://www.cn.wsj.com/gb/20130205/OPN092607.asp. Accessed July 17, 2017.

Yue, X., S. Li, and X. Gao (2013). "How Large Is Income Inequality in China: Assessment on Different Estimates of Gini Coefficient." *China Economic Journal*, 6 (2–3), 112–122.

Yue, X. and T. Sicular (2016). "Weights for 2007 and 2013." China Institute for Income Distribution Working Paper No. 78. http://www.ciidbnu.org/news/201908/20190825121721706.html. Accessed November 6, 2019.

Zhang, X., J. Yang, and S. Wang (2011). "China Has Reached the Lewis Turning Point." *China Economic Review*, 22(4), 542–554.

Zhou, Z. (2015). "China's New Urbanisation Plan." Asia Dialogue, October 14. https://theasiadialogue.com/2015/10/14/chinas-new-urbanisation-plan-2014-2020/. Accessed July 17, 2017.

2

Overview

Incomes and Inequality in China, 2007–2013

Chuliang Luo, Terry Sicular, and Shi Li

2.1 Introduction

China's economic reforms and its transformation from a planned to a market-based economy have been ongoing since 1978. During these decades China has experienced rapid economic growth, substantial structural change, and increased standards of living, as well as rising income inequality. During the early decades of reform, rising inequality was considered an inevitable and acceptable consequence of the economic reforms. As markets replaced planning, income differentiation based on supply, demand, and productivity naturally emerged and provided positive incentives for work, investment, and entrepreneurship. Despite the rise in inequality during the early reform decades, households throughout the income distribution enjoyed rising incomes. Consequently, the benefits of rapid growth were widely shared.

By the early 2000s income inequality reached a level that many viewed as worrisome. In response, China announced the "Harmonious Society" program and embarked on a multi-pronged program to counteract the rising inequality and to create a universal social safety net. Nevertheless, inequality continued to rise such that by 2007 China's Gini coefficient approached 0.5 (Li, Sato, and Sicular 2013; National Bureau of Statistics 2013).

Since 2008 inequality in China appears to have taken a new direction. According to official National Bureau of Statistics (NBS) estimates, the Gini coefficient peaked at 0.49 in 2008-2009 and thereafter progressively declined to 0.46 in 2015, still moderately high by international standards but a return to the level of inequality observed in China during the early 2000s (NBS 2013; NBS 2016). These latest figures suggest that inequality in China may have turned a corner.

Chuliang Luo, Terry Sicular, and Shi Li, *Overview. Incomes and Inequality in China, 2007–2013* In: *Changing Trends in China's Inequality*. Edited by: Terry Sicular, Shi Li, Ximing Yue, and Hiroshi Sato, Oxford University Press (2020). © Oxford University Press.
DOI: 10.1093/oso/9780190077938.003.0002

In this chapter, using data from the CHIP 2007 and 2013 surveys, we take a close look at the recent decline in inequality. The detailed, household-level data in the CHIP surveys allow us to compare the official estimates to alternative, independent estimates and permit a detailed analysis of the factors underlying the recent turnaround in inequality.

Our central estimates of inequality based on the CHIP data confirm the decline in national inequality from 2007 to 2013. Using the CHIP data, we calculate alternative measures of household income that adjust for deficiencies in the official income variable provided by the NBS, and we find that the decline in inequality is robust to these alternative income measures. The decline is also robust to alternative inequality indexes.

Disaggregating among subgroups and sources of income reveals that the decline in inequality reflects underlying changes in several important dimensions of China's income distribution. First, from 2007 to 2013 the urban/rural income gap narrowed, a noticeable change from the past when a secular widening of the urban/rural income gap contributed to the rising national inequality. The narrowing of the urban/rural gap from 2007 to 2013 was the result of rapid growth in rural incomes. Urban incomes also grew, but less quickly. Within the urban and rural sectors, however, income inequality increased. Later chapters in this volume provide more in-depth analyses of the patterns of inequality within each of these sectors (see Chapters 5, 6, and 7).

Second, regional income gaps narrowed. Income growth in the Central and West regions of the country was relatively rapid. Consequently, by 2013 average household income per capita in the West had basically caught up with that in the Central region. These trends were a result of a continuation of the past catch-up among regions and the increased mobility of both people and jobs. Inequality within regions also declined.

Third, inequality declined not only for total household income but also for all its major components—wage earnings, income from agriculture and non-agricultural household businesses, asset income, pensions, and imputed rents on owner-occupied housing. However, the declines in inequality for the individual income components were partially offset by the rapid growth in those income components that are more unequally distributed, importantly, asset income and imputed rents on owner-occupied housing.

We conduct some additional analyses to explore whether the decline in inequality is sensitive to corrections for spatial differences in the cost of living and for a potential understatement of income for the highest-income groups.

These corrections and adjustments require some strong assumptions; thus, we calculate the results by using alternative assumptions to obtain a plausible range of the inequality estimates. We find that these corrections and adjustments reduce the magnitude of the decline in inequality between 2007 and 2013, with some estimates showing an increase in inequality between these two years. Because these estimates are based on strong assumptions and imperfect information, we view these alternative estimates as tentative rather than conclusive. Nevertheless, they indicate that to some extent the recent decline in inequality may be due to differential changes in prices as well as to the increasing underrepresentation of the very rich in the Chinese household survey data.

We begin in Section 2.2 with a brief discussion of the datasets and the measurement issues. Section 2.3 presents our core estimates of income and inequality, paying attention to changes in the composition and distribution of various sources of income and across poorer, middle, and richer subgroups of the population. Section 2.3 also reports estimates of inequality adjusted for spatial price differences. Section 2.4 presents estimates of inequality separately for formal urban residents and for formal rural residents. In view of the growing importance of rural-to-urban migration, we devote Section 2.5 to a discussion of the incomes and inequality of rural-to-urban migrants. In this section we also consider the nationwide effects of rural-to-urban migration on inequality.

Section 2.6 reports changes in urban/rural and regional income gaps as well as their contributions to national inequality. In Section 2.7 we present alternate estimates of inequality that adjust for the underrepresentation of incomes at the top tail of the income distribution. Here we use a standard methodology based on the assumption that the distribution of income for the top-income group takes the shape of a Pareto distribution and can be estimated by using public information about extremely rich individuals. The details of the methodology are provided in Appendix 2.1. We conclude in Section 2.8 with some reflections on the implications of our findings.

2.2 Data, Weights, and Income Definition

In our analysis we use the CHIP 2007 and 2013 household survey data. The CHIP 2007 dataset consists of separate urban and rural samples drawn from the NBS urban and rural household survey samples, plus a sample of rural-to-urban migrants collected from an independent CHIP survey. As noted in Chapter 1, the CHIP 2013 dataset is drawn from the new, integrated NBS household survey sample that differs from the previous CHIP datasets in that it no longer comprises separate urban, rural, and migrant samples. To maintain consistency with the CHIP 2007 survey and to allow for separate analyses by population subgroup, we classify households in the CHIP 2013 sample as urban, rural, and rural-to-urban migrant by the location of the household registration (*hukou*) and the actual location of residence (see Chapter 1). Hereafter, we use the term "migrant" to refer to rural-to-urban migrants.

The sectoral (urban, rural, migrant) and regional (East, Central, West) distributions of the CHIP 2007 and 2013 samples are not entirely consistent with those of China's population, as captured by the national census and the annual population sample surveys. In our national analyses we therefore use population-based two-level region (East, Central, and West) times sector (rural, urban, and migrant) weights (see Chapter 1). For sectoral analyses, we use regional weights and for regional analyses we use sectoral weights.

The target variable in our analysis is household income per capita, that is, household income divided by the number of household members. The CHIP datasets contain estimates of income provided by the NBS (hereafter referred to as "NBS income"). As discussed in Chapter 1, NBS income, widely used by researchers, is a reasonably good measure of household income, but it still has some drawbacks. Consequently, we have constructed alternative estimates of income. First, "adjusted NBS income" adjusts the NBS income variable, the definition of which changed in 2013, so that it is consistent between 2007 and 2013. Second, "CHIP income," which is equal to adjusted NBS income plus estimates of imputed rents on owner-occupied housing and implicit subsidies on subsidized rental housing, is a fuller measure of household income that is more consistent with standard international practices to measure household income. In 2007 and 2013 the amount from urban rental subsidies was small, so that the overwhelming majority of the difference between CHIP income and adjusted NBS income was due to imputed rents. A fuller explanation of these three alternative income variables can be found in Chapter 1.

CHIP income is our preferred measure of income, and we use it for most of the analyses reported in the chapter. One aim of this chapter, however, is to evaluate the official NBS estimates of inequality and to

determine the robustness of the apparent recent decline in national inequality. We therefore also present estimates of income and inequality
calculated with NBS income and adjusted NBS income. A comparison
of the estimates calculated with NBS income to those calculated with
adjusted NBS income reveals the effect of the change in the NBS income
definition on the measured levels of income and inequality. A comparison
of the estimates calculated with adjusted NBS income to those calculated
with CHIP income reveals how a fuller measurement of household income
affects levels of income and inequality.

Prior to 2013 the NBS household survey samples did not adequately
reflect migrants, so in 2007 the CHIP carried out an independent survey
of migrant households. The income variable for migrants in the 2007
data comes from this independent survey and is based on self-reported
responses to questions asking migrant households to recall their annual income and its components. Consequently, migrant income in 2007 may not
be fully consistent with migrant income in 2013 or with rural and urban
incomes in 2007. Because the share of migrants in the population in 2007
was fairly low, this inconsistency is unlikely to have much of an effect on our
national estimates of income and inequality, but readers should keep the
inconsistency in mind when interpreting estimates of migrant incomes and
inequality reported in Section 2.5

2.3 National Incomes and Inequality

2.3.1 Estimates of National Inequality

Table 2.1 reports our estimates of mean incomes and income inequality
in China as a whole in both 2007 and 2013. Estimates are shown for NBS
income, adjusted NBS income, and CHIP income. Mean incomes are in
current year prices; percentage changes in incomes are in constant prices.
In order to check the robustness of the apparent recent decline in national
inequality to the choice of the inequality index, we report estimates of income inequality using three alternative indexes—the Gini coefficient, the
mean logarithmic deviation (MLD), and the Theil index.[1] The Gini coefficient is the most widely used inequality index, so we can easily compare
our estimates to others in the literature. It is relatively sensitive to income
differences around the middle (to be more precise, around the mode) of the

Table 2.1. National average household income per capita and income inequality, 2007 and 2013

	2007	2013	Change (%)
(a) NBS income per capita			
Mean income (yuan)	9353	19,023	+68.7
Gini	0.470	0.448	−4.7
MLD	0.401	0.356	−11.2
Theil	0.380	0.350	−7.9
(b) Adjusted NBS income per capita			
Mean income (yuan)	9432	18,208	+60.2
Gini	0.478	0.436	−8.8
MLD	0.401	0.331	−17.5
Theil	0.388	0.333	−14.2
(c) CHIP income per capita			
Mean income (yuan)	10,934	21,190	+60.8
Gini	0.486	0.433	−10.9
MLD	0.428	0.328	−23.4
Theil	0.405	0.325	−19.8

Notes: Here and elsewhere, calculated by using the CHIP data and weights (see the text). Income levels are in current prices; income changes are in constant prices and deflated by using the NBS national consumer price index, which shows a price level increase of 20.536 percent from 2007 to 2013. The MLD and Theil indexes belong to the general entropy (GE) family of indexes; the MLD is also known as the Theil L or GE(0) index, and the Theil T is known as the GE(1) index.

income distribution. The MLD is relatively sensitive to income differences at the lower end of the income distribution, and the Theil index is equally sensitive to income differences throughout the income distribution. Thus, for example, relatively large changes over time in incomes at the lower end of the income distribution would mean a larger change in the MLD index than in the Gini and Theil indexes. This, in fact, is the case for our estimates of inequality in China between 2007 and 2013.

As shown in Table 2.1, different income definitions yield somewhat different levels of mean income and inequality. In all cases, however, the changes from 2007 to 2013 are consistent—specifically, mean income increased and inequality decreased. For example, CHIP income per capita increased 61 percent from 2007 to 2013, equivalent to an average annual rate of growth of 8 percent over these years. This rate of income growth is rapid by international standards, although slower than that between the CHIP 2002 and the CHIP 2007 surveys, when CHIP income per capita grew at an average annual rate of 13 percent. With respect to inequality, the Gini coefficient for CHIP income declined by 11 percent. The decline in inequality from 2007 to 2013 was even larger for the MLD and Theil indexes.

This change in income inequality from 2007 to 2013 represents the first decline recorded by the CHIP since its initial survey in the late 1980s and it is a sharp turnaround even compared to the immediately preceding years. From 2002 to 2007 the Gini coefficient for CHIP income increased by 5 percent.[2] As a result of the decline, China went from being a high-inequality country (among the 15 percent of countries with the highest Gini coefficients) to a country with moderately high inequality (among the 30 percent of countries with the highest Gini coefficients).[3]

How do our estimates of inequality based on the CHIP sample compare with the official estimates published by the NBS? The official estimates of the national Gini are 0.484 for 2007 and 0.473 for 2013 (Gustafsson, Li, and Sato 2014). These are a bit higher than our estimates using the NBS income variable (Table 2.1). The change in the official Gini from 2007 to 2013 was −23 percent, as compared to −4.7 percent in our estimates using the NBS income variable. In our view, these differences are modest. We conclude that our estimates of inequality using the NBS income variable are reasonably consistent with the official numbers.

Comparisons of our estimates of NBS income, the adjusted NBS income, and the CHIP income based on the CHIP survey data reveal several noteworthy differences. First, income levels and inequality for NBS income and adjusted NBS income are quite similar for 2007, but both income and inequality are lower in 2013 for adjusted NBS income. These differences between the NBS and the adjusted NBS income estimates for 2013 reflect in part the elimination of the NBS's flawed estimates of imputed rents on owner-occupied housing from NBS 2013 income; in 2007 the NBS did not include imputed rents in its income variable (see Chapter 1). We conclude that the 2013 change in the NBS definition of income resulted in an overstatement of the increase in the level of income and an understatement of the decline in inequality from 2007 to 2013.

Second, in both years the mean levels of CHIP income are higher than those for the adjusted NBS income. This result is not surprising, given that imputed rents on owner-occupied housing and implicit rental subsidies are included in the CHIP income but are not included in the adjusted NBS income. With respect to inequality, CHIP 2007 income inequality is higher and CHIP 2013 income inequality is slightly lower than that for the adjusted NBS income. Consequently, the decline in inequality is larger for the CHIP income than it is for either NBS income definition.

Geographic size and market segmentation can result in regional price variations. Consequently, nominal incomes in different regions may not reflect real income differences in terms of purchasing power. In principle, estimates of incomes and inequality should be adjusted for spatial price differences so that they reflect a comparable PPP.

Studies of inequality typically do not adjust incomes for spatial price differences, mainly because of a lack of spatial price data. Available estimates of Chinese spatial price indexes are limited. The most well-known estimates are from Brandt and Holz (2006), who construct a set of spatial price indexes by using geographic price data from about 1990 and then extend them to 2004 by using the provincial rural and urban consumer price indexes published by the NBS. We update the Brandt and Holz indexes to 2013 with the NBS consumer price indexes for more recent years. We then apply the updated indexes to the CHIP income data and calculate the PPP estimates of inequality. The PPP estimates give an indication of how spatial price differences affect measured inequality, but with the caveat that Brandt and Holz's indexes are anchored on very old price data.

Estimates of inequality for NBS and CHIP income with and without spatial price adjustments are reported in Table 2.2. In 2007 PPP estimates of inequality are substantially lower, e.g., for CHIP income the PPP-adjusted Gini is about 11 percent lower and the PPP-adjusted MLD and Theil indexes are more than 20 percent lower than the unadjusted estimates. In 2013 the differences between the PPP-adjusted and the unadjusted estimates are a bit smaller, indicating that from 2007 to 2013 prices rose more rapidly in regions with lower costs of living.

Is the decline in national inequality robust to the PPP adjustments? As shown in the last column of Table 2.2, the answer depends on how income is measured. For NBS income, the PPP adjustments nearly eliminate the decline in inequality. For CHIP income, the PPP adjustments reduce but do not eliminate the decline in inequality. For PPP-adjusted CHIP income, the Gini coefficient declines 7 percent and the MLD and Theil indexes decline 11 percent and 15 percent, respectively, between 2007 and 2013.

Table 2.2. National income inequality with and without spatial PPP adjustments, 2007 and 2013

	2007			2013			Change from 2007 to 2013 (%)	
	Without PPP	With PPP	Difference (%)	Without PPP	With PPP	Difference (%)	Without PPP	With PPP
(a) NBS income per capita								
Gini	0.470	0.417	−11.3	0.448	0.414	−7.8	−4.7	−1.0
MLD	0.401	0.309	−22.9	0.356	0.300	−15.7	−11.2	−2.9
Theil	0.380	0.298	−21.6	0.350	0.299	−14.6	−7.9	0.3
(b) CHIP income per capita								
Gini	0.486	0.431	−11.3	0.433	0.400	−7.6	−10.9	−7.2
MLD	0.428	0.328	−23.4	0.328	0.278	−15.2	−23.4	−15.2
Theil	0.405	0.315	−22.2	0.325	0.280	−13.8	−19.8	−11.1

Note: PPP estimates use urban/rural × province spatial price indexes from Brandt and Holz (2006), updated to 2007 and 2013 by using urban/rural × province consumer price indexes published by the NBS.

Because the spatial price indexes are imprecise, hereafter we focus on estimates of inequality that are not PPP adjusted. Nevertheless, we conclude from the PPP exercise that the decline in national inequality from 2007 to 2013 was partly the result of changes in the relative cost of living among provinces and between urban and rural areas.

2.3.2 Uneven Income Growth

The CHIP data permit us to examine in some detail changes in the underlying distribution of income. Figure 2.1 presents the change in household income per capita for each income decile, from the richest to the poorest. Income levels and the percentage of the change are all in constant 2007 prices. The vertical bars show the income levels for each decile in each year and the curve shows the percentage change in income for each decile between the two years.

Figure 2.1 reveals that incomes increased in real terms for all decile groups. The gains were largest—exceeding 80 percent—for the bottom five deciles.

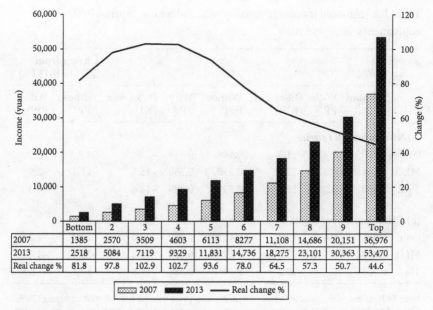

	Bottom	2	3	4	5	6	7	8	9	Top
2007	1385	2570	3509	4603	6113	8277	11,108	14,686	20,151	36,976
2013	2518	5084	7119	9329	11,831	14,736	18,275	23,101	30,363	53,470
Real change %	81.8	97.8	102.9	102.7	93.6	78.0	64.5	57.3	50.7	44.6

▭ 2007   ▬ 2013   —— Real change %

Fig. 2.1 National income per capita by income decile: Level and change from 2007 to 2013 (yuan, %)

Notes: CHIP income per capita. Incomes and income growth are in constant 2007 prices, deflated by using the NBS national average consumer price index, which shows an increase in the price level of 20.536 percent from 2007 to 2013.

For the higher-income deciles, income growth was slower. Thus, the figure reveals that the decline in national inequality from 2007 to 2013 was driven by relatively rapid income gains for the low- and middle-income groups. This pattern differs markedly from the pattern between 2002 and 2007, when income growth disproportionately went to the top four deciles of the income distribution (Figure 2.2 in Li, Luo, and Sicular 2013).

The differences in income growth across deciles of the income distribution are evident in the changes in the Lorenz curve from 2007 to 2013 (Figure 2.2).[4] In the Lorenz curve, the population is arranged in ascending order, from lowest to highest income per capita; the curve shows a plot of the cumulative share of income (the vertical axis) going to the cumulative share of the population (the horizontal axis). The closer the Lorenz curve lies to the 45-degree line, the lower the degree of inequality. With the exception of a small segment at the very bottom of the income distribution, everywhere China's 2013 national Lorenz curve is closer to the 45-degree line than it is in 2007.

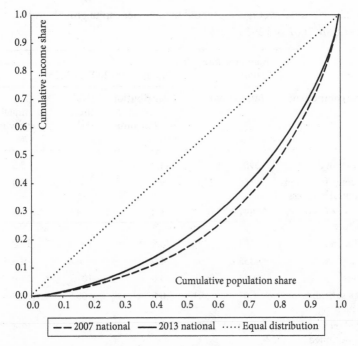

Fig. 2.2 China's national Lorenz curves, 2007 and 2013

Notes: CHIP income per capita. The Lorenz curves for NBS income per capita are very similar.

2.3.3 Inequality Decomposition by Income Sources

Does the decline in inequality reflect changes in the underlying sources of household income? Table 2.3 shows the breakdown of CHIP income by its major components in 2007 and 2013. Wage earnings were the largest component of income in both years. Although they grew more slowly than other components, wages contributed 45 percent of the increase in total household income from 2007 to 2013. The most rapidly growing sources of income were asset income, pensions, and imputed rents from owner-occupied housing. Net income from agriculture increased in nominal terms but it increased more slowly than inflation; therefore, the real change was negative.

To analyze the contributions of different income sources to inequality, we carry out a standard decomposition of the Gini coefficient by factor components, whereby each component's contribution to inequality depends

Table 2.3. National average household income per capita growth and composition, 2007 and 2013

Income component	Mean income (yuan)		Change from 2007 to 2013		
	2007	2013	Contribution to increase in total income (%)	Real increase (%)	Real average annual growth (%)
Wage earnings	6981	11,576	44.9	37.6	5.5
Net income from non-agricultural business	1166	2154	9.6	53.2	7.4
Net income from agriculture	891	1022	1.3	−4.8	−0.8
Asset income	224	722	4.9	167.8	17.8
Net transfers	−355	55	4.0	n.a.	n.a.
Pensions	1066	2669	15.6	107.7	13.0
Implicit subsidies for rental housing	51	101	0.5	65.5	8.8
Imputed rents on owner-occupied housing	912	2881	19.2	162.2	17.4
Total income	10,935	21,180	100.0	60.7	8.2

Notes: CHIP income per capita. Income levels are in current prices; real increases are in 2007 constant prices converted by using the national consumer price index published by the NBS (1.20526). Here and elsewhere imputed rents on owner-occupied housing and pensions are shown as separate income categories (the former are not included in asset income and the latter are not included in net transfer income). The CHIP 2007 data report the income component "other in-kind income" for urban residents, a small item (on average 1 yuan per capita), reflecting mostly in-kind payments by employers. The CHIP 2013 data do not give separate information for "other in-kind income." Therefore, in this and later tables we include this component of 2007 urban income as part of the urban wage income. Net income from agriculture is not reported separately for formal urban residents and migrants. These groups are unlikely to have agricultural income, so we simply categorize the net business income of urban residents and migrants as "net income from non-agricultural household business."

on its share of income and how unequally it is distributed. Specifically, the contribution S_k of income component k to total inequality is given by

$$S_k = \frac{\mu_k}{\mu} C_k,$$
(2.1)

where $\frac{\mu_k}{\mu}$ is the ratio of the mean of income component k to the mean of total household income, or, in other words, income component k's share of total income (Shorrocks 1982). C_k is the Gini concentration coefficient, sometimes called the pseudo-Gini, which measures how unequally the income component is distributed relative to the distribution of total income. For example, if an income component is distributed such that it goes disproportionately to the relatively low-income households in the distribution of total income, then that component will have a small or even negative concentration coefficient.

Comparison of the concentration coefficient of an income component to the Gini coefficient for total income reveals whether the income component is equalizing or disequalizing. Income components with concentration coefficients smaller than the Gini coefficient are considered to be equalizing; income components with concentration coefficients larger than the Gini coefficient are considered to be disequalizing. All else being equal, an income component that constitutes a large share of income will make a large contribution to inequality, and all else being equal, an income component with a high concentration coefficient will make a large contribution to inequality.

Table 2.4 reports income shares, concentration coefficients, and percentage contributions to overall inequality for each income source. Wage earnings are the major contributor to inequality in both years, although their contribution declined from 73 percent in 2007 to 60 percent in 2013. This large contribution indicates that by far wages remained the largest component of household income and the concentration coefficient for wages was higher than the Gini coefficient for total income.

Other components with moderately large contributions to inequality included net income from non-agricultural businesses, pensions, and imputed rents on owner-occupied housing, all of which contributed more than 10 percent of inequality in one or both years. All three of these components had concentration ratios higher than the Gini. The contribution of non-agricultural businesses to overall inequality remained stable at about 11 percent. The contributions to inequality of both pensions and imputed rents increased because their income shares grew. The concentration coefficients of both pensions and imputed rents fell, indicating that they were distributed more equally in 2013 than they were in 2007.

Overall, from 2007 to 2013 the concentration coefficients for most major components of income declined. In some cases, the decline was substantial, e.g., for wage earnings, pensions, and imputed rents. The only exceptions were income from agriculture, which nevertheless continued to be substantially inequality-reducing, and rental housing subsidies, which in both years were a trivial component of income (less than 1 percent). We conclude that the decline in China's overall Gini coefficient from 2007 to 2013 reflected declines in the inequality of most income components, including wage

Table 2.4. Decomposition of national inequality by income source, 2007 and 2013

Income source	2007			2013		
	Share (%)	Concentration coefficient	Contribution to inequality (%)	Share (%)	Concentration coefficient	Contribution to inequality (%)
Wage earnings	63.8	0.554	72.8	54.6	0.477	60.2
Net income from non-agricultural business	10.7	0.506	11.1	10.2	0.471	11.1
Net income from agriculture	8.1	−0.211	−3.5	4.8	−0.169	−1.9
Asset income	2.0	0.592	2.5	3.4	0.572	4.5
Net transfer income	−3.2	0.801	−5.4	0.3	−7.439	−5.3
Pension income	9.7	0.649	13.0	12.6	0.568	16.5
Rental housing subsidies	0.5	0.705	0.7	0.5	0.730	0.8
Imputed rents on owner-occupied housing	8.3	0.516	8.8	13.6	0.448	14.1
Total income	100.0	0.486	100.0	100.0	0.433	100.0

Notes: CHIP income per capita; the decomposition is done by using the standard decomposition of the Gini coefficient (Shorrocks 1982). The (Gini) concentration coefficient is also known as the pseudo-Gini. The concentration coefficient of total income is simply the Gini coefficient of total income.

earnings, net non-agricultural business income, pensions, asset income, and imputed rents.

Income sources associated with public transfer programs require some discussion. Pension income was distributed unequally, reflecting generous pensions to urban households that had relatively high incomes. Nevertheless, the concentration coefficient of pensions declined, a consequence of the expansion and strengthening of pension programs for informal workers and the rural population. Income from other public transfer programs is included in net transfers, which also include private transfers. Net transfers in both years constituted a small share of total income and were, on balance, equalizing. Analysis of the distributional impact of public social welfare and transfer programs is discussed more fully in other chapters (see, for example, Chapter 5).

2.4 Incomes and Inequality within the Rural and Formal Urban Sectors

In this section we examine incomes and inequality separately within the rural and formal urban sectors. By "formal urban" we mean urban residents who hold an urban household registration (*hukou*). Migrants from rural areas who live in cities and who do not have an urban *hukou* are excluded from the analysis in this section and examined separately in the next section. Chapters 6 and 9 discuss incomes and inequality within each of the rural and urban sectors, so we limit our discussion here to those aspects that are most relevant to national inequality.

Table 2.5 shows the levels of income and inequality for rural and urban households. From 2007 to 2013 average CHIP income per capita of rural households doubled in real terms, implying average annual growth of 12.9 percent. This rate substantially outpaced the 7.4 percent average annual growth of rural income from 2002 to 2007 (Li, Sato, and Sicular 2013, Table 1.3). Indeed, this rate approached the rapid pace of rural income growth experienced during the early 1980s when China carried out major rural reforms, including the decollectivization of agriculture; increases in the prices of farm products; the rationalization of agricultural production planning; and the promotion of township and village enterprises.

Average CHIP income per capita for formal urban residents also grew, but more slowly. Formal urban incomes increased 35 percent from 2007 to 2013

Table 2.5. Mean incomes and income inequality within rural, formal urban, and migrant household subgroups, 2007 and 2013

	Rural			Formal Urban			Migrant		
	2007	2013	Change (%)	2007	2013	Change (%)	2007	2013	Change (%)
(a) NBS income per capita									
Mean income (yuan)	4331	9850	85.5	14,982	28,559	59.1	14,986	20,931	16.6
Gini	0.376	0.407	8.2	0.334	0.355	6.3	0.327	0.349	6.7
MLD	0.234	0.273	16.7	0.189	0.212	12.2	0.172	0.184	7.0
Theil	0.253	0.292	15.4	0.192	0.223	16.4	0.189	0.217	14.8
(b) CHIP income per capita									
Mean income (yuan)	4770	12,098	106.82	19,212	30,983	34.6	15,233	22,259	21.9
Gini	0.374	0.405	8.3	0.338	0.349	3.3	0.324	0.348	7.4
MLD	0.232	0.273	17.7	0.191	0.205	7.3	0.168	0.183	8.9
Theil	0.251	0.297	18.3	0.191	0.214	12.0	0.203	0.216	6.4

Notes: Income levels are in current prices; changes are converted to 2007 constant prices by using the rural or urban consumer price index published by the NBS (1.22633 and 1.19829, respectively); 2007 incomes for migrants are self-reported, recalled income from the independent CHIP migrant survey; 2013 incomes for migrants are from the NBS unified household survey collected by using a diary method.

(in constant prices), equivalent to an average annual growth rate of 5 percent. It is worth noting that although the rate of growth in income for formal urban residents was less than half that for rural residents, the absolute increment in income was larger. In constant 2007 prices, the average absolute increment in income per capita of formal urban households was 6647 yuan, as compared to 5095 yuan for rural households.

Contrary to the decline in national income inequality from 2007 to 2013, income inequality within the rural and urban sectors rose. The Gini coefficient for CHIP income in rural China rose by 8 percent, from 0.374 in 2007 to 0.405 in 2013; the MLD and Theil indexes show even larger increases. Increases in inequality measured by using NBS income were similar to those measured by using CHIP income. Among formal urban residents, the Gini coefficient for CHIP income per capita rose by 3 percent, from 0.338 to 0.349.

The magnitude of the increase was slightly larger for NBS income. The MLD and Theil indexes show larger increases in urban inequality than does the Gini, reflecting their sensitivity to income at the tails of the distribution. In both 2007 and 2013 inequality was lower in the formal urban sector than it was in the rural sector.

Thus, from 2007 to 2013 inequality in the rural and formal urban sectors increased, whereas national inequality declined. The decline in national inequality, despite rising within-sector inequality, reflects two forces. First, rapid growth of rural income and slower growth of urban income narrowed the urban/rural income gap, thus reducing inequality between the urban and rural areas. Second, this period was characterized by rising urbanization. Compared with 2007, a smaller share of the population in 2013 belonged to the rural sector, which had higher within-sector inequality, and a larger share of the population belonged to the urban sector, which had lower within-sector inequality

2.5 Rural-to-Urban Migrants and Inequality

Since the late 1990s, rural-to-urban migration has expanded markedly and it has become a significant feature of the Chinese economy. Migration has provided opportunities for employment for the rural population and has contributed to the rising incomes of rural households. Over time, long-term migration has increased, contributing to China's rising level of urbanization. Migration and urbanization can reduce interregional and rural-urban income differentials; however, the movement of relatively low-income workers to the cities may also increase inequality within the urban areas.

In this section, we examine the incomes of and inequality among migrants, and the relationship between migration and national inequality in China. In the CHIP datasets we define migrants as individuals who reside in an urban location for six months or longer but have rural household registrations (*hukou*). As noted in Chapter 1, in 2007 the migrant sample was obtained through an independent survey carried out by the CHIP, and in 2013 migrants were included in the integrated NBS household survey. The migrant samples in the two years were thus selected by using different sampling methods and therefore may not be entirely consistent. Our use of regional sampling weights in all calculations improves comparability, but some inconsistencies undoubtedly still remain.

Not surprisingly, average income per capita of migrant households lies between that of rural and urban households (Table 2.6). From 2007 to 2013, the income of migrant households grew 3 percent per year, more slowly than the income of both formal urban and formal rural individuals. Consequently, the gap between migrant and rural incomes narrowed, whereas the gap between migrant and urban incomes widened.

We note that the relatively slow growth of per capita migrant income reflects in part a change in the structure of migrant households in the CHIP samples. In the 2007 sample, migrant households contained relatively few dependents (19 percent of migrant household members were not employed and thus were dependent); in 2013 half of the migrant household members were dependents (51 percent of migrant household members were not employed). This increase in the proportion of dependents in migrant households offset the relatively rapid growth in migrant earnings per worker. The real increase in wage earnings per employed migrant worker was 6.7 percent per year, substantially higher than the increase in per capita migrant income.

Table 2.6. Migrant household income per capita growth and composition, 2007 and 2013

Income component	Mean income (yuan)		Change from 2007 to 2013		
	2007	2013	Contribution to increase in total income (%)	Real increase (%)	Real average annual growth (%)
Wage earnings	11,480	15,110	51.7	9.8	1.6
Net income from business	4786	5938	16.4	3.5	0.6
Asset income	166	362	2.8	81.7	10.5
Net transfers	−1447	−820	8.9	−52.7	−11.7
Pensions	n.a.	341	4.9	n.a.	n.a.
Imputed rents on owner-occupied housing	352	1328	13.9	214.9	21.1
Total income	15,233	22,259	100.0	21.9	3.4

Notes: CHIP income per capita. Income levels are in current prices; real increases are in 2007 constant prices converted by using the urban consumer price index published by the NBS (1.19829). Information on pensions was not available for migrants in 2007 so we do not calculate the growth rates for this income source; migrant pensions were likely very small or zero in 2007.

This change in migrant household structure in the CHIP data is consistent with the evolution of migration in China from the temporary movement of individual workers to the more permanent residence of workers and their family members in urban areas. It may, however, also reflect the different sampling methods used for migrants in the CHIP surveys in the two years.

Table 2.6 reports information on the composition of migrant income. Most of the growth in migrant income from 2007 to 2013 was contributed by wages and household business income. These sources of income grew relatively slowly but together they accounted for more than 90 percent of total income. The fastest growing component of migrant income was imputed rents on owner-occupied housing, the combined result of rising urban housing values and increased migrant home ownership. In 2013 31 percent of migrant households owned their homes, up from only 3 percent in 2007. Net transfers for migrants remained negative but became less negative from 2007 to 2013. Negative net transfers indicate that on balance migrants send out private transfers and also that their contributions to social programs, such as pensions and health insurance, exceed the benefits they receive.

Inequality among migrants increased between the two years. The Gini coefficient among migrants for CHIP income per capita rose by 7 percent, from 0.324 in 2007 to 0.348 in 2013 (see Table 2.5). Alternative inequality indexes for migrants show increases similar to or larger than that of the Gini coefficient.

How did migration affect nationwide inequality in China? In theory, the movement of workers in response to higher incomes and better employment opportunities will tend to narrow earnings differentials among regions and between urban and rural areas; thus, it may reduce nationwide inequality. Within the urban areas, however, the influx of lower-income workers and their families can increase inequality.

A full analysis of the impact of migration on inequality is beyond the scope of this chapter. We can, however, compare estimates of inequality that exclude migrants with estimates that include migrants. This comparison does not capture the full effects of migration on inequality, e.g., it does not account for the impact of migration on the income of non-migrants. Nevertheless, it provides a back-of-the-envelope indication of the impact.

Table 2.7 shows estimates of urban inequality that include and exclude migrants. In 2007 urban inequality including migrants was not much different from that excluding migrants; in 2013 it was a bit higher. For example, in 2013 the urban Gini for CHIP income including migrants was about

Table 2.7. Estimates of the urban Gini coefficient excluding and including migrants, 2007 and 2013

	2007	2013	change (%)
(a) NBS income per capita			
Gini excluding migrants	0.334	0.355	6.3
Gini including migrants	0.327	0.359	9.8
% difference in Ginis, excluding and including migrants	−2.10	+1.11	—
(b) CHIP income per capita			
Gini excluding migrants	0.338	0.349	3.3
Gini including migrants	0.339	0.356	5.0
% difference in Ginis, excluding and including migrants	+0.30	+2.87	—

Table 2.8. Estimates of the national Gini coefficient excluding and including migrants, 2007 and 2013

	2007	2013	change (%)
(a) NBS income per capita			
Gini excluding migrants	0.476	0.462	−2.94
Gini including migrants	0.469	0.448	−4.48
% difference in Ginis, excluding and including migrants	−1.47	−3.03	—
(b) CHIP income per capita			
Gini excluding migrants	0.502	0.445	−11.35
Gini including migrants	0.486	0.433	−10.91
% difference in Ginis, excluding and including migrants	−3.19	−2.70	—

3 percent higher than that excluding migrants. Whether migrants are included or not, urban inequality increased from 2007 to 2013. The increase in the estimates that include migrants was larger than the increase in the estimates that exclude migrants. Table 2.8 shows estimates of national inequality that include and exclude migrants in the calculation. In both years, including migrants reduces inequality. For CHIP income, for example, the Gini coefficient including migrants is about 3 percent lower than that excluding

migrants. Including migrants reduces inequality because their incomes lie between those of formal urban and rural residents and it reduces the urban/rural income gap. As will be discussed later in the chapter, the urban/rural income gap has been a key factor underlying national inequality in China.

2.6 Urban/Rural and Regional Income Gaps

Segmentation between China's urban and rural sectors has contributed to a large and ongoing income gap between urban and rural households. The urban/rural income gap widened continuously from the late 1980s through 2007 and was a key factor underlying the secular increase in national inequality (Li, Sato, and Sicular 2013). However, rapid growth of rural incomes from 2007 to 2013 reversed this trend.

Table 2.9 shows mean urban and rural incomes per capita and the urban/rural income gap as measured by the ratio of mean urban income to mean

Table 2.9. The urban/rural income gap, 2007 and 2013

	Mean income per capita (yuan)		Change, 2007 to 2013 (%)	Ratio of urban to rural (no PPP adjustment)		Ratio of urban to rural (with PPP adjustment)	
	2007	2013		2007	2013	2007	2013
(a) NBS income per capita							
Urban, excl. migrants	14,982	28,559	59.1	3.46	2.90	2.52	2.20
Urban, incl. migrants	15,298	26,764	46.0	3.53	2.72	2.57	2.06
Rural	4331	9850	85.5	—	—	—	—
(b) CHIP income per capita							
Urban, excl. migrants	19,212	30,983	34.6	4.03	2.56	2.94	1.90
Urban, incl. migrants	18,231	28,843	32.0	3.82	2.38	2.77	1.76
Rural	4770	12,098	106.8	—	—	—	—

Notes: Income levels are in current prices; percentage changes are in constant prices. PPP estimates use the urban/rural × province spatial price indexes from Brandt and Holz (2006), updated to 2007 and 2013 using the urban/rural × province consumer price indexes published by the NBS.

rural income. Estimates are given for both NBS and CHIP income, for urban income excluding and including migrants, and with and without PPP adjustments. In all cases, the increase in rural income far outpaced the increase in urban income and the urban/rural income gap declined substantially. For example, the ratio of CHIP urban (including migrants) income to rural income without PPP adjustments declined from 4.0 in 2007 to 2.6 in 2013.

In view of the difference in costs of living between the urban and rural areas, we report estimates of the urban/rural income gap that are adjusted for spatial price differences (the rightmost two columns of Table 2.9). The PPP adjustment reduces the gap in both years, especially in 2013, but the decline in the urban/rural income gap from 2007 to 2013 is robust to the PPP adjustment. For example, the ratio of urban (including migrants) to rural income for PPP-adjusted CHIP income declined by more than one-third, from 2.9 in 2007 to about 1.9 in 2013.

The narrowing of the urban/rural income gap from 2007 to 2013 was important to the decline in national inequality. We can calculate the contribution of the urban/rural income gap to national inequality by decomposing inequality by subgroup. For this exercise, we use the Theil and MLD inequality indexes because the Gini coefficient cannot be additively decomposed across partitioned groups. The Theil index T can be decomposed into inequality within groups T^{within} and inequality between groups $T^{between}$ as follows:

$$T = \sum_i \frac{y_i}{Y} \ln\left(\frac{y_i}{\mu}\right) \tag{2.2}$$

$$= \sum_j \frac{Y_j}{Y} T^j + \sum_j \frac{Y_j}{Y} \ln\left(\frac{\mu_j}{\mu}\right)$$

$$= T^{within} + T^{between},$$

where y_i is the income of individual i, Y is the total income in the population, μ is the mean income of the population, Y_j is the total income of the population subgroup j, T^j is the Theil index for population subgroup j, and μ_j is the mean income of population subgroup j.

The first line of Equation (2.2) shows the formula for the Theil inequality index. The second line shows its decomposition by population subgroup, which contains two components. The first component T^{within} is equal to the weighted sum of inequality within the population subgroups. The weights are the income shares of each group. The second term $T^{between}$ is equal to the Theil index calculated across the mean incomes of the subgroups. The contribution of between-group inequality to overall inequality, the result of interest here, is equal to between-group inequality $T^{between}$ divided by total inequality T.

The MLD index can be decomposed as follows:

$$
\begin{aligned}
MLD &= \sum_i \frac{1}{N} \ln \frac{\mu}{y_i} \\
&= \sum_j \frac{N_j}{N} MLD^j + \frac{N_j}{N} \ln\left(\frac{\mu}{\mu_j}\right) \\
&= MLD^{within} + MLD^{between},
\end{aligned}
\tag{2.3}
$$

where N is size of the total population, N_j is the population of subgroup j, and MLD^j is the MLD index for population subgroup j.

The first line of Equation (2.3) shows the formula for the MLD inequality index. The second line shows its decomposition by population subgroup. The first component, within-group inequality, or MLD^{within}, is the weighted sum of inequality within the population subgroups, with the weights equal to the population shares of each group. The second term, between-group inequality, or $MLD^{between}$, is the MLD index calculated across the mean incomes of the subgroups and with each subgroup weighted by its population share. Again, the contribution of between-group inequality to total inequality is $MLD^{between}$ divided by total inequality MLD.

We use this methodology to decompose inequality between the urban and rural population subgroups. In this decomposition we include migrants in the urban group. Table 2.10 reports the results. Without PPP adjustments, the contribution of the urban/rural income gap to national inequality was 45–50 percent in 2007 but it declined to 25–30 percent in 2013. PPP adjustments reduced the size of the urban/rural gap and its contribution to national

Table 2.10. Contribution of the urban/rural income gap to national inequality (%)

| | No PPP adjustment | | | | With PPP adjustment | | | |
| | NBS income | | CHIP income | | NBS income | | CHIP income | |
	2007	2013	2007	2013	2007	2013	2007	2013
MLD	47.24	31.71	49.94	26.79	34.63	19.97	38.35	15.11
Theil	46.22	30.72	48.22	25.89	34.98	20.05	38.47	15.02

Notes: Urban includes migrants. The contribution of the urban/rural income gap to national inequality is equal to "between inequality" divided by total inequality. See the main text for an explanation of the inequality decomposition methodology and the formula for "between inequality."

inequality, but the contribution of the urban/rural gap to inequality nevertheless declined substantially, from roughly 40 percent in 2007 to 15 percent in 2013.

Historically, China's economy has been characterized by large regional income differences, with the higher incomes in the more-developed East and the lower incomes in the less-developed West. These regional income differences have contributed to national inequality, although less so than the urban/rural gap. Table 2.11 shows the mean incomes for each of the East, Central, and West regions and the income ratios between the regions, with the West region in the denominator. In both years incomes were highest in the East region and lowest in the West region.

From 2007 to 2013 the income gaps between the East, Central, and West regions narrowed. The PPP-adjusted East/Central income ratio declined from 1.53 to 1.31, and the PPP-adjusted East/West income ratio declined from 1.80 to 1.39. Catch-up was especially marked for the West region, which by 2013 registered incomes that on average were only about 6 percent lower than those in the Central region.

Looking at the regional differences for each of the migrant, formal urban, and rural groups, one finds that by 2013 migrant incomes (PPP adjusted) were quite similar in the three regions, which very likely reflects the mobility of migrant workers and the relocation of jobs among regions. In 2013 formal urban incomes in the Central and West regions were similar, but both remained lower than those in the East. Regional gaps were most persistent for the rural population, although they declined somewhat.

Table 2.11. Household CHIP income per capita by region and regional income gaps, with and without spatial PPP adjustments, 2007 and 2013

Region/sector	2007				2013			
	Urban	Rural	Migrant	All	Urban	Rural	Migrant	All
CHIP income per capita (yuan, current prices, no PPP adjustment)								
East	25,444	6896	16,939	15,574	37,619	16,042	22,805	26,764
Central	15,114	4160	11,536	8514	25,309	10,629	21,274	17,606
West	13,969	3273	12,292	7107	26,320	9556	21,531	16,774
Regional income ratios (no PPP adjustment)								
East/Central	1.68	1.66	1.47	1.83	1.49	1.51	1.07	1.52
East/West	1.82	2.11	1.38	2.19	1.43	1.68	1.06	1.60
Central/West	1.08	1.27	0.94	1.20	0.96	1.11	0.99	1.05
Regional income ratios (PPP adjusted)								
East/Central	1.42	1.52	1.20	1.53	1.30	1.39	0.92	1.31
East/West	1.49	1.92	1.11	1.80	1.23	1.63	0.89	1.39
Central/West	1.05	1.27	0.92	1.17	0.95	1.18	0.97	1.06

Notes: CHIP income per capita. The 2007 urban and rural samples each cover seven East provinces (Beijing, Hebei [rural only], Liaoning, Shanghai [urban only], Jiangsu, Zhejiang, Fujian, and Guangdong), five Central provinces (Shanxi, Anhui, Henan, Hubei, and Hunan), and four West provinces (Chongqing, Sichuan, Yunnan, and Gansu). The 2007 migrant sample covers the five largest migrant outflow provinces (three Central: Anhui, Henan, and Hubei; and two West: Chongqing and Sichuan), and the four largest migrant inflow provinces (all East: Shanghai, Jiangsu, Zhejiang, and Guangdong). The 2013 urban, rural, and migrant samples cover the same provinces: five East (Beijing, Liaoning, Jiangsu, Shandong, and Guangdong), five Central (Shanxi, Anhui, Henan, Hubei, and Hunan), and five West (Chongqing, Sichuan, Yunnan, Gansu, and Xinjiang).

The narrowing of regional income gaps contributed to the decline in national inequality. Table 2.12 shows the results of the decomposition of inequality by regional subgroup. The contribution of between-region income differences was already low in 2007, and it declined further to less than 10 percent of national inequality in 2013.

In addition, within-region inequality declined in all regions. As shown in Table 2.13, within-region inequality was highest in West China, which in 2013 had a regional Gini coefficient that exceeded that of China as a whole. The Gini coefficients of the East and Central regions were lower than that of China as a whole.

Table 2.12. Contribution of regional income gaps to national inequality (%)

	No PPP adjustment				With PPP adjustment			
	NBS income		CHIP income		NBS income		CHIP income	
	2007	2013	2007	2013	2007	2013	2007	2013
MLD	12.95	7.54	14.08	7.29	8.63	4.37	9.88	3.95
Theil	13.84	8.16	15.03	7.72	9.12	4.69	10.48	4.14

Notes: The contribution of the urban/rural income gap to national inequality is equal to "between inequality" divided by total inequality. See the main text for an explanation of the inequality decomposition methodology and the formula for "between inequality."

Table 2.13. Gini coefficients for the East, Central, and West regions, 2007 and 2013

	No PPP adjustments		With PPP adjustments	
	2007	2013	2007	2013
East	0.445	0.415	0.397	0.388
Central	0.444	0.404	0.400	0.376
West	0.485	0.442	0.450	0.424
National	0.486	0.433	0.431	0.400

Note: CHIP income per capita.

High inequality in West China reflected in part its large urban/rural income gap (Table 2.14). In 2007 the urban/rural income ratio without PPP adjustments in the West region was 4.2, compared to 3.3 and 3.5 in the East and Central regions, respectively. The pattern is similar with the PPP adjustments. From 2007 to 2013 the urban/rural income ratio declined substantially in all regions as well as in China as a whole, but it remained highest in the West region.

2.7 Incorporating Top Incomes

Beginning in the 1990s China began economic reforms that opened the door to private ownership and the accumulation of household wealth. Subsequently, income from assets and returns to capital wealth emerged as a new and increasingly important factor affecting China's income distribution (Li, Sato, and Sicular 2013). In China, as elsewhere, income from

Table 2.14. The urban/rural income ratio for the East, Central, and West regions, 2007 and 2013

	No PPP adjustment		With PPP adjustment	
	2007	2013	2007	2013
East	3.27	2.06	2.30	1.51
Central	3.51	2.32	2.69	1.80
West	4.17	2.64	3.27	2.20
National	3.82	2.38	2.77	1.81

Notes: CHIP income per capita. Urban includes migrants. The gaps are a bit larger but follow a similar pattern if migrants are not included as urban.

assets tends to be held disproportionately by individuals at the top tail of the income distribution. Incomes at the top tail of the income distribution, however, are difficult to capture in household surveys. These considerations raise concerns about the possibility of an understatement of the incomes at the top tail of China's income distribution. Such an understatement would cause a downward bias in measured inequality.

In recent years, economists have developed methods to estimate incomes at the top tail of the income distribution and to incorporate them into the inequality measurement (e.g., Alvaredo et al. 2013). In this section, we apply one such method to obtain estimates of inequality for China that are adjusted for the understatement of incomes at the top tail of the Chinese income distribution. The method, applied previously to China by Li and Luo (2011), uses publicly available information about the wealth of the ultra-rich to construct the top tail of the income distribution. This constructed top tail is combined with the household survey data for the rest of the income distribution. Then inequality is then measured over the entire combined distribution.

We begin with a brief overview of this methodology and then report on our findings (see Appendix A2 for additional details). Suppose the true income distribution is as shown in Figure 2.3 and that the household survey sample fully captures only the incomes of households with incomes in Section A of the distribution below some income threshold x_0. Ultra-rich individuals with the very highest incomes (in Section C) are few in number and have a low probability of being selected for the sample through the survey sampling process. This group, however, tends to have high visibility, and some information about its income or wealth is publicly available. The next highest income

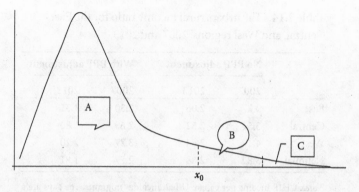

Fig. 2.3 Notional graph of the true income distribution

group (B) is larger numerically than group C. The survey sampling process usually captures some individuals in this group, but they may still be under-represented or their income may not be fully captured in the survey data.

Using publicly available data for very high-income individuals (who populate Section C), and assuming that the top of the income distribution (Sections B and C) takes the shape of a Pareto distribution, one can infer the income distribution of the top sections (B and C) of the income distribution (Creedy 1985; Bronfenbrenner 1971). This inferred income distribution for the top-income individuals can then be combined with the household survey data for the remainder of the income distribution (A) and used to estimate the inequality of the entire population, including the top-income group.

This methodology requires that the researcher choose an income threshold x_0 for the top-income group. It also requires some choices regarding how to incorporate different sources of information on the top-income individuals. For our analysis, we carried out alternative calculations based on three alternative thresholds and incorporating information from two different sources—the *Hurun* rich list and the *Forbes* rich list. We also combined the two rich lists. We thus obtain a range of estimates of the Gini coefficient for different thresholds and sets of information. Appendix A2 provides more explanation regarding these alternatives and the resulting range of estimates.

Table 2.15 reports our low, medium (preferred), and high estimates of the national Gini coefficient, incorporating the top tail of the income distribution. All estimates show a level of inequality that is higher than our original estimates. For 2007 the effect of incorporating the top incomes is modest.

Table 2.15. Estimates of the national Gini coefficient incorporating the top-income group

	Gini adjusted for the top tail		Ratio to original Gini estimate		Increase of adjusted Gini from 2007 to 2013 (%)
	2007	2013	2007	2013	
Low estimate	0.485	0.492	1.032	1.100	1.4
Medium estimate (preferred)	0.494	0.583	1.051	1.301	18.0
High estimate	0.502	0.630	1.068	1.406	25.5

Notes: Estimated by using NBS income per capita; weights are applied to the CHIP sample data. The low estimates are calculated by using information from the *Forbes* list and with x_0 set at the highest observed level of income in the CHIP survey data. The medium estimates use the *Hurun* list and 60,000 yuan. The high estimates use the combined *Forbes* and *Hurun* lists and 120,000 yuan. See Appendix 2 in this chapter for a full explanation. Ratios to the original Gini are calculated by using the Gini of the NBS income per capita of 0.470 in 2007 and 0.448 in 2013 (see Table 2.1).

These estimates range from 0.485 to 0.502, and in all cases they are less than 10 percent higher than our original estimate of the Gini coefficient in that year.[5]

For 2013 the impact of incorporating the top incomes is larger, and the estimates span a wider range. The low estimate is 0.493, 10 percent higher than the original estimate of the Gini without the top incomes, and the high estimate is 0.630, a substantial 41 percent higher than the original estimate of the Gini without the top incomes (Table 2.15).

All our estimates of the Gini incorporating the top-income group show an increase in inequality between 2007 and 2013. For some of the estimates the increase is small—e.g., only 1 percent—for estimates based on the *Forbes* list and a threshold equal to the highest income in the CHIP sample. For some estimates, the increase is large—e.g., 25 percent—for estimates based on the combined list and thresholds of 120,000 yuan and 60,000 yuan. Regardless, adjustments for the top incomes result in trends in inequality that differ from estimates that do not incorporate such adjustments.

The range of our estimates for 2007 is fairly narrow, from about 0.49 to 0.50, and in all cases within 7 percent higher than the Gini without incorporating the top incomes. For 2013 the estimates span a wider range, from 0.49 to 0.63, from 10 percent to 40 percent higher than the Gini without incorporating the top incomes. We conclude that the extent of bias in the standard estimates of inequality in China arising from the underrepresentation of incomes at the top tail of the income distribution was modest in 2007, but by 2013 it became substantial. Because these estimates are based on strong assumptions and rely on incomplete data about the top-income group, we treat them as cautionary rather than definitive.

2.8 Conclusion

Estimates of inequality published by the NBS show a decline in inequality after 2007. Our base estimates corroborate this decline. Alternative estimates using different income definitions (NBS and CHIP) and different inequality indexes (Gini, MLD, and Theil) yield somewhat different levels of inequality, but for all income definitions and for all indexes inequality declined.

We find that the decline reflects reductions in several important dimensions of inequality. The rural/urban income gap narrowed. Regional income gaps between the East, Central, and West regions shrank. Inequality declined for most major components of household income—wage earnings, income from agriculture and non-agricultural household businesses, asset income, pensions, and imputed rents on owner-occupied housing. Reduced inequality in these dimensions contributed to the nationwide decline in overall income inequality. The decline in national inequality would have been even larger if it had not been offset by rising inequality within the urban and rural sectors and by the growing importance of unequally distributed income components, such as income from assets and imputed rents on owner-occupied housing.

In recent years China has experienced a slowdown in macroeconomic growth. According to NBS statistics, average growth in GDP per capita from 2007 to 2013 was 8.5 percent, as compared to 11 percent from 2002 to 2007. Some observers have suggested that the slowdown in GDP growth will have negative implications for household incomes in general and for the middle- and lower-income groups in particular. Our examination of the CHIP data finds that on average, growth in household incomes slowed from 2007 to 2013, but the slowdown was mainly for higher-income groups, especially urban residents (both formal and migrant). For lower- and middle-income households, especially rural residents, income growth accelerated and averaged more than 10 percent per year. Income growth for lower- and middle-income groups occurred despite slow growth in agricultural income; it was the result of solid growth in wage earnings plus robust growth in income from non-agricultural businesses, assets, and pensions, as well as imputed rents on owner-occupied housing.

Although the decline in national inequality is robust across income definitions and alternative inequality indexes, it is sensitive to adjustments for spatial differences in costs of living and for the understatement of incomes at the top tail of the income distribution. When we adjust the estimates to correct for the spatial differences in the cost of living, inequality no longer declines for NBS income and for CHIP income the decline is noticeably reduced. These findings indicate that some of the reduction in inequality from 2007 to 2013 is due to price changes rather than due to changes in real incomes.

Similarly, when we make adjustments that address the understatement of incomes at the top tail of the income distribution, inequality no longer declines from 2007 to 2013. These adjusted estimates require strong assumptions and rely on imperfect data for the top-income group, but they suggest that some, if not all, of the apparent reduction in inequality from 2007 to 2013 is due to the growing importance of the top-income individuals and their incomes. The difficulties of capturing income at the top of China's income distribution through household surveys have been increasing over time. Future analyses of inequality in China must pay attention to this problem.

Our findings raise a series of important questions about the underlying causes of the recent shifts in incomes and inequality. To what extent were incomes and inequality affected by the 2008 Global Financial Crisis? How did the new social programs implemented during the Hu-Wen period— for example, the expansion of medical insurance, pensions, and the minimum livelihood guarantee (*dibao*) programs—contribute to the decline in inequality? What was the role of the ongoing rural-to-urban migration and the government's push to accelerate urbanization? How did changes in human capital and rising education levels affect the growth in wage earnings and thus the income distribution? Some of these questions are addressed in the chapters of this volume and others await further research.

Notes

Note: We acknowledge financial support for this research from the CIGI-INET Program on New Economic Theory, Practice, and Governance.

1. For a further discussion of these inequality indexes, see World Bank (2014, chap. 6).
2. Changes from 2002 to 2007 are from Li, Luo, and Sicular (2013, Table 2.1).

3. Based on country Gini coefficients reported in the *World Bank World Development Indicators Database*, http://wdi.worldbank.org/table/2.9#. Accessed December 11, 2016.

4. See World Bank (2014, chap. 6) for an explanation of the Lorenz curve.

5. Published information on the top-income individuals does not contain any information about the value of their owner-occupied housing, so for this group we cannot estimate imputed rents. Consequently, in this analysis we use the NBS definition of income, and we compare these estimates with our original estimates of the Gini calculated for the NBS income (Table 2.1).

6. The one-year deposit interest rates were 3.465 percent in 2007 and 3.375 percent in 2013. An alternate approach would be to calculate income as the change in wealth from one year to the next, but this approach is problematic because of substantial wealth fluctuations from year to year and because the individuals on the lists change from year to year.

7. Note that the income tax reporting threshold of 120,000 yuan remained unchanged over time, despite changes in the price level. Only 18 and 130 individuals in the CHIP samples had household per capita income over 120,000 in 2007 and 2013 respectively. The proportions (weighted) of the samples are 0.02 percent in 2007 and 0.29 percent in 2013.

8. The number of individuals in the sample with income per capita over 60,000 yuan was 313 in 2007 and 1351 in 2013, equivalent (with weights) to 0.36 percent and 3.02 percent of the population in each year, respectively.

9. The number of individuals with incomes over 120,000 yuan who filed income tax returns in 2007 was reported to be 2.12 million (http://www.chinadaily.com.cn/china/2008-04/19/content_6629213.htm, accessed May 18, 2019). Multiple sources (e.g., Gilley 2017; http://www.kanshangjie.com/article/52811-1.html, accessed April 19, 2019) note that the number of those filing income taxes is unreasonably small, reflecting weak compliance with the personal income tax filing requirements.

10. Statistics on the number of those filing personal incomes taxes are not available for all years. They are not available for 2013; for 2015 the number is 28 million (Gilley 2017; http://www.kanshangjie.com/article/52811-1.html, accessed April 28, 2019). Available reports indicate that the number has grown year over year, so in 2013 the number of those filing taxes is very likely less than 28 million.

References

Alvaredo, F., A. B. Atkinson, T. Piketty, and E. Saez (2013). "The Top 1 Percent in International and Historical Perspective." *Journal of Economic Perspectives*, 27(3), 3–20.

Brandt, L. and C. A. Holz (2006). "Spatial Price Differences in China: Estimates and Implications." *Economic Development and Cultural Change*, 55(1), 43–86.

Bronfenbrenner, M. (1971). *Income Distribution Theory*. Chicago: Aldine Atherton.

Creedy, J. (1985). *Dynamics of Income Distribution*. Oxford: Basil Blackwell.

Gilley, B. (2017). "Taxation and Authoritarian Resilience." *Journal of Contemporary China*, 26(105), 452-464.

Gustafsson, B., S. Li, and H. Sato (2014). "Data for Studying Earnings, the Distribution of Household Income and Poverty in China." IZA Working Paper DP 8244, June. http://ftp.iza.org/dp8244.pdf. Accessed April 27, 2017.

Lambert, P. (1989). *The Distribution and Redistribution of Income.* Oxford: Blackwell.

Li, S. and C. Luo (2011). "Zhongguo shouru chaju jiujing you duoda?" (How unequal is income in China?). *Jingji yanjiu* (Economic research), no. 4, 68-79.

Li, S., C. Luo, and T. Sicular (2013). "Overview: Income Inequality and Poverty in China, 2002-2007," in S. Li, H. Sato, and T. Sicular, eds., *Rising Inequality in China: Challenges to a Harmonious Society*, 44-84. Cambridge and New York: Cambridge University Press.

Li, S., H. Sato, and T. Sicular (2013)."Rising Inequality in China: Key Issues and Findings," in S. Li, H. Sato, and T. Sicular, eds., *Rising Inequality in China: Challenges to a Harmonious Society*, 1-43. Cambridge and New York: Cambridge University Press.

National Bureau of Statistics (NBS) (2013). "Ma Jiantang jiu 2012 nian guomin jingji yun hang qingkuang da jizhe wen" (Press conference with Ma Jiantang on national economic conditions in 2012). January 18. http://www.stats.gov.cn/tjgz/tjdt/201301/t20130118_17719.html. Accessed January 8, 2017.

National Bureau of Statistics (NBS) (2016). "China's Economy Realized a Moderate but Stable and Sound Growth in 2015." January 19. http://www.stats.gov.cn/english/PressRelease/201601/t20160119_1306072.html. Accessed January 8, 2017.

Shorrocks, A. F. (1982). "Inequality Decomposition by Factor Components." *Econometrica*, 50 (1), 193-211.

Sundrum, R. M. (1990). *Income Distribution in Less Developed Countries.* London: Routledge.

World Bank (2014). "Introduction to Poverty Analysis (English)." Washington, DC: World Bank Group. http://documents.worldbank.org/curated/en/775871468331250546/Introduction-to-poverty-analysis. Accessed November 24, 2019.

A2 Appendix

Methodology Used to Incorporate Top Incomes in the Estimation of the Gini Coefficient

A2.1 Methodology

Following the standard approach in the literature, we assume that the income distribution for the top-income individuals follows the Pareto distribution

$$logN = logK - \alpha logx \qquad (A2.1)$$

where N is the number of people with incomes higher than x (Creedy 1985, pp. 24–25). The values of N and x are taken from the available data for the top-income individuals; the parameters K and α are estimated.

For the Pareto distribution, the Gini coefficient among the top-income individuals $Gini_{top}$ is given by the formula (Lambert 1989, p. 29).

$$Gini_{top} = \frac{1}{2\alpha - 1}$$ (A2.2)

Equation (A2.2) reveals that the estimate of the Gini for the top-income group depends entirely on the magnitude of the parameter α. The larger the value of α, the smaller the value of $Gini_{top}$.

Also, for the Pareto distribution the mean income of the top-income group is a function of the income threshold for the top-income group. For any given threshold x_0, the mean income of the top-income group μ_{top} is

$$\mu_{top} = \frac{x_0 \alpha}{\alpha - 1}$$ (A2.3)

To obtain estimates of the parameters K and α of the Pareto distribution, we apply an OLS regression to Equation (A2.1). We then input these estimated parameters into Equations (A2.2) and (A2.3) to calculate the estimates of the Gini coefficient and the mean income of the top-income group. We also use these estimated parameters to predict the population of individuals in the top-income group $\widehat{N}$ for any given x_0 by using the formula

$$\widehat{N} = \exp\left(\widehat{logK} - \widehat{\alpha}logx_0\right)$$ (A2.4)

According to Sundrum (1990), the Gini coefficient for the entire income distribution $Gini_{whole}$ can be calculated on the basis of the Gini coefficients, population shares, and mean incomes of two subgroups as follows:

$$Gini_{whole} = P_1^2 \frac{\mu_1}{\mu} G_1 + P_2^2 \frac{\mu_2}{\mu} G_2 + P_1 P_2 \left| \frac{\mu_2 - \mu_1}{\mu} \right|$$ (A2.5)

In our application, P_1 is the population share of the population represented by the household survey, P_2 is the population share of the top-income group, μ_1 and μ_2 are the mean incomes of these two groups, and μ is the population-weighted mean income of the entire population including both groups. G_1 is the Gini of the population represented by the household survey, and G_2 is the Gini for the top-income group. P_1, μ_1, and G_1 are estimated by using information from the household survey; P_2, μ_2, and G_2 are estimated by using Equations (A2.1) through (A2.4) with publicly available information about the top-income individuals from the *Forbes* and *Hurun* lists.

A2.2   Data for Top-Income Individuals: The *Forbes* and *Hurun* Lists

Each year *Forbes* publishes a list of the 400 richest individuals in China and their wealth. *Hurun* also publishes a list each year, but the number of individuals on the *Hurun* list has increased over time. In 2007 the *Hurun* list contained 797 individuals and in 2013 it contained 1000 individuals. We construct separate estimates based on each of these two lists, as well as estimates based on a combination of the two lists. For the combined list, if an individual appears on both the *Forbes* list and the *Hurun* list, we include that individual on the combined list only once, using the average of the incomes on the two lists. The number of individuals on the combined list is 873 in 2007 and 1040 in 2013.

The *Forbes* and *Hurun* lists report each individual's wealth. We convert wealth into an estimate of the corresponding level of annual income by using the one-year fixed deposit interest rate.[6] We do not have information about these individuals' household size. We assume that on average the top-income households contain two people, which is the average size in the CHIP sample of the ten households with the highest levels of NBS income per capita and also the average size of the top 1 percent of households in the sample. If top-income individuals live in households with more than two people, our estimates of national inequality incorporating the top incomes may be overstated. We also assume that the second household member does not contribute any additional income to the household, i.e., household per capita income in the top-income group is equal to the rich individual's income divided by two. If other household members contribute income to the household, then our estimates of national inequality incorporating the top income may be understated. We checked the sensitivity of our estimates to our assumption of household size. Alternative household sizes of one person and three people change the estimated levels of inequality only modestly and do not change our basic conclusion that inequality increased from 2007 to 2013.

Note that here we use the NBS income definition for all calculations because we have no information on housing for the top-income group and thus we are unable to construct estimates of their CHIP income.

A2.3   Choice of Income Threshold (x_0)

These calculations require that the researcher choose an income threshold x_0 for the top-income group. We follow common practice and set the threshold equal to the highest level of income per capita observed in the survey. The income distribution for individuals with income per capita above this highest observed level is then estimated by using the Pareto distribution with information about very rich individuals that is available in public sources. This approach implicitly assumes that the survey sample accurately captures the income distribution in the population up to the highest income per capita present in the sample.

We also employ an alternative threshold of 120,000 yuan per capita. We choose 120,000 yuan because since 2006 China has required by law that all individuals with annual incomes exceeding 120,000 yuan file annual income tax returns and report their incomes (Gilley 2017). This requirement creates an incentive for individuals with incomes above 120,000 yuan to hide or to underreport their income; in fact, the CHIP samples contain very few individuals with per capita incomes higher than this threshold.[7] Our estimates based on this second threshold assume that the CHIP survey sample accurately captures the income distribution up to, but not above, 120,000 yuan per capita.

For a third set of estimates, we treat 120,000 yuan as the total household income rather than income per capita and we divide it by two to obtain a threshold of 60,000 yuan per capita for the top-income group. The number of individuals in the CHIP sample with income per capita above this threshold remains small.[8] This third set of estimates assumes that the CHIP survey sample accurately captures the income distribution up to but not above 60,000 yuan per capita.

A2.4 Results

Table A2.1 reports the regression estimates for Equation (A2.1), based on the *Forbes, Hurun,* and combined lists. The estimates of α are similar for the three lists, falling between 1.29 and 1.34 in 2007 and between 1.60 and 1.73 in 2013.

Using the parameter estimates in Table A2.1, we calculate estimates of the number of individuals (N), population share (P_2), average income (μ_{top}), and Gini coefficient ($Gini_{top}$) of the top-income group for the *Forbes, Hurun,* and combined lists in 2007 and 2013. Estimates in the top panel of Table A2.2 use a threshold for the top-income group x_0 of 120,000 yuan per capita; the middle panel uses a threshold of 60,000 yuan per capita; the bottom panel uses a threshold equal to the highest income per capita reported in the CHIP survey samples. The highest incomes in the survey are in fact substantially higher than 120,000 yuan, so using this threshold generates higher average incomes and a smaller population in the top-income group. The choice of the cutoff does not, however, affect inequality within the top-income group, because $Gini_{top}$ is based on the parameter α, which is estimated by using information in the *Forbes,* the *Hurun,* and the combined lists.

In all cases, the population of the top-income group is smallest for the estimates based on the *Forbes* list, larger for the estimates based on the *Hurun* list, and largest for the combined list. Also, the population is largest for the lowest cutoff (60,000 yuan) and smallest for the highest cutoff (the highest income in the CHIP sample).

The State Administration of Taxation has published the number of individuals filing taxes, thus providing us with information that we can use to evaluate the alternative estimates based on the 120,000 yuan and 60,000 yuan cutoffs. The State Administration

Table A2.1. OLS estimates of the Pareto distribution

	Forbes			Hurun			Combined		
	logK	α	Adj. R^2	logK	α	Adj. R^2	logK	α	Adj. R^2
2007	28.946	1.294	0.9749	29.461	1.303	0.9740	30.161	1.341	0.9821
	[114.07]	[92.93]		[72.32]	[59.66]		[168.52]	[136.14]	
2013	35.278	1.595	0.9907	36.413	1.634	0.9822	38.124	1.725	0.9919
	[158.02]	[135.02]		[89.29]	[75.72]		[259.47]	[219.18]	

Notes: Estimates of Equation (A2.1) based on information in the *Forbes, Hurun,* and combined lists, assuming that the top-income households contain two members (see the main text); *t*-statistics are reported in brackets; all estimates are significant at the 1 percent level.

Table A2.2. Estimates of the population and distribution of income for the top-income group

	2007	2013	2007	2013	2007	2013
Top income defined as > 120,000 yuan	*Forbes*	*Forbes*	*Hurun*	*Hurun*	Combined	Combined
Top-income population (million)	1.00	16.59	1.50	32.70	1.94	62.44
Share of national population (%)	0.08	1.26	0.11	2.48	0.15	4.73
Average income of top-income group (yuan)	528,657	321,681	516,040	309,274	471,906	285,517
Inequality within the top-income group (Gini)	0.630	0.457	0.623	0.441	0.595	0.408
Top income defined as > 60,000 yuan	*Forbes*	*Forbes*	*Hurun*	*Hurun*	Comb.	Comb.
Top-income population (million)	2.44	50.11	3.71	101.50	4.91	206.41
Share of national population (%)	0.18	3.79	0.28	7.68	0.37	15.62
Average income of top-income group (yuan)	264,328	160,840	258,020	154,637	235,953	142,759
Inequality within the top-income group (Gini)	0.630	0.457	0.623	0.441	0.595	0.408
Top income defined as > highest income in the CHIP sample	*Forbes*	*Forbes*	*Hurun*	*Hurun*	Comb.	Comb.
Top-income population (million)	0.20	1.76	0.30	3.29	0.37	5.52
Share of national population (%)	0.02	0.13	0.02	0.24	0.03	0.41
Average income of top-income group (yuan)	1,814,350	1,312,821	1,771,048	1,262,190	1,619,582	1,165,233
Inequality within the top-income group (Gini)	0.630	0.457	0.623	0.441	0.595	0.408

Notes: Estimated by using Equations (A2.2) through (A2.5) and data from the *Forbes*, *Hurun*, and combined lists.

Table A2.3. Incomes and inequality in the CHIP surveys

	CHIP 2007	CHIP 2013
Entire sample		
Mean income	9353	19,023
Highest income	411,840	489,736
Gini	0.470	0.448
Excluding observations with incomes above 120,000 yuan		
Mean income	9301	18,550
Highest income	120,000	120,000
Gini	0.467	0.437
Excluding observations with incomes above 60,000 yuan		
Mean income	9089	16,923
Highest income	60,000	60,000
Gini	0.458	0.407

Notes: NBS income per capita. Calculated by using CHIP data with weights. The number of individuals in the sample with income per capita greater than or equal to 120,000 yuan was 18 in 2007 and 130 in 2013, equivalent (with weights) to 0.02 percent and 0.29 percent of the population in each year, respectively. The number of individuals in the sample with income per capita greater than or equal to 60,000 yuan was 313 in 2007 and 1351 in 2013, equivalent (with weights) to 0.36 percent and 3.02 percent of the population in each year, respectively.

of Taxation reported that in 2007 the number of individuals in China with incomes over 120,000 yuan who filed income tax returns exceeded 2 million.[9] Assuming a household of two members for each of those filing income tax, we would expect that the population of individuals with income per capita above 120,000 yuan in 2007 should, at the very minimum, be about 4 million (but probably more, due to noncompliance with the tax filing requirements). Consequently, we regard the estimates that use the 120,000-yuan cutoff to yield the top-income populations to be improbably low (all less than 2 million). The estimates based on the 60,000-yuan cutoff and the *Hurun* list and the combined lists give the 2007 top-income populations that in all cases are greater than 2 million yuan and thus more believable.

For 2015 the State Administration of Taxation reported that 28 million individuals with incomes over 120,000 yuan filed taxes.[10] An assumption of two people per household implies the population of this group is 56 million, equivalent to about 4 percent of the 2015 national population (again, likely understated due to noncompliance). In 2013 the number of those filing taxes and their population share would have been a bit lower than that in 2015. On the basis of these numbers, for 2013 we regard the estimated population for the 120,000-yuan cutoff and the *Forbes* and *Hurun* lists to be low (both less than 40 million), and the 60,000-yuan cutoff and the combined list to be high (over 200 million). In our view, then, population estimates for 2007 and 2013 that are based on the

Table A2.4. Estimates of the national Gini coefficient incorporating the top-income group

	2007	2013	2007	2013	2007	2013
	Forbes	Forbes	Hurun	Hurun	Comb.	Comb.
Top income defined as > 120,000 yuan						
Gini including top incomes	0.488	0.523	0.497	0.575	0.502	0.630
Ratio to Gini without top incomes	1.038	1.167	1.057	1.283	1.068	1.406
Top income defined as > 60,000 yuan						
Gini including top incomes	0.483	0.524	0.494	0.583	0.501	0.626
Ratio to Gini without top incomes	1.028	1.170	1.051	1.301	1.066	1.397
Top income defined as > highest income in the CHIP sample						
Gini including top incomes	0.485	0.492	0.491	0.521	0.494	0.553
Ratio to Gini without top incomes	1.038	1.100	1.055	1.183	1.064	1.288

Notes: Estimated by using Equation (A2.5) with data from the Hurun, Forbes, and combined lists and the CHIP data; NBS income per capita; weights are applied to the CHIP sample data.

60,000-yuan cutoff and the Hurun list are most consistent with the reported number of those filing taxes, and they are associated with an adjusted Gini of 0.494 in 2007 and 0.583 in 2013.

Table A2.3 reports information for the rest of the income distribution, based on the CHIP 2007 and 2013 survey data. This information is combined with the estimates for the top-income group in the previous table to estimate $Gini_{whole}$ by using Equation (A2.5).

The top panel of Table A2.3 shows the mean incomes, highest incomes, and Gini coefficients for the full CHIP sample. In both years the highest incomes exceeded 120,000 yuan, although less than 1 percent of the sample had incomes above this threshold; a larger but still small proportion of the sample had incomes above the 60,000-yuan threshold (see the note to Table A2.3).

The bottom two panels of Table A2.3 report the mean income, highest income, and Gini coefficient after dropping those individuals with income per capita above 120,000 yuan or above 60,000 yuan per capita in the CHIP samples. Removing individuals with incomes above 120,000 yuan has only a small impact on the mean income and the Gini coefficient. In 2013, for example, the mean income is only 2.5 percent lower and the Gini is also only 2.5 percent lower than that for the full sample. Removing individuals with incomes above 60,000 yuan makes a greater difference; for example, in 2013 the mean income is 11.0 percent lower and the Gini is 9.2 percent lower than that for the full sample.

Table A2.4 reports our estimates of the national Gini coefficient that combine information from the CHIP datasets with the reconstructed top tail of the income distribution. For 2007 the Gini coefficient ranges from 0.483 to 0.630. Our preferred estimates (x_0 = 60,000, *Hurun* list) are in the middle, at 0.494 in 2007 and 0.583 in 2013.

In all years these estimates are higher than our original estimates (Table 2.1). Furthermore, all these estimates show an increase in inequality from 2007 to 2013, although the extent of the increase varies substantially from 1 percent to 26 percent (Table 2.15).

3

China's Emerging Global Middle Class

Björn Gustafsson, Terry Sicular, and Xiuna Yang

3.1 Introduction

One of the most significant global changes in this millennium has been the substantial increase in the number of Chinese households and persons whose lives in economic terms are similar to those living in the developed world. Most Chinese households no longer worry about how to meet daily living costs and most have savings for a rainy day. Most own a home, and a growing number own a car and can afford to take regular holidays away from home. This change is clearly revealed in studies of worldwide income distribution. Milanovic (2016), for example, reports that globally the largest relative gains in real per capita income between 1988 and 2008 took place at the middle and at the very top of the world's income distribution. To a considerable extent, the gains in the middle were the result of the recent changes in China. In contrast, for the segments between the middle and the top of the global income distribution, income growth was much slower, reflecting the weak growth of income for middle-class households in rich countries.

This chapter seeks to shed new light on the emergence of the Chinese economic middle class. The term "middle class" is used by social scientists in various contexts, as will be further discussed in Section 3.2 and Section 3.3 of this chapter. Here we are in the company of those who take the income of the household as the point of departure, assume a global perspective, and relate the definition of "middle class" to household income levels in those countries with well-established middle classes, that is, the developed countries. We argue that as living standards in China are approaching those in the high-income countries, there is a case to be made to anchor the definition of "middle class" in China to the levels of household income in such countries. More specifically, we define "middle class" as having household income high enough not to be regarded as poor but also low enough not to be regarded as rich in the high-income countries. This approach allows us to consider the

Björn Gustafsson, Terry Sicular, and Xiuna Yang, *China's Emerging Global Middle Class* In: *Changing Trends in China's Inequality.* Edited by: Terry Sicular, Shi Li, Ximing Yue, and Hiroshi Sato, Oxford University Press (2020). © Oxford University Press.
DOI: 10.1093/oso/9780190077938.003.0003

Chinese middle class with an external lens, on the basis of a commonly held notion of the middle class and defined in relation to a standard of living that we believe is the ultimate, long-term objective of China's development process. As will later be explained more fully, this approach yields a threshold for entering the middle class that is equivalent to US $13,140 (PPP) per capita, an annual income that has already been attained or is within reach of many Chinese households.

For a first task, we study the growth of the Chinese middle class from 2007 to 2013. We do this for China as a whole, and then separately for urban residents, rural-to-urban migrants, and rural residents. In order to put this development in perspective, we also look at the growth of the Chinese middle class from 2002 to 2007. For a second task, we simulate how the size of the middle class will develop from 2013 to 2020, assuming there will be uniform income growth of 6.5 percent per annum. The results of this second task allow us to evaluate the extent to which China's population will reach the ranks of the middle classes in the developed world over the medium term. The third task is to investigate to what extent the middle class is distinct and differs from the other classes. We conduct these analyses by using detailed information from the CHIP 2013 survey.

The emerging middle class in China has been the subject of writings by Chinese researchers, most of whom lean toward the long tradition of class analysis in the field of sociology. In contrast, there have been few Chinese attempts to map the middle class on the basis of an analysis that defines middle class on the basis of the level of household disposable income or consumption. In our literature search, we have come across three such studies. Yuan, Wan, and Knor (2012) use the CHIP rural data for 1988, 1995, 2002, and 2007, whereby a rural household is classified as belonging to the middle class if its per capita daily expenditures are from US$4 to US$20 in PPP. Using this definition, these authors find that the middle class in rural China grew from 3 percent in 1988 to 53 percent in 2007. Bonnefond, Clément, and Combarnous (2015) use data from the China Health and Nutrition Survey (CHNS) from 1989 to 2009 to study the urban middle class by using four different definitions, giving some priority to setting the lower cutoff point at 10,000 renminbi (RMB) per year and the upper cutoff point at the 95th income percentile. A cluster analysis for 2009 using household variables indicates that the urban middle class is composed of a significantly higher proportion of households where the household head belongs to the professional and technical worker category, the administrative and executive category, or the office staff category. Somewhat more than two-fifths of middle-class households contain pensioners.[1]

The third study is most similar to ours. Unlike the previous two studies, Chen and Qin (2014) study China as a whole and use the CHIP data for 1995 and 2002 and data from the China Family Panel Study (CFPS) for 2010 and 2012. Households with consumption expenditures in the range of PPP US$10 to US$20 per person per day are classified as upper or global middle class. According to this definition, the Chinese middle class increased from 1 percent in 1995 to 13 percent in 2012. Not surprisingly, the authors find that the proportion of households classified as middle class was highest among urban residents who had an urban *hukou*, followed by migrants living in urban areas, and finally among rural residents.

Turning to our results, according to our definition we find that between 2007 and 2013 the Chinese middle class increased by 159 million persons. This change is larger than the 83 million persons who attained middle-class status between 2002 and 2007. We report that Chinese middle-class persons in 2002 numbered only 12 million, a very small minority of the population. The number of middle-class persons increased to 95 million in 2007 and further to 254 million in 2013. In 2013 one-third of urban persons, but only a small minority of rural and rural-to-urban migrants, belonged to the middle class. A simulation exercise compares the role of income growth versus the role of redistribution in contributing to this expansion of the middle class. For the period from 2007 to 2013 we find that if income growth of all persons had been uniform and equal to the average during that period, then the overall expansion of China's middle class would have been about the same as what in fact occurred; however, the sectoral urban/rural composition of the middle class would have been somewhat different.

Examining the characteristics of China's middle class in 2013, we find that China's middle-class households differed from households with lesser means in various respects, including their savings patterns, sources of income, ownership of consumer durables, geographic distribution, education, and membership in the Chinese Communist Party (CCP). By means of a simulation that assumes incomes for all households will grow at a uniform rate of 6.5 percent per annum (equal to the planned GDP growth per capita), we project the Chinese middle class in 2020 at roughly double its size in 2013, with as much as 60 percent of the urban population belonging to the middle class. In contrast, the size of the rural middle class in 2020 should to remain relatively modest.

In the next section, we discuss how the term "middle class" has been used by Chinese policy makers and in Chinese academic research. Unlike most of the other literature on China's middle class, in this chapter our definition of "middle class" takes a global perspective. Here we follow the approach in the literature on the international distribution of income, which we review in Section 3.3. Section 3.4 discusses the data, our income thresholds for defining the different classes, and our operational assumptions; Section 3.5 reports our findings on the emergence of China's global middle class from 2002 to 2013; Section 3.6 presents an analysis of the growth of China's middle class over time, with projections to 2020. In Section 3.7 we examine the characteristics of China's middle class. Section 3.8 sums up our study and draws some conclusions.

3.2. The Meaning of "Middle Class" in Chinese Policy Making and Academic Studies

For many years the CCP leadership, policy makers, and researchers discussed class in Marxist-Leninist terms of workers, peasants, and intellectuals. The party-state did not acknowledge any social, economic, or political role for the middle class, and its ultimate goal was to create "a classless society." However, during the reform era, beginning in 1978, views began to evolve, and at the Sixteenth Congress of the CCP in 2002, General Secretary Jiang Zemin announced the goal of "control[ling] the growth of the upper stratum of society, expand[ing] the middle stratum, and reduc[ing] the bottom." Thereafter, the CCP developed a state-sponsored discourse on the middle class. The new objective was to achieve an "olive-shaped" middle-class society, in which the bulk of the population would be economically comfortable (*xiaokang*) and society would be harmonious. Goodman notes that this notion of a middle-class society is an aspiration rather than a carefully thought-out idea, but the identification of the middle class as a potential driver of change is clear. "Individuals are being encouraged to pursue new 'social norms of middle-class identity often defined around consumer practices.' The new model citizen is someone with high cultural capital and the economic capacity to consume" (Goodman 2014, p. 27).

The growth of the Chinese middle class may have significant consequences both internationally and domestically. A growing middle class means a growing market for consumer goods and services. It also has potential implications for the geopolitical situation. The history of the Western countries is sometimes used to demonstrate that growth of the middle class is related to the introduction and deepening of political democracy. For example, new research using panel data from many developed and developing countries finds evidence to support the hypothesis that growth in the size of the middle class promotes institutional reform and democratic diffusion (Loayza, Rigolini, and Llorente 2012; Chun et al. 2016).

However, whether and how the growth of a Chinese middle class will affect China's political system is far from clear. For example, Tang (2011) finds that members of the Chinese middle class (defined by occupation and self-identification) pay greater attention to politics and engage more in informal/personal activities in response to conflicts with government policies or officials than those with lesser means. Other studies, however, conclude that the aggregate behavior of the middle class in China is not significantly different from that of other classes when it comes to political activities that require greater civic engagement or confrontation with the political system.[2] If the CCP is able to successfully capture the interests of the middle class, then growth of the Chinese middle class will not necessarily fundamentally challenge China's political system. Indeed, our data reveal that a disproportionately large proportion of China's middle class are members of the CCP (see Section 3.6). Nevertheless, even if growth of the middle class in China leaves the political system intact, a larger proportion of middle-class persons in the society could bring about change in political priorities.

Since the beginning of the new millennium, many sociologists have written about the middle class in China. Li Cheng (2010) cites eleven prominent Chinese researchers who have studied the middle class and discusses their representative works. Research published in 2002 by Lu Xueyi, then director of the Institute of Sociology at the Chinese Academy of Social Sciences (CASS), is considered a landmark study for two reasons. First, for the first time Lu Xueyi categorizes most of the working class as belonging to the lower or lower-middle strata. Such a categorization is new, both politically and ideologically. Second, Lu Xueyi identifies a middle stratum comprised of cadres, managers, private entrepreneurs, technical clerks, and private small-business owners. Using data from 1978, 1988, and 1991, he estimates growth among this group of people. Li Cheng (2010) also comments that in later work Lu Xueyi reports that the proportion of middle-class persons in the Chinese population increased from 15 percent in 2001 to 23 percent in 2009.

Sociologists prefer to define the middle class on the basis of occupation and employment, but they often base such a classification on more than one criterion. Different researchers have proposed many varying definitions of the middle class, which of course yield different pictures of the middle class and have been the source of much debate. An issue in sociological debates regarding the middle class is whether the middle class is merely a statistical category or whether it is a class in a sociological sense. To be a class in a sociological sense, the middle class must have members who develop a coherent identity, class culture, and sociopolitical attitudes and values, and perhaps may take some class-based political actions. Several authors stress the heterogeneity of the Chinese middle class rather than treating it as one single class (Li Cheng 2010). Less attention, with the possible exception of the work by Mackerras (2005), has been paid to possible ethnic diversity among the Chinese middle class.

Economists and business researchers tend to focus on the relationship between the middle class and consumption. Growth of the middle class in China is considered the driver behind the changing consumption patterns and the rising demand for consumer goods. Regular visitors to China have remarked on the stunning changes in the kinds of goods that are now offered to those who have the means. China has become the world's largest market for personal cars, and its market for wine has increased dramatically. Similarly, China has seen a very rapid increase in independent tourism (Chio 2014; Oakes 2016).

Middle-class status is also associated with housing and home ownership. During the planning era from the 1950s to the 1980s, almost all urban households lived in rental apartments provided by their work units. Rents were very low, but so was the quality of their housing. This description no longer holds. Policies initiated by the government in the 1990s gradually introduced privatization of urban housing, as tenants in urban China were given opportunities to buy their apartments at prices typically lower than those in the emerging market. Today, the rate of home ownership in China is very high (Sato, Sicular, and Yue 2013). Moreover, with a boom in the construction industry and the development of residential real-estate markets, many more households now live in housing that is similar in terms of space and quality to that of the middle classes in rich countries. Some members of the upper segment live in gated communities, visibly separated from people with lesser means (for example, see Li Zhang 2010).

In the literature on the middle class in the developed countries, studies define "middle class" on the basis of household disposable income, often in relation to other households within the same country. The various chapters in Gornick and Jäntti (2013) contain a wide variety of definitions along these lines. Indeed, the seventeen authors of the chapters in this volume employ more than twenty different definitions of "middle class." For example, a middle-class household can be defined as having an income between 75 percent and 125 percent of the median.[3] One feature of such an approach is that the definition of the middle class is local, without any reference to universal standards or criteria. This is not the case in this study, as will be discussed in the next section.

3.3 The Meaning of the Global Middle Class

For several decades, researchers at the World Bank have defined poverty on the basis of a global poverty line measured in terms of PPP. Since October 2015 this global poverty line has been set at US$1.9 PPP per person per day, based on the latest round of PPP estimates from the International Comparison Program (ICP) in 2011.[4] The choice of the cutoff for this global poverty line is based on an approximation of the poverty lines in the poorer countries in the developing world.

Several studies now propose using global cutoffs for the middle and upper levels of the income distribution. However, there is no consensus on where exactly to set these cutoffs—that is, how much income a household should have to be considered a member of the middle class, let alone a member of the upper class.[5]

One approach is to define the "middle class" as starting at the income level where poverty ends. By this definition, people living in households with income just above the world poverty line are classified as middle class. Among the more influential papers using this approach is one by Banerjee and Duflo (2008, p. 26), which defines the middle class as living at between US$2 and US$10 per day on the basis of the 1993 PPP. Using microdata on a number of aspects of the middle class in thirteen low- and middle-income countries, these authors conclude that "[n]othing seems more middle class than the fact of having a stable, well-paying job. . . . The middle class . . . spend much more on the education and health of [their] children as well as on their own health." A similar, but not identical, approach is taken by Ravallion (2010), who defines the developing world's middle class as those who are not poor according to the world poverty line but who would be considered poor if they were to live in a high-income country. The latter is operationalized by using the U.S. poverty line, which was set at about US$13 a day in 2005.

A view espoused by other researchers, and shared by this study, is that a global poverty line based on poverty lines in the world's poorest countries is too low to be the starting point of the global middle class. Milanovic and Yitzhaki (2002), for example, define the middle class as people having an income between the mean of Brazil and Italy. Bhalla (2007) postulates that "middle class is where the poor end in the rich world" and places the cutoff at US$10 PPP per person per day. Following this definition, Kharas (2010), in an often-cited study, defines the global middle class as those with daily expenditures from US$10 to US$100 PPP per person. His lower cutoff is set equal to the average poverty line in Portugal and Italy, which is also similar to the poverty line in the United States. His upper cutoff is selected as twice the median income of Luxembourg, the richest country in the European Union.

Unlike Bhalla (2007), Kharas (2010) uses data from 145 countries covering 99 percent of the world's population to estimate the size and regional composition of the world's middle class, but, like Bhalla, he projects future change. Kharas concludes that in 2009 1.8 billion persons belonged to the world's middle class. A majority (54 percent) lived in Europe or North America, 28 percent lived in the Asia-Pacific region, 7 percent lived in Central and South America, and 6 percent lived in the Middle East and North Africa, whereas only 2 percent lived in sub-Saharan Africa. The results from his simulations indicate that the size of this middle class might possibly increase to 3.2 billion by 2020 and to 4.9 billion by 2030. Almost all this projected growth will come from Asia; the size of the middle class in North America is projected to remain roughly constant, as the inflow to the middle class from households with lesser means will be offset by the outflow of middle-class households to the richer classes.

As explained more fully in the next section, for our analysis we define four classes: "poor," "lower class," "middle class," and "upper class." "Poor" refers to standards of living that are poor by developing-country standards as measured by the global poverty line. "Lower class" refers to a standard of living above this global poverty line but still considered poor by standards in the developed countries. "Middle class" refers to a standard of living that is considered in the developed countries as not poor but also not rich. Table 3.1

Table 3.1. Classification of income classes, with comparisons to the literature

Classes used in this chapter	Classes used in the literature: Developing world frame of reference	Classes used in the literature: Developed world frame of reference
Poor	Poor	Ultra-poor
Lower	Vulnerable + middle	Poor + vulnerable
Middle	Upper middle + upper	Middle
Upper	Ultra-rich	Upper + rich

summarizes our classification system and relates it to the terminology found in the literature, which we see as differing from studies that use developing versus developed countries as the frame of reference.

3.4 Data and Operational Assumptions

We use data from the rural, rural-to-urban migrant, and urban samples in the CHIP surveys for the years 2002, 2007, and 2013.[6] Our 2002 estimation sample contains 63,911 individuals, of whom 20,624 are from the urban sample, 37,969 are from the rural sample, and 5318 are from the migrant sample. Our 2007 sample contains 89,804 individuals, of whom 29,553 are from the urban sample, 51,847 are from the rural sample, and 8404 are from the migrant sample. Our 2013 sample has 57,821 individuals, of whom 18,668 are urban, 37,090 are rural, and 2063 are migrant. To some extent, the provincial coverage of the CHIP samples changes across the years of the survey, as do the sampling probabilities. To control for this, in much of the analysis we apply the two-level (region × urban/rural/migrant) population-based sampling weights developed by the CHIP team.[7]

Following previous work by the CHIP project, we use the CHIP definition of household income, which is based on the National Bureau of Statistics (NBS) disposable or net household income data, adjusted to include imputed rents from owner-occupied housing and implicit subsidies on subsidized urban rental housing. As discussed in Chapters 1 and 2, the NBS definition of income changed in 2013. For 2007 we carried out our calculations by using the original and the new income definitions, but we found very little difference in the results. Therefore, for simplicity, here we report our estimates based on the pre-2013 income definition for 2002 and 2007 and based on the new income definition for 2013.

We divide household income by the number of household members, adjusted according to an equivalence scale as discussed more fully later in the chapter. Using the urban consumer price index (CPI) for the urban and migrant samples and the rural CPI for the rural sample, we express income in constant prices over time. In the calculations reported here, we do not adjust for spatial price differences within China.[8]

In our analysis, we use four classes, which we define by applying three cutoffs to the data (Table 3.2). The lowest cutoff, set at PPP US$2 per person per day, closely follows the practice used by the World Bank to define global poverty. To convert to RMB, we use the PPP conversion factor of 3.76 for 2013, which is provided by the Organisation for Economic Co-operation and Development on the basis of estimates from the 2011 International ICP.[9] From this source, we obtain a cutoff in RMB per day, which is 7.52 for 2013.

The second cutoff separates the lower class from the middle class. Here we use as the cutoff the level of income per capita in the EU that separates the poor from the non-poor in 2013. Following EU practices, we put the poverty line at 60 percent of the median income. Information on the median income for fifteen member countries (Austria, Belgium, Denmark, Finland, France, Germany, Greece, Ireland, Italy, Luxembourg, Netherlands, Portugal, Spain, Sweden, and the United Kingdom) is reported by Eurostat.[10] We then apply the PPP conversion factor, which was 0.83 in 2013. This yields a cutoff for 2013 of PPP US$36, or RMB 135.36 per person per day (Table 3.2).

Table 3.2. Cutoffs used in this study (per person per day, 2013 prices)

	First cutoff	Second cutoff	Third cutoff
	Separating the poor from the lower class	Separating the middle class from the lower class	Separating the upper class from the middle class
2013 RMB	7.52	135.36	451.20
2013 US$	2.00	36.00	120.00

Notes: The first cutoff is set close to the World Bank's global poverty line. The second cutoff is set at 60 percent of the median income per equivalized person in fifteen EU countries in 2013. The third cutoff is set at 200 percent of the median income per equivalized person in fifteen EU countries in 2013. Data for the median income in the fifteen EU countries are from Eurostat. See https://appsso. eurostat.ec.europa.eu/nui/show.do?dataset=ilc_di01&lang=en. Accessed November 9, 2019. US dollars are converted to RMB by using the PPP exchange rate. For 2002 and 2007 the cutoffs are equal to the RMB cutoffs converted from 2013 prices to 2002 and 2007 prices by using the urban and rural CPIs published by the NBS.

Definition of the middle class also requires a cutoff between the middle class and the upper class. For this, following other studies in the literature, we use 200 percent of the median household income per capita, as observed in the fifteen EU countries, which in 2013 corresponded to PPP US$120, or RMB 451.2 per person per day. We carried out our analysis by using alternative cutoffs between the middle and upper classes, such as 150 percent and 175 percent of the EU median income. The results are not sensitive to the choice of this upper cutoff because the proportion of Chinese households with incomes above these levels in our data is very small.

Although our procedure for setting the cutoffs for the middle class relative to the median income in the EU is conceptually clear, some details in the calculation require further explanation. First, Eurostat data on median incomes are expressed in terms of an equivalence scale that assumes a value of 1.0 for the first adult in the household, 0.5 for other adults, and 0.3 for each person fourteen years old and younger. Such a procedure typically is not applied in low- and middle-income countries, such as China, and it is not applied by the World Bank in setting the global poverty line. The justification for not using the equivalence scale for low- and middle-income countries is that the scope for economies of scale in low- and middle-income countries is limited because, for example, food consumption makes up a much larger proportion of consumption in low- and middle-income countries than it does in rich countries.

As China is moving in the direction of becoming a country with an income level more similar to that of high-income countries, the use of equivalized income instead of income per capita for analysis of the middle class is appropriate. Our cutoffs for the middle class are based on the Eurostat estimates of median income that use an equivalence scale. Therefore, we apply the same equivalence scale to the Chinese income data when estimating the share of the Chinese population that is middle class versus the share that is upper class. The global poverty line, however, is based on estimates of income per person, not per equivalent person according to an equivalence scale. Therefore, we simply use income per capita when estimating the share of China's population that is poor versus the share that is lower class.

Second, comparisons over time require a decision as to whether to keep the cutoffs constant or to let them change over time, that is, whether to use fixed or moving goalposts. We have chosen to fix the goalposts at 2013 levels. In other words, we define middle class with reference to the recent (2013) standard of being neither poor nor rich in the EU, and our analysis investigates change in China's middle class over time, according to this recent standard. Of course, other approaches are also possible.[11]

3.5 Growth of the Chinese Middle Class

Before turning to the results, we comment on how changes in the size of the middle class are related to trends in income and income inequality, topics addressed in other chapters of this volume. When the middle class is defined relative to absolute cutoffs, as is the case here, then the middle class will expand when income growth for segments of the population below the middle class is sufficient for them to move into the middle class from below the cutoffs, and to do so more rapidly than any outflows from the middle class. Such an expansion of the middle class may or may not reduce inequality. If most of the population is middle class, then the movement of lower-income individuals into the middle class will likely reduce inequality. If most of the population is poor or low-income, however, and if the middle class is located near the top end of the income distribution, then the movement of some lower-income individuals into the middle class could lead to rising inequality. These hypothetical situations suggest a complexity in the relationship between changes in the size of the middle class and inequality.

As we will see later, in 2002 China began with an overwhelming majority of households in the poor and lower classes, very few in the middle class, and extremely few in the upper class. Thereafter, the country experienced rapid economic growth that was not equally shared. During the period from 2002 to 2007 average income growth was rapid and the middle class expanded, but the middle class still remained a relatively small proportion of the population. At this time, growth of China's middle class was accompanied by rising inequality. From 2007 to 2013 incomes continued to grow and China's middle class continued to expand; however, during these years inequality began to decline, as reported in other chapters in this volume.

The relationship between inequality and growth of the middle class in China has been rather different from that in the developed world. In the 1990s many countries in the developed world had large middle classes, but in more recent decades they have experienced unequal income growth that mainly benefited those in the upper segments of the income distribution. Income growth for those in the middle and lower segments has been slow. Consequently, many developed countries have experienced a shrinking of the middle class accompanied by rising inequality.

Figure 3.1 shows how China's income distribution has changed over time in relation to our cutoffs between the poor, lower, middle, and upper classes. For ease of comparison across time, income in all years is expressed in constant 2013 prices. In 2002 the income distribution is concentrated at the left side of the graph and resembles a "pyramid" shape. Most of the income distribution is to the left of the cutoff for the middle class, and much of it is below the poverty line. Moving to 2007 and 2013, the income distribution shifts to the right. Over time, the relative size of those who are considered poor declines and the size of the lower and middle classes grows.

These findings are in line with the objectives of China's policy makers, as discussed in Section 3.2: transformation from a society with an income distribution shaped like a pyramid to a society shaped like an olive, with few at the bottom, many in the middle, and few at the top. China's income

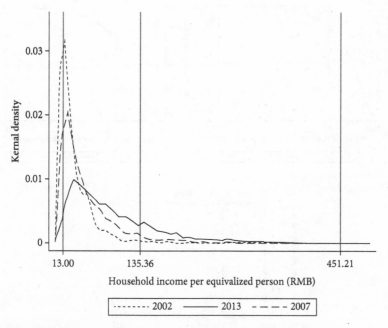

Fig. 3.1 China's income distribution in 2002, 2007, and 2013 (RMB per equivalized person per day)

Note: Income in all years is expressed in 2013 constant prices. The cutoff of RMB 7.52 between the poor and the lower class is calculated in terms of income per person. Here this cutoff is converted into per equivalized person terms by using the average income per equivalent person for observations in the dataset with income per capita between PPP $1.8 and PPP $2.2. This gives a cutoff of RMB 13 per equivalent person.

Source: Authors' calculations using the CHIP data, with weights.

distribution has indeed evolved toward an "olive" shape, although the pyramid's peak remains distinct and is in the lower class, well below our cutoff for the middle class.

Growth of the middle class is visualized in a slightly different way in Figure 3.2, which plots the cumulative distribution of income and also reports the results for both the rural and the urban regions. The cumulative distribution of income shows the proportion of the population with incomes below the level of income at each point on the horizontal axis. For example, at the lower cutoff for the middle class (135.36), the curve on the graph shows the proportion of the population that belongs to the poor and lower classes. Figure 3.2 consists of three panels, one for China as a whole, one for people living in urban locations (urban residents plus migrants), and one for rural residents.

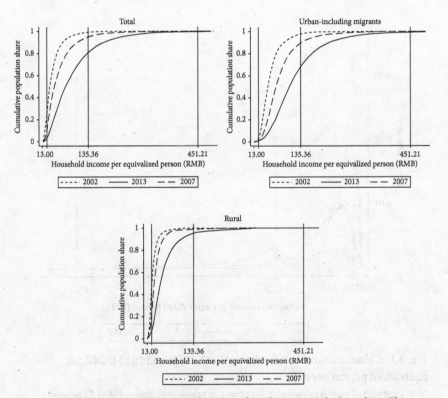

Fig. 3.2 Cumulative distributions of income for China as a whole, urban China, and rural China, 2002, 2007, and 2013 (RMB per equivalized person per day)

Note: Income in all years is expressed in 2013 constant prices. See note to Figure 3.1.

Source: Authors' calculations using the CHIP data, with weights.

Each panel shows the cumulative distribution of income for 2002, 2007, and 2013, with incomes for all years in constant 2013 prices.

One can see that from 2002 to 2007 and again to 2013, the cumulative income distribution shifts downward and to the right. Such shifts indicate that over time the proportion of China's poor and low-income population declined, whereas the share of the population with middle and higher incomes expanded. The shift is most noticeable for the urban sector. For the rural sector, the curves shifted more modestly and remained largely to the left of the cutoff for entering the middle class.

Table 3.3 provides estimates of the nationwide share of the population for each class by year, based on our definitions and also for urban residents, rural residents, and migrants. The Chinese middle class grew from only 1 percent in 2002 to 7 percent in 2007 and further to 19 percent in 2013. In terms of number of people, the middle class consisted of fewer than 12 million Chinese residents in 2002. The size of the middle class increased to 64 million residents in 2007 and expanded rapidly to no fewer than 254 million residents in 2013. Although in percentage terms China's middle class in 2013 remained a relatively modest share of the population, in absolute terms and relative to the size of the world's middle class, it was large.[12]

Concurrently with this growth of the middle class, China's poverty rate decreased from 27 percent in 2002 to 11 percent in 2007 and further to 4 percent in 2013. The lower class expanded from 2002 to 2007, when it exceeded 80 percent of China's population, but it then declined to 77 percent of the population. Despite the growing importance of the Chinese middle class, in all years its size was substantially smaller than that of the lower class, which constituted a large majority of the Chinese population. As of 2013, then, an overwhelming majority of China's population did not yet belong to the global middle class.

An upper class was virtually nonexistent in 2002, and in 2013 it constituted less than 0.5 percent of China's population. However, in absolute terms the number was still sizable (6.8 million) and somewhat larger than the entire population of countries such as Croatia, Denmark, and Ireland. In view of the small proportion of China's population above the highest cutoff, in the following sections we focus on the poor, lower, and middle classes.

As one would expect, growth of China's middle class is seen most clearly in the urban areas. Among urban residents, the share of the population in the middle class increased from 2 percent in 2002 to 34 percent in 2013.[13] The share of migrants who became middle class expanded from 1 percent in

Table 3.3. The shares of the four income classes in China's population as a whole, and among the urban, rural, and migrant populations, 2002, 2007, and 2013 (%)

	All	Urban	Rural	Migrants
A: 2002				
poor	26.88	1.92	40.34	6.95
lower	72.15	95.65	59.44	92.32
middle	0.97	2.43	0.22	0.73
upper	0	0	0	0
all	100	100	100	100
B: 2007				
poor	11.30	0.09	20.58	1.05
lower	81.44	81.21	78.97	93.96
middle	7.16	18.49	0.44	4.74
upper	0.10	0.21	0.01	0.24
all	100	100	100	100
C: 2013				
poor	3.58	0.94	6.65	1.18
lower	77.29	63.71	88.93	79.02
middle	18.66	34.44	4.31	19.49
upper	0.47	0.91	0.11	0.32
all	100	100	100	100

Notes:

1. Calculated with weights. With weights, the urban/rural/migrant population shares are as follows: 2002: 33.65 percent/64.74 percent/1.60 percent; 2007: 34.51 percent/54.21 percent/11.28 percent; and 2013: 40.93 percent/45.77 percent/13.30 percent.

2. For 2002 and 2007 the cutoffs are equal to the RMB cutoffs in Table 3.2 converted from the 2013 prices into 2002 and 2007 prices by using the urban and rural CPIs, as published by the NBS.

3. The first cutoff (between the poor and the lower class) is applied to income per capita (equal to household income divided by the number of persons in the household). The second and third cutoffs are applied to the equivalized income per capita (equal to the household income divided by the number of equivalent individuals in the household). (See the main text.)

4. Here and elsewhere, we do not use spatial price deflators to control for the differences in prices between the rural and urban areas and among the provinces.

Source: Authors' estimates based on the CHIP data.

2002 to 19 percent in 2013. In rural China, the share of the middle class in 2013 remained low, at only 4 percent. Rural China, however, was characterized by a rapid reduction in poverty, from 40 percent to 7 percent, and by an expansion of the lower class from 60 percent to 89 percent of the population between 2002 and 2013.

How do our estimates of the size and development of the middle class relate to information reported by others? Table 3.4 summarizes several previous estimates. Because Yuan, Wan, and Khor (2012) used the lowest cutoffs, it comes as no surprise that they report higher proportions of middle-class persons in rural China than we report or than Chen and Qin (2014) report. As a whole, our estimates of the size of the middle class in China are similar to those reported by Chen and Qin (2014) and Kharas (2010). Kharas (2010) finds that less than 12 percent of the Chinese population was middle class in 2009, a percentage that corresponds to our estimate of 12 percent in 2013. Chen and Qin (2014) report a middle-class share of 13 percent in 2012. The preferred estimate of Bonnefond, Clément, and Combarnous (2015) for 2009 is substantially larger; however, this estimate reflects their low cutoff for entering the middle class. Their preferred cutoff of only RMB 10,000 per year translates to only RMB 27 per day, much lower than our cutoff of RMB 135 per day.

Only Chen and Qin (2014) report the size of the middle class separately for the rural, urban, and migrant sectors. For the most recent year (2012 for Chen and Qin 2014; 2013 for us), we find a smaller rural middle class and larger urban and migrant middle classes than they do.[14]

3.6 Analyzing the Growth of the Chinese Middle Class

To what extent is the growth of China's middle class due to growth in average incomes versus redistribution toward the middle of the income distribution? Both growth and redistribution have taken place during the period of our analysis. As shown in other chapters in this volume, from 2007 to 2013 household income growth in China was broad-based. We also know, however, that some redistribution took place, because from 2007 to 2013 income growth was more rapid at the lower end and in the middle than at the top of the income distribution, as well as more rapid in the poorer rural sectors than in the richer urban areas (see Chapter 2).

Table 3.4. Estimates of the Chinese middle class in the literature

Author(s)	Definition of the middle class	Year of measurement	Data	Size of the middle class (% of population)			
				Rural	Urban	Migrants	All of China
Kharas (2010)	10–100 US$ per person per day	2009	Merging information on household income data for deciles with national account data on mean expenditures	NE	NE	NE	Less than 12 percent
Bonnefond, Clément, and Combarnous (2015)	Four different definitions, with a preference for RMB 10,000 per person per year to the 95th percentile	1989–2009	China Health and Nutrition Survey	—	—	NE	Approximately 50 percent of the urban households in 2009 may be said to belong to the middle class
Yuan, Wan, and Khor (2012)	4–10 US$ per person per day	1988	CHIP	3			
		1995		5			
		2002		15			
		2007		53			
Chen and Qin (2014) ("upper middle class")	10–20 US$ PPP per person per day	1995	CHIP	<0.5	2		1
		2002	CHIP	<1	3		2
		2010	CFPS	5	14	10	8
		2012	CFPS	9	20	14	13
This study	36–120 US$ per person per day	2002	CHIP	<0.5	3		1
		2007		<0.5	12		6
		2013		4	34	20	19

Notes: CFPS: China Family Panel Survey. NE: not estimated. Estimates by Chen and Qin (2014) refer to consumption, not income, and the percentage of households, not individuals.

In order to explore the role of average income growth versus redistribution, we carry out a simulation exercise (see Table 3.5) that begins with the 2007 distribution of income and assumes that from 2007 to 2013 all persons experienced the same annual income growth rate. We set the uniform annual growth rate at 7.97 percent, equal to the average rate of growth of per capita household income during this period. This simulation yields a hypothetical distribution of income for 2013 that assumes no redistribution of income. We then compare the size of the middle class in this hypothetical distribution to that in the observed income distribution for 2013.

Interestingly, we find that the size of China's middle class in the hypothetical distribution is virtually the same as that observed in 2013. We also find, however, that this result masks some differences in the composition of the hypothetical middle class versus the observed middle class. Using the assumption of uniform growth yields a middle class in urban China that is substantially larger (45 percent, not 34 percent) and a middle class in rural China that is somewhat smaller (2 percent, not 4 percent) than that which was observed in 2013. We conclude that although redistribution did not affect growth in the overall size of China's middle class from 2007 to 2013, it increased the proportion of the middle class that was rural as opposed to the

Table 3.5. The simulated shares of the four classes in 2013, assuming that the incomes of all individuals grew at the same rate between 2007 and 2013 (%)

	Total	Urban	Rural	Migrants
Poor	4.01	0.02	7.25	0.68
Lower	76.38	53.16	90.62	79.01
Middle	18.71	44.57	2.08	19.49
Upper	0.90	2.25	0.05	0.83
All	100	100	100	100

Notes: This simulation yields a hypothetical distribution of income for 2013 that assumes income grew at the same rate for all persons and there was no income redistribution between 2007 and 2013. To calculate the simulated shares, we start with the 2007 distribution of income and assume that from 2007 to 2013 all persons experienced the same annual rate of income growth. We use a uniform income growth rate of 7.97 percent, which is equal to the average annual rate of growth of household income per capita during this period. The urban/rural/migrant population shares are assumed to remain unchanged at their 2007 values. This assumption yields the simulated income for each equivalent person in 2013. Using the cutoffs shown in Table 3.2, we then obtain the share of the population in each class.

proportion that was urban. These results reflect the relatively rapid growth of rural incomes vis-à-vis the growth of urban incomes during this period.

How large will China's middle class grow? We answer this question by projecting from 2013 to 2020 under an assumption of uniform 6.5 percent income growth per year for all households. We use 6.5 percent growth for the projection because China's Thirteenth Five-Year Plan (2016–2020) established a 6.5 percent target GDP growth rate and because this growth rate is in line with standard forecasts, e.g., the International Monetary Fund predicted China's GDP growth of 6.5 percent in 2016 and slowing gradually to 6.0 percent in 2020.[15]

The results from this exercise are reported in Table 3.6. A comparison with the numbers in Table 3.3 indicates that in the seven years from 2013 to 2020, the share of the middle class in China should almost double—from 19 percent to 36 percent of the population, or from 254 million to 509 million persons (assuming a population growth of 0.5 percent per annum). By 2020 more than half of urban China would be middle class, with 60 percent of urban residents thus classified. Reflecting the persistent gap in income between the urban and rural areas, rural China in 2020 would remain overwhelmingly lower class, with only 13 percent of rural inhabitants classified

Table 3.6. The simulated shares of the four classes in 2020, assuming that the incomes of all individuals grew at the same rate between 2013 and 2020 (%)

	All	Urban	Rural	Migrants
Poor	1.70	0.65	2.86	0.95
Lower	59.81	34.36	84.20	54.21
Middle	36.18	60.31	12.50	43.43
Upper	2.31	4.69	0.43	1.41
All	100	100	100	100

Notes: This simulation yields a hypothetical distribution of income for the year 2020, based on the assumption that income grows at the same rate for all persons and there is no redistribution of income. To calculate the simulated shares, we start with the 2013 distribution of income and assume that from 2013 to 2020 all persons will experience an annual income growth rate of 6.5 percent rate. The urban/rural/migrant population shares are assumed to remain unchanged at their 2013 values. This assumption yields the simulated income for each equivalent person in 2013. Using the cutoffs shown in Table 3.2, we then obtain the share of the population in each class.

Source: Authors' estimates based on the CHIP data.

as middle class.[16] These projections indicate that in the near future China's middle class will remain mainly an urban phenomenon.

3.7 Characteristics of China's Middle Class

In this section, we use the 2013 survey data to identify the distinctive characteristics of China's middle class in comparison to the lower and poor classes. First, we note that the Chinese middle class contains relatively high savers, with an average savings rate of 35 percent.[17] Figure 3.3 shows the relationship between savings rate and income by using a plot of the median savings rate

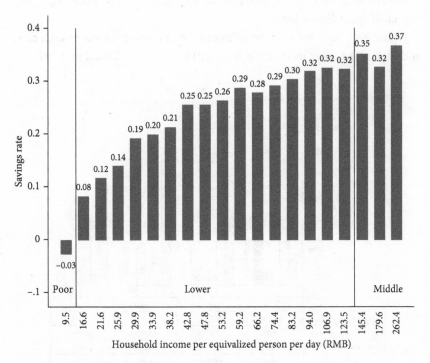

Fig. 3.3 Savings rate by ventile in the income distribution, 2013

Notes: Each bar presents the median savings rate for each ventile (5 percentile group) in the income distribution. Labels on the horizontal axis are the median income of each ventile (in RMB). The vertical lines indicate the income cutoffs between the classes. No cutoff is shown between the middle and upper classes because the upper class constitutes only 0.47 percent of the population and thus is a small component of the top ventile. Note that the savings rates are calculated by using the NBS income variable, which does not include imputed rents on owner-occupied housing or imputed subsidies on subsidized rental housing.

Source: Authors' calculations using the CHIP data, with weights.

by ventile of the income distribution. The median income per capita for each ventile is shown on the horizontal axis. The vertical lines delineate between the poor and the lower classes and between the lower and the middle classes. The median savings rate is negative for the poor, it increases from about 10 percent to 30 percent for the lower class, and it then reaches 35–40 percent for the middle class. On the basis of Figure 3.3, we conclude that an expansion of the middle class may not lead to a rising rate of consumption relative to income, although the absolute level of consumption may nevertheless increase.[18]

In the remainder of this section, we examine five sets of characteristics: a.) sources of income, b.) housing and ownership of consumer durables, c.) location of residence, d.) demographic and education characteristics, and e.) membership in the CCP. We find that the middle class is distinct in many, but not all, of these dimensions.

Figure 3.4 shows the average composition of income for the middle class and each of the other income classes in 2013.[19] The middle and upper classes

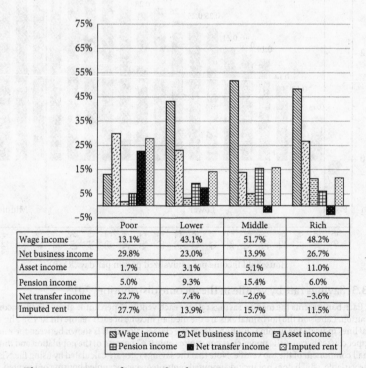

	Poor	Lower	Middle	Rich
Wage income	13.1%	43.1%	51.7%	48.2%
Net business income	29.8%	23.0%	13.9%	26.7%
Asset income	1.7%	3.1%	5.1%	11.0%
Pension income	5.0%	9.3%	15.4%	6.0%
Net transfer income	22.7%	7.4%	-2.6%	-3.6%
Imputed rent	27.7%	13.9%	15.7%	11.5%

Wage income ◩ Net business income ⊡ Asset income
⊞ Pension income ■ Net transfer income ⊠ Imputed rent

Fig. 3.4 The composition of income by class, 2013
Source: Authors' calculations using the CHIP data, with weights.

differ from the poor and lower classes in terms of the importance of income from wage employment. For the middle and upper classes, wages contribute on average more than one-half of total income.

For the middle class, pensions are also a significant source of income, contributing 15 percent of income, compared to 9 percent for the lower class and only 5 to 6 percent for the poor and upper classes. Since pensions are typically linked to past employment, this point underscores the central role of employment as a source of income for the middle class. Together, wage and pension income account for 67 percent of middle-class income, as compared to about 50 percent for the upper and lower classes and only 18 percent for the poor. We note, however, that the heavy reliance of the middle class on employment for income has declined over time. In 2007 the sum of wages plus pensions constituted a substantially larger share (80 percent) of middle-class income.

The middle class also differs from other classes in terms of the relative unimportance of income from household businesses. In 2013 business income on average accounted for 14 percent of middle-class income. For the other classes, business income was noticeably more important, in all cases higher than 20 percent of income. Business income is most concentrated in the rich and poor classes. We conclude that, in general, China's middle class is a salaried rather than an entrepreneurial class.

Table 3.7 shows housing characteristics and ownership of consumer durables by class. The differences in housing among the classes are revealed very clearly in the market rental values of their housing (self-reported). On average, middle-class individuals live in housing that is valued more than three times that of the housing of the lower class, and almost ten times that of the housing of the poor. The upper class, however, lives in housing with an average rental value that is double that of the middle class. Modern housing conditions, as measured by the presence of piped water and a flush toilet, are nearly universal for the middle and upper classes but not so for the lower and poor classes. Fuel used for cooking also differs considerably. Exceedingly few middle- and upper-class individuals use firewood or coal for cooking, as compared to one-third of the lower class and two-thirds of the poor individuals.

With respect to consumer durables, ownership of the two major household appliances, refrigerators and washing machines, is widespread among the upper, middle, lower, and even poor classes. Large differences emerge, however, with respect to other durables. Most of the middle class owns air

Table 3.7. Housing and ownership of consumer durables by income class, 2013

	Total	Poor	Lower	Middle	Upper
Estimated monthly market rent of dwelling (RMB)	797	202	533	1917	3901
Piped water in dwelling (%)	82.9	50.4	80.4	98.8	97.0
Flush toilet in dwelling (%)	60.9	20.9	54.6	94.2	94.9
Ownership of refrigerator (%)	82.6	54.0	80.7	95.4	97.9
Ownership of washing machine (%)	84.3	69.2	82.2	95.4	100.0
Ownership of air conditioner (%)	47.5	19.8	41.3	77.5	84.6
Main fuel for cooking is firewood or coal (%)	27.6	66.2	32.2	2.1	2.4
Ownership of computer connected to the Internet (%)	40.6	14.0	33.8	72.9	81.8
Ownership of private car (%)	20.2	9.3	14.6	44.2	74.3

Note: Means are calculated over individuals in each class.
Source: Authors' estimates based on the CHIP data, with weights.

conditioners and a computer with Internet connections. These items are al-most universal among the upper class but they are not typical for the two lower classes. Almost one in two middle-class individuals lives in a house-hold that owns a personal car; however, car ownership is unusual among the lower classes. Therefore, in terms of ownership of consumer durables, China's middle class is somewhat distinct from China's lower classes and resembles the middle classes in the developed world.

China's middle class is geographically concentrated (Table 3.8); 90 percent of middle-class persons are urban residents (including migrants). Similarly, 90 percent of the upper class is urban. In comparison, 85 percent of the poor are rural residents. Regionally, the middle classes are concentrated in the East, with three out of five middle-class persons living in the East, as com-pared to only one out of five of the poor. The upper class is even more concen-trated in the East.

The geographic distribution of China's middle class is related to the spatial variations in levels of economic development and urbanization. To investi-gate this relationship, we calculate the share of the middle class in each of the fourteen provinces covered by the CHIP 2013 survey and plot it against the provincial per capita GDP, the provincial average disposable household

Table 3.8. Composition of the income classes by location, 2013 (%)

	Total	Poor	Lower class	Middle class	Upper class
Sector					
Urban	40.9	10.7	33.7	75.5	80.3
Rural	45.8	84.9	52.7	10.6	10.6
Migrants	13.3	4.4	13.6	13.9	9.1
Total	100	100	100	100	100
Region					
East	41.5	20.9	37.6	60.4	85.4
Central	31.5	34.6	34.0	21.0	9.9
West	27.0	44.5	28.4	18.6	4.7
Total	100	100	100	100	100

Sources: Authors' estimates based on the CHIP data, with weights. Calculated for individuals.

income per capita (as reported by the NBS in its statistical yearbooks), and the provincial rate of urbanization (Figure 3.5). The graphs indicate the expected relations: the size of the middle class increases with the provincial per capita GDP, average provincial household income, and provincial urbanization.

Note that Beijing is an extreme outlier located far in the northeast corner of all the figures. Not only does Beijing have a substantially higher GDP per capita, income per capita, and rate of urbanization than the thirteen other provinces in the sample, but it also has a markedly larger middle class. The share of the middle class in Beijing exceeds 50 percent, as compared to 30 percent in second-place Jiangsu. This gap in the size of the middle class between Beijing and the other provinces reveals that impressions of China's income distribution that are based solely on its capital city present a misleading picture of the importance of the middle class in China as a whole.

With respect to demographic variables, the middle class is not very different from the other classes (Table 3.9). China's ethnic minorities are less frequently represented among the middle class than among the other classes. Children make up a slightly smaller proportion and adults make up a slightly larger proportion of the middle class than they do in the overall population. Years of education are relatively high for adults in the middle class, at 11.7 years, as compared to 8.7 years for those in the lower class and 7.6 years

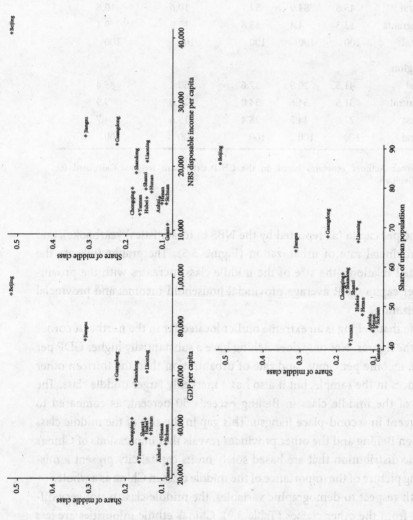

Fig. 3.5 The size of the middle class by province plotted against provincial GDP per capita, household disposable income per capita, and the rate of urbanization, 2013 (%)

Notes: Provincial GDP per capita, NBS disposable income per capita, and the share of the urban population are based on statistics published by the NBS. Provincial shares of the middle class are calculated by the authors using the CHIP data, with weights.

Table 3.9. Composition of the classes by demographic variables, 2013

Table 3.9-1: All

	All	Poor	Lower	Middle	Upper
Ethnicity (%)					
Han	93.1	87.2	92.8	95.6	92.4
Minority	6.9	12.8	7.2	4.4	7.6
Age group (%)					
Child	15.1	17.3	15.4	13.4	16.4
Adult	75.9	72.6	75.6	77.1	79.9
Elderly	9.0	10.1	9.0	8.9	3.7
Average education among adults (years)	9.3	7.6	8.7	11.7	13.0

Table 3.9-2: Urban (including migrants)

	All	Poor	Lower	Middle	Upper
Ethnicity (%)					
Han	94.5	89.7	94.0	95.8	91.5
Minority	5.5	10.3	6.0	4.2	8.5
Age group (%)					
Child	14.9	15.1	15.5	13.6	16.3
Adult	76.3	75.0	75.8	77.3	79.9
Elderly	8.8	9.9	8.7	9.2	3.8
Average education among adults (years)	10.5	9.1	9.7	12.0	13.3

Table 3.9-3: Rural

	All	Poor	Lower	Middle
Ethnicity (%)				
Han	91.5	86.7	91.8	93.7
Minority	8.5	13.3	8.2	6.3
Age group (%)				
Child	15.3	17.7	15.3	12.3
Adult	75.5	72.1	75.5	81.3
Elderly	9.2	10.2	9.3	6.4
Average education among adults (years)	7.8	7.3	7.7	9.4

Notes: Calculated for individuals. Ethnicity is based on the ethnicity information of each person, not the ethnicity of the household head. Age groups are defined as follows: children (age < 16); adults (16 ≤ age ≤ 65); elderly (age > 65). The number of rural upper-class observations in the sample is extremely small, so it is not reported here.

Source: Authors' estimates based on the CHIP data.

for those in the poor class. In other words, completion of high school is typical for adults in the middle class, as compared to completion of junior middle school for adults in the lower and poor classes. In contrast, on average adults in the upper class have completed 13 years of education.

Communist Party membership is highest in the middle class. Table 3.10 shows that not less than one in five middle-class persons is a party member, compared with 16 percent of the upper class and less than 10 percent of the lower class and less than 5 percent of the poor. Party membership is most prevalent among the formal urban residents. Among China's urban middle class, almost one in four is a party member. Table 3.11 shows the class composition of CCP members. Overall, the majority of party members (58 percent) belong to the lower class; however, a substantial minority (40 percent)

Table 3.10. Membership in the Chinese Communist Party by class and by urban/rural/migrant in 2013 (%)

	All	Poor	Lower	Middle	Upper
Total	9.1	4.2	6.7	19.5	16.4
Rural	4.7	3.4	4.7	7.7	NA
Migrants	2.7	0.0	2.3	4.9	NA
Urban	16.0	11.5	11.8	23.8	NA

Notes: The percentages refer to the share of individuals who are members of the Chinese Communist Party. "All" includes all four classes. Because of the small number of upper-class observations in the sample and thus the very few observations in each sector, we do not report urban/rural/migrant breakdowns for the upper class.

Source: Authors' estimates based on the CHIP data, with weights.

Table 3.11. Communist Party members belonging to each class in 2013 (%)

	All	Poor	Lower	Middle	Upper
Total	100	1.7	57.5	39.9	0.9
Rural	100	4.9	87.8	7.0	NA
Migrant	100	0.0	65.3	34.0	NA
Urban	100	0.7	47.0	51.1	NA

Notes: The percentages refer to the share of individuals who are members of the Chinese Communist Party. "All" includes all four classes. Because of the small number of upper-class observations in the sample and thus the very few in each sector, we do not report the urban/rural/migrant breakdown for the upper class.

Source: Authors' estimates based on the CHIP data, with weights.

is middle class. In rural areas, party membership is dominated by the lower class; in urban areas, the middle and lower classes constitute roughly equal shares of party membership. Together, the lower and middle classes comprise 97 percent of party members; the upper class and the poor account for the exceedingly small remainder.

3.8 Conclusions

Various studies in the literature use different definitions of the middle class. Our definition is based on household income and it is anchored to the levels of household income in high-income countries. Specifically, we define the middle class as having a per capita income that if living in Europe is high enough not to be classified as poor and low enough not to be classified as upper class. The cutoff for belonging to the middle class is 60 percent of the median income and the cutoff for belonging to the upper class is 200 percent of the median income in fifteen EU countries, as observed in 2013. In some sense, this definition is rather generous. Not all observers would agree that people in Europe with an income of over 60 percent of the median, equivalent to a modest US$13,140 (PPP) per capita, are middle class.

We subdivide those individuals with incomes below the middle-class cutoff into two groups. The "poor" are defined as those living in a household with an income that is below PPP US$2 per day. The "lower class" consists of people with an income above PPP US$2 per day but not high enough to be classified as middle class.

Using these definitions, we measure the sizes of the middle- and other-income classes in China in 2002, 2007, and 2013, and we trace the changes in their relative importance during the period of China's substantial economic growth. We find that during this eleven-year period the middle class grew extremely rapidly, increasing from only 12 million persons in 2002 to 254 million persons in 2013. Most of this increase occurred between 2007 and 2013. By 2013 the absolute size of China's middle class was large, equivalent to 80 percent of the entire population of the United States.

This expansion of the middle class was accompanied by a change in the shape of China's income distribution from a distinct pyramid shape to an olive shape, but still with a marked peak in the share of the population that falls within the lower-income class. At 77 percent of the population, the lower class remained by far China's largest class in 2013. Despite the rapid expansion of the middle class, in 2013 the middle class still constituted a relatively modest share—20 percent—of the Chinese population.

As of 2013, China's middle class was very much an urban phenomenon. Most of China's middle-class persons were urban residents. Most of the rural population belonged to the lower-income class. A clear majority of China's poor lived in the rural areas.

We have investigated how the characteristics of the middle class compare to those of the other classes. The middle class earned most of its income from wage employment and was less involved in business and self-employment than the poorer classes. Variations among the classes across some demographic variables were modest. Children, adults, and the elderly made up proportions of the middle class similar to those in the overall population. Education levels were noticeably higher among adults in the middle class than among those in the lower and poor classes. We find that one in five persons in the middle class was a member of the CCP, a considerably higher proportion than among the lower-income class and the poor. However, in 2013 the CCP continued to be largely made up of lower-class individuals.

We project that if household incomes grow at a uniform average rate of 6.5 percent per annum, then by 2020 the proportion of Chinese households classified as middle class would be almost double the proportion in 2013, reaching over 500 million persons and accounting for about one-third of the total population. If such an expansion occurs, which is not unlikely given China's recent GDP growth rates, then by 2020 China should be the single largest contributor to the global middle class. It is not unreasonable to assume that this quantitative expansion will have consequences in terms of the evolution of tastes and habits of middle-class consumers in other countries. We note, however, that China's population in the near future will continue to belong predominately to the global lower-income class.

It has been observed that the growth of a middle class is important for China's shift from an investment-led to a consumption-led growth model. In fact, we find that China's middle-class households are large savers, saving on average more than one-third of their income and with savings rates higher than those of the lower classes. Consequently, the expansion of China's middle class may not necessarily be an engine of consumption growth and could conceivably be an obstacle to China's shift to a consumption-led growth model unless it is accompanied by other changes that alter savings behavior. Nevertheless, the expansion of China's middle class will reflect rising absolute incomes, so that even if the share of income spent on consumption declines, the absolute levels of consumption will rise. In addition, the composition of consumption will very likely change as the level of demand for items associated with middle-class consumption in China (and elsewhere), such as housing improvements, household appliances, electronic equipment, and automobiles, increases.

Notes

Note: Previous versions of this paper were presented at the CHIP Workshop, Beijing Normal University, Beijing, May 7–8, 2016, and at the IARIW General Conference, Dresden, Germany, August 22–26, 2016. We are grateful for the useful comments we received on those occasions. We acknowledge financial support for this research from the CIGI-INET Program on New Economic Theory, Practice and Governance.

1. Bonnefond and Clément (2014) use the same definition and data to study body weight among members of the Chinese urban middle class. They conclude that only one sub-category ("the new middle class"—the highest earners and the best educated) is relatively well protected from obesity.
2. Tang and Unger (2013, p. 109) write, "The Chinese educated middle class has, as a whole, become a bulwark of the current regime. As a consequence, regime change or democratization should not be expected any time soon. The rise of China's educated middle class blocks the way." Nathan (2016, p. 17) writes, "What middle-class persons dread is an economic or military crisis or an internal power struggle that triggers a breakdown of order. It is the fear of such a crisis that explains why a middle class that increasingly embraces liberal values still supports an authoritarian regime."
3. Anderson et al. (2016) define middle class in China on the basis of an econometric approach using information on disposable income.
4. https://siteresources.worldbank.org/ICPINT/Resources/270056-1183395201801/Summary-of-Results-and-Findings-of-the-2011-International-Comparison-Program.pdf. Accessed March 24, 2017. See also Ferreira et al. (2016).
5. In the relatively large literature on top-income earners, they are typically defined as those who belong to the upper one-tenth or upper one-hundredth of the income distribution. See, for example, Atkinson, Piketty, and Saez (2011).
6. For an introduction to the household income surveys in China including the CHIP, see Gustafsson, Li, and Sato (2014).
7. We use CHIP sampling weights that assume a middle estimate of the size of the rural-to-urban migrant population.
8. We carried out the calculations with adjustments for the spatial price differences, which somewhat changed the relative shares of the urban/rural/migrant populations in the middle class, but otherwise did not substantially change our overall findings.
9. http://siteresources.worldbank.org/ICPINT/Resources/270056-1183395201801/Summary-of-Results-and-Findings-of-the-2011-International-Comparison-Program.pdf. Accessed March 24, 2017.

10. We use the median for fifteen EU countries (18,219 € per person per year) because it covers long-term, stable members of the EU and because it is the only multiple-country median that Eurostat reports for the years prior to 2005, thus allowing us to conduct some sensitivity analyses. The median for the EU-15 is close to that for the EU-18, as well as that for Germany, the EU's largest member-state. In 2013 the median income of the EU-15 was 5 percent higher than the median income of the EU-18 and 7 percent lower than the median income for Germany. Eurostat's median income statistics can be found at https://appsso.eurostat.ec.europa.eu/nui/show.do?dataset=ilc_di01&lang=en. Accessed November 9, 2019.

11. Gustafsson, Sicular, and Yang (2017) report results from an exercise in which the cutoffs are based on the medians in the EU countries in 2002, 2007, and 2013. The results of this alternative approach using moving goalposts for the most part are similar to those using fixed goalposts because income growth in the fifteen EU countries from 2002 to 2013 was relatively modest.

12. Kharas (2010) estimates a global middle class of 1.8 billion in 2009.

13. Gustafsson, Sicular, and Yang (2017) report results from a sensitivity analysis in which the second and third cutoffs are set in accordance with the changes in the median incomes in the fifteen EU countries from 2002 and from 2007, i.e., using moving goalposts. This alternative approach produces faster growth of the middle class in urban China from 2002 to 2007 than is reported in this section and slower growth from 2007 to 2013 than is reported in this section.

14. We note that our estimates are based on income, whereas those of Chen and Qin (2014) are based on consumption expenditures. Another difference is that the estimates of Chen and Qin (2014) are for households, whereas ours are for individuals.

15. See the IMF World Economic Outlook, April 2016, http://www.imf.org/external/pubs/ft/weo/2016/01/. Accessed March 24, 2017.

16. It should be remembered that these results assume that the income cutoffs defining the middle class remain unchanged at the median income levels observed in the EU countries in 2013. To the extent that households in the EU experience income growth between 2013 and 2020, one could argue that the criteria for being classified as middle class in China should be revised upward, which would reduce China's 2020 projected share of the middle class.

17. The savings rate is estimated to be equal to the average savings rate among individuals. Each individual's savings rate is equal to its household savings rate, and the household's savings rate is calculated as household disposable income minus consumption expenditures, divided by household disposable income. To calculate the savings rate, we use the NBS income variable that does not include imputed rents on owner-occupied housing or imputed subsidies on subsidized rental housing.

18. The median savings rate reported here for urban China in 2013 (33 percent) is slightly higher than that reported in Chapter 4. In both chapters the estimated saving rates increase with household income. The reasons for the slight differences in the saving rates in the two chapters include: 1.) differences in the definition of income and whether income is calculated per equivalent persons or per capita; 2.) for each decile here we report the median value, whereas Chapter 4 reports the mean; and 3.) differences in the treatment of the few households that have negative incomes.

19. We calculate the share of income by income component for each household, and then we take the average of the shares over the households in each income class. Consequently, the shares reported in the figures do not add up to 100 percent.

References

Anderson, G., A. Farcomeni, M. G. Pittau, and R. Zelli, (2016). "A New Approach to Measuring and Studying the Characteristics of Class Membership: Examining Poverty, Inequality and Polarization in Urban China." *Journal of Econometrics*, 191(2), 348–359.

Atkinson, A., T. Piketty, and E. Saez (2011). "Top Incomes in the Long Run of History." *Journal of Economic Literature*, 49(1), 3–71.

Banerjee, A. V. and E. Duflo (2008). "What Is Middle Class about the Middle Classes around the World?" *Journal of Economic Perspectives*, 22(2), 3–28.

Bhalla, S. S. (2007). "Second among Equals: The Middle Class Kingdoms of India and China." Unpublished manuscript, Peterson Institute for International Economics, Washington, DC. https://www.researchgate.net/profile/Surjit_Bhalla/publication/228386466_Second_among_Equals_The_Middle_Class_Kingdoms_of_India_and_China/links/555b53aa08aec5ac223225ea.pdf. Accessed March 24, 2017.

Bonnefond, C. and M. Clément (2014). "Social Class and Body Weight among Chinese Urban Adults: The Role of the Middle Classes in the Nutrition Transition." *Social Science & Medicine*, 112 (July), 22–29.

Bonnefond, C., M. Clément, and F. Combarnous (2015). "In Search of the Elusive Chinese Urban Middle Class: An Exploratory Analysis." *Post-Communist Economics*, 27(1), 41–59.

Chen, C. and B. Qin (2014). "The Emergence of China's Middle Class: Social Mobility in a Rapidly Urbanizing Economy." *Habitat International*, 44 (October), 528–535.

Chio, J. (2014). *A Landscape of Travel: The Work of Tourism in Rural Ethnic China*. Seattle: University of Washington Press.

Chun, N., R. Hasan, M. H. Rahman, and M. A. Ulubaşoğlu (2016). "The Role of Middle Class in Democratic Diffusion." *International Review of Economics and Finance*, 42 (March), 536–548.

Ferreira, F. H. G., S. Chen, A. Dabalen, Y. Dikhanov, N. Hamadeh, D. Jolliffe, A. Narayan, E. B. Prydz, A. Revenga, P. Sangraula, U. Serajuddin, and N. Yoshida (2016). "A Global Count of the Extreme Poor in 2012: Data Issues, Methodology and Initial Results." *Journal of Economic Inequality*, 14(2), 141–172.

Goodman, D. S. G. (2014). *Class in Contemporary China*, Cambridge, UK: Polity Press.

Gornick, J. C. and M. Jäntti (2013). *Income Inequality: Economic Disparities and the Middle Class in Affluent Countries*, Stanford, CA: Stanford University Press.

Gustafsson, B., S. Li, and H. Sato (2014). "Data for Studying Earnings, the Distribution of Household Income and Poverty in China." *China Economic Review*, 30, 419–431.

Gustafsson, B., T. Sicular, and X. Yang (2017). "China's Emerging Global Middle Class." Centre for Human Capital and Productivity. CHCP Working Papers, 2017-14. London, Canada: Department of Economics, University of Western Ontario.

Kharas, H. (2010). "The Emerging Middle Class in Developing Countries." OECD Development Centre Working Paper No 285. https://www.oecd.org/dev/44457738.pdf. Accessed March 24, 2017.

Li, C. (2010). "Chinese Scholarship on the Middle Class: From Social Stratification to Political Potential," in C. Li, ed., *China's Emerging Middle Class: Beyond Economic Transformation*, 55-83. Washington DC: Brookings Institution Press.

Li, Z. (2010). *In Search of Paradise: Middle-Class Living in a Chinese Metropolis*. Ithaca, NY: Cornell University Press.

Loayza, N., J. Rigolini, and G. Llorente (2012). "Do Middle Classes Bring About Institutional Reforms?" *Economic Letters*, 116(3), 440-444.

Mackerras, C. (2005). "China's Ethnic Minorities and the Middle Classes: An Overview." *International Journal of Social Economics*, 32(9), 814-826.

Milanovic, B. (2016). *Global Inequality: A New Approach for the Age of Globalization*. Cambridge, MA: Belknap Press of Harvard University Press.

Milanovic, B. and S. Yitzhaki (2002). "Decomposing World Income Distribution: Does the World Have a Middle Class?" *Review of Income and Wealth*, 48(2), 155-178.

Nathan, A. J. (2016). "The Puzzle of the Chinese Middle Class." *Journal of Democracy*, 27(2), 5-19.

Oakes, T. (2016). "Ethnic Tourism in China," in X. Zang, ed., *Handbook on Ethnic Minorities in China*, 291-315. Cheltenham, UK: Edward Elgar.

Ravallion, M. (2010). "The Developing World's Bulging (but Vulnerable) Middle Class." *World Development*, 38(4), 445-454.

Sato, H., T. Sicular, and X. Yue (2013). "Housing Ownership, Incomes, and Inequality in China, 2002-2007," in S. Li, H. Sato, and T. Sicular, eds., *Rising Inequality in China: Challenges to a Harmonious Society*, 85-141. Cambridge and New York: Cambridge University Press.

Tang, B. and J. Unger (2013). "The Socioeconomic Status, Co-optation and Political Conservatism of the Educated Middle Class: A Case Study of University Teachers," in M. Chen and D.S.G. Goodman, eds., *Middle Class China: Identity and Behavior*, 90-109. Cheltenham, UK: Edward Elgar.

Tang, M. (2011). "The Political Behavior of the Chinese Middle Class." *Journal of Chinese Political Science*, 16(4), 373-387.

Yuan, Z., G. Wan, and N. Khor (2012). "The Rise of Middle Class in Rural China." *China Agricultural Economic Review*, 4(1), 36-51.

4

The Increasing Inequality of Wealth in China

John Knight, Shi Li, and Haiyuan Wan

4.1 Introduction

Which country in the world has the most dollar billionaires? If you are willing to believe the *Hurun Rich List 2016* and its sources, the answer is China, with 570 (mainland China 470), now surpassing the United States by 30. Which city in the world has the most dollar billionaires? The answer is Beijing, with 100, now exceeding New York. Is this a matter for national pride or for policy concern?

Our main argument is that the inequality of wealth in China has increased rapidly since the late 1990s and there are convincing explanations for this increase. Prior to the economic reforms that began in 1978, all Chinese households possessed negligible wealth. China therefore presents a fascinating case study of how inequality of wealth increases rapidly as economic reforms take place, marketization occurs, and capital accumulates. Wealth inequality and its growth deserve examination by using data from two twenty-first-century CHIP national household surveys—2002 and 2013. We opt for 2002 rather than 2007 because the CHIP 2002 survey is the first comprehensive data source on wealth, because the CHIP 2007 does not have full and comparable wealth data, and because it is more interesting to take a longer-term view of trends in wealth.

We proceed as follows. Section 4.2 of this chapter sets out the relevant literature on wealth inequality. Section 4.3 outlines the possible reasons that inequality is hypothesized to have increased. Section 4.4 explains the two comparable datasets that will be used to test the hypotheses. Because of the economic differences between urban and rural China and the differences in survey design and implementation, we distinguish urban and rural wealth

John Knight, Shi Li, and Haiyuan Wan, *The Increasing Inequality of Wealth in China* In: *Changing Trends in China's Inequality*. Edited by: Terry Sicular, Shi Li, Ximing Yue, and Hiroshi Sato, Oxford University Press (2020). © Oxford University Press.
DOI: 10.1093/oso/9780190077938.003.0004

throughout, as well as reporting on national wealth. The national wealth estimates require a weighting of the urban and rural samples.

In Section 4.5 we examine the level and structure of wealth in our two survey years, 2002 and 2013, and its growth over that period. Section 4.6 measures the distribution of wealth in the two years, by decile and by other indicators of inequality. This analysis leads to a decomposition of wealth inequality in each year in Section 4.7. Section 4.8 contrasts the urban and rural sectors, distinguishing between—and within—sector wealth inequality.

Section 4.9 attempts to explain the results, in particular by examining the processes by which wealth inequality increased over the eleven years. Several hypotheses are tested: for instance, that relative house price inflation generates unequal capital gains, that the savings rate is a positive function of income per capita and of wealth per capita, and that a growing share of income from wealth concentrates wealth. Section 4.10 provides estimates of wealth inequality in 2013 both without and with correction for underreported wealth at the top of the wealth distribution. Section 4.11 draws out the implications of the research and concludes.

4.2 Literature

Little has been written on the inequality of wealth in China, mainly because of a lack of data. In the pre-reform period China had virtually no private property or personal wealth. However, the economic reforms—relating to land use, housing, finance, entrepreneurship, etc.—allowed Chinese people to become property owners. The changes were rapid, making it difficult to maintain the collection of accurate data.

McKinley (1993) and Brenner (2001) analyze the inequality of rural (net) wealth by using the 1988 and 1995 CHIP surveys, respectively. Rural household members did not (and do not) own their land; they merely had (and have) use of land, which they hold on long leases. Nor was there an active land rental market during the early stages of the reforms. The value of land to the household had to be calculated on the basis of output from the land. The policy of ensuring rough per capita equality of landholding within a local community made land "ownership" an equalizing force. Financial assets had a disequalizing effect on total wealth but the effect was small, as financial assets accounted for only 3 percent of wealth in 1988 and 11 percent in 1995. When wealth is measured on a comparable basis, the Gini coefficient of wealth in rural China rose from 0.30 in 1988 to 0.35 in 1995.

Urban analysis became possible only after the privatization of urban housing, which began in the early 1990s and was largely completed by the late 1990s. The first urban study was based on the CHIP 1995 survey (Gustafsson, Li, and Wei 2006). Only 42 percent of households reported a positive housing value: the urban wealth Gini reflected that source of housing inequality at this time of ongoing privatization. Official selling prices to urban resident households were very low and simply based on house area and not on quality or location, but the values became more unequal as market prices were established. In 1995 the ratio of market price to official selling price averaged 7.7 to 1 (Zhao and Ding 2008, p. 128). Inequality of housing values was created because housing was allocated according to official rank and political power. The windfall gains meant that housing wealth became unequal.

Li and Zhao (2007) and Zhao and Ding (2008) examine rural, urban, and national wealth inequality by drawing on the CHIP 2002 survey, and Sato, Sicular, and Yue (2013) use the CHIP 2007 survey to examine housing inequality. Xie and Jin (2015) estimate China's inequality of household wealth per capita by means of the China Family Panel Study (CFPS) survey of 2012. However, China's degree of wealth inequality and its evolution deserve increasing research attention as this inequality becomes more pronounced, more obvious, and politically more important.

Our analysis in this chapter, although based on household microdata, connects with the important book *Capital in the Twenty-First Century* (2014), by Thomas Piketty. In it he analyzes why inequality of wealth has risen in Western countries since about 1980 and why, he predicts it will go on rising. It is central to Piketty's argument that wealth increases more rapidly than income, and that it increases more rapidly for those who are wealthier. He uses sources of data, such as statistics on estates and income tax, that differ from our sources. Nevertheless, in Section 4.9 we shall use the household surveys to consider whether his ideas have relevance to China.

4.3 China's Rising Inequality of Wealth and Its Possible Causes

Table 4.1 reports the basic facts of national wealth inequality as measured by the Gini coefficient. Wealth inequality is shown both on a household basis (the first three columns) and on a household per capita basis (the last three columns). The Gini coefficient of household wealth per capita is generally

Table 4.1. Gini coefficient of wealth and income inequality

	Household level			Household per capita level		
	Actual	CPI adjusted	PPP + CPI adjusted	Actual	adjusted	adjusted
2002 wealth	0.454	0.443	0.402	0.508	0.495	0.445
2013 wealth	0.583	0.583	0.541	0.617	0.617	0.574
2002 income	0.384	0.371	0.328	0.437	0.424	0.370
2013 income	0.411	0.411	0.382	0.444	0.444	0.414

Source: In this table and in all subsequent tables and figures the estimates for 2002 are derived from the CHIP 2002 survey and the estimates for 2013 are derived from the CHIP 2013 survey.

3 or 5 percentage points higher than that per household. Consider the per capita results. The Gini coefficient expressed in nominal terms rose from 0.51 to 0.62 over the period.[1] Expressing 2002 wealth in 2013 consumer prices makes little difference: the 2002 Gini falls by about 1 percentage point as a result. However, when wealth is corrected for province, urban, and rural consumer price differences (based on Brandt and Holz [2006] and adjusted to our two years), the 2002 Gini becomes 0.45 and the 2013 Gini becomes 0.57. Wealth inequality did indeed increase sharply, by some 11 or 12 Gini percentage points over those eleven years, i.e., by about 1 percentage point each year.

To put China's inequality of wealth in international perspective we draw on Davies et al. (2008). The authors report estimates of the Gini coefficient of household wealth in the major economies, focusing on the year 2000. The degree of wealth inequality is generally higher than that of income inequality. China's unadjusted Gini of 0.62 in 2013 is exceeded by no fewer than 20 of the 26 countries. The average value of the Gini for all the countries is 0.68. China's degree of wealth inequality is moderated by its remarkably high rate of home ownership in both urban and rural areas compared to most countries, and by its relatively high—almost universal—rate of land "ownership" in rural areas. The inequality of wealth in China is not exceptional. What might be exceptional, however, is its rate of increase.

A combination of various factors might be responsible for this rising inequality of wealth. China has experienced very rapid physical capital accumulation; since 2000 the proportion of GDP that is invested has generally exceeded 40 percent. Wealth has therefore risen rapidly; the question is whether the increase in wealth has accrued unequally among households.

Inequality of household income per capita has grown fast, with the Gini coefficient rising from 0.42 in 2002 to 0.49 in 2007. It fell to 0.45 in 2013 but mainly because the ratio of urban to rural incomes narrowed: within both urban and rural China inequality rose (see Chapter 2). If wealth is positively related to income, the rise in income inequality over the period 2002–2013 might have contributed to the rise in wealth inequality.

A relative rise in the price of wealth goods—property and in particular housing—enriched those who held wealth and enriched most those who held the most wealth. China has experienced a great surge in housing prices, and this trend is likely to have increased the inequality of housing wealth. Financial markets in China remain imperfect, thus providing opportunities to acquire wealth for those with preferential access to funds or with the ability to save a high proportion of their income. If the savings rate is positively related to income, the result provides a channel that is likely to disequalize wealth-holding.

The share of profits in national income has been high throughout the period, being 37 percent in 2007 (Knight and Ding 2012, p. 164). Some profits accrued to the state, some accrued to shareholders, and some were saved. Some of these savings raised the value of personal holdings of company shares. If shareholding is unequally distributed among households, paid-out profits and capital gains will probably contribute to the rising inequality of household wealth in China. If there is a higher savings rate out of income from wealth than out of other income, that too can increase wealth inequality.

Insofar as the available data permit, hypotheses to explain the observed rise in inequality of wealth are examined in Section 4.9.

4.4 The Data

We decided to compare wealth inequality by using the CHIP 2002 and CHIP 2013 national surveys.[2] We need the 2002 and 2013 data to be as comparable as possible. Fortunately, the variables relating to wealth are very similar in the two surveys. Thus, the estimates of wealth distributions can be compared, given appropriate weighting. The weightings used were almost the same as those applied generally in the CHIP 2002 and 2013 surveys to achieve national representativeness.[3]

Nevertheless, various issues had to be resolved. Some issues were simple to deal with. For instance, because the NBS changed its definition of "migrants" in 2012, we reclassified the affected 2013 migrants to be comparable with those in 2002. All provinces in each survey are covered, with one exception. Because the 2013 Xinjiang sample lacks information on wealth, both Xinjiang samples are excluded. Thus, 21 provinces are included in 2002 and 14 provinces are included in 2013.

Other issues were more difficult. Valuing wealth—and in particular housing and land wealth—inevitably encountered problems. Net housing is housing value minus housing loans. This calculation is based on the respondents' reported values (of both owner-occupied and other housing) in each year, despite the weakness of the housing market in rural China.

No information was gathered in the surveys on the asset value of rural land: households merely have user rights to their land. It is possible to base the valuation of rural land (defined as cultivated land, pastures, and forests) on reported net agricultural income. As is explained in Appendix A.4, which describes the components of wealth, the formula for the conversion from net agricultural income to the value of rural land is based on previous research findings. Land assets in urban areas are defined to be zero.

The missing values had to be interpolated. For instance, where a housing value is missing, the imputation of the housing value is on the basis of price per square meter at the local (county, city, or municipal district) level. Local averaging is also used for missing financial assets. Where the value of net income from agricultural operations is missing, we use the county-level value. Where consumer durables are listed but not valued, they are valued by using local consumer durable prices, derived from households that reported both values and quantities.

Comparative real wealth is obtained by reflating 2002 nominal wealth by the NBS's consumer price indexes, so as to express the 2002 values in 2013 prices. We use province-level consumer price indexes, distinguishing also between urban and rural indexes. Throughout the chapter our discussion of wealth is real wealth, i.e., measured at 2013 constant CPI-adjusted prices. The wealth concept of most interest is not total household wealth but household wealth per capita. Thus, when we refer to the term wealth, we mean real household wealth per capita.

It will become evident later in this chapter that the growth of housing wealth has made a considerable contribution to the growth of inequality of household wealth. It is therefore important to examine the role of housing price inflation in this process. The task is complicated by the fact that our two datasets do not constitute a panel.

Two approaches were tried. One was to use data published by the Ministry of Housing and Construction, which show the value of sales of commercialized buildings, and the corresponding sold floor space, at district and county level. From this information it was possible to construct a housing inflation index. The other approach was to calculate housing prices from the CHIP surveys for each of the urban and rural areas within each included province. Districts within cities were used in the case of metropolitan areas. Reflecting the data available, each subsample was divided into ranked subgroups based on average housing value per square meter, and these subgroups were compared in 2002 and 2013. If an area was not included in both years, another location with a very similar housing price was substituted. The resultant housing price inflation index was then applied to all households in each area. Robustness tests were passed. The results obtained by the two approaches were fairly similar. Our estimates of housing price inflation are based on the second approach.

Because wealth in 2002 and 2013 is calculated in real terms by using 2013 constant prices, 2002 housing prices are already raised by the consumer price index. Our interest is therefore in the relative housing price inflation, measured as housing price inflation divided by consumer price inflation.

At several points in this chapter household wealth is related to household income, both expressed in per capita terms. We follow the CHIP income definition in the 2013 survey except that imputed rents on owner-occupied housing are not included. Partly because of the NBS's reform of statistics in 2012, income in 2002 and in 2013 was defined differently. We adjusted the 2002 definition of income to be consistent with that of 2013.

We confine our analysis to the rural and urban samples of the CHIP. Although there was a rural/urban migrant sample in both 2002 and 2013, the 2002 migrant questionnaire contained little information relating to income and, especially, to wealth. Since our objective is to examine the rise in wealth inequality between the two years and its causes, it is necessary to exclude rural/urban migrants from the analysis. Insofar as the rural surveys include households containing absent migrants, their wealth is covered by the rural questionnaire.

4.5 The Level of Wealth and Its Growth, 2002 and 2013

Table 4.2 has six columns: the first three (A–C) relate to the level of wealth per capita in 2002, the next two (D and E) relate to the level of wealth in 2013,

Table 4.2. Level and growth of wealth per capita

Category	Actual 2002 (A)	CPI adjusted 2002 (B)	PPP + CPI adjusted 2002 (C)	Actual 2013 (D)	PPP adjusted 2013 (E)	Annual real growth rate, 2002–2013 F = (D–B)
Urban						
Overall net wealth	36,764	49,517	36,042	273,841	195,607	16.8
Financial assets	9921	13,357	9731	38,996	28,697	10.2
Net housing	22,639	30,483	22,146	214,021	151,423	19.4
Productive fixed assets	712	973	761	4041	3181	13.8
Consumer durables	3088	4160	3006	15,071	11,085	12.4
Other assets	648	878	652	2334	1708	9.3
Non-housing debt	−244	−334	−254	−622	−487	5.8
Rural						
Overall net wealth	13,666	19,576	20,521	83,489	80,127	14.1
Land	3862	5590	5903	8263	8297	3.6
Financial assets	2076	2972	3122	16,112	15,906	16.6
Net housing	5680	8074	8406	49,336	46,430	17.9
Productive fixed assets	1192	1722	1812	4931	4772	10.0
Consumer durables	1072	1529	1602	5690	5550	12.7
Non-housing debt	−216	−311	−324	−843	−828	9.5

National					
Overall net wealth	21,565	29,815	25,829	162,829	128,261	16.7
Land	2541	3678	3884	4819	4839	2.5
Financial assets	4759	6523	5382	25,650	21,238	13.3
Net housing	11,480	15,738	13,105	117,978	90,192	20.1
Productive fixed assets	1027	1466	1452	4560	4109	10.9
Consumer durables	1761	2429	2083	9600	7857	13.3
Other assets	222	300	223	973	712	11.3
Non-housing debt	−225	−319	−300	−751	−686	8.1

Note: In this table and all subsequent tables and figures wealth is defined as household wealth per capita.

and the final column (F, derived from D and B) shows the real annual growth rate of wealth over the eleven years. National, urban, and rural wealth per capita are shown separately, and wealth is reported by type as well as total wealth.

We begin with urban wealth. Overall real net wealth per capita grew at 16.8 percent per annum. The fastest growth is seen in net housing (19.4 percent), followed by consumer durables and productive fixed assets. Further insights are obtained in Table 4.3, which shows the structure of household wealth in the two years. We see that the share of urban net housing in total urban wealth rose from 62 percent in 2002 to 78 percent in 2013. This was the most striking change. The next largest share was financial assets, but this share fell, from 27 percent in 2002 to 14 percent in 2013.

Total net wealth per capita in rural China grew by 14.1 percent per annum (Table 4.2). This growth rate was fastest for net housing (17.9 percent), followed by financial assets (16.6 percent). Again, net housing was the predominant form of wealth-holding, rising from 41 percent to 59 percent of the total (Table 4.3). The share of land wealth fell drastically, from 29 percent to 10 percent of the total.

Similar patterns are found at the national level. Overall net wealth per capita increased by 16.7 percent per annum, and net housing increased fastest (20.1 percent). The share of net housing rose from 53 percent to 73 percent of the total. Clearly, housing plays a central role in China's accumulation of wealth. It will be important to inquire whether it also plays a central role in the rising inequality of wealth.

4.6 The Distribution of Wealth, 2002 and 2013

The distribution of household wealth by wealth per capita decile is reported in Table 4.4. Consider first the urban decile shares. Remarkably, the poorest wealth decile of households held 0.44 percent of total wealth in 2002 and 0.58 percent in 2013. By contrast, the richest decile owned 32 percent in 2002 and 42 percent in 2013, a rise of 10 percentage points. In fact, only the top decile experienced a substantial increase in share over the period. A similar pattern is found in rural China. The top decile increased its share from 29 percent to 43 percent, and the shares of the lowest eight deciles fell. At the national level, the share of the richest decile rose from 37 percent to 48 percent and the share of all the other deciles fell.

Table 4.3. Structure of household wealth by type of wealth asset (%)

Category	Urban 2002	2013	Rural 2002	2013	National 2002	2013
Overall net wealth	100	100	100	100	100	100
Land	NA	NA	28.6	9.9	12.3	3.0
Financial assets	27.0	14.2	15.2	19.3	21.9	15.8
Net housing	61.6	78.2	41.2	59.1	52.8	72.5
Productive fixed assets	2.0	1.5	8.8	5.9	4.9	2.8
Consumer durables	8.4	5.5	7.8	6.8	8.1	5.9
Other assets	1.8	0.9	NA	NA	1.0	0.6
Non-housing debt	–0.7	–0.2	–1.6	–1.0	–1.1	–0.5

Notes: In this table and all subsequent tables and figures we show only CPI deflated wealth, i.e., in both 2002 and 2013 wealth is reported in constant 2013 prices.

Table 4.4. Household wealth share by wealth decile (%)

Wealth decile from lowest to highest	Urban 2002	2013	Rural 2002	2013	National 2002	2013	National wealth per capita (yuan) 2002	2013
1	0.4	0.6	2.2	0.7	1.2	0.4	3742	7688
2	2.0	1.9	3.8	2.1	2.6	1.4	8223	22,575
3	3.6	2.8	5.0	3.1	3.6	2.2	11,584	33,397
4	5.0	3.8	6.1	4.1	4.6	3.0	15,003	45,232
5	6.5	4.9	7.2	5.2	5.7	4.0	18,858	59,417
6	8.3	6.4	8.6	6.6	7.0	5.4	23,577	77,474
7	10.5	8.4	10.1	8.3	8.9	7.4	30,210	104,428
8	13.6	11.6	12.3	11.0	11.8	10.7	40,365	148,946
9	18.5	17.9	15.8	16.4	17.5	17.2	59,001	238,683
10	31.5	41.8	29.0	42.7	37.1	48.4	119,630	701,955

The final column of Table 4.4 reports the national wealth per capita by decile. The ratio of the highest to the lowest decile was 32 times in 2002 and no fewer than 91 times in 2013. The ratio of the tenth to the ninth decile rose from 2.0 to 2.9.

Figures 4.1, 4.2, and 4.3 show the Lorenz curve for wealth per capita of urban, rural, and national households. In each case, the 2013 curve is more

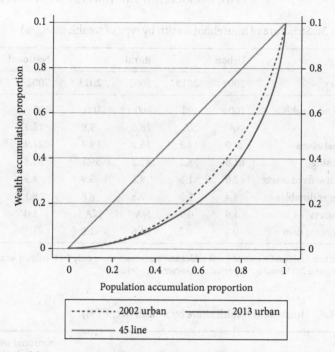

Fig. 4.1 Wealth Lorenz curves for urban households

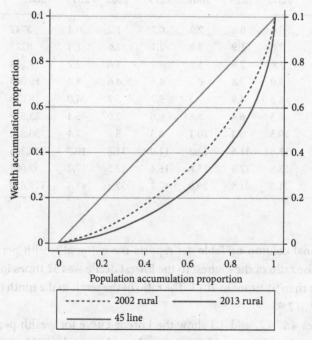

Fig. 4.2 Wealth Lorenz curves for rural households

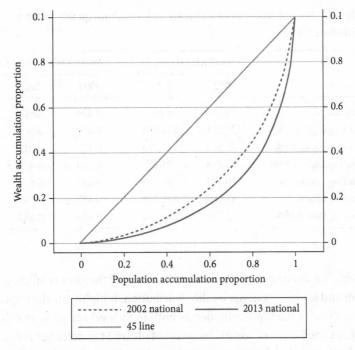

Fig. 4.3 Wealth Lorenz curves for national households

Table 4.5. Wealth Gini coefficients, 2002 and 2013

Sample	2002	2013	Change 2002–2013	
			Percentage points	Percentage
Urban	0.472	0.557	0.09	18.03
Rural	0.384	0.548	0.16	42.54
National	0.494	0.617	0.12	25.06

bowed than the 2002 curve throughout its range, indicating a rise in inequality throughout the wealth distribution.

Table 4.5 reduces the Lorenz curve to a single number, that is, the Gini coefficient. In urban China the Gini coefficient increased by 9 percentage points, from 0.47 to 0.56 over the eleven years. In rural China the increase was even greater, by 17 percentage points, from 0.38 to 0.55. Rural wealth inequality is almost the same as urban wealth inequality in 2013, whereas the rural Gini was lower (by 9 percentage points) in 2002. The national Gini (rising from 0.49 to 0.62) exceeds both the urban and rural Ginis because of the difference between the average urban and the average rural household wealth per capita.

Table 4.6. The sensitivity of wealth level and wealth inequality to the tails of the wealth distribution

Category	Wealth level (yuan)		Wealth inequality (Gini)	
	2002	2013	2002	2013
Entire sample	29,815	16,2829	0.494	0.617
Excluding highest 1%	27,971	144,433	0.470	0.581
Excluding highest 5%	23,905	113,573	0.419	0.518
Excluding highest 10%	20,848	93,429	0.380	0.473
Excluding lowest 1%	30,147	164,693	0.487	0.611
Excluding lowest 5%	31,289	171,358	0.472	0.598
Excluding lowest 10%	32,733	180,135	0.456	0.582

Table 4.6 illustrates the degree of sensitivity of the Gini coefficient to the upper and lower tails of the wealth distribution. It highlights the importance of the share of the top wealth decile, both in its level and in its rise. In 2002 the Gini coefficient of wealth inequality falls by 11 percentage points if the top decile is excluded from the sample, and in 2013 its fall is by no fewer than 15 percentage points, from 0.62 down to 0.47.

Information in tables is sometimes easier to absorb if it is also shown in corresponding figures. Relating the share of wealth to income deciles instead of wealth deciles, Figure 4.4 shows the share held by each household income per capita decile. With only a trivial exception, there is a monotonic rise in this share with income per capita. For instance, at the national level, in 2002 the share of the lowest income per capita decile was 2.9 percent and that of the highest decile was 26.6 percent, and in 2013 the share ranged from 2.9 percent to 36.1 percent. The ninth decile and, in particular, the tenth decile increased their shares of total wealth in all three cases. Figure 4.4 shows clearly how inequality of wealth among the income groups increased in the urban, rural, and national samples.

4.7 Decomposition of Wealth Inequality, 2002 and 2013

Table 4.7 and Table 4.8 employ the standard method for the decomposition of inequality among different components, in this case forms of wealth

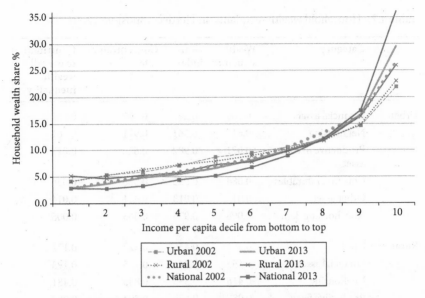

Fig. 4.4 Household wealth share by income per capita decile (%)

holding.[4] In each table, the first column shows the share of each item in total wealth, the second column shows the Gini coefficient for that item, and the third column shows the concentration coefficient, reflecting the correlation between the income of that item and total income. The final column is derived from the product of these three variables, yielding the result of most interest: the contribution of each item to overall wealth inequality.

We examine first the urban results. Net housing makes by far the greatest contribution to wealth inequality in 2002 (66 percent). It is followed by financial assets (24 percent). Productive fixed assets are very unequally held but their contribution to total wealth inequality is small (3 percent), owing to their small share of total wealth. The contribution of net housing is as high as 83 percent in 2013, increasing because all three components—its share of wealth, its concentration coefficient, and its Gini coefficient—rose. The contribution of financial assets fell over the period (to 11 percent) because its share of total wealth fell. Other wealth assets contributed only 6 percent to total inequality of wealth. The extreme importance of housing in explaining the inequality of urban wealth is clear.

Housing made the largest contribution also to the rural wealth inequality. Its contribution increased from 48 percent in 2002 to 65 percent in 2013. By

Table 4.7. Household wealth inequality and its decomposition, 2002

	Category	Wealth structure	Gini index	Concentration rate	Contribution to overall wealth inequality
Urban	Financial assets	0.269	0.596	0.707	0.237
	Net housing	0.617	0.561	0.911	0.661
	Productive fixed assets	0.021	0.982	0.626	0.027
	Consumer durables	0.084	0.555	0.566	0.056
	Other assets	0.017	0.913	0.411	0.014
	Non-housing debt	−0.008	−0.975	0.365	0.006
Rural	Land	0.281	0.455	0.522	0.172
	Financial assets	0.155	0.641	0.755	0.193
	Net housing	0.416	0.533	0.843	0.481
	Productive fixed assets	0.087	0.675	0.594	0.089
	Consumer durables	0.078	0.466	0.642	0.060
	Non-housing debt	−0.016	−0.918	0.140	0.005
National	Land	0.101	0.691	0.004	0.001
	Financial assets	0.228	0.688	0.796	0.250
	Net housing	0.545	0.636	0.914	0.636
	Productive fixed assets	0.044	0.847	0.424	0.032
	Consumer durables	0.082	0.569	0.672	0.063
	Other assets	0.011	0.963	0.625	0.014
	Non-housing debt	−0.011	−0.951	0.254	0.005

contrast, the contribution of land fell from 17 percent to 5 percent, essentially because the share of land in total rural wealth fell. The contributions of other wealth assets were both minor and stable.

The urban and rural results are reflected in the national pattern. The contribution of net housing rose, being 64 percent in 2002 and 78 percent in 2013. The only other form of wealth-holding of importance was financial assets: its contribution fell, from 25 percent to 13 percent, reflecting the rising contribution of net housing.

Table 4.8. Household wealth inequality and its decomposition, 2013

	Category	Wealth structure	Gini index	Concentration coefficient	Contribution to overall wealth inequality
Urban	Financial assets	0.145	0.606	0.681	0.108
	Net housing	0.778	0.608	0.967	0.828
	Productive fixed assets	0.016	0.979	0.608	0.017
	Consumer durables	0.055	0.704	0.580	0.041
	Other assets	0.008	0.765	0.451	0.005
	Non-housing debt	−0.003	−1.482	0.201	0.001
Rural	Land	0.114	0.552	0.412	0.050
	Financial assets	0.189	0.618	0.730	0.164
	Net housing	0.580	0.635	0.907	0.646
	Productive fixed assets	0.061	0.909	0.699	0.075
	Consumer durables	0.067	0.728	0.648	0.061
	Non-housing debt	−0.011	−1.085	0.215	0.005
National	Land	0.039	0.714	−0.012	−0.001
	Financial assets	0.160	0.647	0.763	0.130
	Net housing	0.711	0.702	0.960	0.785
	Productive fixed assets	0.031	0.942	0.608	0.029
	Consumer durables	0.059	0.746	0.685	0.049
	Other assets	0.006	0.915	0.695	0.006
	Non-housing debt	−0.005	−1.212	0.203	0.002

4.8 Wealth Inequality within and between the Urban and Rural Sectors

Table 4.9 uses the Theil index of inequality because it can decompose inequality precisely into between-group and within-group inequality, whereas the Gini coefficient cannot do so. The groups in this case are urban and rural China. In 2002 within-group inequality of household wealth per capita accounted for 78 percent of national wealth inequality, and between-group inequality

Table 4.9. National wealth inequality decomposition: Urban and rural

	Year, index	National inequality	Within-group inequality	Between-group inequality
2002	Theil index	0.429	0.332	0.096
	Proportion (%)	100	77.5	22.5
2013	Theil index	0.728	0.547	0.182
	Proportion (%)	100	75.1	24.9

accounted for the remaining 22 percent. In 2013 the contributions were 75 percent and 25 percent respectively. The proportions of the total contributed by within-urban and within-rural wealth inequality fell a little, whereas the contribution made by the difference between urban and rural wealth rose correspondingly. The more important point, however, is that the Theil index, and both of its components, rose substantially between 2002 and 2013.

In both years the national Gini coefficient exceeded both the urban and the rural Gini coefficient because the difference between urban and rural household wealth per capita extended the wealth range. Recall that in 2002 the national, urban, and rural Gini coefficients for household wealth per capita were 0.49, 0.47, and 0.38 respectively, and that in 2013 the corresponding values were 0.62, 0.56, and 0.55.

The ratio of urban to rural wealth per capita increased over the period, from 2.69 to 3.20. This widening spatial wealth disparity contributed to the rise in national inequality of wealth. That rise is consistent with the absolute rise (from 0.10 to 0.18) and the rise in the share (from 22.5 percent to 24.9 percent) of between-group inequality in the Theil index. The findings for the wealth Gini contrast with those for the income Gini: the urban/rural disparity in income per capita narrowed after 2007, and this narrowing was mainly responsible for the fall in China's income Gini during the period 2007–2013 (Chapter 2; Knight 2017).

4.9 Explaining the Results

4.9.1 The Wealth/Income Ratio

How does wealth relate to income? Do households with higher income per capita have proportionately higher wealth per capita? If that is the case, what

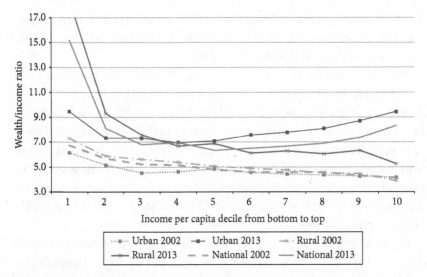

Fig. 4.5 Wealth/income ratio by income per capita decile

are the mechanisms that produce this result? Figure 4.5 shows the wealth/income ratio by income decile (both expressed in per capita terms) in 2002 and 2013. Causation cannot be attributed to the relationship: causation might run from income to wealth or from wealth to income, or in both directions. Nevertheless, the results are informative.

We see from the figure that in 2002 the wealth/income ratio was very similar for the urban, rural, and national samples. The ratio was highest for the poorest income decile but beyond the second decile the ratio was fairly constant, declining only slightly. In China as a whole the average ratio was 4.9. The high ratio for the poorest two income deciles might be due to the egalitarian system of landholding and the possibility that income fluctuations raised the ratio of wealth (for instance, land and housing) relative to the income of households in temporary income poverty (for example, instances of negative net income). The analysis by income decile reveals a relationship that might otherwise be obscured.

The wealth/income ratio was generally higher in 2013, notably for the poorest and the richest households. In particular, the urban ratio increased beyond the median income level, and the same U-shape is seen in the national sample. A tendency for the wealth/income ratio to rise with income (beyond a low-income level) is observable in 2013 but not in 2002. The country's wealth/income ratio in 2013 was 7.4, having increased rapidly—by no less than 2.5—over the eleven years. China's ratio then exceeded the private wealth/income ratio in the developed economies, which generally varied between 5 and 6 (Piketty 2014, p. 50).

The same exercise is conducted for the housing wealth/income ratio in Figure 4.6. In 2002 the ratio is highest for the poorest income decile, is similar for all three cases, and is fairly constant beyond the second decile. For the 2013 sample, the middle deciles are pivotal. Beyond them, the rural ratio is fairly constant but the urban ratio, and thus also the national ratio, tend to rise. Thus, there is a tendency for the housing wealth/income ratio to rise with income decile in the upper half of the urban and national income distributions.[5] Over the period 2002–2013 the housing wealth of households outpaced their incomes in China as a whole.

Figure 4.7 reports the growth of real wealth per capita by income per capita decile. In the rural sample the lowest decile shows the highest growth rate and in the urban and national samples it is the highest decile that grows the fastest. In the urban and national samples the growth rate rises after the fifth and second deciles, respectively. There is a tendency for China's income-rich to become relatively wealth-richer.

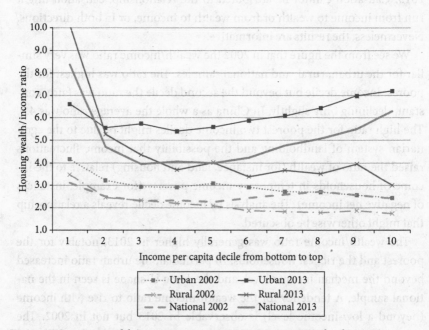

Fig. 4.6 Housing wealth/income ratio per income per capita decile

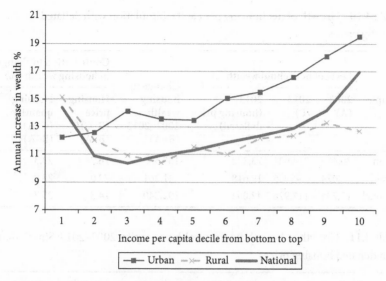

Fig. 4.7 Annual percentage increase in wealth by income per capita decile

4.9.2 The Role of Housing Price Inflation

Table 4.10 divides the increase in housing wealth into that part which is due to relative housing price inflation and that part due to a real increase in housing. However, our measure of relative housing price inflation necessarily includes the value of housing improvements per square meter: it is not a pure price effect. Thus, the real increase (the increase in housing quantity) represents an increase in the average number of square meters reported. Insofar as part of the increase in housing values is due to housing improvements, these improvements represent a form of wealth-holding that yields high returns to the investment.

In China as a whole, after elimination of the effect of relative housing price inflation (74.3 percent of the increase), 25.7 percent is due to the increase in the volume of housing wealth. We see that the proportions are very similar to the national case in both urban and rural China. Much of China's rapid growth in housing wealth can be attributed to a relative increase in housing values.

The effect of relative housing price inflation seems important enough to examine its effect on the growth of household wealth as a whole. Thus, Table 4.11 divides the change in household wealth over the eleven years into that part which is due to housing price inflation (relative to consumer price

Table 4.10. Growth of net housing per capita: Simulation with deflated
housing prices

Sample	Level of household wealth			Change in housing wealth 2002–2013 (B–A)	Contribution to change in housing wealth (%)	
	2002 (A)	2013 (B)	2013 (housing price deflated) (C)		Housing price (B–C)/ (B–A)	Housing quantity (C–A)/ (B–A)
Urban	30,483	214,021	73,322	183,538	76.7	23.3
Rural	8074	49336	19,618	41,261	72.0	28.0
National	15,738	117,978	42,002	102,240	74.3	25.7

Table 4.11. Growth of household net wealth per capita, 2002–2013: Simulation
with deflated housing prices

Sample	Level of household wealth			Change in wealth 2002–2013 (B–A)	Contribution to change in wealth (%)	
	2002 (A)	2013 (B)	2013 (house price deflated) (C)		House price (B–C)/ (B–A)	Other (C–A)/ (B–A)
Urban	49,517	273,840	133,786	224,323	62.4	37.6
Rural	19,575	834,88	53,747	63,913	46.5	53.5
National	29,815	162,829	871,08	133,014	56.9	43.1

inflation) and other factors. In urban China, 62.4 percent of the rise in household wealth is due to (relative) inflation of housing prices and 37.6 percent is
due to other factors. In rural China we see that 46.5 percent of the rise results
from housing price inflation and 53.5 percent results from other factors. At
the national level, 56.9 percent of the increase in household wealth reflects
the relative housing price index and 43.1 percent reflects other influences.
We see the great importance of relative housing price inflation for the growth
of household wealth in China.

Figure 4.8 shows the housing price (per square meter) in 2002 on the horizontal axis, with regions (county, city, or municipal district) of the country,
ordered from the lowest priced region in 2002 on the left to the highest
priced region on the right; the prices (in 10,000 yuan) range from 0 to 0.6.
The regions to the far right are the four included municipalities: Beijing,
Shanghai, Tianjin, and Chongqing. The vertical axis (also measured in

Fig. 4.8 Housing price by common area in 2002 and 2013

10,000 yuan, but ranging from 0 to 4.0) shows the housing price of each region in 2013. The best fit to the points is curvilinear, curving upward. Areas with higher initial housing prices benefited from proportionately faster housing price inflation.

Figure 4.9 shows, by wealth per capita decile, the percentage increase in relative housing price inflation (derived for each household by the method explained previously) during the eleven-year period in urban areas, rural areas, and China as a whole. In the rural sample, housing price inflation is fairly constant over the whole range. In the urban sample, there is an almost monotonic increase with the wealth decile, and in the national sample the increase occurs after the eighth wealth decile. In both the urban and the national samples there is a very sharp rise in the top decile. Households in the wealthiest deciles have experienced the greatest capital gains from housing price inflation.

Table 4.12 shows the impact of housing price inflation on the Gini coefficient. Columns A and B report the Gini as previously estimated. Column C reports the Gini for 2013 if wealth is deflated by the relative rise in housing prices between 2002 and 2013. Column D shows the rise in the undeflated Gini over the eleven years (B–A). Columns E and F measure the contributions to the rise in the Gini that are due to the rise in housing prices (B–C) and to other factors (C–A). Relative housing price inflation accounted

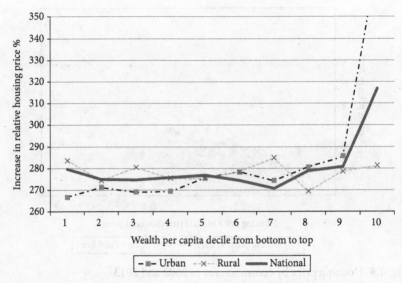

Fig. 4.9 Increase in relative housing price by wealth per capita decile (%)

Table 4.12. Impact of relative housing price inflation on wealth inequality

Sample	Gini coefficient of household wealth				Contribution to change in Gini (%)	
	2002 (A)	2013 (B)	2013 (housing price deflated) (C)	Change in Gini 2002–2013 D = (B–A)	Housing price inflation (B–C)/ (B–A)	Other (C–A)/ (B–A)
Urban	0.472	0.557	0.510	0.085	55.1	44.9
Rural	0.384	0.548	0.520	0.164	17.2	82.8
National	0.494	0.617	0.561	0.124	45.3	54.7

for 55 percent of the rise in urban China, 17 percent in rural China, and 45 percent at the national level. Again, it is clear that the excess of housing price inflation over consumer price inflation is very important to our story.

An underlying question that deserves further research is the following: why has housing price inflation been so rapid? One possible explanation is the rapid increase in demand for housing and housing land in relation to supply. Another possibility is that the housing market has grown stronger over time. Part of the housing price inflation over this period might have represented some market undervaluation in 2002 and subsequent movement toward equilibrium market values. A third possible reason for the substantial rise in housing prices is speculative demand, which accentuated the underlying rise.

4.9.3 Differential Savings

Another channel by which wealth inequality can increase is through differential savings: the rich might save a higher proportion of their income than the poor. Figure 4.10 shows the savings rate (i.e., savings as a percentage of income) by income per capita decile, and Figure 4.11 does the same by wealth per capita. Figure 4.10 displays a monotonic rise in the savings rate in all six cases as we move up the income deciles. At the national level, in 2002 the savings rate rose from –29.3 percent in the first decile to 17.7 percent in the fifth decile and to 32.6 percent in the tenth decile, and in 2013 it rose correspondingly from –72.0 percent to 32.8 percent, to 57.2 percent, and to 55.9 percent. In both years the savings rate is highly sensitive to income level. Some negative savings are to be expected in the lowest decile if there is transient poverty.

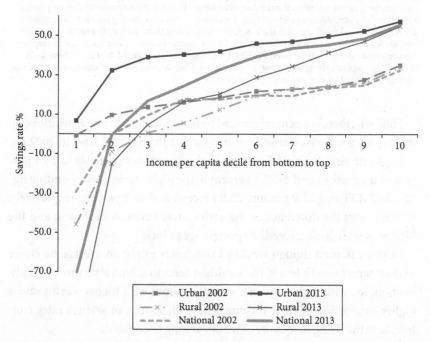

Fig. 4.10 Savings rate by income per capita decile (%)

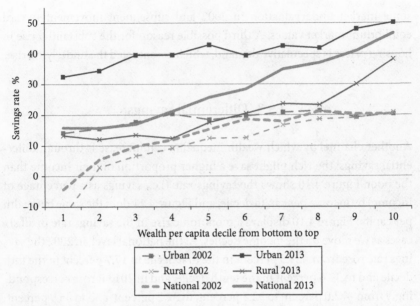

Fig. 4.11 Savings rate by wealth per capita decile (%)

Notes: The savings rate is calculated as $(Y–C)/Y$ where Y is household income per capita and C is household consumption per capita, with imputed rent of owner-occupied housing excluded from both income and consumption. Expenditures on consumer durables are not part of measured consumption; rather, it is treated instead as an addition to wealth. We estimate the average savings rate for each income decile as a whole. Negative income yields a misleading positive value, as both the numerator and the denominator are negative. Fortunately, there are very few negative-income households in either survey, so the poorest decile has positive income. There is a minor discrepancy between Figure 3.3 in Chapter 3 and Figure 4.10, owing to different methods of estimation. Both show the savings rate rising with income, but Chapter 3 uses income per equivalized person and the median household savings rate in the income ventile,

Similarly, there is a general upward trend in the savings rate as we move up the wealth-per-capita deciles. For instance, at the national level in 2002 the savings rate rises from –4.3 percent in the lowest wealth decile to 15.4 percent in the median and to 20.4 percent in the highest, the corresponding figures in 2013 being 15.9 percent, 25.8 percent, and 46.7 percent, respectively. In both years the difference in the savings rate between the lowest and the highest wealth decile exceeds 20 percentage points.

In general, even though wealthy households might on average be closer to their target wealth levels, the wealthier tend to accumulate more quickly. Households with higher income as well as those with higher wealth save a higher proportion of their income. These disparities in savings rates contribute to the rising inequality of wealth among households.

4.9.4 The Ratio of Wealth Income to Non-Wealth Income

Piketty (2014) examines the ratio of wealth to income over time and establishes the conditions required for the ratio to increase. He argues that in since about 1980 such conditions have been satisfied in the advanced economies. As the ratio rises, the share of income from wealth in total income rises as well. If the savings rate for income from wealth is higher than that for income from non-wealth, this difference generates proportionately faster growth of wealth for those with more of their income derived from wealth. Piketty regards this mechanism to be an important explanation for the recent growth of wealth inequality in the advanced economies.

We have adduced evidence that the ratio of wealth to income increased sharply during the 2002–2013 period. Nevertheless, the Piketty effect is unlikely to be important in the Chinese case. We define income from wealth as interest, dividends, and rent received.[6] In 2002, for the urban sample the proportion of income from wealth was very low, at 4.6 percent for the urban sample and 3.0 percent for the rural sample, and for the two combined it was 3.6 percent; in 2013 the corresponding figures were 9.5 percent, 4.0 percent, and 6.3 percent, respectively (Table 4.13). Thus, it is to be expected that in 2002 the proportion of income from wealth would have a negligible effect on savings, and even in 2013 it would have only a small effect.

In order to investigate Piketty's argument further, we estimated OLS equations with the savings rate as the dependent variable and the share of income from wealth as an explanatory variable. In 2013 at least, there is a higher propensity to save out of income from wealth than out of other income. However, this significant positive coefficient on income from wealth could be a non-causal association resulting from the positive relation between the share of income from wealth and income on the one hand and between income and the savings rate on the other hand. Indeed, the addition of income

Table 4.13. Income from wealth as a share of household income

	Urban		Rural		National	
	2002	2013	2002	2013	2002	2013
%	4.64	9.54	3.04	4.04	3.59	6.34

Note: We use CPI-deflated wealth and income, both household per capita. Income from wealth is defined here as interest, dividends, and actual rent.

per capita in the estimated equation removes the significant positive effect of the share of income from wealth. Overall, we find little support for Piketty's explanation of the rise in wealth inequality.

4.10 Correction for Underrepresentation and Underreporting in 2013

China has enough dollar billionaires to influence measures of income and wealth distributions if they are included in the national household surveys on which estimates of inequality are based. However, it is most unlikely that any are included and, if any are included, it is unlikely that their wealth can be accurately recorded. It is worth exploring scientific ways of correcting for survey inaccuracies near the top of the income distribution.

Atkinson, Piketty, and Saez (2011), using income tax data for the major economies, measure the income share of the top 5 or 1 or 0.1 percent. They identify these precise top shares by imputing them using the Pareto distribution. They use the actual distribution below 5 (or 1 or 0.1) percent but apply the Pareto distribution for the top incomes. Their justification is that "a number of top income studies conclude that the Pareto approximation works remarkably well."

The Pareto law for top incomes is given by the cumulative density function $F(y)$:

$$1 - F(y) = (k/y)^{\alpha} \quad (k > 0, \alpha > 0) \tag{4.1}$$

where α is the Pareto parameter. The corresponding density function $f(y)$ is

$$F(y) = \alpha k^{\alpha} / y^{(1+\alpha)} \tag{4.2}$$

The key property of Pareto distributions is that the ratio of average income $y^*(y)$ of individuals with income above y, to y, does not depend on the income threshold y.

$$y^* = \alpha y / (\alpha - 1)$$

$$\text{i.e., } y^*(y) / y = \beta = \alpha / (\alpha - 1) \tag{4.3}$$

Thus, if we know β, we can calculate α. A higher value of β implies a fatter upper tail.

Atkinson, Piketty, and Saez (2011) assumed that records are accurate (i.e., there is no nonresponse and no underreporting), but our concern is to conduct simulations that assume underrepresentation and underreporting.

Consider, first, the correction for underrepresentation. Given that the top households tend to avoid a survey of this sort, reweighting can be used to correct for such a nonresponse bias. Assume that the nonresponse rate among the top-wealth households is (say) 50 percent. We can then expand the top 5 percent of households to become the top 7.5/102.5 = 7.32 percent, and we thus get a new frequency distribution of household wealth. This expansion involves randomly repeating every second high-wealth household. It is then possible to calculate the Gini with the assumed nonresponse uncorrected and also corrected, and to measure the sensitivity of the Gini to this assumption.

Table 4.14 reports the results of this exercise. The rows indicate the top percentile to be expanded. The first row shows no expansion, then the expansion of the top 0.5 percent, 1.0 percent, and 5.0 percent of the wealth distribution. The columns show the mean value of the simulated sample and its Gini coefficient if the top subsample is first doubled and then tripled. Consider the effect of doubling the number of wealthy households. The Gini coefficient of the actual sample is 0.62. It rises to 0.65 when the number of the top 5 percent of households is doubled. If instead a tripling is assumed, the Gini rises to 0.67 in the case of the top 1 percent of households but it actually falls to 0.66 in the case of the top 5 percent. As a kernel density function suggests, beyond about 1 percent of households, a tripling of the top households begins to dilute inequality.

Now consider a correction for an underreporting of wealth by respondents. Semi-parametric analysis can be used: actual data below the top x percent

Table 4.14. Simulated correction for nonresponse by the wealthy in 2013

	Top subsample doubled		Top subsample tripled	
	Mean	Gini	Mean	Gini
No expansion	162,829	0.617	162,829	0.617
Expand top 0.5%	176,310	0.639	189,621	0.657
Expand top 1%	183,888	0.647	204,423	0.668
Expand top 5%	212,058	0.650	255,719	0.657

and simulated data for the top x percent, with values taken from the corresponding Pareto function. The observed and the simulated frequencies should be the same at the changeover point. We now have the means to correct for possible underreporting of household wealth. The actual value of β is derived from the survey. A higher value—a fatter tail—can be assumed on the assumption that there is underreporting.

Table 4.15 shows four rows. In the first row there is by assumption no underrepresentation of the wealthy, i.e., no expansion of the richest subsample takes place. In the other three rows it is assumed that the number of those in the top 0.5 percent, 1.0 percent, and 5.0 percent, respectively, of the sample are tripled. The value of β in the actual sample is 1.51. Column 1 shows the results if the value of β takes almost its actual value (assumed $\beta = 1.5$); column 2 assumes a fatter tail ($\beta = 2.0$), owing to assumed underreporting of wealth; and column 3 is a still fatter tail.

As might be expected, simply replacing the actual data with simulated data has little effect on the Gini coefficient. This ineffectiveness is evident in the Gini value (0.613) of the (first row, first column) cell in the table. Looking across the first row, we find that the Gini coefficient increases from 0.62 (actual distribution) to 0.64 when $\beta = 2.0$ and to 0.66 when $\beta = 0.25$. This row shows the degree of sensitivity of the Gini to possible underreporting. When the assumption of underreporting is combined with the assumption of underrepresentation, the effect is magnified. Consider a tripling of the top 1 percent of wealthy households (row 3). The Gini rises from 0.67 with the actual value of β to 0.69 with $\beta = 2.0$ and to 0.72 with $\beta = 2.5$. On that last assumption, the Gini coefficient is 9 percentage points above its reported value. Expanding the top 5 percent is again found to dilute inequality.

Table 4.15. Simulated correction for nonresponse plus underreporting by the wealthy in 2013

The top subsample is tripled	$\beta = 1.5$		$\beta = 2.0$		$\beta = 2.5$	
	Mean	Gini	Mean	Gini	Mean	Gini
No expansion	160,679	0.613	172,353	0.637	184,028	0.659
Expand top 0.5%	190,583	0.659	201,664	0.677	212,745	0.693
Expand top 1%	205,039	0.669	222,775	0.694	240,511	0.715
Expand top 5%	256,270	0.657	272,737	0.677	289,204	0.694

The table cannot produce the "true, corrected" Gini coefficient of wealth. However, it does show the considerable sensitivity of the Gini to plausible assumptions of the degree of underrepresentation of and underreporting by wealthy households.

A different method of correcting for underrepresentation at the top of China's wealth distribution is employed by Xie and Jin (2015). They use the *Hurun Rich List 2012*, which reports the wealth of the thousand richest households in China. The Pareto distribution is then applied to estimate the wealth of the top 0.1 percent and, with appropriate weights, this result is combined with wealth data from the CFPS national survey of 2012 for the remaining 99.9 percent of households (Xie and Jin 2015, p. 209). The unadjusted Gini coefficient of wealth among households is estimated to be 0.64 and the Gini adjusted for underrepresentation at the top is 0.73—a difference of 9 percentage points (Xie and Jin 2015, table 2). Their estimates correspond well to our unadjusted Gini in 2013 (0.62) and our adjusted estimate when it is based on the assumptions that the top 1 percent is tripled and that $\beta = 2.5$ (0.71)—also a difference of 9 percentage points.

4.11 Conclusion

Between 2002 and 2013 (real) household net wealth per capita in China increased by 17 percent per annum, and net housing wealth increased by no less than 20 percent per annum. Our comparison of China's inequality of household wealth per capita in the two years shows that this inequality has risen rapidly in the twenty-first century. For instance, the share of the top wealth decile increased from 37 percent to 48 percent of total wealth. A decomposition of the sources of wealth inequality shows the great importance of net housing in its share of wealth and in its contribution to wealth inequality, and to their rise over time: the share rose from 53 percent to 73 percent and the contribution rose from 64 percent to 79 percent.

This chapter is one of the first attempts not only to describe China's rapidly rising inequality of wealth but also to explain the phenomenon. Setting aside the poorest income groups, we find a tendency for the wealth/income ratio to rise with income in 2013, and for the wealth/income ratio to rise sharply over the eleven-year period under examination. The rise in relative housing prices plays an important part in widening the distribution of wealth. The capital gain derived from the relative housing price inflation accrues disproportionately to households in the upper income deciles and the upper wealth deciles. The tendency for the savings rate to rise with income as well as with wealth provides another mechanism for the growth of wealth inequality. Households having more income and more wealth save more proportionately and thus they accumulate wealth more rapidly. Although from the CHIP 2007 and 2013 surveys China's inequality of income appears now to be on the decline, the preceding results provide reasons to expect that the inequality of wealth will continue to rise. This is a phenomenon of growing socioeconomic importance, and it deserves more extensive study in the future.

Possible policy implications also deserve attention. These might include reform of the banking and financial system: such reform can have the effect of reducing inequality in opportunities to secure access to funds, thus reducing unfair wealth inequality. It is worth exploring the feasibility of introducing serious wealth, property, or inheritance taxes. Furthermore, corruption among the powerful is likely to have increased wealth inequality. The current anticorruption campaign (described by Manion [2016]) that was introduced in 2013 is likely to temper the rise in wealth inequality that would otherwise stem from this source.

Notes

Note: We are grateful to the editors and referees for helpful comments on this chapter.
1. The Gini of 0.62 in 2013 contrasts with the Gini of 0.76 in 2010 obtained by Li and Wan (2015) by using the CFPS survey 2010. Their high figure is sensitive to the inclusion of some 300 implausibly or suspiciously large housing values. If they are excluded, the Gini falls by some 10 percentage points.
2. See Chapters 1 and 2 for a description of the CHIP 2013 survey data and Gustafsson, Li, and Sicular (2008) for a description of the CHIP 2002 survey data.
3. The CHIP samples were stratified by two criteria: urban/rural and East/Central/West. A set of sampling weights was created on the basis of population numbers in each stratum in 2002 and in 2013. Our samples are representative of urban and rural areas and of provinces, and they are representative within each province.
4. Chapter 2 explains this decomposition methodology.
5. The curious fall in the ratio in the 2013 rural sample is likely to have an institutional explanation, e.g., the difficulty of owning more than one house in the village, or the difficulty of reporting a market-based rather than a cost-based value.

6. We exclude imputed rent because it dominates the series, especially in the lower-income deciles, and imputed wealth income is unlikely to affect savings to the same extent as wealth income actually received.

References

Atkinson, A., T. Piketty, and E. Saez (2011). "Top Incomes in the Long Run of History." *Journal of Economic Literature*, 49(1), 3–71.

Brandt, L. and C. Holz (2006). "Spatial Price Differences in China: Estimates and Implications." *Economic Development and Cultural Change*, 55(1), 43–86.

Brenner, M. (2001). "Re-examining the Distribution of Wealth in Rural China," in C. Riskin, R. Zhao, and S. Li, eds., *China's Retreat from Equality*, 245–275. New York: M. E. Sharpe.

Davies, J. B., S. Sandstrom, A. F. Shorrocks, and E. N. Wolff (2008). "The World Distribution of Household Wealth." UNU–WIDER Working Paper 3/2008, February.

Gustafsson, B., S. Li, and T. Sicular, eds. (2008). *Inequality and Public Policy in China.* Cambridge and New York: Cambridge University Press.

Gustafsson, B., S. Li, and Z. Wei (2006). "The Distribution of Wealth in Urban China and in China as a Whole." *Review of Income and Wealth*, 52(2), 173–188.

Knight, J. (2017). "China's Evolving Inequality." *Journal of Chinese Economic and Business Studies*, 15(4), 307–322.

Knight, J. and S. Ding (2012). *China's Remarkable Economic Growth.* Oxford: Oxford University Press.

Li, S. and H. Wan (2015). "Evolution of Wealth Inequality in China." *China Economic Journal*, 8(3), 264–287.

Li, S. and R. Zhao (2007). "Changes in the Distribution of Wealth in China, 1995–2002." UNU–WIDER Research Paper No. 2007/03, January.

Manion, M. (2016). "Taking China's Anticorruption Campaign Seriously." *Economic and Political Studies*, 4(1), 3–18.

McKinley, T. (1993). "The Distribution of Wealth in Rural China," in K. Griffin and R. Zhao, eds., *The Distribution of Income in China*, 116–134. London: Macmillan.

Piketty, T. (2014). *Capital in the Twenty-First Century.* Cambridge, MA: Harvard University Press.

Sato, H., T. Sicular, and X. Yue (2013). "Housing Ownership, Incomes, and Inequality in China, 2002–2007," in S. Li, H. Sato, and T. Sicular, eds., *Rising Inequality in China: Challenges to a Harmonious Society*, 85–141. Cambridge and New York: Cambridge University Press.

Xie, Y. and Y. Jin (2015). "Household Wealth in China." *Chinese Sociological Review*, 47(3), 203–329.

Zhao, R. and S. Ding (2008). "The Distribution of Wealth in China," in B. Gustafsson, S. Li, and T. Sicular, eds., *Inequality and Public Policy in China*, 118–144. Cambridge and New York: Cambridge University Press.

A4 Appendix

Measurement of Wealth per Capita in CHIP 2002 and CHIP 2013

In all cases we divide each component of wealth by the number of household members to obtain household wealth per capita. For 2002 we follow very closely the definitions set out in the data appendix to Zhao and Ding (2008, pp. 140–144). The definitions used in 2013 are set out as follows.

A4.1 Net Housing Value

Net housing value is calculated as housing value minus housing loans. As a few households (3.5 percent of all households) have more than one house, we sum the net value for each household—the reported market value of both owner-occupied and any other owned housing. For those who report housing area but not housing value, we multiply by the average value per square meter in the county. Those who have no ownership rights but report housing area are recorded as having a housing value of zero.

A4.2 Net Financial Assets

The questionnaire asks separately for the total value of financial assets and for the separate components. Where the sum of the components is not equal to the reported total value, we use the sum of the components. Financial assets include spot cash, demand deposits, time deposits, endowment insurance, government bonds, other bonds, stocks, funds, futures, money lent (not including business loans), and other financial assets.

A4.3 Non-Housing Debt

Comparing reported gross non-housing debt with the sum value of its components, we use the value of the debt components when the two are not equal. Missing values are treated as zero.

A4.4 Fixed Productive Assets

We take the estimated net present value of agricultural and non-agricultural fixed productive assets as reported on the questionnaire to record the fixed productive assets.

A4.5 Consumer Durables

We take the estimated market value of household "movable properties" from the questionnaire as the value of consumer durables, which comprises private (non-business) automobiles and various other consumer durables.

A4.6 Rural Land Value

The variable household net agricultural income, recorded in the NBS survey, is used to calculate rural land value in 2013. However, because we lack direct information on net household agricultural income in 2002, we follow Zhao and Ding (2008) in assuming that one acre of irrigated land equals two acres of dry land and calculating net household agricultural income as gross agricultural income minus production costs. Furthermore, following earlier research we assume that 25 percent of net agricultural income comes from land and the return rate of land is 8 percent (McKinley 1993; Zhao and Ding 2008). Therefore, we get land value from net household agricultural income times 25/8.

A4.7 Other Assets

The questionnaire items "other precious metals and jewelry (including gold ornaments)," and "other assets" are not included in either financial assets or fixed productive assets or consumer durables. Accordingly, we define these items as our variable "other assets."

A4.8 Total Net Wealth

The total value of net wealth is the sum of the wealth components listed and defined previously: net housing wealth, net financial assets, non-housing debt, fixed productive assets, consumer durables, rural land value, and other assets.

5

Social Policy Reforms and Economic Distances in China

Qin Gao, Sui Yang, Fuhua Zhai, and Yake Wang

5.1 Introduction

Between 2002 and 2013, the Chinese government launched a series of social policy reforms that aimed to provide basic social protection to its citizens and to unify the long-segregated social benefit systems across the urban/rural divide. Part of the reason for the expansion of the social policies was China's rapidly rising income inequality that had surpassed conventional alarm levels and was thought to threaten political stability and social harmony, both of which are high on the agenda of the ruling Chinese Communist Party. China's national Gini coefficient rose from 0.44 in 2000 to 0.49 in 2007, and then declined somewhat to 0.43 in 2013, but China remained among the most unequal third of all countries (Chapter 2; Li and Sicular 2014). The fast-growing number of Internet and social media users during this period helped expose the widening income gaps and the imbalances in social benefits enjoyed by various groups, promoting awareness and demand for greater social protection among Chinese citizens.

To address these challenges and shift away from focusing solely on economic growth, the government launched significant social policy reforms that expanded social insurance and social assistance programs to extend coverage from urban employees to urban non-employees, rural residents, and, to some extent, rural-to-urban migrants. In 2006, on the basis of a series of initiatives to improve the livelihood of rural residents, the government implemented an extensive campaign to "Build a New Socialist Countryside." Additionally, enactment of the 2008 Labor Contract Law required that all employers sign labor contracts with employees and provide social insurance coverage for employees, including migrant workers.

Qin Gao, Sui Yang, Fuhua Zhai, and Yake Wang, *Social Policy Reforms and Economic Distances in China* In: *Changing Trends in China's Inequality*. Edited by: Terry Sicular, Shi Li, Ximing Yue, and Hiroshi Sato, Oxford University Press (2020).
© Oxford University Press.
DOI: 10.1093/oso/9780190077938.003.0005

How successful was this series of social policy reforms in redistributing resources and narrowing the economic distance between the rich and poor? Existing studies have examined the redistributive effects of selected social benefits but have not examined the set of social benefits in its entirety. In addition, most existing studies rely on the widely used Gini coefficient to capture the redistributive effects of the social benefits on overall income distribution. However, none of the studies have focused specifically on the economic distance between the rich and the poor, the two ends of the income distribution.

In this chapter, we use data from the China Household Income Project (CHIP) surveys in 2002, 2007, and 2013 to investigate how the social policy reforms affected the economic distance between the rich and poor from 2002 to 2013, a period that witnessed a significant expansion of social policies under the leadership of President Hu Jintao and Premier Wen Jiabao (Gao, Yang, and Zhai 2019). Instead of focusing on the national sample, we examine the respective urban, rural, and migrant samples to better understand the different effects of these social policy changes on the various populations. We use an innovative and revealing method to examine the economic distance between low- and high-income households within the urban, rural, and migrant populations to shed light on aspects of the income distribution that are beyond the overall level of inequality as captured by the Gini coefficient.

5.2 Social Policy Reforms and Their Redistributive Effects: 2002–2013

Scholars largely agree that the social policy reforms during the 2002–2013 period represent a significant expansion and shift in the policy direction from focusing on economic growth to focusing on social development (Besharov and Baehler 2013; Carrillo and Duckett 2011; Leung and Xu 2015; Liu and Sun 2015; Ngok and Chan 2015; Saich 2008, 2015; Shue and Wong 2007). Duckett (2012) characterizes these reforms as a compromise between the social and economic agendas, whereas Frazier (2014) emphasizes the role of urbanization in driving the unification of the urban/rural social benefit systems. This literature, however, also points out the persistent urban/rural/migrant disparities in terms of social provisions and benefit levels and the gaps across employees and non-employees in the urban areas. Empirical evidence based on the CHIP 2002–2007 data suggests that social policy reforms during this period moved in the direction of progressivity, but the urban/ rural gaps remained substantial and migrants continued to be left behind in terms of social protection (Gao, Yang, and Li 2013).

First, during this period a comprehensive social insurance system began to take shape, with significant expansions of pensions and health insurance to urban non-employees, rural residents, and migrants. Specifically, the urban pension system gradually moved from covering only civil servants and employees of public institutions and state-owned enterprises (SOEs) to a dual system of social pooling (i.e., earnings-based and pay-as-you-go) and individual accounts (with mandatory individual contributions). In 2012, a nationwide urban resident pension system, funded by both government subsidies and individual contributions, was established for urban non-employees. The New Rural Social Pension System (NRSPS) was launched in 2009 to provide pension coverage for rural residents. It also offered a national framework to allow participation by migrant workers. This system was fully funded (in the Central and West regions) or half-funded (in the East region) by the central government and a highly subsidized personal savings account. In 2014, the rural and urban pension systems were unified to allow equal access and equal quality of pension systems for urban and rural residents and to facilitate rural/urban mobility. Nevertheless, average benefit levels for urban non-employees and rural residents remained very low and varied substantially across localities, whereas urban employees received pension benefits in accordance with their job positions and ranks (Dorfman, Holtzmann, and O'Keefe 2012; Leung and Xu 2015; Liu and Sun 2016).

Another major development in the social insurance system was the expansion of health insurance. In particular, the Urban Employee Basic Medical Insurance (UEBMI) was expanded from covering only employees and retirees with urban *hukou* to covering migrant workers (Hu and Ljungwall 2013). The Urban Resident Basic Medical Insurance (URBMI), with significantly lower premiums and benefits than those of the UEBMI (Fang 2014; Ministry of Health 2010) was implemented nationwide in 2010 to provide health coverage for urban non-employees, including children, older adults who were ineligible for the UEBMI, and the poor and disabled. The New Rural Cooperative Medical System (NRCMS) was introduced in 2002 and implemented nationwide in 2008. Heavily subsidized by the central and local governments, it is a voluntary health insurance program for rural residents, with low premiums and benefits (Barber and Yao 2010; Fang 2014). By 2013, the coverage rate of the NRCMS reached 98.7 percent of the country and covered 802 million participants (National Bureau of Statistics of China 2014).

Wang and his colleagues (Wang 2013; Wang et al. 2016), using survey data from 2012, have examined the redistributive effects of social insurance programs. They found that social insurance income lowered the Gini coefficient by 6.4 percent. This social insurance income included pensions, health, maternity, work injury, and unemployment insurance. However, the redistributive effects differed greatly for the urban/rural/migrant populations: social insurance helped reduce the urban Gini coefficient by 12 percent, the rural Gini coefficient by 3 percent, and the migrant Gini coefficient by only 0.1 percent. Pensions contributed the most to income redistribution, lowering the Gini coefficient by 5.88 percent. Much of this reduction (5.30 percent) was due to the pensions for urban employees and retirees, whereas the pensions for urban non-employees and rural residents had minimal effects (reductions in the Gini coefficient by 0.24 percent and 0.32 percent, respectively). It is important to note that this equalizing effect of pensions was concentrated on the urban employees and retirees, but it was disequalizing across groups of urban employees/retirees, urban non-employees, and rural residents, as the latter groups had no or a minimal level of pensions. This finding is echoed by findings in Chapter 2 in this volume (see Table 2.4), as pensions disproportionately go to the richer urban population. The studies by Wang and his colleagues—as well as the present study—find pensions to be equalizing because, other than pensions, pensioner households have little or no pre-transfer income.

Wang and his colleagues (Wang 2013; Wang et al. 2016) also found that health insurance lowered the Gini coefficient by 0.49 percent, with 0.27 percent, 0.20 percent, and 0.02 percent, respectively, due to the NRCMS, UEBMI, and URBMI. Maternity, work injuries, and unemployment insurance together helped reduce the overall Gini coefficient by only 0.04 percent. It is also important to note that these social insurance programs are closely tied to employment status and rank and they disproportionately benefit the richer, urban citizens.

Second, this period also saw the establishment and expansion of a comprehensive social assistance system. The centerpiece of this system, the minimum livelihood guarantee, or *dibao*, was initially established in cities in 1999 but was expanded significantly in 2001–2002. It was further expanded to the rural areas in 2007. Meanwhile, the government also launched a series of supplementary social assistance programs to offer extra support to families in need and to integrate the traditional "three withouts" (*sanwu*, i.e., those without an income, without a working ability, or without a legal guardian in the urban areas) and the "five guarantees" (*wubao*, i.e., guarantees to provide food, clothing, shelter, medical care, and burial services for rural residents who have no working ability or income source) into this system. These include medical, education, and housing assistance as well as temporary assistance to provide subsidies and service referrals for individuals and families facing urgent or extreme difficulties (Gao 2017; Liu 2010).

Using data from the CHIP 2007 survey, Li and Yang (2009) found that the urban *dibao* had a very small impact on reducing income inequality, lowering the overall Gini coefficient by only 0.46 percent and the ratio between the average income of the highest and lowest income deciles by only 3.19 percent. A growing number of recent studies on the rural *dibao* focus on its targeting performance and its antipoverty effectiveness (Golan, Sicular, and Umapathi 2017; Han and Gao 2019; Han, Gao, and Xu 2016; Han and Xu 2013, 2014; Liu and Xu 2016), but none of these studies examine its impact on income inequality. Given the small size of the *dibao* benefits, it is reasonable to speculate a similar small impact on inequality in the case of the urban *dibao*.

Using data from the 2009 China Health and Nutrition Survey, Lu and her colleagues (Lu et al. 2013) investigated how pensions and social assistance affect income inequality. They found that pensions substantially helped lower the Gini coefficient (by 0.0595), whereas social assistance, including the *dibao* and disability subsidies, lowered the Gini coefficient by only 0.0046. However, pensions were distributed regressively, helping to raise the ratio of those in the top-quintile income to those in the bottom-quintile income from 15.99 to 17.60. Social assistance also helped reduce this ratio from 15.99 to 14.80. In addition, the authors, in an examination of in-kind subsidies that were mostly employment-based (e.g., assistance for food, gas, coal, electricity, and child care), found that in-kind subsidies played a small but positive role in reducing overall income inequality and in narrowing the top-bottom income gap.

Third, in addition to expanding social insurance and social assistance, the government launched a major campaign to Build a New Socialist Countryside through a series of initiatives to narrow the urban/rural gap and to improve the livelihood of rural residents. These initiatives included the abolition of agricultural taxes, the elimination of tuition and fees for rural compulsory education, increased investments for rural infrastructure, and the provision of direct subsidies to support the production and welfare of farmers (Fock and Wong 2008; Frazier 2014; Lardy 2012; Lin and Wong

2012; Wallace 2014; World Bank 2007). On the basis of an analysis of all five waves of the CHIP data, Chapter 6 in this volume by Hoken and Sato finds substantial improvements in the redistributive and poverty impacts of public transfers in the rural areas, signifying a historic reversal in the long-term urban-biased public policy in contemporary China.

Two other studies have examined the redistributive effects of specific components of these policies in rural China. Lin and Wong (2012) focus on direct subsidies to farmers, which include subsidies for farmland production, social welfare, and public services (e.g., pensions, health, education, and *dibao*) and subsidies for living conditions. Using administrative data from 2003 to 2009 published by the various Chinese commissions and ministries as well as in the *China Statistical Yearbooks*, they found that over time these subsidies played an increasingly large role in narrowing the urban/rural income gap. However, their analysis of a 2005 Ministry of Agriculture survey dataset reveals these subsidies to have a strikingly regressive effect, with higher-income households, households with a party member, and households in richer regions reaping greater benefits from these subsidies.

Using the CHIP 2002 and 2007 data, Li and Sicular (2014) focus on the redistributive effects of the abolition of agricultural taxes. They find the average tax rate paid by rural households decreased from 2.8 percent in 2002 to 0.3 percent in 2007, suggesting that the abolition of agricultural taxes and fees had positive distributional effects. They also find that this policy change was particularly beneficial to low-income groups, with the average tax rate for those in the lowest income decile decreasing from 6.2 percent in 2002 to 0.3 percent in 2007, whereas the average tax rate for those in the highest-income decile declined from 1.5 percent to 0.4 percent during the same period. However, they found this policy to have virtually no effect on overall income inequality in the rural areas.

Fourth, the government also made efforts to improve labor conditions for migrant workers. The 2008 Labor Contract Law requires that employers sign labor contracts with employees and provide them with social insurance. Migrant workers, who previously had been largely ineligible for such protection, benefited the most from these stipulations because both their labor conditions and their subjective well-being improved (Cheng, Smyth, and Guo 2015; Gallagher et al. 2015; Gao, Yang, and Li 2012, 2017; Li and Freeman 2015). Luo and Sicular (2013) use the CHIP 2002 and 2007 data to find that income from migrant employment contributed to robust economic growth in rural households and helped to reduce income inequality and to narrow the urban/rural income gap. Because of this law, migrant workers are more likely to sign labor contracts, receive higher wages, and enroll in pension, health, work injury, and unemployment insurance.

In summary, existing evidence shows that social insurance—especially pensions—played a dominant role in reducing income inequality during this period, whereas social assistance had a negligible effect in narrowing inequality gaps. Both the campaign to Build a New Socialist Countryside and the efforts to support migrants helped improve the living conditions of rural residents and migrants and to reduce income inequality. Building on this body of literature, in this chapter we use the CHIP 2002, 2007, and 2013 data to offer new evidence on the effects of these social policy reforms on the economic distance between the rich and the poor among the urban, rural, and migrant populations during the 2002–2013 period. We hypothesize that social insurance, particularly pensions, played the most prominent role in narrowing the economic distance between the rich and poor, whereas social assistance played only a minimal role. We also hypothesize that the economic distance between the rural and migrant samples were reduced due to the social policy reforms that aimed to increase living standards, especially among the most vulnerable population groups.

5.3 Data and Methods

5.3.1 CHIP Data

This study uses the three recent waves of the CHIP data, which collected information regarding family income, consumption, and demographics for 2002, 2007, and 2013 (see Chapters 1 and 2 and also Gustafsson, Li, and Sicular [2008] and Li, Sato, and Sicular [2013] for a detailed description and discussion of the CHIP data for these years). Because CHIP 2002 and 2007 intentionally sampled migrants, they contained relatively large samples for migrant households (2000 and 5000 respectively). In the unified CHIP 2013 national sample, rural residents constituted the rural sample, urban residents with an urban *hukou* constituted the urban sample, and urban residents with a rural *hukou* constituted the migrant sample. Because migrants were not intentionally sampled, their sample size was quite small (957 households). The analyses in this chapter are based on the separate, mutually exclusive urban, rural, and migrant samples. We use data from all provinces contained

Table 5.1 Sample sizes of the China Household Income
Project (CHIP) survey, by year

	2002	2007	2013
Urban			
Households	6835	10,235	6,762
Individuals	20,632	30,340	20,414
Provinces	12	16	15
Rural			
Households	9,200	13,000	10,456
Individuals	37,928	51,847	39,869
Provinces	21	16	15
Migrants			
Households	2000	5000	957
Individuals	5318	8404	2609
Provinces	12	9	15

Notes: The sample sizes reported are total sample sizes, which are used in
our analyses. As CHIP income data are collected by using a diary method,
any nonresponses to income questions are assumed to represent receiving
zero income in that category.

in the respective waves and apply sampling weights so that the results are nationally representative for each of the urban/rural/migrant subgroups. Table
5.1 presents the CHIP sample sizes for the three years that are examined in
this study.

5.4 Measuring Social Benefits and Their Effects
on Economic Distance

Taking advantage of the detailed income measures available in the CHIP
data, we define household final income as the sum of market income, social
benefit income, and private transfers, minus taxes, fees, and payments for
social insurance contributions.[1] Market income includes wage income, net
business income, property income, and the rental value of owner-occupied
housing. Social benefits include pensions, health insurance, unemployment
insurance, supplementary income, social assistance, in-kind housing and

food benefits, and other in-kind benefits.[2] The inclusion of these various cash and in-kind benefits enables us to provide a comprehensive examination of the recent social policy changes as reflected at the household level. In addition, private transfers include remittance income sent back by household members working away from home, elderly support, alimony, and other gifts from family and friends. All incomes are calculated at the per capita household level and are adjusted by the provincial price deflators compiled by Brandt and Holz (2006), which we updated to 2013.[3]

We measure the size of the total social benefits by the percentage of social benefit income in the household final income. This measure has the advantage of taking into consideration changes in the overall income level over time and gauging the relative contribution of the social benefit income. The structure of social benefits is measured by the percentages of specific social benefits in the household final income.

Following recent studies that use the same method (Gao 2010; Gao, Yang, and Li 2013; Garfinkel, Rainwater, and Smeeding 2010), we calculate the economic distances at the bottom (i.e., the 10th percentile) and at the top (i.e., the 90th percentile) of the income distribution based on pre- and post-transfer incomes, respectively. Because the calculations are based on different income distributions, the relative positions (or percentile ranks) of the households may change from the pre- to post-transfer income, reflecting the dynamic and relative nature of income inequality. We then compare the economic distances calculated by using the pre- and post-transfer incomes to understand the redistributive nature of the social benefits and to detect whether the 2002–2013 social policy reforms were progressive (i.e., supporting the poor) or regressive (i.e., favoring the rich). Because the economic distances are calculated on the basis of the respective pre- and post-transfer incomes, the results show that some major social benefit transfers, such as pensions, are equalizing because the pre-transfer income for many urban pensioners are low, but their substantial pension transfers can move them into relatively high post-transfer income brackets.

We use eight income definitions to examine how the cumulative inclusion of each additional income component changed the economic distance between the rich and the poor within the respective urban, rural, and migrant populations. These income definitions are 1.) market income (i.e., pre-transfer, pre-tax income); 2.) plus pensions; 3.) plus health insurance; 4.) plus social assistance; 5.) plus supplementary income and in-kind benefits; 6.) plus private transfers; 7.) plus other transfers; and 8.) minus taxes and fees (i.e., post-transfer, post-tax income). Because these benefits and transfers are added cumulatively, it is important to note that the order in which they are added will affect the results. A comparison between the results that are based on the first definition (i.e., market income, or pre-transfer, pre-tax income) and the last definition (i.e., final income, or post-transfer, post-tax income) reveals the redistributive effects of the entire set of social benefits and transfers.

On the basis of each income definition, we identity the 10th, 50th (i.e., median), and 90th percentile incomes and use bar charts to capture the economic distance between rich and poor households within the urban, rural, and migrant populations, respectively. The bottom end of the bar has the ratio of the income of the households in the 10th percentile relative to the median multiplied by 100 (i.e., p10/p50*100). The top end of the bar has the ratio of the income of the households in the 90th percentile relative to the median multiplied by 100 (i.e., p90/p50*100). The length of the bar, reflecting the economic distance between these two ends, is calculated as the difference between the two (i.e., p90/p50*100–p10/p50*100). An increase at the lower end of the bar and a reduction at the higher end of the bar due to social benefits and transfers indicate progressivity, whereas the opposite case reflects regressivity (Gao 2010; Gao, Yang, and Li 2013; Garfinkel, Rainwater, and Smeeding 2010). By comparing the length of the pre- and post-transfers bars and understanding whether the shift occurred at the lower or higher end of the bars, we can understand the extent to which the social benefits helped reduce the economic distance between the rich and poor and whether the social benefits were progressive or regressive.

5.5 The Size and Structure of the Social Benefits

Before delving into an analysis of the effects of the social benefits on the economic distance, we first present the results regarding the changes in the size and structure of the social benefits during the 2002–2013 period. As measured by the percentage of social benefit income in the household final income, the size of urban social benefits decreased from 2002 to 2013, whereas social benefits for rural and migrant families increased, a reflection of the social policy reforms that aimed to broaden social protection for these groups. However, the urban/rural/migrant gaps persisted, with the size of the urban social benefits still substantially larger than the rural and migrant social benefits. Across the three groups, pensions dominated the social benefit package, with noticeable gains by rural and migrant families in 2013. Rural families also gained transfer income through the Building a New Socialist Countryside initiative.

Table 5.2 presents the changes in the size and structure of social benefits for the urban, rural, and migrant samples from 2002 to 2013, respectively. For urban families, the share of social benefits in household final income decreased on average from 26.92 percent in 2002 to 20.05 percent in 2007 and then to 17.46 percent in 2013. In all three years, pensions were the dominant social benefit for urban families, constituting 14.80 percent of urban household final income in 2002 and increasing to 16.97 percent in 2007. But in 2013 pensions declined to 15.61 percent of urban household final income. This fluctuation reflects the requirement that urban employees had to shoulder more pension contributions through the urban employee pension system, which included both social pooling and individual accounts. Health benefits, however, declined sharply for urban families, from 7.29 percent of household final income in 2002 to 1.60 percent in 2007 and 0.45 percent in 2013. This decline is partly because our measure of health benefits

Table 5.2. Size and structure of social benefits measured as a percentage of household final income (%)

	Urban			Rural			Migrants		
	2002	2007	2013	2002	2007	2013	2002	2007	2013
Pensions	14.80	16.97	15.61	0.58	—	3.59	—	0.02	1.44
Health	7.29	1.60	0.45	0.02	—	0.73	—	0.11	0.07
Unemployment insurance	0.27	0.15	—	—	—	—	—	—	—
Social assistance	0.53	0.16	0.18	0.06	—	0.51	—	0.01	0.02
Supplementary income	0.69	—	0.12	—	—	1.30	—	—	0.08
Housing	2.68	0.77	0.79	—	—	0.01	—	—	0.05
Food	0.54	0.32	—	—	—	—	—	—	—
Other in-kind	0.13	0.07	0.31	0.05	—	0.28	—	0.42	0.72
Total Social Benefits	**26.92**	**20.05**	**17.46**	**0.71**	**2.13**	**6.42**	**2.96**	**0.57**	**2.39**

Notes: Household final income refers to post-transfer, post-tax income, calculated as the sum of market income, social benefit income, and private transfers, minus taxes, fees, and payments for social insurance contributions. All income and social benefits are calculated at the per capita household level and are adjusted by the provincial price deflators compiled by Brandt and Holz (2006), which we updated to 2013. Some categories of social benefits were not reported in the selected waves and samples of the data and thus their cells remain empty in the table. The total social benefits are the sums of the respective columns.

captures only the self-estimated cash value of medical care expenses covered by employers or the government and does not reflect the value of health insurance coverage that was available but not utilized or claimed. Therefore, our estimate of health benefits is an underestimate, especially for urban residents, who on average had access to much broader coverage than their rural and migrant counterparts. Housing benefits also declined sharply from 2.68 percent in 2002 to about 0.78 percent in the later years, mainly because of the privatization of housing that was launched in the 1990s and was completed shortly after 2002. Other social benefits—including social assistance—remained a small proportion of household final income in urban China despite the policy expansions during this period.

Unlike the trends for urban residents, however, rural and migrant families both gained significantly from social benefits during this period, especially from 2007 to 2013, as indicated by Table 5.2. In 2002 social benefits accounted for only 0.71 percent of rural families' final income, but this figure rose to 2.13 percent in 2007. By 2013 social benefits constituted 6.42 percent of rural families' final income, a significant increase from the earlier years, because of the expansion of social insurance and social assistance as well as the Building a New Socialist Countryside initiative. Specifically, pensions increased from 0.58 percent of rural household final income in 2002 to 3.59 percent in 2013, a sixfold jump during the eleven-year period. Health benefits also increased substantially, from 0.02 percent in 2002 to 0.73 percent in 2013, because of implementation of the NRCMS. Social assistance rose from 0.06 percent in 2002 to 0.51 percent in 2013, also a significant increase, mainly due to the implementation and expansion of the rural *dibao* since 2007. In 2013, supplementary income in the form of agricultural and livelihood subsidies, an income item that was nonexistent in previous years, constituted 1.30 percent of rural households' final income.[4]

For the migrants, social benefits constituted 2.96 percent of household final income in 2002.[5] However, most of these benefits were employer-provided food and housing, which in effect were wages paid in-kind. The same items were included in the wage income for 2007 and 2013. Social benefits for migrants increased significantly, from 0.57 percent in 2007 to 2.39 percent in 2013. The biggest boost came from pension income, which increased from 0.02 percent in 2007 to 1.44 percent in 2013. Other in-kind benefits increased from 0.42 percent in 2007 to 0.72 percent in 2013.

Despite the significant gains in social benefits for rural residents and migrants during this period, especially from 2007 to 2013, they still lagged considerably behind the gains of their urban peers. In 2013 an average of 17.46 percent of urban families' household final income came from social benefits, but for rural families it was only 6.42 percent and for migrant families it was a mere 2.39 percent. It is important to note that not only did rural households receive social benefits that constituted a much smaller share of their final income than that of their urban peers but also their final household income was much lower. Indeed, across the three years, after adjusting for consumer price differences the final household income of rural families on average remained less than one-half that of urban families. A much smaller share in the amount of final household income meant that the value of rural social benefits, as opposed to the value of urban social benefits, was also much smaller. The persistent urban/rural/migrant gap in social benefits indicates the continuing challenges to achieving a truly unified and balanced social welfare system in China.

5.6 The Effects of Social Benefits on Economic Distance

We now turn to the effects of social benefits on reducing the economic distance between rich and poor families in the urban, rural, and migrant samples, respectively. Figure 5.1 presents the results for urban China. Overall, we find that market forces played a dominant role in widening the economic distance between the urban rich and poor during the 2002–2013 period, suppressing the redistributive effects of the social benefit package as a whole. Among the social benefits, pensions consistently helped narrow the economic distance over the years, whereas other social benefits—including health insurance, social assistance, supplementary income, and in-kind benefits—had little or no redistributive impact despite the recent social policy expansions in these areas.

First and foremost, both the pre- and post-transfer economic distance between the urban rich and poor continued to increase from 2002 to 2013. This gap was clearly driven by market forces. The pre-transfer economic distance, as measured by the length of the bar, increased from 186 in 2002 to 199 in 2007 and 216 in 2013, a 16 percent increase during the eleven-year period. The social benefit transfers helped narrow the economic distance somewhat, but the post-transfer economic distance continued to rise over time, from 151 in 2002 to 159 in 2007 and 179 in 2013, a 19 percent increase during this

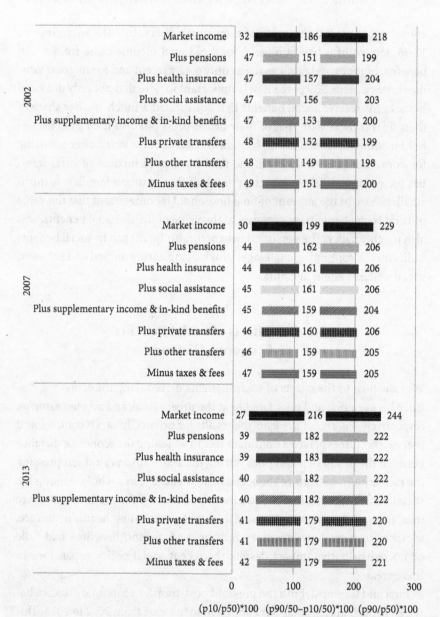

Fig. 5.1 Impact of social benefits on the economic distance between low- and high-income households in urban China

Notes: For each income definition, the bottom end of the bar gives the ratio of the household income in the 10th percentile relative to the median multiplied by 100 (i.e., p10/p50*100). The top end of the bar gives the ratio of the household income in the 90th percentile relative to the median multiplied by 100 (i.e., p90/p50*100). The length of the bar reflects the economic distance between these two ends and is calculated as the difference between the two (i.e., p90/p50*100–p10/p50*100). The percentiles and medians change on the basis of the respective income definitions.

period. These trends suggest that the disequalizing force of the market dominated the equalizing role of the social benefits during the 2002–2013 period in urban China, producing a much more unequal society as measured by the economic distance between the rich and poor.

Second, throughout the period pensions functioned as the primary equalizing social benefit that consistently narrowed the economic distance between the rich and poor in urban China. In 2002 pensions reduced the economic distance by 35 (from 186 to 151), as measured by the length of the bar. That reduction increased to 37 in 2007 (from 199 to 162) but the increase was slightly less in 2013 at 34 (from 216 to 182). However, the redistributive effects of pensions still trumped that of any other social benefits or transfers across all three years. It is important to note that this equalizing effect of pensions is because pre-transfer income is based only on market income. In reality, urban pensions favored those who had better and more stable jobs.

Third, all the other social benefits and transfers—including health insurance, social assistance (mainly *dibao*), supplementary income and in-kind benefits, private transfers, and other transfers that cannot be designated as public or private as well as taxes and fees paid—had little impact on the economic distance between the rich and poor across all three years, suggesting that the social policy reforms and expansions during the 2002–2013 period in these areas were ineffective in terms of income redistribution. Specifically, in 2002 health insurance helped lift the relative positions of the rich (from 199 to 204), mainly because health insurance was closely tied to employment status and position and those with better jobs tended to have better health coverage. By 2007 and 2013, health insurance had a minor impact on economic distance. In 2002, supplementary income and in-kind benefits helped narrow the economic distance somewhat, mainly because the in-kind benefits tended to go to the less advantaged, but their redistributive role diminished to become almost nonexistent by 2013. None of the other benefits or transfers played a noticeable role in changing the economic distance between the rich and poor in urban China during the period of this study.

Figure 5.2 presents the results of the effects of social benefits on the economic distance between rich and poor families in the rural areas. Rural social benefits were regressive in 2002 but they became slightly progressive in 2007 and substantially progressive in 2013. In 2002, social benefits—mainly pensions—helped increase the p10/p50 ratio from 43 to 44, thus slightly lifting the relative position of low-income households, but they also raised the relative position of high-income households, increasing the p90/p50

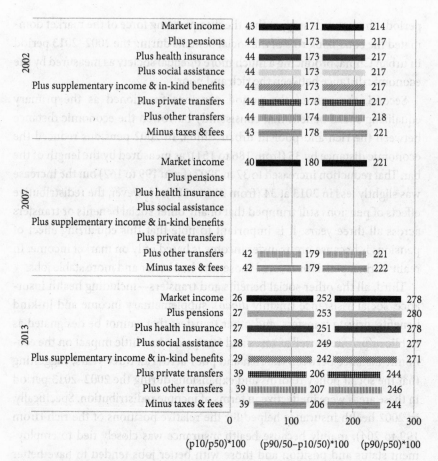

Fig. 5.2 Impact of social benefits on the economic distance between low- and high-income households in rural China

Notes: For each income definition, the bottom end of the bar gives the ratio of the household income in the 10th percentile relative to the median multiplied by 100 (i.e., p10/p50*100). The top end of the bar gives the ratio of the household income in the 90th percentile relative to the median multiplied by 100 (i.e., p90/p50*100). The length of the bar reflects the economic distance between these two ends and is calculated as the difference between the two (i.e., p90/p50*100–p10/p50*100). The percentiles and medians change on the basis of the respective income definitions. In the rural 2007 survey, separate information on the different types of social transfers is not reported. All social transfers are reported as a single, sum amount, which we refer to as "other transfers" in this figure.

ratio from 214 to 217. Taxes and fees were also regressive in 2002: they lowered the relative position of low-income families by 1 (from 44 to 43) and raised the relative position of high-income families by 3 (from 218 to 221). In 2007 rural social benefits became slightly progressive and shortened the economic distance bar by 1 (from 180 to 179).

The social policy reforms since 2007 changed the redistributive nature of rural social benefits to become substantially progressive by 2013. Overall, social benefits and transfers helped narrow the economic distance between rich and poor families from 252 to 206, a 46-point reduction, which was larger than the reduction due to social benefits in urban China in any of the three years under study.

Among the social benefits, supplementary income and in-kind benefits in the form of agricultural and livelihood subsidies played the most significant redistributive role, shortening the length of the bar by 7 points. Pensions remained regressive, benefiting the rich more than the poor and slightly increasing the economic distance. Health benefits and social assistance each helped narrow the economic distance by 2 points. Private transfers had the largest redistributive role, narrowing the economic distance by 36 points. Such transfers included remittance income sent back by household members working away from home, elderly support, alimony, and other gifts from family and friends. It is noteworthy that these private transfers played a dominant redistributive role in rural China in 2013, probably supplementing the still inadequate redistributive role of public transfers.

Despite the larger redistributive effects of both private and public transfers in 2013 in the rural areas, the post-transfer economic distance (206) was still substantially wider than that in earlier years (178 in 2002 and 179 in 2007), suggesting that market forces had become much more disequalizing by 2013, a trend that was similar to that in urban China. The pace of social policy expansions lagged behind the pace of market forces.

Figure 5.3 presents the results of the effects of social benefits on economic distances among migrants. Similar to the trends in the rural areas, migrant social benefits also changed from regressive in 2002 to progressive in 2013, although to a lesser extent as compared to the rural social benefits. In 2002 social benefits for migrants helped widen the economic distance between rich and poor families from 154 to 162, an 8-point increase. In 2007, social benefits played a minimal role in impacting the economic distance, whereas private transfers helped lift the relative position of rich families. In 2013 health insurance helped narrow the economic distance by 1 point (from 166 to 165), private transfers reduced the economic distance by 2 points, and taxes and fees further reduced the economic distance by 4 points. Social benefits still played a very limited redistributive role, but they did become progressive.

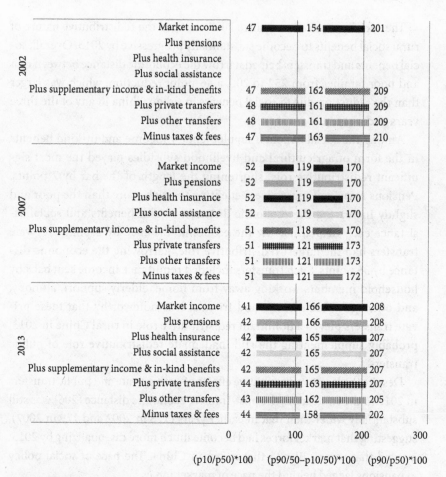

Fig. 5.3 Impact of social benefits on the economic distance between low- and high-income households among rural-to-urban migrants in China

Notes: For each income definition, the bottom end of the bar gives the ratio of the household income in the 10th percentile relative to the median multiplied by 100 (i.e., p10/p50*100). The top end of the bar gives the ratio of the household income in the 90th percentile relative to the median multiplied by 100 (i.e., p90/p50*100). The length of the bar reflects the economic distance between these two ends and is calculated as the difference between the two (i.e., p90/p50*100–p10/p50*100). The percentiles and medians change on the basis of the respective income definitions.

5.7 Conclusion and Discussion

Using data from the CHIP 2002, 2007, and 2013 surveys, this chapter examines the effects of a series of social policy reforms on the economic distance between the rich and poor among urban, rural, and migrant families during this period. These social policy reforms included expansion of social insurance and social assistance programs to extend coverage from urban employees to urban non-employees, rural residents, and migrants, provision of agricultural and livelihood subsidies to rural residents through the Building a New Socialist Countryside initiative, and enactment of the 2008 Labor Contract Law to offer greater social protection to migrant workers.

We find that pensions in urban areas consistently helped narrow the economic distance among urban households over the years, whereas other social benefits—including health insurance, social assistance, supplementary income, and in-kind benefits—had little or no redistributive impact. Both rural and migrant social benefits changed from regressive in 2002 to progressive in 2013. In the rural areas, supplementary income and in-kind benefits, in the form of agricultural and livelihood subsidies, played the most significant redistributive role among all social benefits in 2013, but private transfers helped narrow the economic distance substantially. For migrants, health benefits and taxes and fees helped narrow the economic distance in 2013, although to a lesser extent as compared to the rural social benefits.

Despite the series of social policy expansions during this period, in both urban and rural China market forces still played a dominant role in widening the economic distance between the rich and poor and trumped the redistributive effects of the social benefits. These results suggest that China's future social policy reforms will face continued challenges in terms of attempting to adjust the imbalances in the urban/rural/migrant systems and to keep pace with the disequalizing market forces. Urban social benefits are larger in size and more comprehensive in coverage, and they play a consistently larger redistributive role, as compared to the social benefits for rural residents and migrants. It will take strong political will and a serious fiscal commitment to address the disparities in social protection among the urban/rural/migrant populations and to respect their equal rights.

Meanwhile, it is alarming that the levels of the pre-transfer income inequality in both urban and rural areas continued to rise and that the expanding social benefits were unable to sufficiently curtail this trend. Despite a decline in national inequality from 2007 to 2013, an underlying factor behind which was the narrowing of the urban-rural gap, the rising income inequality within the respective urban and rural areas is of critical concern and may threaten social stability and harmony. Given China's unique blend of socialist rule and state capitalism, an elevated level of income inequality may have more direct and serious political and social consequences in China than it does in other countries. This possibility is partly why the government promoted the social policy reforms as part of an effort to provide a basic level of social protection and as an equalizer across the urban/rural boundaries and income groups. The balancing act between economic growth and social harmony remains a serious challenge for current and future administrations in China.

Notes

Note: We thank the research team of the China Household Income Project (CHIP)—in particular, Shi Li, Chuliang Luo, Terry Sicular, and Ximing Yue—for helping clarify income definitions and for sharing the imputed rental value of owned housing and weights. We also acknowledge Yalu Zhang for capable research assistance. We are grateful for the support from two National Social Science Fund of China Key Programs (Grant Numbers: 15AJY006 and 16AJY007). We thank the funders of the multiple waves of the CHIP surveys, which provided the data used in this study.

1. In some cases, the CHIP questionnaire did not specify whether transfer income was from public or private sources; these items are grouped as "other transfer income," as explained in the following section describing the results.
2. Some of these social benefits are measured differently across the various waves and across the urban, rural, and migrant samples. They are explained in the following section on results.
3. As these provincial price deflators are somewhat outdated, we attempted to use the official urban and rural CPIs to adjust the prices. The results are not reported here but are very consistent with our main results.
4. The CHIP 2007 rural survey did not ask about specific social benefits. Therefore, for 2007 we are able to estimate only the size and redistributive effects of total social benefits in the rural areas but not the effects of specific items.
5. Similarly, the CHIP 2002 migrant survey also did not ask about specific social benefits.

References

Barber, S. L. and L. Yao (2010). "Health Insurance Systems in China: A Briefing Note." Geneva: World Health Organization Background Paper, no. 37.

Besharov, D. J. and K. Baehler, eds. (2013). *Chinese Social Policy in a Time of Transition.* New York: Oxford University Press.

Brandt, L. and C. A. Holz (2006). "Spatial Price Differences in China: Estimates and Implications." *Economic Development and Cultural Change*, 55(1), 43–86.

Carrillo, B. and J. Duckett, eds. (2011). *China's Changing Welfare Mix: Local Perspectives.* London: Routledge.

Cheng, Z., R. Smyth, and F. Guo (2015). "The Impact of China's New Labour Contract Law on Socioeconomic Outcomes for Migrant and Urban Workers." *Human Relations*, 68(3), 329–352.

Dorfman, M. C., R. Holzmann, and P. O'Keefe (2012). "China's Pension System: A Vision." Washington DC: World Bank.

Duckett, J. (2012). "China's 21st-Century Welfare Reform." *Local Economy,* 27(5–6), 645–650.

Fang, H. (2014). "Insurance Markets in China," in S. Fan, R. Kanbur, S.-J. Wei, and X. Zhang, eds., *The Oxford Companion to the Economics of China,* 279–284. New York: Oxford University Press.

Fock, A. and C. Wong (2008). "Financing Rural Development for a Harmonious Society in China: Recent Reforms in Public Finance and Their Prospects." World Bank Policy Research Working Paper, no. 4693.

Frazier, M. W. (2014). "State Schemes or Safety Nets? China's Push for Universal Coverage." *Daedalus,* 143(2), 69–80.

Gallagher, M., J. Giles, A. Park, and M. Wang (2015). "China's 2008 Labor Contract Law: Implementation and Implications for China's Workers." *Human Relations,* 68(2), 197–235.

Gao, Q. (2010). "Redistributive Nature of the Chinese Social Benefit System: Progressive or Regressive?" *China Quarterly,* no. 201, 1–19.

Gao, Q. (2017). *Welfare, Work and Poverty: Social Assistance in China.* New York: Oxford University Press.

Gao, Q., S. Yang, and S. Li (2012). "Labor Contracts and Social Insurance Participation among Migrant Workers in China." *China Economic Review,* 23(4), 1195–1205.

Gao, Q., S. Yang, and S. Li (2013). "The Chinese Welfare State in Transition: 1988–2007." *Journal of Social Policy,* 42(4), 743–762.

Gao, Q., S. Yang, and S. Li (2017). "Social Insurance for Migrant Workers in China: Impact of the 2008 Labor Contract Law." *Economic and Political Studies,* 5 (3), 285–204.

Gao, Q., S. Yang, and F. Zhai, (2019). "Social Policy and Income Inequality during the Hu-Wen Era: A Progressive Legacy?" *China Quarterly,* no. 237, 82–107.

Garfinkel, I., L. Rainwater, and T. M. Smeeding (2010). *Wealth and Welfare States: Is America a Laggard or Leader?* New York: Oxford University Press.

Golan, J., T. Sicular, and N. Umapathi (2017). "Unconditional Cash Transfers in China: Who Benefits from the Rural Minimum Living Standard Guarantee (Dibao) Program?" *World Development,* 93 (May), 316–336.

Gustafsson, B., S. Li, and T. Sicular, eds. (2008). *Inequality and Public Policy in China.* Cambridge and New York: Cambridge University Press.

Han, H. and Q. Gao (2019). "Community-based Welfare Targeting and Political Elite Capture: Evidence from Rural China." *World Development,* 115 (March), 145–169.

Han, H., Q. Gao, and Y. Xu (2016). "Welfare Participation and Family Consumption Choices in Rural China." *Global Social Welfare,* 3(4), 223–241.

Han H. and Y. Xu (2013). "Nongcun zuidi shenghuo baozhang zhidu de miaozhun xiaoguo yanjiu: Laizi Henan, Shanxisheng de diaocha" (A study on the poverty targeting of the Minimum Living Standard Security Scheme [MLSS] in rural China: Evidence from Henan and Shanxi provinces). *Zhongguo renkou kexue,* no. 4, 117–125, 128.

Han, H. and Y. Xu (2014). "Zhongguo nongcun dibao zhidu de fanpinkun xiaoying yanjiu: Laizi zhongxi bu wu sheng de jingyan zhengju" (The anti-poverty effectiveness of the Minimum Living Standard Assistance Policy in rural China: Evidence from five Central and Western provinces). *Jingji pinglun,* no. 6, 63–77.

Hu, S. and C. Ljungwall (2013). *China's Healthcare System: Overview and Quality Improvements.* Östersund, Sweden: Swedish Agency for Growth Policy Analysis.

Lardy, N. R. (2012). *Sustaining China's Economic Growth after the Global Financial Crisis.* Washington, DC: Peterson Institute for International Economics.

Leung, J. C. B. and Y. Xu (2015). *China's Social Welfare: The Third Turning Point.* Cambridge, UK: Polity Press.

Li, S., H. Sato, and T. Sicular, eds. (2013). *Rising Inequality in China: Challenges to a Harmonious Society.* Cambridge and New York: Cambridge University Press.

Li, S. and T. Sicular (2014). "The Distribution of Household Income in China: Inequality, Poverty and Policies." *China Quarterly,* no. 217, 1–41.

Li, S. and S. Yang (2009). "Zhongguo chengzhen dibao zhengce dui shouru fenpei he pinkunde yingxiang zuoyong" (Impacts of China's urban *dibao* policy on income distribution and poverty). *Zhongguo renkou kexue,* no. 5, 19–27, 111.

Li, X. and R. B. Freeman (2015). "How Does China's New Labour Contract Law Affect Floating Workers?" *British Journal of Industrial Relations,* 53(4), 711–735.

Lin, W. and C. Wong (2012). "Are Beijing's Equalization Policies Reaching the Poor? An Analysis of Direct Subsidies under the 'Three Rurals' (*Sannong*)." *China Journal,* no. 67, 23–45.

Liu, F. and Y. Xu (2016). "Shui zai xiangyou gonggong jiuzhu ziyuan? Zhongguo nongcun dibao zhidu de miaozhun xiaoguo yanjiu" (Who are beneficiaries of public assistance? The performance of the targeting mechanism of China's rural *dibao* program). *Gonggong guanli xuebao,* 13(1), 141–150, 160.

Liu, T. and L. Sun (2015). "An Apocalyptic Vision of Ageing in China: Old Age Care for the Largest Elderly Population in the World." *Zeitschrift für Gerontologie und Geriatrie,* 48(4), 354–364.

Liu, T. and L. Sun (2016). "Pension Reform in China." *Journal of Aging & Social Policy,* 28(1), 15–28.

Liu, X. (2010). "Jianguo 60 nian lai woguo shehui jiuzhu fazhan licheng yu zhidu bianqian" (China's development process and institutional change in social assistance during the last sixty years). *Huazhong shifan daxue xuebao (renwen shehui kexue ban),* 49(4), 19–26.

Lu, S., Y. T. Lin, J. H. Vikse, and C.-C. Huang (2013). "Effectiveness of Social Welfare Programmes on Poverty Reduction and Income Inequality in China." *Journal of Asian Public Policy,* 6(3), 277–291.

Luo, C. and T. Sicular (2013). "Inequality and Poverty in Rural China," in S. Li, H. Sato, and T. Sicular, eds., *Rising Inequality in China: Challenges to a Harmonious Society,* 197–229. Cambridge and New York: Cambridge University Press.

Ministry of Health (2010). *Zhongguo weisheng tongji nianjian* (China public health statistical yearbook). Beijing: Peking Union Medical College Press.

National Bureau of Statistics of China (2014). *China Statistical Yearbook 2014.* Beijing: China Statistics Press. http://www.stats.gov.cn/tjsj/ndsj/2014/indexch.htm. Accessed November 14, 2019.

Ngok, K. L. and C. K. Chan, eds. (2015). *China's Social Policy: Transformation and Challenges.* London: Routledge.

Saich, T. (2008). *Providing Public Goods in Transitional China.* New York: Palgrave Macmillan.

Saich, T. (2015). *The Governance and Politics of China,* 4th ed. New York: Palgrave Macmillan.

Shue, V. and C. Wong, eds. (2007). *Paying for Progress in China: Public Finance, Human Welfare and Changing Patterns of Inequality.* London: Routledge.

Wallace, J. L. (2014). *Cities and Stability: Urbanization, Redistribution, and Regime Survival in China.* New York: Oxford University Press.

Wang Y., ed. (2013). *Zhongguo shehui baozhang shouru zai fenpei zhuangkuang diaocha* (Study on the redistribution of social security income in China). Beijing: Shehui kexue chubanshe.

Wang Y., Y. Long, C. Jiang, and Q. Xu (2016). "Zhongguo shehui baozhang shouru zai fenpei xiaoying yanjiu" (Redistributive effects of social security income in China). *Jingji yanjiu,* no. 2, 4–15.

World Bank (2007). "China: Public Services for Building the New Socialist Countryside." Washington, DC: East Asia and Pacific Regional Office, World Bank.

6

Public Policy and Long-Term Trends in Inequality in Rural China

Hisatoshi Hoken and Hiroshi Sato

6.1 Introduction

Rapid and prolonged economic development in China has dramatically changed the economic structure in the rural areas. Since implementation of the "reform and opening" policy in the late 1970s, rural households have been released from the constraints of collective farming and have been granted autonomy over their agricultural production and marketing, thus resulting in improved production incentives. Furthermore, the rapid growth of township and village enterprises (TVEs) and manufacturing enterprises in the urban areas has presented huge opportunities for the rural labor force to engage in off-farm employment in both the rural and urban areas. Recently, the boom in investment in real estate and stock markets has been gradually spreading to the rural areas, particularly those areas surrounding the large cities. These prolonged and drastic changes in the rural economy have influenced socioeconomic inequalities among rural households. Income inequalities in rural areas have also been rising because of structural changes in the rural economy, thereby increasing the importance of effective rural public policy for reducing inequality in order to maintain sustainable economic development and social stability in China.

This chapter examines long-term changes in the distribution of rural income in China from the late 1980s to the mid-2010s. It focuses on changes in the redistributive and poverty impacts of public policy as well as the structural evolution of rural income and the contribution of the major income components to overall inequality. Implementation of a series of pro-rural (*huinong*) policies during the first decade of the 2000s marked a historical change in contemporary China's public policy, which during both the Mao and the post-Mao eras was heavily biased to the urban areas. This change in

Hisatoshi Hoken and Hiroshi Sato, *Public Policy and Long- Term Trends in Inequality in Rural China* In: *Changing Trends in China's Inequality*. Edited by: Terry Sicular, Shi Li, Ximing Yue, and Hiroshi Sato, Oxford University Press (2020). © Oxford University Press.
DOI: 10.1093/oso/9780190077938.003.0006

policy was due to the enhancement of state capacity brought about by economic development and systemic transition during the reform era.[1] To elucidate the historical policy changes during the first decade of the 2000s, this chapter extends its scope to the long-term dynamics of income inequality from 1988 to 2013. This expansion will help us better understand the policy background for the inequality trends between 2007 and 2013.

It is thus important to examine to what extent the new public transfers, such as production/living subsidies and social security benefits, have affected the distribution of rural income. Although the pro-rural policies in the 2000s have been a common focus of research, relatively few studies examine the empirical significance of these policies from the perspective of income distribution. Among such studies, Wang (2010), in an examination of the redistributive impact of pro-rural policies, finds that the income redistribution brought about by these policies mitigated rural income inequalities and reduced urban/rural income disparities. Qi (2011) investigates the effects of the newly introduced public medical insurance system on rural income inequalities. Lin and Wong (2012), in an examination of government transfers to rural households, confirm the positive impact of subsidies and reimbursements on rural household income.

Given that this study shares a focus with the previous literature, in this chapter we utilize more recent nationally representative CHIP (China Household Income Project) survey data, which include comprehensive coverage of income and transfer payments. The data are compiled from the rural household components of the five rounds of the CHIP surveys, that is, 1988, 1995, 2002, 2007, and 2013. The survey database covers rural households across the twenty-five-year period from 1988 to 2013, which was a time of rapid and prolonged changes in the rural economy in terms of the structure of household income as well as in the implementation of public policies affecting rural households.

Two major empirical approaches are adopted in this chapter. First, using inequality decomposition methodologies, we identify the major components of income that affect income inequality in rural China. We separate household income into six components: net income from agriculture, net income from non-agricultural self-employment/business, wage earnings, asset income, imputed rental income from owner-occupied housing (hereafter referred to as "imputed rent"), and net transfer payments.

The first two components are the amounts of income earned from family farming or non-agricultural self-employment/business, after deducting input costs (seeds, fertilizer, pesticides, other material costs, rental fees, etc.). Wage earnings consist of both wages from local employment and wages from migrant jobs. Asset income includes interest, dividends, and other income from assets. Imputed rent from owner-occupied housing is estimated on the basis of a rate-of-return approach. We have adjusted the imputed rent to maintain consistency among the five rounds of the CHIP survey.[2] Net transfer payments are defined as the sum of transfers to households (social security benefits/reimbursements, other transfers from government/ collectives and private transfers) minus transfers from households to the public sector (taxes, levies/fees, social security contributions, and other payments to the government/collectives), and private transfers to relatives and friends. Unlike in the analysis in Chapter 2, we include the amount of pension income in 2013 in the net transfer payments.[3]

Second, we examine the impacts of public transfers on income inequality and poverty by comparing inequality and poverty measures with and without specific public transfers. If transfers from households exceed payments to households, net transfer payments will be negative; such cases occurred in the 1990s and the early 2000s when there was a heavy peasant burden from taxes and levies/fees. We will examine the contributions of positive or negative net public transfers to income inequality and to the poverty indexes by comparing the outcomes with and without specific public transfers.

It should be noted that there are limitations to our study with respect to the estimation of net transfer payments. First, invisible public transfers through institutional/policy interventions, such as the compulsory grain purchase quota at below-market prices (*dinggou renwu*), are not counted as taxation on rural households. The interventions in grain marketing, a legacy of the Mao era, continued until the beginning of the 2000s (Ikegami 2012; Hoken 2014).[4] Second, the subsidies for compulsory education that targeted rural households are also not examined in this chapter, because it is difficult to estimate the amounts of school fees that were exempt. Moreover, information on boarding students is unavailable in the data.[5] Third, although unpaid labor contributions (*yiwugong*) were a non-negligible component of rural taxation until the early 2000s, here we do not include the monetary value of such labor contributions to tax and levy/fee collections, because of a lack of consistent data in the CHIP surveys.[6]

The structure of this chapter is as follows. Section 6.2 presents an overview of income inequality in rural China from 1988 to 2013. Section 6.3 decomposes total income inequality into its major components to capture the structural changes in rural household income during the dual processes of economic development and systemic transition in China. Special attention is paid to public transfer payments and the changing redistributive effects of these transfers. Section 6.4 summarizes the structure of the pro-rural policies in the 2000s, and Section 6.5 investigates the redistributive and poverty impacts of various types of public transfers. The conclusion in Section 6.6 describes policy implications relevant to addressing inequality in rural China.

6.2 Trends in Income Inequality from the Late 1980s through 2013

6.2.1 Income per Capita and the Gini Coefficients in the CHIP Surveys

Table 6.1 shows the average income per capita for rural households during the five rounds of the CHIP surveys, based on the previous income definition. We utilize regional weights to estimate the national average of per capita income and the Gini coefficients for rural households (not including migrant households). Regional (East, Central, and West) weights, which are calculated on the basis of the sizes of the provincial and regional rural populations, were prepared by the CHIP research team for 2007 and 2013. We extend these weights by using the same procedures for the previous CHIP rounds.

The long-term trend in income inequality in rural China measured by the Gini coefficients can be summarized as follows. A substantial rise in the Gini coefficients in the CHIP survey is observed between 1988 and 1995, increasing from 0.353 in 1988 to 0.419 in 1995. In 2002, the Gini coefficient

Table 6.1. Income per capita and the Gini coefficients for rural households

	1988	1995	2002	2007	2013
Rural income per capita (yuan)	779	2076	2775	5054	13,505
Gini coefficient	0.353	0.419	0.376	0.385	0.417

Notes: Whole rural household observations (not including migrant households) are utilized to estimate the per capita income (in current prices) and the Gini coefficient. Regional weights are calculated on the basis of the share of the provincial agricultural population to the regional agricultural population.

Sources: Authors' estimations based on the CHIP surveys.

dropped considerably to 0.376. Thereafter, the coefficient rose again, reaching 0.385 in 2007 and 0.417 in 2013, which was the second highest in all the rounds. In comparison, the Gini coefficients reported by the NBS on the basis of the NBS rural household survey exhibited a gradual rise from the 1980s to the 1990s; thereafter, beginning in the early 2000s they remained stable at a relatively elevated level (Guojia tongjiju, Zhuhu diaocha bangongshi 2014).

6.2.2 Annual Growth of per Capita Income by Income Decile

To understand income inequality in China, it is necessary to look at the differences in income growth among the different income strata. Figure 6.1 shows the annual real growth of adjusted per capita income between each CHIP survey by income deciles. It is apparent that the annual income growth rates between 2007 and 2013 are much higher than those in the previous years for all income deciles. The growth rates between 2007 and

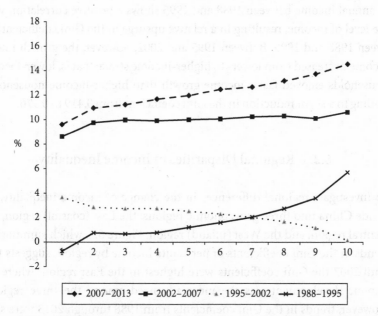

Fig. 6.1 Real annual growth rates of income between survey rounds, by income decile

Notes: Income is adjusted by the regional weights. Per capita income is deflated by the rural CPI (2013 = 100). The rural CPI is from Guoji tongjiju (various years).

Sources: Authors' estimation based on the CHIP surveys.

annual 2013 reach approximately 10–14 percent and they are distributed proportionally among the income deciles. As will be discussed in the following section, the rapid growth of real income between 2007 and 2013 was mainly caused by an upsurge in the share of wage income in total income. The continuous increase in the number of rural migrant laborers as well as in the number of local off-farm laborers explains this trend. According to the NBS monitoring survey report on rural migrants, rural laborers working out of their home townships increased from 140.41 million people in 2008 to 166.10 million people in 2013. Aggregate real monthly wages of migrant laborers increased approximately 61 percent between 2009 and 2013.[7] In addition to wage earnings, the share of imputed rent and asset income in total income, new sources of inequality, also increased rapidly between 2007 and 2013.

Relatively even income growth among the income deciles is observed between 2002 and 2007, and the growth rates during this period are lower than those from 2007 to 2013. In contrast, the distribution of annual income growth from 1988 through 2002 among the income deciles is different than that after 2002. Specifically, except for the lowest-income decile, the real growth rate of annual income between 1988 and 1995 shows a positive correlation with the level of income, resulting in a relative upsurge in the Gini coefficient between 1988 and 1995. Between 1995 and 2002, however, the growth rate of income decreased from lower- to higher-income strata: that is, lower-income households enjoyed faster income growth than higher-income households, leading to a slight reduction in the Gini coefficient from 0.419 to 0.376.

6.2.3 Regional Disparities in Income Inequality

To investigate regional differences in the change of income inequality, we divide China into three geoeconomic regions: the East (coastal) region, the Central region, and the West (inland) region. Figure 6.2, which summarizes trends in the Gini coefficients of per capita income by region, suggests that until 2007 the Gini coefficients were highest in the East region, where economic development was the most advanced among the three regions. However, trends in the Gini coefficients from 1988 through 2013 were similar across regions. Specifically, the Gini coefficients increased from 1988 to 1995 in all three regions. Thereafter, the Gini coefficients gradually dropped

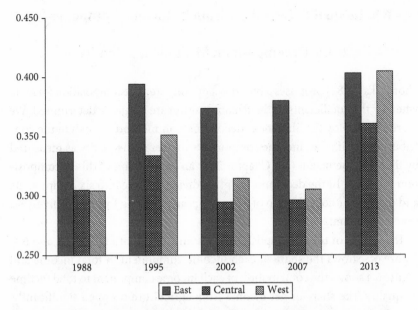

Fig. 6.2 Gini coefficients of adjusted income per capita by region

Notes: 1.) The regional classifications are as follows: East region (Beijing, Tianjin, Hebei, Liaoning, Shanghai, Jiangsu, Zhejiang, Fujian, Shandong, Guangdong, and Hainan), Central region (Shanxi, Jilin, Heilongjiang, Anhui, Jiangxi, Henan, Hubei, and Hunan), West region (Inner Mongolia, Guangxi, Chongqing, Sichuan, Guizhou, Yunnan, Tibet, Shaanxi, Gansu, Qinghai, Ningxia, and Xinjiang). 2.) Income is adjusted by the regional weight and the PPP index.

Sources: Authors' estimations based on the CHIP surveys.

in the 2000s, but then rose again between 2007 and 2013, especially in the Central and West regions.

It should be noted that the exacerbation of income inequalities in the Central and West regions from 2007 to 2013 was correlated with the changes in the income structure. The shares of imputed rent in total income surged from 7.8 percent to 14.4 percent in the Central region and from 7.5 percent to 15.0 percent in the West region, whereas the shares of net income from agriculture were reduced dramatically, from 42.6 percent to 19.1 percent in the Central region and from 47.0 percent to 28.5 percent in the West region. With respect to the East region, although the change in income composition is less distinct, the share of imputed rent increased slightly from 11.4 percent to 18.0 percent. To more closely investigate the contributions to income inequality by income source, in the next section we employ the Shorrocks decomposition method.

6.3 Inequality Decomposition by Income Components

6.3.1 Decomposition Methods and Results

Shorrocks (1982) proposes a theoretically consistent decomposition formula whereby the coefficients of the decomposition are uniquely determined. We therefore employ the Shorrocks decomposition method to analyze the contribution of different income components to overall inequality as measured by the Gini coefficient (see Chapter 2 for an explanation of this decomposition method). In the decomposition, we divide income into six components and discuss the contribution of each component during the twenty-five-year span of our data.

The results of the decomposition are summarized in Figures 6.3 and 6.4. Figure 6.3 shows the share of each income component in total income and Figure 6.4 shows the contribution of each income component to total income inequality. The share of net income from agriculture dropped significantly, from 74.0 percent in 1988 to 56.4 percent in 1995, and its contribution to total income inequality also declined from 41.6 percent in 1988 to 24.8 percent in

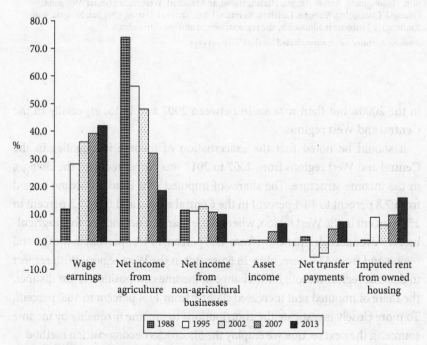

Fig. 6.3 Shares of income components in total income

Sources: Authors' estimations based on the CHIP surveys.

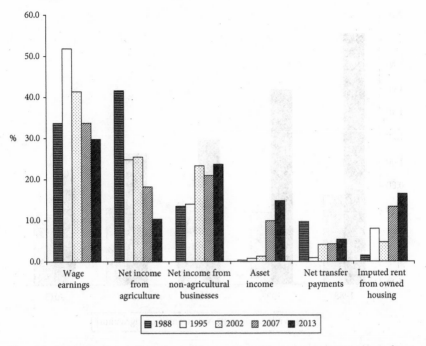

Fig. 6.4 Contributions of income components to income per capita inequality
Sources: Authors' estimations based on the CHIP surveys.

1995.[8] Both the share in total income and the contribution to total income inequality continued to decline in 2007 and 2013. Between 2007 and 2013, the share of agricultural income in total income dropped from 31.2 percent to 18.5 percent, while its contribution to total income inequality dropped from 18.2 percent to 10.3 percent.

Unlike the share of agricultural income and its contribution to total inequality, the concentration coefficient (the pseudo-Gini coefficient) for net income from agriculture remained almost unchanged from 1988 until 2013 (Figure 6.5). This consistency suggests that inter-household disparities in agricultural production were gradually decreasing as the relative share of the agricultural sector declined. It should also be noted that regional disparities in the distributive effects of net income from agriculture have expanded. Specifically, the concentration coefficients for net income from agriculture in 1988 were 0.633 in the East region, 0.799 in the Central region, and 0.895 in the West region, suggesting that agricultural activities were rather homogeneous among all regions. In 2013, however, the relevant figures were 0.384 in the East region, 0.706 in the Central region, and 0.833 in the West region. The variation in agricultural activity was largest in the less-developed regions.

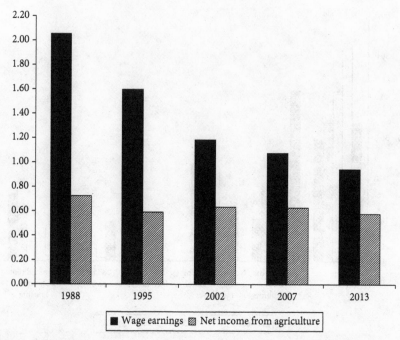

Fig. 6.5 Comparison of concentration coefficients of per capita income between agriculture and wage earnings
Sources: Authors' estimations based on the CHIP surveys.

These changing regional patterns in agricultural income reflect the implementation of the "agro-industrialization" (*nongye chanyehua*) agricultural policy in the late 1990s. Central and local governments evaluated the integration of small farmers by agribusiness enterprises through contract farming, and began to officially support the establishment of agricultural conglomerates through contract farming. These agricultural policies were aimed at increasing the profitability of agricultural production and improving the living standards of rural residents (Fock and Zachernuk 2006; Nongyebu, Nongye chanyehua bangongshi, Nongyebu nongcun jingji yanjiu zhongxin 2008).

The penetration of agro-industrialization appears to facilitate the diversification of agricultural production into large-scale specialized farming and self-supported small-scale farming. According to our calculations using published data (Nongyebu 2010, 2014), the shares of leased-in farmland to total contracted farmland have been increasing rapidly since the end of the 2000s, with the share rising from 12.0 percent in 2009 to 25.7 percent in 2013. Related to these data, institutional arrangements that allow and encourage the development of rental markets for farmland are a source of the diversification of farming structures; namely, implementation of the Rural Cultivated Land Contracting Law in 2003 and policy support for farmland rental transactions facilitated the diversification of agricultural production (Gao, Huang, and Rozelle 2012). These agricultural structural changes are reflected in the changes of the concentration coefficients for net income from agriculture.

In contrast to agricultural income, a different trend is revealed in wage earnings, including migration wage income. The share of wage earnings in total income jumped from 11.4 percent in 1988 to 36.0 percent in 2002, and its contribution to total income inequality increased from 33.7 percent in 1988 to 51.8 percent in 2002. The contribution of wage earnings to total inequality was higher than its share in total income between 1988 and 2002, indicating that wage earnings rapidly expanded to become the most influential income component. At the same time, it should be noted that the concentration coefficient for wage earnings had been declining from a considerably elevated level of 2.05 in 1988 to 1.19 in 2002 (see Figure 6.5). This finding reflects the expansion of non-agricultural job opportunities. As shown by Zhang (2001) and Li (2001), the development of rural industries, such as TVEs, remained geographically unbalanced, and opportunities to secure off-farm occupations were relatively limited until the early 2000s.[9] Therefore, rural households that were located in relatively developed areas or laborers who had more opportunities to migrate appear to have benefited from wage income more than others, thus accelerating income inequalities among rural households.

From 2002 to 2013, however, off-farm opportunities, including migrant jobs, continued to expand and spread widely; hence the relatively easy access to off-farm jobs mitigated the disparity effects of wage earnings. More specifically, the share of wage earnings in total income continued to increase, from 36.0 percent in 2002 to 41.8 percent in 2013, and the concentration coefficients decreased from 1.19 in 2002 to 0.94 in 2013, resulting in a gradual decrease in the contribution of wage earnings to total income inequality, from 41 percent in 2002 to 28.7 percent in 2013. Luo and Sicular (2013) point out that the contributions from migration and local employment were quite different between 2002 and 2007, but our estimates show that the total contributions from wage earnings, including migration income, dropped gradually from 2002 to 2013.

Because of data limitations in the CHIP 2013, we could not disaggregate the contributions from migrant and local employment to wage earnings. However, considering the previously mentioned ongoing increase in migrant laborers, it is highly likely that an increasing contribution of migration income was offset by a reduction in the contribution of local employment. This evolution of off-farm employment from initial scarcity to increasing prevalence as well as the continuous growth of migrant labor appears to characterize the change in overall income inequality in rural China.

Meanwhile, net income from non-agricultural businesses became a major factor contributing to income inequality in rural China since 2002. The contributions of net income from non-agricultural businesses jumped to 23.3 percent in 2002 and remained at this level thereafter; nevertheless, the shares of non-agricultural businesses in total household income remained at about 10 percent during the five rounds of the CHIP surveys. The rising contribution of non-agricultural business income to inequality reflects the increasingly unequal distribution of this component of income among rural households, for which the concentration coefficient increased substantially from 1.17 in 1995 to 1.45 in 2002, and 1.54 in 2013.

With respect to asset income, the share in total income remained at less than 1.2 percent until 2002. Although the share of asset income in total income was still relatively small in 2013, its contribution to total income inequality became more significant after 2000, at 9.8 percent in 2007 and 14.7 percent in 2013. In addition, the contribution of imputed rent on owner-occupied housing began to increase rapidly from the beginning of the 2000s. The share of imputed rent in total income increased from 6.4 percent in 2002 to 16.1 percent in 2013, while its contribution to total income inequality increased from 4.7 percent to 16.4 percent between 2002 and 2013. Although the reform of property rights for rural land and housing is still at an early experimental stage, the increase in imputed rent suggests that rural housing may possibly become a new source of inequality in the future.

6.3.2 Change in the Public Transfer Policy

We can trace changes in the direct effects of public policy on households by analyzing the impact of transfers on total income. Here we examine the trend in the share of net transfers in total income and its contribution to income inequality. As reported in Figure 6.3, the share of net transfers in 1988 was slightly positive at an average of 2.0 percent, whereas its contribution to income inequality was 7.9 percent, larger than its income share.

Yet one should focus on the differences in the shares of net transfers in total income among the different income strata. Table 6.2 summarizes the changes in the shares of net transfers by income deciles during the five rounds of the CHIP surveys. As shown in the table, in 1988 the shares of net transfers for the bottom and second deciles were –12.34 percent and –3.32 percent respectively, while those for the top deciles were 6.73 percent. These findings indicate that net transfers were distributed regressively, playing a disequalizing role during the initial stages of the economic reforms.

During the 1990s and the beginning of the 2000s, the direct impact of rural public policy on rural household income became "exploitive" and more regressive. The shares of net transfers in total income in 1988 were close to zero for the middle-income deciles. However, in 1995 the shares of net transfers in total income became negative for all income deciles. Moreover,

Table 6.2. Shares of net transfer income by region and decile (%)

		1988	1995	2002	2007	2013
Total average		2.62	–5.11	–4.00	4.77	7.67
Region	East	4.31	–3.36	–2.71	5.39	6.94
	Central	–0.54	–9.07	–6.55	3.77	8.40
	West	1.62	–4.15	–3.23	4.99	8.33
Decile	Bottom	–12.34	–26.65	–28.19	8.45	3.67
	2nd	–3.32	–11.73	–8.61	6.04	10.27
	3rd	–2.67	–10.61	–7.73	4.37	9.65
	4th	–0.32	–8.60	–6.83	4.59	7.86
	5th	–0.04	–8.49	–6.72	4.01	8.00
	6th	1.01	–6.67	–5.57	4.69	7.98
	7th	1.60	–6.51	–4.36	4.68	7.98
	8th	1.99	–6.11	–4.34	4.17	7.49
	9th	3.25	–4.27	–3.07	5.31	8.01
	Top	6.73	–1.05	0.86	5.14	6.98

Notes: 1.) Net transfer payments are defined as the sum of transfers to households (social security benefits/reimbursements, other transfers from the government/collectives, and private transfers) minus transfers from households to the public sector (taxes, levies/fees, social security contributions, and other payments to the government/collectives) and private transfers to relatives and friends. 2.) Post-transfer per capita income is utilized as the denominator to calculate the net transfer share.

Sources: Authors' estimations based on the CHIP surveys.

negative public transfers, which became substantially larger for the lower-income deciles in 1995, accounted for -26.65 percent and -11.73 percent for the bottom and second deciles respectively. After 1995, the regressivity of the transfers remained and it still had not been eliminated by 2002. Even excluding the amount of private net transfers from net transfer income, regressive trends of net income transfers are observed from 1988 to 2002.

These findings clearly illustrate the increasing and heavily regressive taxes and local levies/fees on the "peasant burden" during the 1990s and the beginning of the 2000s, a penalty that created serious social tensions in rural China. The urban-biased fiscal and investment policies of local governments, which were stimulated by competition over interregional economic growth under the fiscal decentralization policies of the post-Mao era as well as by the weak fiscal redistributive ability of the central government, placed a heavy financial burden on county-, township-, and village-level authorities and led to the "peasant burden" problem (Bernstein and Lü 2003; Lü 1997; Sato, Li, and Yue 2008; Yep 2004).

Against this background, pro-rural public policies were implemented, first by the rural taxation reform in 2002 and then by a series of public transfer programs. As a result, the structure of public transfers changed fundamentally during the first decade of the 2000s. According to our analysis of the CHIP 2007 and 2013 surveys, the signs of the shares of net transfers became positive: 4.77 percent and 7.67 percent respectively. Their contributions to inequality appear to be neutral, and slightly lower than the shares. As shown in Table 6.2, the shares are also positive for all income deciles, with the shares relatively favorable to the lower income deciles (except for the bottom decile). Specifically, the shares for the bottom decile in 2007 and 2013 were 8.45 percent and 3.67 percent, and those for the second decile were 6.04 percent and 10.27 percent respectively. To further investigate the direct impacts of rural public policies on structural changes in rural household incomes, in the following section we will discuss the effects of the public transfer programs.

6.4 Rural Policy and Inequality

6.4.1 Institutional and Policy Background

Table 6.3 summarizes the major pro-rural public policies in China during the 2000s. Pro-rural public policies during this period are well captured by the

Table 6.3. Major pro-rural public policies in the 2000s

	Period of nationwide implementation	Number of beneficiaries/ participants, millions of persons (% of rural residents in parentheses)		
		2005	2010	2013
Policy of "Taking less"				
Tax-for-fee (*feigaishui*) reform	2002	na	na	na
Abolition of agricultural taxes	2006	—	na	na
Policies of "Giving more"				
Direct subsidies for agricultural production*	2002	na	na	na
Subsidies for the sloping land conversion (SLC) program	2002	na	na	na
New Rural Cooperative Medical System (NRCMS)	2003	179 (18.8)	836 (96.0)	802 (99.0)
Rural minimum living standard guarantee (*dibao*)	2007	8.3 (1.1)	52.1 (7.8)	53.9 (8.6)
Newly defined conventional rural social assistance (*wubao*, five-guarantee assistance)	2006	—	5.6 (0.8)	5.4 (0.9)
New rural public pension insurance (PPI) program	2009	—	102.8 (15.3)	497.5 (79.0)**

Notes: 1.) * Direct subsidies for agricultural production include a subsidy for food grain production, comprehensive subsidies for agricultural production materials, subsidies for improved seeds, subsidies for the purchase of agricultural machinery, and other local subsidies for staple agricultural products. 2.) ** includes urban residents, and the share is calculated by the total population.

Sources: Li, Sato, and Sicular (2013); Lin and Wong (2012); Guojia tongjiju (various years).

slogan "giving more, taking less, and allowing peasants more opportunities" (*duoyu shaoqu fanghuo*) (Zhonggong zhongyang and Guowuyuan 2005).

Policies for "taking less" began with the tax-for-fee (*feigaishui*) reform at the beginning of the 2000s and ended with the nationwide abolition of agricultural taxes at the beginning of 2006. The reform of rural taxation can be divided into two phases (Sato, Li, and Yue 2008; Tian 2009). The first phase (2000–2003) involved imposing newly defined agricultural taxes in place of local levies and fees, resulting in some reduction in the total "peasant burden." The second phase (2004–2006) involved first a gradual reduction in the agricultural tax (including the special agricultural tax and the livestock tax) and then its complete abolition in January 2006, whereby the previously urban-biased institutional arrangements were transformed into rural- (or agriculture)-supportive arrangements.

Despite completion of the rural taxation reform and the increase in fiscal budgets for rural areas under the New Socialist Countryside Construction scheme, village collectives and townships still must collect money from peasants when fiscal inputs from the central/local governments are limited. This newly defined local levy, called the "one issue, one discussion collection of money and labor services" (*yishi yiyi chouzi choulao*), is monitored and controlled by the auditing department of the "peasant burden" at the county level, along with various other fees imposed on rural households. Therefore, although the level of rural taxation was fundamentally reduced after the rural taxation reform, the "peasant burden" remained a policy issue.[10]

Policies for "giving more" consist of various public transfer programs to rural households, which can be categorized in two groups: (a) production-related transfers, and (b) social security transfers. In addition, following Lin and Wong (2012), we can further classify public transfers, in terms of the three types of targeted beneficiaries: (1) universal, (2) pro-poor, and (3) reimbursable. Universal transfers provide benefits without counterpart fees/contributions to almost all rural households without regard to their economic status. Pro-poor transfers, which are means tested, target eligible poor households. Reimbursable transfers provide partial reimbursement for eligible household expenditures.

Classifications of the public transfers covered in this chapter are summarized in Table 6.4. It should be noted that there is one other group of public transfers: living/consumption-related transfers. These include subsidies for boarding students and subsidies to purchase durable goods and facilities, such as the subsidy for biogas digesters, the subsidy for electrical appliances (*jiadian xiaxiang*), and the subsidy for automobiles (*qiche xiaxiang*). Although these subsidies influence the level of household income as well as income inequality in rural China, the CHIP surveys do not contain detailed data about them. Therefore, in this chapter we concentrate on production-related and social security transfers

Production-related transfers include both universal and reimbursement types of subsidies. The direct subsidies for food grain production and comprehensive subsidies for agricultural production materials are classified as

Table 6.4. Classifications of the pro-rural public transfers in this study

	(1) Universal types of transfers	(2) Pro-poor types of transfers	(3) Reimbursement types of transfers
(a) Production-related transfers	Direct subsidies for food grain production, comprehensive subsidies for agricultural production materials, SLC subsidies		Subsidies for purchasing improved seeds, subsidies for purchasing agricultural machinery
(b) Social security transfers		*Dibao, wubao,* poverty alleviation fund, medical relief fund	NRCMS, rural PPI

Sources: Lin and Wong (2012); Sato and Wang (2014).

universal transfers. Subsidies for the sloping land conversion program (SLC), providing for the restoration of forests and grasslands, are also regarded as universal transfers. However, subsidies for purchasing improved seeds and agricultural machinery are classified as reimbursable transfers.

Among the social-security-related transfers, the New Rural Cooperative Medical System (NRCMS) and the new rural public pension insurance (PPI) program are categorized as reimbursable transfers. As shown in Table 6.3, because of powerful policy support from central and local governments for large subsidy distributions, the NRCMS rapidly expanded its coverage, from 18.8 percent of rural residents in 2005 to 96.0 percent of rural residents in 2010. Coverage reached 99.0 percent in 2013, suggesting that most rural residents were participating in this program. Although the subsidies for the NRCMS premium are distributed universally by both the central and local governments as a fixed amount (or a fixed ratio) to all participants, household medical expense transfers can also be classified as reimbursable transfers. This classification is because they depend on the medical expenses that households have paid.

Under the rural PPI program, pension benefits are determined by the subsidies from the central and local authorities as well as by the pension premium paid by the participants. Therefore, payments from the rural PPI can be categorized as reimbursable transfers. Because the rural PPI was at an experimental stage in 2010, the program covered only 102.8 million rural residents, constituting 15.3 percent of the rural residents at that time. Since then, the rural PPI program has been merged with the urban PPI program, and the total number of participants has grown dramatically, reaching 497.5 million participants in 2013.

The *dibao* program is an important pro-poor subsidy. This program was introduced in the urban areas in the early 1990s; selected rural localities (especially the more developed localities) began to initiate the *dibao* program later, in the early 2000s. However, the *dibao* program has been widespread since 2006, mainly because of the intensification of policy support for rural households as well as the transfer of authority for the *dibao* program from the provincial governments to the central government (Luo and Sicular 2013).

The number of households that receive *dibao* increased rapidly from 8.3 million to 52.1 million between 2006 and 2010. The share of *dibao* households in the rural total reached 7.8 percent in 2010. Thereafter, the expansion gradually slowed, with the share reaching 8.6 percent of the total in 2013. In addition to *dibao*, pro-poor programs for rural residents also include the rural social assistance program for the elderly (*wubao*), which is the conventional rural social assistance program for food, clothing, housing, medical care, and burial expenses that began during the collective era but has recently been redefined; the poverty alleviation fund (*fupinkuan*); the medical relief fund (*yiliao jiuzhu*); and other social assistance programs.[11]

In the following sections, we first examine the impact of the rural taxation reform ("taking less") and then investigate the redistributive and poverty impacts of public transfers ("giving more"). In the investigation of the impacts of public transfers, we confine our analysis to public transfers that are universal, pro-poor, and reimbursements rather than production-related or social security transfers. This approach is because we are better able to specify the beneficiaries of each policy for the former, allowing for an evaluation of the policy impacts on income inequality in rural China.

6.4.2 Impacts of "Taking Less" Policies

To examine policy changes and their effects on the various income strata, we disaggregate rural households into income deciles and calculate the taxation rate (the percentage of pretax income paid as agricultural taxes and other taxes and local levies/fees). As shown in Table 6.5, in both 1988 and 1995 taxation

Table 6.5. Tax rates by region and decile (%)

		1988	1995	2002	2007	2013
Total average		3.77	4.04	3.18	0.22	0.24
Region	East	3.05	2.62	2.40	0.17	0.22
	Central	6.40	6.81	4.23	0.35	0.24
	West	2.56	3.95	3.33	0.25	0.28
Decile	Bottom	14.82	14.22	8.27	0.27	1.49
	2nd	7.72	8.20	5.82	0.39	0.40
	3rd	6.43	7.67	5.13	0.23	0.37
	4th	5.12	6.79	4.81	0.27	0.35
	5th	4.86	6.35	4.34	0.25	0.34
	6th	4.06	5.73	3.82	0.26	0.30
	7th	3.90	4.90	3.56	0.35	0.17
	8th	3.47	4.52	2.96	0.14	0.17
	9th	2.70	3.21	2.52	0.20	0.17
	Top	2.06	1.37	1.41	0.18	0.17

Notes: 1.) Tax payments include agricultural taxes, other taxes, and local levies/fees paid to local governments and collectives. 2.) Pretax income is used as the denominator to estimate the tax rate.
Sources: Authors' estimation based on the CHIP surveys.

rates for the bottom decile were the highest among all income deciles, constituting 14.82 percent and 14.22 percent of pretax income respectively, and the shares declined for the higher-income deciles. Comparing the shares between 1988 and 1995, we find that the shares in 1995 were considerably higher than those in 1988 for most of the income deciles, although the gaps between 1988 and 1995 still declined progressively for the higher-income deciles. These outcomes suggest that tax and fee payments were levied regressively and the burdens were most serious for the lower-income deciles.

A notable change in tax rates is observed in both 2007 and 2013. Specifically, the tax rates were reduced drastically for all income deciles, and the average shares decreased to 0.22 percent and 0.24 percent respectively. These changes reflect the impacts of the comprehensive rural tax and the fee reforms implemented after 2000. Although the tax rates in 2007 and 2013 were slightly regressive, the rates were less than 1 percent for all deciles, except for the lowest decile in 2013. These findings suggest that the "taking less" policies succeeded in resolving the problem of higher tax burdens for poor households in the 2000s.

6.4.3 Impacts of "Giving More" Policies

In our examination of the "giving more" policies, we focus on the CHIP 2013 to estimate the effects by comparing income inequality and the poverty index with/without specific transfers. Although the pro-poor public transfers were introduced in the early 2000s, because the CHIP survey was not designed to track the same households during the period, it is difficult to evaluate the impact of specific pro-poor public transfers in a before-and-after analysis. In addition, the CHIP 2007 data do not include the disaggregated amounts of the transfers, such as the universal, pro-poor, and reimbursable transfers. Therefore, we utilize disaggregated public transfers in 2013 to examine the impacts on income inequality.

The CHIP 2013 questionnaire asked each household member whether he or she participated in social security programs. Table 6.6 reports the percentages of households that were beneficiaries of specific types of social security programs.

Among rural households, 6.2 percent were recipients of *dibao* transfers. When other types of social relief (i.e., *wubao*, and so forth) are added, the share of recipient households increased to 8.0 percent.[12] Participants in public medical insurance, including both the NRCMS and the employee insurance program, constituted 98.9 percent of all rural households, of which participants in the NRCMS accounted for 90.3 percent of all rural households. The pension participation rate was 87.3 percent, including participants in the

Table 6.6. Shares of rural households that received specific types of social security, 2013

	% of beneficiaries/participants
Dibao or social relief	8.0
Dibao	6.2
Medical insurance	98.9
NRCMS	90.3
Public pension insurance	87.3
Rural PPI	76.0

Note: The observations for Xinjiang province are not included in the table, because of differences between the Xinjiang questionnaires and those distributed elsewhere.

Source: Authors' estimations based on the CHIP 2013 survey.

employee pension scheme and other public pension programs, while the participation rate in the rural PPI was 76.0 percent. Participation rates in social insurance programs in the CHIP 2013 rural sample are generally consistent with those described in the official national statistics, as shown in Table 6.3.[13]

Table 6.7, based on income data from the CHIP 2013 survey, summarizes households that received public transfers, by both transfer types and regions. The upper part of Table 6.7 shows that the share of households benefiting from reimbursable transfers among the total sample of households was the highest of all types of public transfer programs, at 60.2 percent. The shares were slightly higher in the less-developed provinces, i.e., those in the Central and West regions. Among the reimbursable transfers, the share of rural PPI beneficiary households was higher than that for public medical insurance in all regions and provinces.[14]

As shown in Table 6.7, universal transfers were widely spread and affected almost one-half of the rural households (46.2 percent). The share of universal transfer beneficiary households was relatively low in the advanced provinces, such as Beijing, Guangdong, and Jiangsu. The beneficiary households receiving pro-poor transfers were also a substantial proportion of the entire sample, constituting 36.4 percent. The share of rural households that received

Table 6.7. Shares of beneficiary households among all rural households, 2013

	Universal transfers	Pro-poor transfers	Dibao	Reimbursable transfers	PPI	Medical insurance
(a) Share of beneficiaries among all rural households (%)						
Total	46.2	36.4	7.5	60.2	32.4	11.3
East	34.6	34.3	2.8	56.7	38.2	8.7
Central	57.3	35.4	7.7	61.3	29.4	14.8
West	45.0	40.1	12.3	62.7	29.8	9.9
(b) Average amount from public transfers for beneficiaries (yuan)						
Total	524	1204	1603	3446	4801	2739
East	635	767	1770	5310	6733	3816
Central	393	929	1240	2628	3614	2382
West	638	1920	1846	2589	3540	2369

Notes: 1.) The average amount from public transfers is calculated only for households that receive transfers. 2.) Households that received the transfers but the amounts were zero are excluded from the estimation. 3.) It is possible that the average amount of the subtotal exceeds the total.

Source: Authors' estimation based on the CHIP 2013 survey.

antipoverty relief through the *dibao* program was 7.5 percent, slightly lower than the national average (8.6 percent). Also, the share of households that received *dibao* was higher in the less-developed provinces, such as Gansu and Sichuan in the West region.

The average amounts of public transfers to beneficiary households are summarized in the lower part of Table 6.7. The average amount of reimbursable transfers was 3446 yuan per household per year, making it the largest of all types of public transfers. It is noteworthy that households in the East region enjoyed significantly larger transfers. The same pattern is observed for rural PPI and public medical insurance. These results indicate that reimbursable transfers appear to increase income inequality in rural China.

Meanwhile, the average pro-poor transfer was relatively large for households in the West region, reaching 1920 yuan per household. However, there were no significant differences in the average amount of *dibao* transfers between the East and West regions, probably because, consistent with its higher minimum living costs, the East region had a relatively stronger local fiscal capacity. The average universal transfer was much lower than the average of the other types of transfers and larger amounts were distributed in the East and West regions.

6.5 Impacts of Public Transfers on Income Inequality and the Poverty Index

To identify the impacts of public transfers on income inequality in rural China, we estimate the Gini coefficients with/without public transfers, assuming all else being equal. Because public transfers appear to be more important for lower-income households, especially households whose income is below the poverty line, we also estimate the Foster-Greer-Thorbecke poverty indexes (FGT indexes) with/without public transfers.[15] The FGT indexes are defined as follows:

$$FGT(\alpha) = \frac{1}{N} \sum_{i=1}^{H} \left(\frac{z - y_i}{z} \right)^\alpha$$

where z denotes the poverty threshold, which was defined as 2300 yuan per capita in 2010 prices by the NBS (Guojia tongjiju, Zhuhu diaocha bangongshi

2015) and we extended this to 2013 by using the weighted average of the rural CPI and the rural Food CPI. N is the number of households, H is the number of poor households, and y_i is the income per capita of household i. With the parameter $\alpha = 0$, FGT(0) corresponds to the head-count ratio, which is a fraction of the households below the poverty line and the most commonly used measure of poverty. FGT(1) corresponds to the poverty gap index, referred to as a measure of "poverty depth" because it measures how far, on average, the poor fall below the poverty line. FGT(2) corresponds to the squared poverty gap index (or "poverty sensitivity") because squaring puts more weight on households that fall below the poverty line. Therefore, the higher the value of parameter α, the greater the weight placed on poorer households. Because the official poverty level is determined according to NBS household income, we exclude imputed rent from our CHIP household income to calculate the FGT indexes.

In estimating the Gini coefficients and the poverty indexes, as discussed in previous subsections, the impacts of public transfers on income inequality differ according to the type of transfers. Therefore, to calculate the indexes, we classify public transfers into (1) universal, (2) pro-poor, and (3) reimbursable transfers. Because of a lack of detailed data on public transfers, examination of the decomposition of public transfers is limited for 2013.

Initially, we calculated the Gini coefficients with/without net transfers to compare 2002 and 2013. As described in the previous section, because negative transfers were implemented between the 1990s and the early 2000s, a comparison of 2002 and 2013 will enable us to evaluate the impacts of the transformation of public policy on income inequality. Table 6.8 reports the estimation results. It shows that there is slight change in the Gini coefficients between these years with or without net transfers, regardless of region. However, the Gini coefficients for 2013 without net transfers are approximately 3.60 percent larger than those with net transfers, and the gaps are larger in the Central and West regions. These findings indicate small but substantial improvements in the redistributive impacts of public transfers between 2002 and 2013. Moreover, the strength of the redistributive impacts is not proportional to the level of regional development, with the greatest impact being in the Central region and the least impact in the East region. Therefore, it can be argued that implementation of pro-rural public policies during the first decade of this century represented a historical reversal of the urban-biased public policy in contemporary China.

Table 6.8. Comparison of per capita income Gini coefficients with and without public transfers, 2002–2013

	2002			2013		
	(a) Gini coefficient with transfers	(b) Gini coefficient without transfers	(c) % change of Gini coefficient	(a) Gini coefficient with transfers	(b) Gini coefficient without transfers	(c) % change of Gini coefficient
All households	0.366	0.367	0.24	0.411	0.426	3.60
East	0.374	0.373	−0.23	0.396	0.408	2.89
Central	0.292	0.293	0.50	0.358	0.379	5.83
West	0.314	0.313	−0.33	0.395	0.413	4.43

Sources: Authors' estimations based on the CHIP 2002 and 2013 surveys.

Next, we calculated the Gini coefficients with/without the three types of public transfers; the results are summarized in Table 6.9. The contributions of both pro-poor and reimbursable transfers in 2013 are high compared with the contributions of universal transfers, both for total households and for all regions. The largest reduction in the Gini coefficient is observed in the Central region, at 3.19 percent. However, the impact of pro-poor transfers on improvements in income inequality was relatively low, although the contribution was more important (at 1.86 percent) in the West region. The impact of universal transfers on income inequality accounted for only 0.49 percent, and the regional differences of the impacts are not obvious.

Although the impacts of specific public transfers on total income inequality are not large, they tend to be targeted at relatively poor households and so may have a more distinct impact on the level of poverty. Thus, we calculate the FGT poverty indexes, using the official rural poverty threshold as the poverty line.[16] Table 6.10 summarizes the estimated results for the FGT indexes in 2013, with and without the specific types of public transfers. The poverty impacts of universal transfers are limited at best. Improvements in the FGT indexes when universal transfers are included are 6.7 percent for the poverty head-count ratio (FGT[0]), 7.5 percent for the poverty gap (FGT[1]), and 7.2 percent for the squared poverty gap (FGT[2]). The poverty impacts of universal transfers differ among regions, with those in the Central region higher than those in the East and West regions.

The poverty impact from pro-poor transfers is relatively larger for all regions. The improvement in FGT(1) when pro-poor transfers are included

Table 6.9. Per capita income Gini coefficients with and without specific public transfers, 2013

	Total	East	Central	West
Gini coefficients with transfers	0.411	0.396	0.358	0.395
Gini coefficients without specific public transfers				
(i) Universal	0.413	0.397	0.361	0.398
(ii) Pro-poor	0.416	0.398	0.363	0.403
(iii) Reimbursable	0.418	0.403	0.369	0.402
% change in Gini coefficients				
(i) Universal	0.49	0.27	0.75	0.59
(ii) Pro-poor	1.29	0.56	1.58	1.86
(iii) Reimbursable	1.59	1.82	3.19	1.75

Source: Authors' estimation based on the CHIP 2013 survey.

was 13.2 percent in the East region, 25.5 percent in the Central region, and 21.4 percent in the West region. This finding suggests that the targeting of pro-poor transfers worked more effectively in the Central region, where the incidence of poverty was moderate.

Improvements in the poverty indexes when public transfers are included were larger for reimbursable transfers than for the other two types of public transfers. Changes in the FGT indexes improved when reimbursable transfers were included: 36.8 percent (FGT[0]), 50.5 percent (FGT[1]), and 63.2 percent (FGT[2]). The poverty impacts from reimbursable transfers differ from the impacts of other types of public transfers, that is, the redistribution effects are much larger in the Central and East regions than they are in the West region. The impact is noteworthy in the Central and East regions, where reimbursable transfers produce 74.2 percent and 59.4 percent reductions in FGT(1), respectively.

6.6 Conclusion

This study examines long-term changes in the distribution of rural income in China from the late 1980s to the mid-2010s. The major results are summarized as follows. First, we find rapid growth of real income in rural households between 2007 and 2013, growth that was mainly caused by an

Table 6.10. Poverty index with and without specific public transfers, 2013

	Total			East			Central			West		
	FGT(0)	FGT(1)	FGT(2)	FGT(0)	FGT(1)	FGT(2)	FGT(0)	FGT(1)	FGT(2)	FGT(0)	FGT(1)	FGT(2)
Poverty index with transfers	0.039	0.011	0.005	0.017	0.006	0.003	0.041	0.011	0.005	0.063	0.017	0.008
Poverty index without specific public transfers												
(i) Universal	0.042	0.012	0.005	0.018	0.006	0.003	0.047	0.012	0.005	0.064	0.019	0.008
(ii) Pro-poor	0.046	0.013	0.006	0.020	0.006	0.003	0.050	0.014	0.006	0.073	0.021	0.010
(iii) Reimbursable	0.054	0.017	0.008	0.027	0.009	0.005	0.062	0.019	0.009	0.076	0.022	0.011
% change in poverty index												
(i) Universal	6.7	7.5	7.2	6.1	0.7	-4.0	13.4	10.7	11.7	1.8	7.6	9.2
(ii) Pro-poor	17.8	21.4	23.9	14.9	13.2	12.1	22.2	25.5	29.6	15.5	21.4	25.2
(iii) Reimbursable	36.8	50.5	63.2	59.1	59.4	63.1	49.0	74.2	102.6	20.4	29.8	35.8

Note: The poverty indexes are estimated by employing per capita income.

Source: Authors' estimations based on the CHIP 2013 survey.

upsurge in wage earnings, asset income, and imputed rent from owner-occupied housing. The rising share of wage earnings in total household income was the most fundamental trend in rural income distribution from 1988 to 2013. Rapid increases in asset income and imputed rent represent new noteworthy trends that were observed between 2007 and 2013.

Second, with regard to the results of a decomposition analysis of income inequality, we found contrasting trends in the contributions of agricultural income and wage earnings, which reflect the rapid change in the income structure of rural households caused by the dual processes of economic development and systemic transition during the post-Mao era. Both the share of total income and the contribution to total income inequality from agricultural income were decreasing rapidly between 1988 and 2013. In contrast, both the share of total income and the contribution to inequality from wage earnings were increasing rapidly between 1988 and 2002, and by 2002 wage earnings had become the largest disequalizing component of income. Between 2002 and 2013, the contribution of wage income was declining gradually, whereas the share of wage income in total income was continuing to increase.

Third, the rapid increase in income inequality between 2007 and 2013 can be attributed not only to the larger income growth of the higher-income deciles but also to the expansion of income inequality within the geoeconomic regions. In addition, the increasing contribution of asset income and imputed rent from owner-occupied housing to income inequality suggests that wealth inequality is becoming increasingly important to understanding income inequality in rural China.

Fourth, there were small but substantial improvements in the redistributive impacts of public transfers between 2002 and 2013. Implementation of pro-rural public policies during the first decade of this century marked a historic reversal of the long-term urban-biased public policy of contemporary China. Comparing the redistributive impacts among the several types of public transfers in 2013, we found that the contribution of reimbursable transfers was the largest and the contributions of universal and pro-poor transfers were limited.

Last, our estimations of the impacts of public transfers on poverty in 2013 reveal comparable results to those of the redistributive impacts of public transfers. Improvements in the poverty indexes were largest for reimbursable transfers in the moderately developed regions, even though pro-poor public transfers improved the poverty indexes and the impact of poverty was relatively larger in the less-developed regions. Therefore, when examining appropriate policy interventions to reduce rural poverty and income inequality, it is crucial to estimate the impact of specific public transfers according to their geoeconomic characteristics.

This study is based on aggregated indicators, such as the Gini coefficient and the FGT indexes. To further investigate the dynamics of income inequality in rural China, in the future it will be necessary to carry out further econometric examinations, controlling for the socioeconomic attributes of households.

Notes

1. Reform of the household registration system (*hukou*) was implemented in the mid-1980s and, along with the urbanization of the rural areas, has been enforced since the early 2000s, resulting in a rapid expansion of rural/urban migration as well as a gradual decline in the rural population. It may be that the qualitative attributes of rural households gradually changed during this period because of natural selection and selective urbanization (e.g., older and less-educated people tended to remain in the rural areas). Rigorous examination of the selection bias caused by the structural changes in the rural economy, a subject requiring further research, is beyond the scope of this chapter.

2. We construct our own estimates of imputed rent from owner-occupied housing (R) to maintain consistency of the estimations among the five rounds of the survey. More specifically, according to Sato, Sicular, and Yue (2013), we adopt the following formula:

$$R = i(V - M)$$

where V denotes the market value of owner-occupied housing, M denotes the amount of mortgage loans, and i is the rate of return from housing. The rate of return is the interest rate on thirty-year government bonds. The interest rates in 2002, 2007, and 2013 were 3.2028 percent, 4.3625 percent, and 4.8992 percent respectively. Because of the lack of market value data for owner-occupied housing and the relevant interest rates for government bonds in 1988 and 1995, following Khan and Riskin (2001) we substitute the book value of housing construction (or purchase) cost and 8 percent of the market value as the rate of return in each year to calculate the imputed rents. In addition, mortgage loan data are not included in the CHIP 2007 survey. Because the distribution of mortgage loans in 2002 and 2013 are substantially skewed to the right (i.e., higher values), substituting the mean share of mortgage loans in the construction value in 2002 and 2013 for 2007 is not suitable for the estimations. Therefore, we do not deduct the mortgage loans from the construction value to calculate the imputed rent. It should be noted that the amounts of imputed rent for 2007 tend to be somewhat overestimated. On average, our estimates of imputed rent in 2007 and 2013 are 20.3 percent and 29.0 percent respectively, larger than the CHIP estimates used elsewhere in this volume. (See Chapters 1 and 2 for a discussion of the CHIP estimates of imputed rents on owner-occupied housing.)

3. Since the amount from private transfer payments was not included in the CHIP 1988 questionnaire, the average amount of net transfer payments in 1988 may be relatively overestimated. Prior to 2013, China did not have a pension program in the rural areas, so rural pension income was zero in the earlier years.

4. A major reason that invisible public transfers through grain marketing are not included as public payments is the lack of detailed information on grain sales in the CHIP surveys. A relatively detailed questionnaire survey on sales of agricultural products was distributed only in the CHIP 1988 survey, and few households sold the same products through different marketing channels (such as grain quotas, contract sales with the government, and sales through the free market). Therefore, identification of the appropriate market prices for specific grains will produce considerable measurement errors, resulting in an inaccurate measurement of agricultural income. However, agricultural inputs tended to be distributed at discount prices to farmers who met the grain quota, inputs that partially supplemented the hidden losses stemming from the grain quota. Because the CHIP survey does not contain detailed price and quantity data on agricultural inputs, it is difficult to come up with an accurate measurement of the invisible public transfers through grain marketing channels in terms of both input and output markets.

5. Indirect public transfers based on the policy of "two exemptions and one subsidy" (liangmian yibu) were implemented nationwide in 2006. The subsidy consists of an exemption from tuition and textbook fees for all rural households and subsidies for poor boarding students in rural areas. Li and Luo (2007), by utilizing the urban/rural income gap in China based on the average public education expenditure in the urban and rural areas as an estimate of the direct subsidies to households, argue that the urban/rural income gap increased when public education expenditures and other social services were incorporated into household income.

6. See Sato, Li, and Yue (2008) for a discussion of regressivity in rural taxation in 2002, including the unpaid labor contributions.

7. See National Bureau of Statistics (2014). The corresponding nominal monthly wage of migrant laborers was 1417 yuan in 2009 and 2609 yuan in 2013. The total number of rural off-farm laborers including those who were employed within their home townships was 225.4 million in 2008 and 268.9 million in 2013.

8. It should be noted that self-consumption of agricultural products by rural households accounted for a large share of total and farm management income. Specifically, the shares of self-consumption of agricultural products in farm management and total income accounted for 62.6 percent in 1988 and 47.1 percent in 1995. An evaluation of self-consumption involves the problem of how to estimate "market prices." The CHIP 1988 survey questionnaire required that respondents evaluate the value of self-consumption of agricultural products by market price. Because the development of

agricultural markets remained at a preliminary stage during the late 1980s, the estimated values contain relatively large measurement errors.

9. As discussed in Glauben, Herzfeld, and Wang (2008) and Yang (1997, 2004), the probability of obtaining off-farm occupations was determined significantly by the attributes of the rural households (i.e., age, educational level, and household size) as well as by the economic conditions in each locality.

10. According to our calculations using Nongyebu (2014), the average level of levies, fees, and other "social burdens"—43.7 yuan per capita in 2013—fell for the first time after the abolition of agricultural taxes.

11. There are also pro-poor programs that provide income to poor households, such as the cash-for-work program (Chen et al. 2014). Unfortunately, we are unable to distinguish wages from these programs from other wage earnings.

12. Luo and Sicular (2013) use the CHIP 2007 dataset to conduct a detailed analysis of *dibao* households. Because the estimated results from our re-examination of *dibao* households in 2007 are consistent with those of Luo and Sicular (2013), we omit the descriptions for 2007.

13. According to Golan, Sicular, and Umapathi (2015), who employ the CHIP 2007 and a related survey for 2008 and 2009, *dibao* participation rates in their dataset are notably lower than those in the official data during this period, as contrasted with our results for 2013. The discrepancy might be due to improvements in the *dibao*, both in terms of enforcement as well as because of increasing recognition of the *dibao* institution by rural farmers. A detailed investigation of *dibao* coverage over time is left for future research.

14. The occurrence of reimbursable transfers through medical insurance was considerably lower in Beijing, Shanxi, and Gansu.

15. See Foster, Greer, and Thorbecke (2010) for a review of the literature on the FGT indexes.

16. The current official poverty threshold is an annual per capita income of 2300 yuan, in 2010 constant prices.

References

Bernstein, T. and X. Lü (2003). *Taxation without Representation in Contemporary Rural China*. Cambridge and New York: Cambridge University Press.

Chen, Y., S. Démurger, F. Sjöholm, and J. Zheng (2014). "Pro-rural Policies, Income, and Inequality: Evaluating a Cash-for-Work Program in Rural China." *Asian Economic Papers*, 13(3), 87–114.

Fock, A. and T. Zachernuk (2006). "China—Farmers Professional Associations: Review and Policy Recommendations." World Bank EASRD Working Paper Series.

Foster, J., J. Greer, and E. Thorbecke (2010). "The Foster–Greer–Thorbecke (FGT) Poverty Measures: 25 Years Later." *Journal of Economic Inequality*, 8(4), 491–524.

Gao, L., J. Huang, and S. Rozelle (2012). "Rental Markets for Cultivated Land and Agricultural Investments in China." *Agricultural Economics*, 43(4), 391–403.

Glauben, T., T. Herzfeld, and X. Wang (2008). "Labor Market Participation of Chinese Agricultural Households: Empirical Evidence from Zhejiang Province." *Food Policy*, 33(4), 329–340.

Golan, J., T. Sicular, and N. Umapathi (2015). "Unconditional Cash Transfers in China: An Analysis of the Rural Minimum Living Standard Guarantee Program." World Bank Policy Research Working Paper, no. 7374.

Guojia tongjiju (National Bureau of Statistics), ed. (various years). *Zhongguo tongji nianjian* (China statistical yearbook). Beijing: Zhongguo tongji chubanshe.

Guojia tongjiju, Zhuhu diaocha bangongshi (Department of Household Surveys of the NBS), ed. (2014). *Zhongguo zhuhu diaocha nianjian 2014* (China yearbook of household survey 2014). Beijing: Zhongguo tongji chubanshe.

Guojia tongjiju, Zhuhu diaocha bangongshi (Department of Household Surveys of the NBS), ed. (2015). *Zhongguo nongcun pinkun jiance baogao 2015* (Poverty monitoring report of rural China 2015). Beijing: Zhongguo tongji chubanshe.

Hoken, H. (2014). "Grains: Marketing Systems and Agricultural Technologies for Low Prices," in M. Watanabe, ed., *The Disintegration of Production: Firm Strategy and Industrial Development in China*, 241–274. Cheltenham, UK: Edward Elgar.

Ikegami, A. (2012). *Chūgoku no shokuryō ryūtsū shisutemu* (The food grain distribution system of China). Tokyo: Ochanomizu Shobō.

Khan, A. R. and C. Riskin (2001). *Inequality and Poverty in China in the Age of Globalization*. New York: Oxford University Press.

Li, S. (2001). "Labor Migration and Income Distribution in Rural China," in C. Riskin, R. Zhao, and S. Li, eds., *China's Retreat from Equality: Income Distribution and Economic Transition*, 303–328. Armonk, NY: M. E. Sharpe.

Li, S. and C. Luo (2007). "Zhongguo chengxiang jumin shouru chajude chongxin guji" (Re-estimating the income gap between urban and rural households in China). *Beijing daxue xuebao (zhexue shehui kexueban)*, 44(2), 111-120.

Li, S., H. Sato, and T. Sicular, eds. (2013). *Rising Inequality in China: Challenges to a Harmonious Society*. Cambridge and New York: Cambridge University Press.

Lin, W. and C. Wong (2012). "Are Beijing's Equalization Policies Reaching the Poor? An Analysis of Direct Subsidies under the 'Three Rurals' (*Sannong*)." *China Journal*, no. 67, 23-45.

Lü, X. (1997). "The Politics of Peasant Burden in Reform China." *Journal of Peasant Studies*, 25(1), 113-138.

Luo, C. and T. Sicular (2013). "Inequality and Poverty in Rural China," in S. Li, H. Sato, and T. Sicular, eds., *Rising Inequality in China: Challenges to a Harmonious Society*, 197-229. Cambridge and New York: Cambridge University Press.

National Bureau of Statistics (NBS), Department of Household Surveys, ed. (2013). *China Yearbook of Household Survey 2013*. Beijing: China Statistics Press.

National Bureau of Statistics (NBS) (2014). *Nongmingong jiance diaocha baogao 2013* (Monitoring survey report on migrant labor in 2013). http://www.stats.gov.cn/tjsj/zxfb/201405/t20140512_551585.html. Accessed July 16, 2018.

Nongyebu (Ministry of Agriculture), ed. (2010). *Zhongguo nongye tongji ziliao 2009* (China agriculture statistical report 2009). Beijing: Zhongguo nongye chubanshe.

Nongyebu (Ministry of Agriculture), ed. (2014). *Zhongguo nongye tongji ziliao 2013* (China agriculture statistical report 2014). Beijing: Zhongguo nongye chubanshe.

Nongyebu, Nongye chanyehua bangongshi, Nongyebu nongcun jingji yanjiu zhongxin (Ministry of Agriculture, Office for Agricultural Industrialization, Research Center for the Rural Economy in the Ministry of Agriculture), ed. (2008). *Zhongguo nongye chanyehua fazhan baogao* (Development report on Chinese agricultural industrialization). Beijing: Zhongguo nongye chubanshe.

Qi, L. (2011). "Xinxing nongcun hezuo yiliao de jianpin zengshou he zaifenpei xiaoguo yanjiu" (A study of the effects of the new rural cooperative medical system on poverty alleviation, income growth, and income redistribution). *Shuliang jingji jishu jingji yanjiu*, no. 8, 35–52.

Riskin, C., R. Zhao, and S. Li, eds. (2001). *China's Retreat from Inequality: Income Distribution and Economic Transition*. Armonk, NY: M. E. Sharpe.

Sato, H., S. Li, and X. Yue (2008). "The Redistributive Impact of Taxation in Rural China, 1995–2002: An Evaluation of Rural Taxation Reform at the Turn of the Century," in B. Gustafsson, S. Li, and T. Sicular, eds., *Inequality and Public Policy in China*, 312–336. Cambridge and New York: Cambridge University Press.

Sato, H., T. Sicular, and X. Yue (2013). "Housing Ownership, Incomes, and Inequality in China," in S. Li, H. Sato, and T. Sicular, eds., *Rising Inequality in China: Challenge to a Harmonious Society*, 85–141. Cambridge and New York: Cambridge University Press.

Sato, H. and Y. Wang (2014). "The Redistributive Impact of Pro-Rural Policies in the Western Ethnic Minority Regions of China." Mimeograph.

Shorrocks, A. F. (1982). "Inequality Decomposition by Factor Components." *Econometrica*, 50(1), 193–211.

Tian, J. Q. (2009). "Reorganizing Rural Public Finance: Reforms and Consequences." *Journal of Current Chinese Affairs*, 38(4), 145–171.

Wang, Z. (2010). "Xin nongcun jianshe de shouru zaifenpei xiaoying" (The income redistribution effects from construction of the new socialist countryside). *Jingji yanjiu*, no. 6, 17–27.

Yang, D. T. (1997). "Education and Off-Farm Work." *Economic Development and Cultural Change*, 45(3), 613–632.

Yang, D. T. (2004). "Education and Allocative Efficiency: Household Income Growth during Rural Reforms in China." *Journal of Development Economics*, 74(1), 137–162.

Yep, R. (2004). "Can 'Tax-For-Fee' Reform Reduce Rural Tension in China? The Process, Progress and Limitations." *China Quarterly*, no. 177, 42–70.

Zhang, P. (2001). "Rural Interregional Inequality and Off-Farm Employment in China," in C. Riskin, R. Zhao, and S. Li, eds., *China's Retreat from Equality: Income Distribution and Economic Transition*, 213–228. Armonk, NY: M. E. Sharpe.

Zhonggong zhongyang and Guowuyuan (Central Committee of the Communist Party of China and the State Council) (2005). "Zhonggong zhongyang guowuyuan guanyu jinyibu jiaqiang nongcun gongzuo tigao nongye zonghe shengchan nengli ruogan zhengce de yijian" (Comments by the Central Committee of the Chinese Communist Party and the State Council on reinforcing rural work and improving comprehensive agricultural productivity), December 31, 2004. http://www.gov.cn/gongbao/content/2005/content_63347.htm. Accessed January 7, 2017.

7

New Patterns in China's Rural Poverty

Shi Li, Peng Zhan, and Yangyang Shen

7.1 Introduction

Since the Chinese reform and opening policies, the number of Chinese poor people as well as China's poverty rate have declined dramatically, thus contributing to global poverty reduction. After promulgation of the policies of the "National Eight-Seven Poverty Alleviation Program (1994–2000)" (*Guojia baqi fupin gongjian jihua* [1994-2000]) and "China's Rural Poverty Alleviation and Development Project (2001-2010)" (*Zhongguo nongcun fupin kaifa gangyao* [2001-2010]) (Zhonggong zhongyang and Guowuyuan 2011), in 2010 the Chinese government released "China's Rural Poverty Alleviation and Development Project (2011–2020)," with the goals of "achieving no worries about food and clothing, and guarantees for compulsory education, basic medical care, and housing" (*liang bu chou, san baozhang*) by 2020. In 2015 the Chinese government released its "Decision on Winning the Anti-Poverty Battle" (*Guanyu daying tuolu gongjianzhan de jueding*), further supplementing the goal of "ensuring that all rural subjects will escape poverty under current standards" (Zhonggong zhongyang and Guowuyuan 2015). Regarding specific actions, the "five measurements" (*wuge yipi*) were raised by President Xi Jinping at the Poverty Reduction and Development Forum on October 16, 2015. However, after many years of effort the structure of poverty has changed and the difficulties of antipoverty work have gradually increased (World Bank 2009). To achieve future goals, we need to better understand existing poverty patterns.

With respect to the poverty patterns, there are two key issues: first, the geographical distribution of poverty has become more dispersed than it was during the early stage of reform and opening, when most of the rural population was living in poverty. The result is that poverty targeting now faces new challenges. The targets of the poverty alleviation policies must be more precise. Second, the Chinese economy has now become the second largest

Shi Li, Peng Zhan, and Yangyang Shen, *New Patterns in China's Rural Poverty* In: *Changing Trends in China's Inequality*. Edited by: Terry Sicular, Shi Li, Ximing Yue, and Hiroshi Sato, Oxford University Press (2020). © Oxford University Press.
DOI: 10.1093/oso/9780190077938.003.0007

economy in the world, and economic conditions, the economic structure, and government efforts to implement rural social security are much different from what they were in the 1980s. There are now more options for antipoverty policies. Against this background, we must have a better understanding of poverty achievements and difficulties vis-à-vis the problems in the past.

The Chinese government, the World Bank, and independent researchers have estimated China's poverty head-count ratio. The World Bank has released poverty indexes for more than 100 countries, in which China's poverty indexes are grouped according to consumption rather than according to the original microdata.[1] Furthermore, the World Bank reports only national, rather than rural, poverty indexes. According to these national data and the poverty level of US$1.9 per day, the proportion of the Chinese population living in poverty to the world's total declined from 43.95 percent in 1981 to 9.75 percent in 2012 (Wang 2012). China's National Bureau of Statistics (NBS) releases annual head-count ratios to support the antipoverty projects.[2] According to the NBS results using the new poverty line of 2300 yuan in 2010 prices, the rural head-count ratios were 97.5 percent, 78.3 percent, 73.5 percent, 60.5 percent, 49.8 percent, 30.2 percent, and 4.5 percent in 1978, 1985, 1990, 1995, 2000, 2005, and 2016, respectively. China has clearly made remarkable achievements since the 1980s.

For rural areas, the Chinese government has released estimates of annual head-count ratios based on the new poverty line,[3] but they are insufficient to determine the poverty alleviation trends during the past decades. Using a subsample of the Rural Household Survey of the NBS, Ravallion and Chen (2007) have estimated the head-count ratios from 1980 to 2001, based on an annual poverty level of 850 yuan per person at 2002 prices; and Chen and Ravallion (2008) have estimated the head-count ratios from 1980 to 2005 at US$1.25 per day and at US$2 per day. The standard of 850 yuan at 2002 prices is a little less than the low poverty level in this chapter.[4] According to this standard, the head-count ratios were 75.7 percent in 1980, 23.15 percent in 1988, and 12.5 percent in 2001. Other recent research has also reported estimates of China's level of poverty. Luo and Sicular (2013) calculated the head-count ratios in rural China for the years 2002 to 2007 on the basis of alternate measures: 1.) the measure of absolute poverty—using the standard of US$1.25 per day, and 1196 yuan per year at 2008 prices, and 2.) the measure of relative poverty, with the poverty line set at 50 percent or 60 percent of the median income, a measure that is one of the few academic efforts that estimates China's relative rural poverty. On the basis of additional national survey data, Zhang et al. (2014) estimated China's head-count ratios in 2009 and 2010. For their analysis, they used microdata from three independent surveys: the China Family Panel Survey (CFPS), the Chinese General Social Survey (CGSS), and the China Household Finance Survey (CHFS). They find that the head-count ratios calculated using data from these independent surveys are higher than the official rates.

On the basis of the background of China's poverty alleviation efforts and the findings in the existing literature, this chapter uses data from various years of the CHIP survey to analyze China's new poverty patterns and to discuss the implications for current and future poverty alleviation work in China. We ask two principal questions: 1.) What are the features of the population living in poverty? 2.) What are the reasons for poverty and how have they changed compared to in the past?

The next section will introduce the poverty standards, evaluation approaches, and the CHIP data. The third section will report on the distribution of poverty in China on the basis of Chinese official data and the CHIP data. Section 7.4 describes the structure of poverty during the various periods. Section 7.5, based on a probit regression model, examines the principal factors associated with poverty. Finally, Section 7.6 presents our conclusions.

7.2 Background and Evaluation Approaches

7.2.1 Poverty Standards

All China's official poverty standards, including the 1978 standard, the 2008 standard, and the 2010 standard, are absolute poverty standards (Wang 2015). These official poverty standards are based on 625 yuan per year at prices in the year 2000, 1196 yuan per year at prices in the year 2008, and 2300 yuan per year at prices in the year 2010. We call these poverty standards the "dire poverty level," the "low poverty level," and the "new poverty level." The NBS has also calculated poverty levels for some other years by using a consumer price index (CPI) for rural poor households. These poverty estimates are reported in the *Chinese Household Survey Yearbook* and the *China Rural Poverty Monitoring Report*. However, the NBS has not released details about the calculation process. In the *China Rural Poverty Monitoring Report* (Guojia tongjiju, Zhuhu diaocha bangongshi 2015), the current poverty standard is equal to 60 percent of the cost of food (Wang 2015) (see Table A7.1).

On the basis of this information, we define a "Chinese rural poor household consumption price index (CRHCPI)" which is equal to Rural CPI × 0.4 + Rural Food CPI × 0.6.[5] The rural food CPI was not published prior to 1996, so for earlier years we replace it with the national food CPI. Using the CRHCPI, we derive the poverty standards in the other years, as reported in Table 7.1.

In terms of international comparisons, the accepted standards have been introduced by the World Bank. In 2008, on the basis of the average poverty levels in the fifteen poorest countries, the World Bank formulated a global poverty standard of US$1.25 per day. This figure indicates a basic subsistence level, referring to minimal expenditures for basic food and basic non-food needs (Wang 2015). The US$1.25 and US$2 per day figures are based on the 2005 PPP. In December 2015 the World Bank updated the two standards to US$1.9 per day and US$3.1 per day according to the 2011 PPP exchange rates from the 2011 International Comparison Program.[6] Using the 2011 PPP and China's CPI,[7] we arrive at the values for the other years (see Table 7.1). For consistency with the NBS poverty standards, we also use the CRHCPI as the price deflators

Table 7.1. Poverty standards, yuan per person per year

	World Bank		Official Chinese		Relative poverty level
Year	US$1.9 per day	US$3.1 per day	Low poverty level	New poverty level	
1988	544	888	368	651	229
1995	1262	2059	855	1510	723
2002	1272	2075	869	1522	1045
2007	1636	2669	1067	1957	1713
2013	2270	3703	1505	2736	3838

Notes: 1.) The poverty standards (poverty lines) in this table were adjusted by rural China's PPP from the 2011 International Comparison Program; the PPP values are found in the World Bank database. 2.) The "new poverty level," "low poverty level," and "relative poverty level" are 2300 yuan at 2010 prices, 1196 yuan at 2008 prices, and 50 percent of the median income in each year, respectively. 3.) The values of the World Bank standards, the "new poverty level" in 1988, 1995, 2002, and 2007, and the "low poverty level" in 1988, 1995, and 2013 are adjusted by the CPI of the rural poor households, as explained in Table A7.2.

Sources: Authors' calculations.

In addition, this chapter considers the relative poverty standards, which place more emphasis on the households' relative income levels rather than on absolute income or basic food and clothing needs. Relative poverty standards do not consider basic needs and so implicitly assume that basic needs do not define poverty. When the level of real income in a society has increased sufficiently so that basic needs are met for virtually all of the population, the relative poverty level is useful and targets a more important segment of the population. Thus, as income levels grow relative poverty standards become more relevant. On the basis of other research, we use 50 percent of the median income as the relative poverty line.

7.2.2 Evaluation Approaches

As in Chapter 6, the index that we use to evaluate poverty is the FGT index (Foster, Greer, and Thorbecke 1984):

$$\text{FGT}(\alpha) = \frac{1}{N} \sum_{i=1}^{H} \left(\frac{z - y_i}{z} \right)^{\alpha}$$

in which N is the number of people, H is the number of people below the poverty line, z is the poverty line, y_i is the income of person i, and α is the poverty aversion coefficient.[8] The larger the value of α, the greater the aversion to poverty, or the more weight placed on low-income individuals. FGT(0) is the head-count ratio usually reported in the literature. FGT(1) is sometimes called the poverty gap or poverty depth, and FGT(2) is sometimes called the squared poverty gap or the weighted poverty gap. Compared to FGT(0), which counts only the number of people who are poor, FGT(1) considers the income gap between the per capita income of poor households and the poverty line; compared to FGT(1), FGT(2) gives higher weights for lower per capita income. Therefore, if the per capita incomes of most of the poor households are concentrated near zero and far below the poverty line, the poverty gap and the squared poverty gap will be very large. In other words, larger values for FGT(1) and FGT(2) mean that extreme poverty is higher.

7.3 Rural Data

We use the data from the 1988, 1995, 2002, 2007, and 2013 waves of the CHIP surveys. In our analysis we use all provinces in the samples. The provinces differ somewhat during the various waves of the CHIP survey; we employ regional (East/West/Central) population weights to achieve results at the national level that are comparable over time (see Chapter 1). The target variable for our calculations is per capita household income. Some chapters in this volume use the CHIP income definition, which includes imputed housing income and in-kind subsidies. Since the poverty standards of the NBS and the World Bank do not consider these additional components, in this chapter we use the NBS income definition.

For the analysis of poverty trends, we use all five waves of the CHIP survey data, but we use only the CHIP 2002 and the CHIP 2013 for the relation-- ship analysis and the causal analysis. There are three reasons for this: 1.) The questionnaires for the CHIP 1988 and the CHIP 1995 were quite different from the other questionnaires. 2.) There are two parts to the CHIP 2007: 8000 households in the CHIP questionnaire and 5000 households selected from the NBS database. Together the two parts of the survey are nationally rep-resentative, but each part is not nationally representative. Unfortunately, the main household information, except for income and expenditures, in these two parts is different. 3.) The Chinese government issued the National Program for Rural Poverty Alleviation (2001-2010) in 2001 and the National Program for Rural Poverty Alleviation (2011-2020) in 2011. The analysis based on the data from the CHIP 2002-2013 can be used as a reference to evaluate the practical effects of the poverty alleviation policies during this initial period of the new century.

We also consider interregional price disparities and adjust the normal in-come values by the regional PPP in each year. The adjusted results are com-pared to the normal results to provide two pieces of additional information: 1.) When the regional price differences are removed, how are the head-count ratio and the poverty gap affected? 2.) What is the impact of interregional price disparities and their trends on the overall poverty situation? Brandt and Holz (2006) give estimates of the 1990 PPP and the 2000 PPP indexes.[9] We adjusted the 2000 PPP to 2002, 2007, and 2013 by the provincial rural CPI. However, we did not find the provincial rural CPI for the years prior to 1996. Thus, we assume the 1988 PPP to be equal to the 1990 PPP and the 1995 PPP to be equal to the average of the 1990 PPP and the 2000 PPP.

7.4 Poverty Distribution

7.4.1 Poverty Trends in the Years since 1988

Since the start of China's reform and opening policies, the population living in poverty and the rate of poverty have both decreased significantly. Figure 7.1 shows the official poverty statistics over time. According to the earliest official poverty standard (the "dire poverty level" in this chapter), the incidence rate of rural poverty fell from 30.7 percent in 1978 to 1.6 percent in 2007. In 2008 the Chinese government raised the poverty standard to 1196 yuan per year (the "low poverty level" in this chapter). The head-count ratio at this new standard was 10.2 percent in 2008 but it decreased to 2.8 percent in 2010. In 2011 the poverty standard changed to 2300 yuan per year at 2010 prices (the "new poverty level" in this chapter). The head-count ratio at this new standard reached 17.2 percent but by 2017 it had decreased to 3.2 percent. No matter which standard is used, the population living in poverty declined dramatically. It should be noted that this decline slowed down from 2010 to 2014 but then accelerated in 2015, when 14.42 million persons escaped poverty and the head-count ratio declined by 1.5 percentage points. Based on the 2010–2014 trends, the reduction in 2015 can be considered

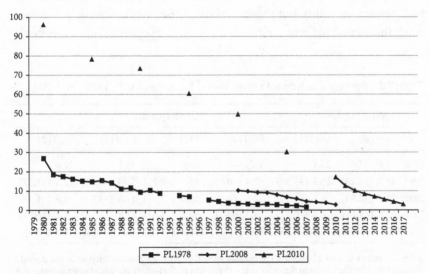

Fig. 7.1 Head-count ratio trends in China, 1978-2017 (%)
Source: Guojia tongjiju, Zhuhu diaocha bangongshi (2018).

amazing. Furthermore, this reduction continued in 2016. The main reason is the government's strengthening of its poverty alleviation efforts in 2015, for example, with the "five measurements" program introduced by President Xi Jinping.

From the comparability of the estimates of the poverty head-count ratios over the long run, the *China Rural Poverty Monitoring Report* (Guojia tongjiju, Zhuhu diaocha bangongshi, various years) released by the NBS in recent years reports trends in the incidence of Chinese rural poverty since the reform and opening on the basis of the 2010 poverty standard. However, one single indicator is insufficient to understand the overall changing characteristics of China's poverty patterns. Therefore, on the basis of the CHIP data we re-computed some comparable evaluation indexes during different periods. The results are shown in Table 7.2 and Table 7.3.[10] These are helpful to understand the current poverty situation from a retrospective perspective. The following are our main findings.

1.) The head-count ratios fell sharply between 1988 and 2013. According to the 2010 new poverty standard, the head-count ratios fell from 75.6 percent in 1988 to 8.8 percent in 2013. Our 2013 result is similar to the NBS result of 8.5 percent. This implies that the CHIP data can be considered representative of Chinese rural poverty. However, despite China's remarkable achievements in poverty reduction, there is still considerable pressure for future work. The total head-count ratio reduction between 1988 and 2013 was 66.8 percentage points, but the annual reduction rates slowed down. Before 2002, the annual reduction rate was 3.2 percentage points, but thereafter it

Table 7.2. Poverty head-count ratios, World Bank standards, 1988-2013 (%)

	US$1.9 per day			US$3.1per day		
	FGT(0)	FGT(1)	FGT(2)	FGT(0)	FGT(1)	FGT(2)
1988	63.6	23.5	12.3 —	89.0	45.1	27.0
1995	41.3 (−3.19)	13.8 (−1.38)	7.4 (−0.69)	73.4 (−2.23)	31.3 (−1.96)	17.4 (−1.37)
2002	21.4 (−2.84)	6.1 (−1.10)	2.6 (−0.69)	49.5 (−3.41)	17.6 (−1.96)	8.5 (−1.26)
2007	13.3 (−1.61)	4.4 (−0.32)	5.5 (0.57)	34.3 (−3.03)	11.8 (−1.16)	7.1 (−0.27)
2013	6.2 (−1.18)	3.5 (−0.15)	16.6 (1.85)	15.9 (−3.06)	6.3 (−0.91)	9.3 (0.35)

Note: The values in parentheses are the average annual percentage point reduction in the poverty indexes, equal to (the results in the latter year − the results in the former year)/(the years between the former year and the latter year).

Sources: Calculated from the rural CHIP data for 1988, 1995, 2002, 2007, and 2013.

Table 7.3. Poverty head-count ratios, NBS standards, and relative standards, 1988–2013 (%)

	New poverty level			Low poverty level			Relative poverty level		
	FGT(0)	FGT(1)	FGT(2)	FGT(0)	FGT(1)	FGT(2)	FGT(0)	FGT(1)	FGT(2)
1988	75.6	31.1	16.9	33.6	11.2	6.0	11.5	4.6	3.2
1995	53.3 (−3.18)	19.3 (−1.68)	10.2 (−0.95)	19.7 (−1.98)	5.7 (−0.78)	4.6 (−0.19)	13.0 (0.22)	3.8 (−0.10)	4.6 (0.19)
2002	30.5 (−3.25)	9.3 (−1.42)	4.1 (−0.86)	8.5 (−1.59)	2.2 (−0.50)	0.9 (−0.53)	13.4 (0.06)	3.6 (−0.02)	1.5 (−0.43)
2007	19.4 (−2.22)	6.4 (−0.59)	5.4 (0.25)	4.8 (−0.74)	2.2 (0)	8.4 (1.50)	14.7 (0.25)	4.9 (0.25)	5.4 (0.77)
2013	8.8 (−1.76)	4.2 (−0.36)	12.6 (1.19)	2.6 (−0.36)	3.1 (0.16)	33.6 (4.19)	17.0 (0.38)	6.6 (0.28)	9.1 (0.61)

Notes: 1.) "New poverty level," "low poverty level," and "relative poverty level" are respectively 2300 yuan in 2010 prices, 1196 yuan in 2008 prices, and 50 percent of the median income in each year. 2.) The values in parentheses are the average annual percentage point change, equal to (the results in the latter year − the results in the former year)/(the years between the former year and the latter year).

Sources: Calculated from the rural CHIP data for 1988, 1995, 2002, 2007, and 2013.

decreased to 2 percentage points per year. However, this slowdown does not indicate that the Chinese government's poverty reduction efforts have weakened. In fact, a poverty reduction of 2 percentage points for over ten years can be considered an impressive achievement. As the population living in poverty has been reduced, most of the people left living in poverty are those who are extremely poor and geographically dispersed, and thus very difficult to lift out of poverty. They therefore present a major challenge to antipoverty work during the new period. Similar conclusions based on the World Bank standards can be drawn. With the use of the relatively high US$3.1 standard, the head-count ratio reached 89.0 percent in 1988 and 15.9 percent in 2013, a cumulative decrease of 73.1 percentage points. The difference is that the decline in the poverty rate seems to have been a relatively high rate over twenty-five years, even during the 2007–2013 period, and the annual reduction may be close to 3 percentage points. Compared with the decreasing speed of the head-count ratios between the new poverty standard and the US$3.1 standard, the income of low- and middle-income groups grew slightly faster than that of the extremely poor.

2.) The number of people living in poverty declined substantially from 1988 to 2013, but the poverty gap and squared poverty gap did not continue to decline accordingly. The poverty gap calculated according to the new poverty standard declined year by year, but the average annual decline decreased from –1.68 percentage points per year during the 1988–1992 period to –0.36 percentage points per year during the 2007–2013 period. However, if the low poverty standard is used, the poverty gap hardly changed during the 2002–2007 period and it rose during the 2007–2013 period. The increasing trend during the latter period implies additional difficulties for the extremely poor groups to benefit from the poverty-reduction activities. The squared poverty gap suggests a similar conclusion. During the 2002–2007 and 2007–2013 periods, the squared poverty gap increased, reaching 12.6 percent in 2013. Similar conclusions can be drawn by using the World Bank standards. Even with the relatively high US$3.1 standard, the squared poverty gap rose during the 2007–2013 period, reaching 9.3 percent in 2013.

3.) Relative poverty has continued to increase since 1998. At present, China does not have an official relative poverty standard, but this omission does not mean that a relative measure is not important in the new era. In 2014 the Chinese government proposed that poverty would be eliminated under the current standards by 2020. According to official estimates, the poverty head-count ratio in rural areas fell to only 1 percent in 2018. After 2020, therefore, the use of a relative measure may be relevant. In general, the incidence of relative poverty has gradually increased along with the trend of increasing income inequality—from only 11.5 percent in 1988 to 17.0 percent in 2013. If this trend continues, it will remain a difficult task to eliminate poverty after 2020. From the perspective of the poverty gap and the squared poverty gap, there was an increase between 2002 and 2013. This increase shows that among the relatively poor, the extremely poor can be considered to be still a very serious problem. The poverty gap and the squared poverty gap under the relative poverty standard of 2013 reached 6.6 percent and 9.1 percent respectively.

7.4.2 Geographical Distribution

Because of the development gaps among the different regions, geographical differences among the population living in poverty are expected. Table A7.2 and Table A7.3 report the head-count ratios in different regions.

7.4.2.1 Regional Poverty Disparities

Figure 7.2 shows the provincial head-count ratios and log per capita GDPs in 2014. It reveals an overall negative relationship between the head-count ratio and the log per capita GDP: the head-count ratio is higher at a lower level of economic development. On the basis of this figure we can roughly classify the provinces into five groups: 1.) the highest head-count ratio and the lowest economic level, including Tibet, Gansu, Guizhou, and Yunnan; 2.) the relatively high head-count ratio and the relatively low economic level, including Guangxi, Qinghai, Shaanxi, Shanxi, Ningxia, Hunan, Hubei, Hainan, Jiangxi, Anhui, Henan, Heilongjiang, Hebei, Chongqing, and Jilin; 3.) the relatively low head-count ratio and the relatively high economic level, including Inner Mongolia, Liaoning, Shandong, Fujian, Guangdong, Jiangsu, and Zhejiang; 4.) a zero head-count ratio and the highest economic level, including Beijing, Tianjin, and Shanghai; 5.) provinces that are outliers and do not fit the general pattern, a category that includes only Xinjiang province, with almost the highest head-count ratio but a relatively low economic level. The various province groups face different situations and require different antipoverty strategies. Almost all the West provinces are classified in Group 1, Group 2, and Group 5. Gansu, Guizhou, and Yunnan remain the main poverty strongholds. Because Xinjiang province faces a complex ethnic problem, the difficulties in antipoverty work are further exacerbated.

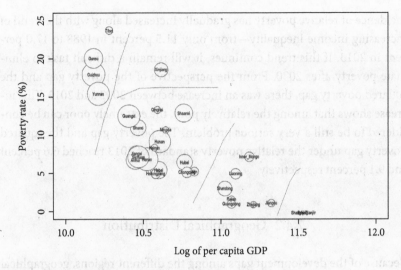

Fig. 7.2 Regional head-count ratios in China, 2014

Note: The area of the circles reflects the size of the provincial poverty population.

Sources: The provincial poverty populations and rates come from the Leading Group of the Office of Poverty Alleviation and Development of the State Council. Per capita GDP comes from the NBS website.

The CHIP results in Table 7.4 provide additional information for the years 1988 to 2013, including results based on other poverty standards.[11] With respect to differences in regional poverty levels, the head-count ratios in the West are 1.5 times higher than those in the East, and the head-count ratios in Central China are about double those in the East.

7.4.2.2 Trends in Poverty Reduction in Different Regions

The speed of poverty reduction in the East and Central regions was faster than that in the West region before 2002, whereas the speed of poverty reduction in the West region was faster than that in other regions after 2002. According to the results for the new poverty standard, the annual decline in the East region from 1988 to 2002 was about 2.91 percentage points, but it was reduced to 1.13 percentage points from 2002 to 2007 and then to 0.82 percentage point from 2007 to 2013. However, the speed in the West region was 2.44, 3.81, 2.86 and 3.03 percentage points during the four periods. The results based on the poverty standard of US$1.9 per day reveal the same phenomenon.

There may be two reasons for the differential pattern of poverty reduction among regions: 1.) During the early periods, the government emphasized

Table 7.4. Regional head-count ratios, new poverty level, 1988-2013 (%)

		New poverty level					
		FGT(0)		FGT(1)		FGT(2)	
East	1988	57.7	—	21.3	—	11.4	—
	1995	37.7	(−2.86)	13.3	(−1.14)	8.1	(−0.46)
	2002	15.5	(−3.17)	4.9	(−1.20)	2.3	(−0.83)
	2007	9.8	(−1.13)	4.4	(−0.09)	9.6	(1.46)
	2013	4.9	(−0.82)	2.9	(−0.24)	14.4	(0.79)
Central	1988	82.9	—	33.3	—	17.5	—
	1995	52.3	(−4.37)	17.2	(−2.29)	8.6	(−1.27)
	2002	30.9	(−3.05)	8.6	(−1.22)	3.6	(−0.71)
	2007	17.7	(−2.64)	5.1	(−0.71)	2.3	(−0.25)
	2013	9.0	(−1.44)	3.9	(−0.19)	4.6	(0.38)
West	1988	88.9	—	40.7	—	22.8	—
	1995	71.7	(−2.44)	28.5	(−1.74)	14.4	(−1.20)
	2002	45.0	(−3.81)	14.5	(−1.98)	6.6	(−1.11)
	2007	30.7	(−2.86)	9.7	(−0.96)	4.6	(−0.40)
	2013	12.5	(−3.03)	5.8	(−0.65)	19.5	(2.48)

Notes: 1.) The "new poverty level" is 2300 yuan in 2010 prices. 2.) The values in parentheses are the average annual changes in the head-count ratios, equal to (the results in the latter year – the results in the former year)/(the years between the former year and the latter year).
Sources: Calculated from the rural CHIP data for 1988, 1995, 2002, 2007, and 2013.

development in the East, resulting in an increase in the income of residents in the East. 2.) During the early periods, the main purpose of the poverty alleviation projects was economic development, thus benefiting the middle low-income residents more than the extremely low-income residents who were mainly concentrated in the West. With respect to the latter, until the beginning of the new century we find some evidence that coverage of the pension system and medical insurance in the rural regions was far below that in the urban regions. Meanwhile, the agricultural tax was not abolished until 2006 (Luo and Sicular 2013). During the first ten years of the new century, with the abolition of the agricultural tax, the strengthening of the rural minimum living security system, and the promotion of many transfer policies, the speed of poverty reduction in the West region that could not benefit from economic growth was accelerating.

7.4.2.3 Poverty Gaps in Different Regions

The extreme poverty problems are mainly concentrated in the East and Central regions. The squared poverty gaps in those regions are relatively high. Under the new poverty line, the squared poverty gaps are 14.4 percent and 19.5 percent in the East and West regions, respectively. If the low poverty standard is used, the squared poverty gaps may exceed 40 percent. This result suggests that there are households with disposable income or net income that is very close to zero or even negative. One likely reason for the fairly high squared poverty gap in the East region is that the benefits of economic development in the East region did not adequately reach the extremely poor households. Another possible reason is that with the development of a market economy, there may be more households with negative net income from production and operations because of market reasons. In the West region, a likely reason was the special characteristics of many West households that weakened the effects of the poverty alleviation programs. For example, many minority nationalities reside in the West region and some of their habits and customs are quite different from those of the people living in the East.

7.4.2.4 Relative Head-Count Ratios in Different Regions

Most of those who live in relative poverty are concentrated in the West region, where the rates of relative poverty have not changed significantly since the 1990s. In contrast, the relative head-count ratios in the Central region increased dramatically: from 1995 to 2013 annual growth was about 0.06 percentage point. At the same time, annual growth in the relative head-count ratio was only 0.13 percentage point in the East region. The trend in the relative head-count ratio in the West region was less clear, since the relative head-count ratio increased from 1988 to 1995 and from 2002 to 2007 but decreased during the other periods. When the policy emphasis changed to relative poverty, the West and Central regions remained the focal points.

7.5 The Impact of Regional Prices

When we consider regional prices and adjust household income by the regional PPP indexes, in some years the head-count ratios changed considerably. We call these the "adjusted head-count ratios," as opposed to the previous unadjusted head-count ratios. Most of the adjusted head-count ratios are higher than the unadjusted rates (Table 7.5). In 2013 the former were about 21 percent higher than the latter, and in the West region the gap between the two was even larger at about 27 percent (Table 7.7).

Why are most of the head-count ratios higher after adjusting for the regional prices? The reason is that some low-income provinces have higher prices. Figure 7.3 and Figure 7.4 examine the relationship between the provincial PPP price index and per capita GDP and between the provincial PPP price index and per capita income. The provincial per capita GDP was reported by the NBS, and the provincial per capita income was calculated using the CHIP data. Regardless of which indicator is used to reflect the level of regional development, the PPP index in some low-income provinces such as Gansu and Shaanxi is higher than that in other provinces. We also fit a cubic polynomial curve for the data in each year and show the curve in the figures. It is very clear that these curves assume a significant "U-shape" in 2002 and 2013, especially in 2002, whereas it is not significant in 1988. The consequence of this phenomenon is that the gap between the adjusted head-count ratios and the unadjusted head-count ratios has been increasing since 1988. When we divide the country into the East, Central, and West regions, we find the gaps in the West to be more serious.

However, the adjusted squared poverty gaps produce a different outcome. We report the results of FGT(2) in the table. The trend in the ratios between the adjusted squared poverty gaps and the unadjusted squared poverty gaps

Table 7.5. Poverty head-count ratios with PPP adjustments, World Bank standards, 1988-2013 (%)

	US$1.9 per day			US$3.1 per day		
	FGT(0)	FGT(1)	FGT(2)	FGT(0)	FGT(1)	FGT(2)
1988	63.4	23.3	12.1	90.0	45.2	27.0
1995	42.6 (−2.96)	14.6 (−1.24)	7.9 (−0.59)	74.1 (−2.26)	32.2 (−1.86)	18.1 (−1.26)
2002	24.2 (−2.62)	7.7 (−0.98)	3.5 (−0.63)	51.8 (−3.19)	19.6 (−1.79)	10.0 (−1.15)
2007	15.1 (−1.81)	5.4 (−0.45)	5.9 (0.49)	36.3 (−3.08)	13.2 (−1.27)	8.1 (−0.38)
2013	7.7 (−1.24)	3.9 (−0.24)	14.9 (1.49)	18.8 (−2.91)	7.4 (−0.97)	9.1 (0.16)

Notes: The values in parentheses are the average annual changes in the poverty evaluations. They are equal to (the results in the latter year − the results in the former year)/(the years between the former year and the latter year).

Sources: Calculated from the rural CHIP data for 1988, 1995, 2002, 2007, and 2013.

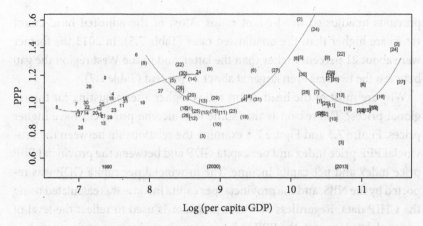

Fig. 7.3 The relationship between the PPP price index and per capita GDP (log) at the provincial level, 1990-2013

Note: The lines in the figure are the fitted cubic polynomial curves.

Sources: The regional PPP is from Brandt and Holz (2006), with further calculations by the authors. Per capita GDP is from the NBS.

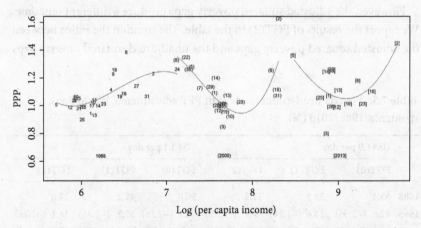

1 Anhui; 2 Beijing; 3 Chongqing; 4 Fujian; 5 Gansu; 6 Guangdong; 7 Guangxi; 8 Guizhou; 9 Hainan; 10 Hebei; 11 Heilongjiang; 12 Henan; 13 Hubei; 14 Hunan; 15 Inner Mongolia; 16 Jiangsu; 17 Jiangxi; 18 Jilin; 19 Liaoning; 20 Ningxia; 21 Qinghai; 22 Shaanxi; 23 Shandong; 24 Shanghai; 25 Shanxi; 26 Sichuan; 27 Tianjin; 28 Tibet; 29 Xinjiang; 30 Yunnan; 31 Zhejiang

Fig. 7.4 The relationship between the PPP price index and per capita income (log) at the provincial level, 1988-2013

Note: The lines in the figure are the fitted cubic polynomial curves.

Sources: The regional PPP is from Brandt and Holz (2006), with further calculations by the authors. Per capita income is calculated from the CHIP data for 1988, 2002, and 2013.

Table 7.6. Poverty head-count ratios with PPP adjustments, NBS standards, 1988–2013 (%)

	New poverty levels			Low poverty levels			Relative poverty levels		
	FGT(0)	FGT(1)	FGT(2)	FGT(0)	FGT(1)	FGT(2)	FGT(0)	FGT(1)	FGT(2)
1988	76.0	31.0	16.7	33.5	11.0	5.9	11.1	4.5	3.2
1995	54.3 (−3.09)	20.2 (−1.54)	10.8 (−0.84)	21.3 (−1.74)	6.4 (−0.66)	4.8 (−0.16)	14.5 (0.49)	4.3 (−0.03)	4.6 (0.19)
2002	33.3 (−3.00)	11.2 (−1.29)	5.3 (−0.79)	10.9 (−1.47)	3.1 (−0.47)	1.3 (−0.49)	16.9 (0.33)	4.9 (0.08)	2.1 (−0.35)
2007	21.7 (−2.32)	7.5 (−0.72)	6.1 (0.16)	6.4 (−0.91)	2.7 (−0.08)	8.6 (1.45)	17.0 (0.03)	5.9 (0.20)	5.9 (0.75)
2013	10.6 (−1.84)	4.8 (−0.45)	11.6 (0.92)	3.4 (−0.50)	3.2 (0.09)	29.5 (3.48)	19.9 (0.47)	7.8 (0.31)	9.0 (0.51)

Notes: 1.) The "new poverty level," "low poverty level," and "relative poverty level" were 2300 yuan in 2010 prices, 1196 yuan in 2008 prices, and 50 percent of the median income in each year. 2.) The values in parentheses are the average annual changes in the head-count ratios. They are equal to (the results in the latter year − the results in the former year)/(the years between the former and latter years).

Sources: Calculated from the rural CHIP data for 1988, 1995, 2002, 2007, and 2013.

was greater than 100 percent in 2002 but less than 100 percent in 1988 and 2013. The ratio of the adjusted versus unadjusted squared poverty gap was lower than 100 percent, but the ratio for the head-count ratio was higher than 100 percent, indicating that the extremely low-income households had a lower PPP, whereas the less extremely low-income households had a higher PPP. This situation appears in 2013 but not in either 2002 or 2007. In about 2002, regional prices of most of the extremely low-income households were still very high. This trend was more obvious in the West area. It may be a consequence of the economic development and poverty alleviation programs since 2007. This result requires further analysis.

7.6   Further Analysis of Rural Poverty

7.6.1   Income Sources in Poor Households

Table 7.8 reports the income sources in poor and non-poor households in 2002 and 2013. Three findings emerge: 1.) The proportion of primary (agricultural) industry net business income was very high in the poor households, and far higher than that in the non-poor households. In particular, in the West region this proportion reached 67 percent. 2.) The proportion of wage income in poor households was generally lower than that in non-poor households. A related problem is that fewer retirement payments covered the low-income households. Since on occasion the amount of the retirement payments was relatively high, the effect on reducing poverty could be significant (see Table 7.9). Increasing the job stability and wage income of low-income laborers seemed to cause poverty to decline permanently. 3.) Compared to 2002, transfer income in 2013 was much larger. Transfer income includes both private transfers and public transfers from the government. The proportion of transfer income for poor households increased from almost 0 percent in 2002 to 37 percent in 2013. According to the estimation by Li, Zhan, and Yang (2016), in 2013 private transfers reduced the head-count ratio by 12 percentage points and public transfers reduced the head-count ratio by about 4 percentage points (see Table 7.9). To some extent, government efforts to alleviate poverty have been effective.

Table 7.7. The impact of regional prices on poverty head-count ratios, 1988–2013

		FGT(0)			FGT(2)		
		PPP	noPPP	Ratio	PPP	noPPP	Ratio
All	1988	76.0	75.6	100.5	16.7	16.9	98.8
	1995	54.3	53.3	101.9	10.8	10.2	105.9
	2002	33.3	30.5	109.2	5.3	4.1	129.3
	2007	21.7	19.4	111.9	6.1	5.4	113.0
	2013	10.6	8.8	120.5	11.6	12.6	92.1
East	1988	63.1	57.7	109.4	13.0	11.4	114.0
	1995	40.9	37.7	108.5	8.5	8.1	104.9
	2002	16.3	15.5	105.2	2.2	2.3	95.7
	2007	10.3	9.8	105.1	9.6	9.6	100.0
	2013	5.7	4.9	116.3	14.4	14.4	100.0
Central	1988	81.0	82.9	97.7	16.5	17.5	94.3
	1995	52.1	52.3	99.6	8.7	8.6	101.2
	2002	32.5	30.9	105.2	4.0	3.6	111.1
	2007	19.6	17.7	110.7	2.7	2.3	117.4
	2013	10.3	9.0	114.4	4.8	4.6	104.3
West	1988	86.0	88.9	96.7	21.5	22.8	94.3
	1995	71.9	71.7	100.3	15.9	14.4	110.4
	2002	51.4	45.0	114.2	9.8	6.6	148.5
	2007	35.3	30.7	115.0	6.3	4.6	137.0
	2013	15.9	12.5	127.2	16.2	19.5	83.1

Notes: (1.) We use the "new poverty level" in this table. (2.) "PPP" refers to the adjusted head-count ratios, whereas "noPPP" refers to the unadjusted head-count ratios. (3) The ratio is equal to (PPP results)/(no PPP results) × 100%.
Sources: Calculated from the rural CHIP data for 1988, 1995, 2002, 2007, and 2013.

7.6.2 Expenditure Structure in Poor Households

The consumption structure of poor families differs significantly from that of non-poor households (Table 7.10). Their specific consumption patterns are as follows: 1.) The proportion of food, tobacco, and alcohol consumption expenditures of poor households is significantly higher than that of non-poor households. The ratio of food consumption expenditures to

Table 7.8. Income sources in poor and non-poor households

Year	Items	Nation		East		Center		West	
		Poor	Not Poor	Poor	Not Poor	Poor	Not Poor	Poor	Not Poor
2002	Per capita disposable income (yuan)	1077	3210	1077	4061	1115	2763	1049	2533
	Wage income (%)	28.41	39.16	28.88	46.44	29.28	32.33	27.56	31.66
	Net business income (%)	72.32	59.80	69.86	51.70	73.35	68.41	72.36	66.60
	Primary (%)	65.80	43.98	61.02	33.37	66.85	52.84	66.62	56.54
	Secondary (%)	1.78	5.53	1.23	6.92	2.41	5.32	1.48	2.46
	Tertiary (%)	3.41	8.54	5.06	9.67	3.01	3.01	2.60	6.22
	Net property income (%)	0.08	0.68	0.04	1.15	0.09	0.29	0.08	0.14
	Net transfer income (%)	−0.81	0.36	1.22	0.70	−2.72	−1.03	0.00	1.60
2013	Per capita disposable income (yuan)	1878	10694	1967	13504	1825	9464	1886	9012
	Wage income (%)	23.41	44.08	34.37	51.82	25.46	43.30	17.71	32.40
	Net business income (%)	41.31	36.61	37.11	32.60	39.09	34.80	44.56	45.28
	Primary (%)	38.69	23.16	37.94	17.24	34.61	22.36	42.04	33.74
	Secondary (%)	0.92	3.44	−4.08	4.61	4.15	3.24	0.40	1.80
	Tertiary (%)	1.69	10.01	3.26	10.75	0.33	9.20	2.12	9.75
	Net property income (%)	0.38	5.67	2.61	6.14	−2.11	4.97	1.40	5.72
	Net transfer income (%)	36.91	13.64	25.91	9.44	37.56	16.94	36.34	16.60

Sources: Authors' calculations from the rural CHIP 2002 and 2013 data.

total consumption expenditures, also called the Engel coefficient, in low-income families is generally relatively large. In 2002, the Engel coefficient of poor families was close to 50 percent and that of non-poor households was 38 percent. In 2013 the Engel coefficient of poor families fell to 38 percent, reaching the level of non-poor families in 2002. However, the Engel coefficient of non-poor households fell further to 33 percent in 2013. This result shows that the overall consumption structure is improving and the

Table 7.9. The poverty reduction effects from transfer income, 2013

Per capita income	National		East		Central		West	
	FGT(0)	Change	FGT(0)	Change	FGT(0)	Change	FGT(0)	Change
Excluding transfer income	24.67	—	15.8	—	26.31	—	30.68	—
+ Private transfers	12.69	-11.98	7.69	-8.11	13.07	-13.24	16.66	-14.02
+ Retirement payments	11.65	-1.04	6.91	-0.78	11.70	-1.37	15.77	-0.89
+ New rural pensions	10.67	-0.98	6.03	-0.88	10.54	-1.16	14.90	-0.87
+ Other pensions	10.56	-0.11	5.84	-0.19	10.48	-0.06	14.79	-0.11
+ Minimum living guarantee	9.92	-0.64	5.35	-0.49	9.96	-0.52	13.91	-0.88
+ Reimbursements	9.70	-0.22	5.23	-0.12	9.51	-0.45	13.83	-0.08
+ Cash subsidies	9.50	-0.20	5.19	-0.04	9.40	-0.11	13.42	-0.41
+ In-kind subsidies	9.34	-0.16	5.11	-0.08	9.08	-0.32	13.35	-0.07
+ Direct food subsidies	8.87	-0.47	4.95	-0.16	8.45	-0.63	12.77	-0.58
+ Subsidies for returning farmland to forests and grassland	8.76	-0.11	4.91	-0.04	8.38	-0.07	12.55	-0.22
+ Other policy subsidies	8.43	-0.33	4.43	-0.48	8.21	-0.17	12.08	-0.47

Notes: 1.) The poverty standard in this table is the "new poverty level." 2.) The final head-count ratio in this table is somewhat different from that elsewhere in this chapter. The main reason is that Li, Zhan, and Yang (2016) apply different weights to consider the distribution of low-income households.

Source: Li, Zhan, and Yang (2016).

Table 7.10. The structure of consumption for poor and non-poor households (%)

	2002		2013	
	Poor	Non-poor	Poor	Non-poor
Food, tobacco, alcohol consumption	49.78	37.72	37.54	33.07
Clothing consumption	5.03	6.14	5.67	6.72
Residence-related consumption	12.47	17.11	22.17	20.66
Rental rent	—	—	0.26	0.35
Housing repair and management	—	—	3.93	3.78
Consumption of daily necessities and services	3.32	3.91	5.47	6.55
Traffic communication consumption	3.98	7.54	10.53	12.48
Transportation consumption	—	—	6.86	8.29
Communication consumption	—	—	3.66	4.18
Education, culture, and entertainment consumption	9.17	7.44	9.20	9.66
Education consumption	—	—	7.51	6.88
Preschool education consumption	—	—	0.61	0.60
Primary education consumption	—	—	0.85	0.79
Junior high-school education consumption	—	—	1.59	0.98
High-school education consumption	—	—	1.87	1.56
Secondary vocational education	—	—	0.24	0.30
College and above education consumption			1.82	2.34
Adult education consumption			0.30	0.30
Health care consumption	5.45	5.58	7.41	8.78
Outpatient medical expenses			2.16	2.24
Total hospitalization expenses			2.53	4.01
Consumption of other supplies and services	10.80	14.57	2.02	2.08
Total	100.00	100.00	100.00	100.00

Sources: Authors' calculations from the rural CHIP data for 2002 and 2013.

Engel coefficient difference between poor families and non-poor families is gradually narrowing. 2.) The proportion of education expenditures of poor families is relatively high. In 2002 the ratio of consumption expenditures for education, culture, and entertainment to total consumption expenditures (9.17 percent) was nearly 2 percentage points higher than that of non-poor households. In 2013 the proportion of consumption expenditures for education, culture, and entertainment of poor households was lower than that of non-poor households, but the ratio of education expenditures to total consumption (7.51 percent) was still higher than that of non-poor households (6.88 percent). Among the education expenditures, the shares of preschool education consumption, primary education consumption, junior high-school education consumption, and high-school education consumption were all larger than those of non-poor households. The shares of adult education consumption (0.30 percent) between poverty households and non-poverty households were almost the same. This finding means that basic education and adult education are a major consumption burden for poor households. 3.) In 2002 the share of residence-related consumption of poor households was lower than that of non-poor households, but in 2013, its share exceeded that of non-poor families. In 2013 the proportion of residence-related household consumption expenditures of poor households reached 22.17 percent and that of non-poor households was 20.66 percent. Both were higher than the proportion in 2002, and the increase for poor families was even higher. Probably because of the rapid development of the real estate market after 2003, the share of residence-related expenditures in the household consumption structure increased significantly. The impact on poor rural families seems to be stronger. In the 2013 residence-related consumption composition, the poor households' share of housing repairs and management to total consumption was larger than that of the non-poor households. This result may be related to the price increase for related commodities. 4.) The share of medical expenditures in the total consumption of poor households is lower than that of non-poor households, but the share of outpatient medical expenses is very close to that of non-poor households. Excluding food consumption, poor households will spend more on outpatient medical care than non-poor families. Whether a family spends more on medical consumption depends on the medical expenses that are necessary for illnesses and on the luxury consumption expenditures that result from a higher economic income. The latter may lead to excessive medical problems. It is conceivable that the rich are more likely to require extravagant consumption for medical issues. After deduction of this part, the burden of medical expenditures in the consumption expenditures of poor families will be relatively high.

We also estimate the ratios of various components of consumer spending to household disposable income (Table 7.11). It should be noted here that since the proportion of poor people in 2013 was much lower than that in 2002, the relationship between consumption expenditures and the income

Table 7.11. Ratio of various types of consumption to disposable income (%)

	2002		2013	
	Poor	Non poor	Poor	Non poor
Food, tobacco, alcohol consumption	52.84	25.34	117.48	24.51
Clothing consumption	5.34	4.12	17.75	4.98
Residence-related consumption	13.24	11.50	69.37	15.32
Rental rent	—	—	0.80	0.26
Housing repair and management	—	—	12.31	2.80
Consumption of daily necessities and services	3.52	2.62	17.11	4.85
Traffic communication consumption	4.22	5.07	32.95	9.25
Transportation consumption	—	—	21.47	6.14
Communication consumption	—	—	11.45	3.10
Education, culture, and entertainment consumption	9.74	5.00	28.80	7.16
Education consumption	—	—	23.52	5.10
Preschool education consumption	—	—	1.90	0.45
Primary education consumption	—	—	2.67	0.58
Junior high-school education consumption	—	—	4.96	0.72
High-school education consumption	—	—	5.86	1.16
Secondary vocational education	—	—	0.75	0.22
College and above education consumption	—	—	5.68	1.74
Adult education consumption	—	—	0.95	0.22
Health care consumption	5.79	3.75	23.19	6.51
Outpatient medical expenses	—	—	6.76	1.66
Total hospitalization expenses	—	—	7.92	2.97
Consumption of other supplies and services	11.46	9.79	6.32	1.54

Sources: Authors' calculations from the rural CHIP data for 2002 and 2013.

composition of poor households are not strictly comparable; they are related to the characteristics of the consumption structures for the different segments of the income distribution. Thus, the change in the ratio of consumer spending to disposable income of poor households in 2002 and 2013 does not make much sense. We focus on the differences between poor and non-poor families during the same year. Surprisingly, the per capita food consumption expenditures of poor households in 2013 exceeded their per capita disposable income, with a ratio of 117.48 percent. In contrast, the ratio of food consumption to per capita disposable income of non-poor households was only 24.51 percent. The ratio of residence-related consumptionforpoorhouseholdswasalmost70percent.Amongthedisposable income of poor households, the share of education consumption and health care consumption accounted for about one quarter of consumption. For non-poor households the shares were only 5.10 percent and 6.51 percent respectively.

7.6.3 Household Characteristics of Poverty Households

Table 7.12 reports the characteristics of poor and non-poor households during the 2002–2013 period. In general, poor families have a weak labor force, face health conditions, or live in poor geographical areas. The details are as follows: 1.) The number of years of education for poor and non-poor households has increased significantly, rising by about 0.6 years and 0.35 years respectively. The gap between poor and non-poor families is narrowing. However, the "labor ratio" of poor households is 3 percentage points lower than that of non-poor households. This ratio widens the gap between poor and non-poor households with regard to income earnings. The proportion of disabled and unhealthy adults in poor families is higher than that in non-poor families. These families in many ways are limited in terms of living and working conditions. 2.) The proportion of poor families in the mountainous areas is higher. They are relatively far from townships, stations, and transportation terminals, and the cost of obtaining employment is higher. 3.) Because of the relatively poor geographical location of poor families, their labor force is more likely to flow to distant places—the proportion of migrant workers outside the province from poor families is notably higher than that of non-poor families. This phenomenon is particularly evident in 2013. In general, engaging in non-agricultural employment is more likely to generate higher income sources. However, limited by labor force and geographical constraints, the proportion of non-agricultural wages and non-agricultural business income of poor households is much lower than that of non-poor households. This feature existed in both 2002 and 2013. 4.) The economic burden of poor families is heavy. Their old-age dependency ratio, child dependency ratio, and disability support ratio are 7 percent, 16 percent, and 35 percent higher respectively than non-poor families. The proportion of poor families with disabled and unhealthy children is also higher, which may lead to a greater economic burden. 5.) Forty-one percent of the housing structures in poor households are made of brick or mud, which is a

Table 7.12. Characteristics of poor and non-poor households, 2002–2013

	2002			2013		
	Poor	Non poor	Ratio	Poor	Non poor	Ratio
Laborers						
Average years of education	7.06	7.90	0.89***	7.68	8.25	0.93***
Average health scores	3.93	4.03	0.97***	3.95	4.03	0.98
Proportion of laborers (%)	65.76	69.73	0.94***	64.87	67.74	0.95***
Proportion of households with disabled adults (ages 16–60) (%)	4.77	3.39	1.40**	5.83	3.17	1.83***
Proportion of households with unhealthy adults (ages 16–60) (%)	12.81	8.99	1.42***	14.95	10.41	1.43***
Conditions						
Land conditions: mountainous	—	—	—	34.88	22.10	1.57***
Roads (%)	—	—	—	99.10	99.26	0.99
Clinics existing in the village (%)	—	—	—	82.02	87.14	0.94***
Distance to the county town (km)	—	—	—	30.32	23.80	1.27***
Distance to the nearest train/bus station or wharf (km)	—	—	—	18.37	15.83	1.16***
Work						
Proportion of outside laborers (%)	25.49	28.57	0.89**	57.55	34.86	1.65***
To other villages in the county	3.18	3.70	0.85*	5.80	5.00	1.16
To other counties in the province	8.21	10.94	0.75***	21.60	14.08	1.53***
To other provinces	18.25	16.39	1.11*	35.30	17.80	1.98***
Proportion of non-agricultural laborers (%)	48.04	65.67	0.73***	30.69	59.78	0.51***
Non-agricultural wage laborers	38.11	50.99	0.74***	21.64	49.27	0.43***
Non-agricultural business laborers	4.83	11.78	0.40***	11.03	18.42	0.59***
Household structure						
Household size	4.87	4.28	1.13***	5.01	4.19	1.19***
Proportion of disabled (%)	1.80	1.45	1.24***	2.16	1.60	1.35***
Proportion of children (%)	24.47	19.70	1.24***	21.56	18.59	1.16***
Proportion of elderly (%)	9.09	7.77	1.17***	13.02	12.08	1.07***
Proportion of disabled elderly (%)	2.20	0.92	2.39***	3.02	2.24	1.35*
Proportion of disabled children (%)	0.90	0.48	1.88**	0.61	0.29	2.12
Proportion of unhealthy elderly (%)	10.97	7.05	1.55***	18.22	10.30	1.76***
Proportion of unhealthy children (%)	1.39	0.36	3.89***	0.98	0.49	1.99
Others						
Brick or mud houses (%)	72.10	63.44	1.13***	41.43	33.33	1.24***

Notes: 1.) "Health scores" are derived from the following question in the CHIP survey: "What was your health situation last year?"; the options were "very bad," "bad," "okay," "good," and "very good." These answers were transferred into scores between 1 and 5 respectively. 2.) ***, **, and * indicate that, based on the *t*-test, the difference between the values for the poor and non-poor was statistically significant at the 0.01, 0.05, or 0.10 level respectively.

Sources: Authors' calculations from the rural CHIP data for 2002 and 2013.

significant decline compared to that in 2002. However, it is clear that in 2013 the government's housing security target had not yet been met.

7.7 Factors Related to Poverty

7.7.1 Approach

In a statistical sense, which variables are related to poverty when other conditions are controlled? The answer to this question will be helpful to determine the correct direction for future poverty alleviation projects. In this section, we create a probit model to answer this question by using the CHIP 2002 and 2013 data. Because of the high correlation between the variables "disabilities" and "being unhealthy," we estimate two models: models (1)–(3) contain the explanatory variables "household with disabled elderly" and "household with disabled children," but they do not contain the explanatory variables "household with unhealthy elderly" and "household with unhealthy children"; models (4)–(6) contain the latter but not former.

Our main approach is a probit regression model that can determine the average impact of the independent variables on the probability of poverty. The estimation equation for the model is the following:

$$\Pr\left(Y = poverty \,|\, X\right) = \Phi\left(\beta_0 + \beta_1 \cdot X + \mu\right)$$

where $\Phi(.)$ is the cumulative distribution function (CDF) of a standard normal distribution for transforming the distribution into probabilities. X indicates the independent variables that may impact the probability of poverty. $\Pr(Y = poverty|X)$ indicates the conditional probability of poverty. The estimated values of the coefficients do not have precise economic meanings, but our emphasis is on their statistical significance, which reflects the significance of each variable's association with poverty.

For consistency with the previous discussion, we focus on the first two groups of factors that may impact poverty status. Theoretically, the third group, "housing status," is merely the result of poverty and not the reason for poverty. But we still use this variable as a control variable. Another control variable is the province of residence. The main estimated results are reported in Table 7.13. Additional results are found in Table A7.2 and Table A7.3.

Table 7.13. Results of the probit models, 2002 and 2013

	2002 Estimates	Std. errors	Marginal effects (dy/dx)	2013 Estimates	Std. errors	Marginal effects (dy/dx)
Laborers						
Average years of education	-0.086***	(0.009)	-0.025	-0.019*	(0.010)	-0.002
Average health scores	-0.036	(0.035)	-0.010	-0.003	(0.034)	0.000
Proportion of laborers (%)	-0.259**	(0.120)	-0.075	-.457***	(0.125)	-0.053
Proportion of disabled adults (ages 16–60) in the household (%)	0.051	(0.101)	0.015	0.225**	(0.106)	0.031
Proportion of unhealthy adults (ages 16–60) in the Household (%)	0.079	(0.067)	0.023	-0.020	(0.074)	-0.002
Conditions						
Land conditions: mountainous	—	—	—	0.130**	(0.055)	0.016
Clinic existing in the village (%)	—	—	—	-0.111*	(0.057)	-0.014
Distance to the county town (km)	—	—	—	0.001	(0.001)	0.000
Distance to the nearest train/bus station or wharf (km)	—	—	—	0.000	(0.001)	0.000
Work						
Proportion of outside laborers (%)						
Working in other villages in the county	0.068	(0.104)	0.020	0.049	(0.092)	0.006
Working in other counties in the province	0.012	(0.067)	0.003	0.355***	(0.059)	0.050
Working in other provinces	-0.020	(0.055)	-0.006	0.405***	(0.053)	0.057

Proportion of non-agricultural laborers (%)				
Non-agricultural wage laborers	-0.130***	-0.038	-0.420***	-0.048
	(0.038)		(0.047)	(0.047)
Non-agricultural business laborers	-0.431***	-0.107	-0.207***	-0.022
	(0.064)		(0.064)	(0.064)
Household structure				
Proportion of children (%)	0.730***	0.211	0.391**	0.045
	(0.130)		(0.158)	(0.158)
Proportion of elderly (%)	0.114	0.033	0.045	0.005
	(0.117)		(0.098)	(0.098)
Proportion of unhealthy elderly in the household (%)	0.184**	0.056	0.131*	0.016
	(0.074)		(0.070)	(0.070)
Proportion of unhealthy children in the household (%)	0.368	0.120	0.249	0.035
	(0.251)		(0.246)	(0.246)
Others (control variables)				
Brick or mud houses (%)	0.250***	0.070	0.074	0.009
	(0.041)		(0.046)	(0.046)
Provinces	Yes		Yes	
Constant	-1.252***		-1.642***	
	(0.312)		(0.305)	
Obs.	7106	—	8865	—

Note: The marginal effect is the effect of a small change in the independent variable on the probability of being poor.

Sources: Authors' calculations based on the rural CHIP data for 2002 and 2013.

7.7.2 Results

7.7.2.1 Factors That May Reduce Household Income

In general, the average number of years of education of household laborers, the proportion of laborers, and the health status of household members between the ages of 16 and 60 are significant; the probability of poverty in households with non-agricultural laborers will be lower and that in households living in mountainous areas will be higher.

The number of effective laborers in a household obviously impacts the income level. As the average years of education increase by one year, the probability of poverty decreases by 0.025 in 2002 and by 0.003 in 2013. Even though the size of the marginal effect decreased dramatically, in both years the estimated coefficients were statistically significant. After the addition of the variables indicating the local development conditions, the effect of education decreases somewhat. Among the variables indicating the local development conditions, "land conditions: mountainous" is significant, indicating that poverty is associated with the relatively low levels of education in mountainous areas.

"Clinic existing in the village" was significant in 2013. The probability of poverty in a village without a clinic increased by 0.014. This does not mean that the probability of poverty will be immediately reduced after adding a clinic in the village. An improvement in the causal relationship between access to medical care and poverty is likely to be long term and gradual.

The higher the proportion of the labor force in the household, the lower the probability of poverty in both 2002 and 2013. The coefficients in both years were significant and the marginal effects were very high, −0.075 in 2002 and about −0.050 in 2013. Furthermore, the variable "households with disabled members between the ages of 16 and 60" was significant in 2013. If one member is disabled, the probability of poverty will increase by about 0.030, which is large compared with the other variables. The estimated coefficient of the variable "households with unhealthy members between the ages of 16 and 60" was not significant but it was positive and weakly raised the probability of poverty.

Participation in non-agricultural work is greatly associated with the probability of poverty. The negative relationship between poverty and business income was about three times that of agricultural wages in 2002. However, in 2013 the effect of agricultural wages on alleviating poverty was about twice that of business income. During the recent period, agricultural wages appear to be more effective in reducing poverty. In the model, the coefficients of migrant workers have a positive sign and they are statistically significant. But we cannot say that migrant workers increase poverty. According to counterfactual analyses in other literature, the earnings of migrant workers are higher than that of onsite workers (Li, Sato, and Sicular 2013). The results of the probit model merely reflect the differences between poor households and non-poor households; they do not reveal the differences between households with migrant laborers and those without migrant laborers. Thus, the results show that the probability of poverty was greater in 2013 when outside laborers were working in other counties or other provinces. This information leads to a further question—why are laborers from low-income households more likely to be working in other counties or provinces? Do they have fewer opportunities in their hometown counties?

7.7.2.2 Factors That May Raise Consumption Expenditures

In general, the proportion of children, disabled elderly and their health status, and disabled children and their health status are significantly related to the probability of poverty. In 2002 and 2013 the marginal effects of the "proportion of children" were both very large—if an ordinary household had one more child between the age of 0 and 15 (the explanatory value changes about 0.25 in 2002), its probability of poverty increases by about 0.05 (0.205 × 0.25). Even though the coefficients of the proportion of elderly are not significant in either year, the proportion of elderly has a weak positive effect on the probability, according to the standard errors. Since rural social security policies did not undergo large-scale expansion until 2007, the health problems of the elderly and of children greatly impacted the probability of poverty in 2002. The coefficients in models (1) and (4) are both significant. However, rural public services were improved in 2013, and there were many special transfer policies targeting low-income households, especially households with disabled members or members with serious health condition. Thus, the impact of disabled elderly or disabled children was no longer significant. But if the elderly had serious health problems, the probability of poverty increased. The latter may result in two consequences: first, increases in medical expenditures; second, a rise in the amount of time other members of the household must devote to health care and hence a reduction in the time available for effective work. Problems due to the aging population and the reduction in the size of households will continue in the future.

7.8 Discussion and Conclusions

This chapter analyzes the CHIP data to shed light on Chinese poverty problems during different periods. The results of the research can be summarized by the answers to the following three questions: 1.) What were the trends and achievements of antipoverty work in China since the reform and opening? 2.) After the years of poverty alleviation work since 1988, which segments of the population are still living in poverty? 3.) What are the most important sources of poverty? Answers to these questions allow us to evaluate the antipoverty and related policies in recent decades and provide ideas regarding future poverty programs.

The poverty head-count ratio in China has been decreasing since the start of the reform and opening policies. Three additional phenomena are particularly noteworthy. First, the poverty gap increased after 2007, an indication that the beneficiaries of poverty alleviation work since that year were the middle low-income households but not the extremely low-income households. Second, poverty alleviation is becoming more challenging and the speed of poverty reduction has been decelerating in the recent decades. Third, relative poverty has continued to rise since 1988. Along with the decrease in the absolute head-count ratio, the relative poverty problem will gradually become more prominent. Regional comparisons reveal regional differences in the speed of poverty reduction. The speed of poverty reduction in the East and Central regions was higher than that in the West region between 1995 and 2002 but it was lower between 2002 and 2013. The relative poverty head-count ratio in the Central region has increased notably in the recent decades.

Our findings show that the quality of household laborers is relevant to household income. We should pay attention to the proportion of disabled, unhealthy, and other ineffective laborers. Also, it is difficult for households in the mountainous areas to overcome poverty. The design of suitable policies should take these issues into consideration. Non-agricultural work can have a significant impact on raising income levels. According to the literature, the proportions of migrants in poor and non-poor households are similar, but migrant work is still an effective way to raise incomes. The problem of unhealthy elderly significantly impacts the poverty status of rural households. Along with the aging population, elderly-related policies are important. In terms of children, their proportions may raise consumption expenditures and thus will have an impact on the probability of poverty.

In an attempt to solve China's poverty problems, the Chinese government declared the goal of not worrying about food and clothing, and of guaranteeing compulsory education, basic medical care, and housing by the year 2020. This goal not only considers absolute poverty (not worrying about food and clothing) but also focuses on the quality of life. The results in this chapter reveal the specific factors that should be incorporated into the design of suitable poverty alleviation policies in the new period.

Notes

Note: We thank the research members of the May 7, 2016 CHIP workshop, especially Chuliang Luo, Jin Song, Terry Sicular, John Knight, Björn Gustafsson, and Hiroshi Sato for their helpful comments. We also thank those researchers who provided very detailed comments in November 2016.

1. See the description of China's poverty head-count ratio at http://data.worldbank.org/country/china. Accessed April 12, 2017.
2. See Figure 7.1 and Table A7.1.
3. See Figure 7.1 and Table A7.1.
4. See Table 7.1.
5. The NBS employs a similar method to adjust the poverty levels in different years. Unfortunately, we do not have information about its calculation process. Our approach may create some errors. But it is still better than using the rural CPI or the national CPI, and it should be closer to the NBS approach.
6. Following Ferreira et al. (2016), the World Bank began to use US$1.9 per day and US$3.1 per day. See http://iresearch.worldbank.org/PovcalNet/index.htm. Accessed January 10, 2017.
7. The process: 1.) Adjust the US$1 in 1993 to the value in 2011 by the CPI in the United States; 2.) exchange the value to RMB by the 2011 PPP; 3.) adjust the values in the other years by using the CPI of China's rural population. In 2011, the PPP (actual individual consumption) in rural China was 3.04 (yuan per US$), according to the World Bank data at http://data.worldbank.org/country/china and working paper http://documents.worldbank.org/curated/en/360021468187787070/pdf/WPS7432.pdf. Accessed January 10, 2017. The PPP (actual individual consumption) in China in 2005 was 4.087 (yuan per US$), according to the World Bank data at http://data.worldbank.org/country/china. Accessed January 10, 2016; and the United Nations MDG Indicators at http://unstats.un.org/unsd/mdg/Default.aspx. Accessed January 10, 2017.
8. For more details on the FGT index, see Chapter 6 of this volume.
9. It is regrettable that we cannot locate regional price data close to the year 2013. When we use the regional CPI adjusted to the 2000 PPP for the 2013 PPP, we will inevitably encounter some errors.
10. Because the estimated sample is different from that of the Chinese government, the head-count ratios in each year are different from the official rates. But the structural characteristics and trends are almost same.
11. More estimates are available in Li, Zhan, and Shen (2017).

References

Brandt, L. and C. A. Holz (2006). "Spatial Price Differences in China: Estimates and Implications." *Economic Development and Cultural Change*, 55(1), 43–86.

Chen, S. and M. Ravallion (2008). "China Is Poorer Than We Thought, But No Less Successful in the Fight against Poverty." World Bank Policy Research Working Paper, no. 4621.

Ferreira, F. H. G., S. Chen, A. Dabalen, et al. (2016). "A Global Count of the Extreme Poor in 2012: Data Issues, Methodology and Initial Results." *Journal of Economic Inequality*, 14(2), 141–172.

Foster, J., J. Greer, and E. Thorbecke (1984). "A Class of Decomposable Poverty Measures." *Econometrica*, 52(3), 761–766.

Guojia tongjiju, Zhuhu diaocha bangongshi (Department of Household Survey, National Bureau of Statistics), ed. (various years). *Zhongguo nongcun pinkun jiance baogao* (China rural poverty monitoring report). Beijing: Zhongguo tongji chubanshe.

Li, S., H. Sato, and T. Sicular (2013). *Rising Inequality in China: Challenges to a Harmonious Society*. Cambridge and New York: Cambridge University Press.

Li, S., P. Zhan, and Y. Shen (2017). "New Patterns in China's Rural Poverty." Centre for Human Capital and Productivity. CHCP Working Papers, 2017-17. London, Canada: Department of Economics, University of Western Ontario.

Li, S., P. Zhan, and C. Yang (2016). "Zhongguo nongcun gonggong zhuanyi shouru de jianpin xiaoguo" (The poverty reduction effect of China's public transfer income in the rural areas). *Zhongguo nongye daxue xuebao (shehui kexueban)*, no. 5, 71–80.

Luo, C. and T. Sicular (2013). "Inequality and Poverty in Rural China," in S. Li, H. Sato, and T. Sicular, eds., *Rising Inequality in China*, 197–229. Cambridge and New York: Cambridge University Press.

Ravallion, M. and S. Chen (2007). "China's (Uneven) Progress against Poverty." *Journal of Development Economics*, 82(1), 1–42.

Wang, P. (2015). "Pinkun biaozhun wenti yanjiu" (Research on the issue of poverty standards), in Guojia tongjiju, Zhuhu diaocha bangongshi (Office of Household Survey, National Bureau of Statistics), ed., *Zhongguo nongcun pinkun jiance baogao 2015* (China rural poverty monitoring report 2015). Beijing: Zhongguo tongji chubanshe.

Wang, X. (2012), "Pinkun biaozhun ji quanqiu zhuangkuang" (Poverty standards and the status of global poverty). *Jingji yanjiu cankao*, no. 55, 41–50.

World Bank. 2009. "From Poor Areas to Poor People: China's Evolving Poverty Reduction Agenda. An Assessment of Poverty and Inequality in China." Poverty Reduction and Economic Management Department, East Asia and Pacific Region, Report 47349-CN.

Zhang, C., Q. Xu, X. Zhou, X. Zhang, and Y. Xie (2014). "Are Poverty Rates Underestimated in China? New Evidence from Four Recent Surveys." *China Economic Review*, 31(December), 410–425.

Zhonggong zhongyang and Guowuyuan (Central Committee of the Communist Party of China and the State Council) (2011). *Zhongguo nongcun pinkun kaifa gangyao (2011-2020)* (China's rural poverty alleviation and development project [2011–2020]). http://www.gov.cn/jrzg/2011-12/01/content_2008462.htm. Accessed January 7, 2017.

Zhongguo zhongyang and Guowuyuan (2015). *Guanyu daying tuolu gongjianzhan de jueding* (Decision on winning the anti-poverty battle). http://news.xinhuanet.com/politics/2015-12/07/c_1117383987.htm. Accessed January 7, 2017.

A7 Appendix Tables

Table A7.1. Poverty estimates in the existing literature, 2002–2015

Source	Data	Standard	Index	2002	2003	2004	2005	2006	2007	2008	2009	2010	2011	2012	2013	2014	2015
Guojia tongjiju, Zhuhu diaocha bangongshi (2015)	Rural Household Survey by the NBS	Dire poverty level	FGT(0)	3.0	3.1	2.8	2.5	2.3	1.6	—	—	—	—	—	—	—	—
		Low poverty level	FGT(0)	9.2	9.1	8.1	6.8	6.0	4.6	4.2	3.8	2.8	—	—	—	—	—
		New poverty level	FGT(0)	—	—	—	—	—	—	—	—	17.2	12.7	10.2	8.5	7.2	5.7
World Bank	National consumption data from the NBS; urban and rural combination; consumption; 2011 PPP	US$1.9	FGT(0)	32.0	—	—	18.8	—	—	14.7	—	11.2	7.9	6.5	1.9	—	—
		US$1.9	FGT(1)	10.2	—	—	4.9	—	—	3.9	—	2.7	1.8	1.4	0.4	—	—
		US$3.1	FGT(0)	56.4	—	—	41.8	—	—	33.0	—	27.2	22.2	19.1	11.1	—	—
		US$3.1	FGT(1)	23.8	—	—	14.7	—	—	11.6	—	9.1	6.9	5.7	2.5	—	—
Chen and Ravallion (2008)	Subsample of the rural Household Survey by the NBS; consumption; 2005 PPP	US$1.25	FGT(0)	40.1	—	33.9	26.4	—	—	—	—	—	—	—	—	—	—
		US$2	FGT(0)	58.4	—	52.2	46.7	—	—	—	—	—	—	—	—	—	—
Luo and Sicular (2013)	China Household Income Project	US$1.25	FGT(0)	27.5	—	—	—	—	13.9	—	—	—	—	—	—	—	—
			FGT(1)	8.4	—	—	—	—	4.7	—	—	—	—	—	—	—	—
			FGT(2)	3.7	—	—	—	—	5.0	—	—	—	—	—	—	—	—

(continued)

Table A7.1. Continued

Source	Data	Standard	Index	2002	2003	2004	2005	2006	2007	2008	2009	2010	2011	2012	2013	2014	2015
		Low poverty level	FGT(0)	11.2	—	—	—	—	5.6	—	—	—	—	—	—	—	—
			FGT(1)	3.0	—	—	—	—	2.3	—	—	—	—	—	—	—	—
			FGT(2)	1.3	—	—	—	—	7.1	—	—	—	—	—	—	—	—
		50% of the median income	FGT(0)	13.7	—	—	—	—	14.3	—	—	—	—	—	—	—	—
			FGT(1)	3.8	—	—	—	—	4.8	—	—	—	—	—	—	—	—
			FGT(2)	1.6	—	—	—	—	5.0	—	—	—	—	—	—	—	—
		60% of the median income	FGT(0)	20.8	—	—	—	—	21.1	—	—	—	—	—	—	—	—
			FGT(1)	6.0	—	—	—	—	6.9	—	—	—	—	—	—	—	—
			FGT(2)	2.6	—	—	—	—	5.3	—	—	—	—	—	—	—	—
Zhang et al. (2014)	China Family Panel Survey	New poverty level	FGT(0)	—	—	—	—	—	—	—	18.3	—	—	—	—	—	—
			FGT(1)	—	—	—	—	—	—	—	6.5	—	—	—	—	—	—
			FGT(2)	—	—	—	—	—	—	—	3.4	—	—	—	—	—	—
	Chinese General Social Survey	New poverty level	FGT(0)	—	—	—	—	—	—	—	23.2	—	—	—	—	—	—
			FGT(1)	—	—	—	—	—	—	—	8.0	—	—	—	—	—	—
			FGT(2)	—	—	—	—	—	—	—	4.0	—	—	—	—	—	—
	China Household Finance Survey	New poverty level	FGT(0)	—	—	—	—	—	—	—	—	26.3	—	—	—	—	—
			FGT(1)	—	—	—	—	—	—	—	—	9.7	—	—	—	—	—
			FGT(2)	—	—	—	—	—	—	—	—	5.2	—	—	—	—	—

Notes: (1) NBS refers to the National Bureau of Statistics in China. (2) Poverty levels: "$" refers to dollars per person per day, and "yuan" refers to yuan per person per year. (3) "New poverty levels," "Low poverty levels," and "Dire poverty levels" are 2300 yuan at 2010 prices, 1196 yuan at 2008 prices, and 625 yuan at 2000 prices respectively. (4) The World Bank data are from http://data.worldbank.org. Accessed April 12, 2017. According to the World Bank descriptions, the data for 2013 and 2012 are not comparable, because the NBS altered its survey approach. Furthermore, the results for the World Bank data are national poverty indexes, not rural indexes.

Table A7.2. Results of the probit models, part A, 2002 and 2013

	(1) 2002			(2) 2013			(3) 2013		
	Estimates	Std. errors	Marginal effects (dy/dx)	Estimates	Std. errors	Marginal effects (dy/dx)	Estimates	Std. errors	Marginal effects (dy/dx)
Laborers									
Average years of education	0.085***	(0.009)	−0.025	−0.024**	(0.010)	−0.003	−0.018*	(0.010)	−0.002
Average health scores	−0.047	(0.035)	−0.014	−0.015	(0.033)	−0.002	−0.017	(0.033)	−0.002
Proportion of laborers (%)	−0.284**	(0.119)	−0.082	−0.470***	(0.122)	−0.052	−0.495***	(0.123)	−0.057
Proportion of disabled adults (ages 16–60) in the Household (%)	0.048	(0.101)	0.014	0.222**	(0.105)	0.029	0.216**	(0.106)	0.029
Proportion of unhealthy adults (ages 16–60) in the household (%)	0.077	(0.067)	0.023	−0.011	(0.074)	−0.001	−0.017	(0.074)	−0.002
Conditions									
Land conditions: mountainous	—	—	—	—	—	—	0.133**	(0.055)	0.016
Clinic existing in the village (%)	—	—	—	—	—	—	−0.113**	(0.057)	−0.014
Distance to the county town (km)	—	—	—	—	—	—	0.001	(0.001)	0.000
Distance to the nearest train/bus station or wharf (km)	—	—	—	—	—	—	0.000	(0.001)	0.000
Work									
Proportion of outside laborers (%)									
Other villages in the county	0.065	(0.104)	0.019	0.047	(0.091)	0.005	0.052	(0.092)	0.006
Other counties in the province	0.009	(0.067)	0.003	0.370***	(0.058)	0.051	0.360***	(0.059)	0.051
Other provinces	−0.019	(0.055)	−0.005	0.428***	(0.053)	0.059	0.413***	(0.053)	0.059

(continued)

Table A7.2. Continued

	(1) 2002			(2) 2013			(3) 2013		
	Estimates	Std. errors	Marginal effects (dy/dx)	Estimates	Std. errors	Marginal effects (dy/dx)	Estimates	Std. errors	Marginal effects (dy/dx)
Proportion of non-agricultural laborers (%)									
Non-agricultural laborers	-0.127***	(0.038)	-0.037	-0.438***	(0.047)	-0.048	-0.419***	(0.047)	-0.048
Non-agricultural business laborers	-0.426***	(0.064)	-0.106	-0.224***	(0.063)	-0.022	-0.209***	(0.064)	-0.022
Household structure									
Proportion of children (%)	0.710***	(0.130)	0.205	0.387**	(0.155)	0.043	0.380**	(0.157)	0.044
Proportion of elderly (%)	0.173	(0.111)	0.050	0.086	(0.092)	0.009	0.100	(0.093)	0.012
Proportion of disabled elderly in the household (%)	0.459***	(0.164)	0.154	0.074	(0.131)	0.009	0.059	(0.133)	0.007
Proportion of disabled children in the household (%)	0.447**	(0.216)	0.149	0.277	(0.328)	0.038	0.264	(0.327)	0.037
Others (control variables)									
Brick or mud houses (%)	0.246***	(0.041)	0.069	0.096**	(0.046)	0.011	0.074	(0.046)	0.009
Provinces	Yes	—	—	Yes	—	—	Yes	—	—
Constant	-1.210***	(0.312)	—	-1.580***	(0.296)	—	-1.569***	(0.303)	—
Obs.	7106	—	—	8865	—	—	8865	—	—

Sources: Authors' calculations from the rural CHIP data for 2002 and 2013.

Table A7.3. Results of the probit models, part B, 2002 and 2013

	(4) 2002			(5) 2013			(6) 2013		
	Estimates	Std. errors	Marginal effects (dy/dx)	Estimates	Std. errors	Marginal effects (dy/dx)	Estimates	Std. errors	Marginal effects (dy/dx)
Laborers									
Average years of education	-0.086***	(0.009)	-0.025	-0.025**	(0.010)	-0.003	-0.019*	(0.010)	-0.002
Average health scores	-0.036	(0.035)	-0.010	-0.001	(0.033)	0.000	-0.003	(0.034)	0.000
Proportion of laborers (%)	-0.259**	(0.120)	-0.075	-0.430***	(0.124)	-0.048	-0.457***	(0.125)	-0.053
Proportion of disabled adults (ages 16–60) in the household (%)	0.051	(0.101)	0.015	0.232**	(0.105)	0.030	0.225**	(0.106)	0.031
Proportion of unhealthy adults (ages 16–60) in the household (%)	0.079	(0.067)	0.023	-0.013	(0.074)	-0.001	-0.020	(0.074)	-0.002
Conditions									
Land conditions: mountainous	—	—	—	—	—	—	0.130**	(0.055)	0.016
Clinic existing in the village (%)	—	—	—	—	—	—	-0.111*	(0.057)	-0.014
Distance to the county town (km)	—	—	—	—	—	—	0.001	(0.001)	0.000
Distance to the nearest train/bus station or wharf (km)	—	—	—	—	—	—	0.000	(0.001)	0.000
Work									
Proportion of outside laborers (%)									
Other villages in the county	0.068	(0.104)	0.020	0.044	(0.092)	0.005	0.049	(0.092)	0.006
Other counties in the province	0.012	(0.067)	0.003	0.364***	(0.058)	0.050	0.355***	(0.059)	0.050
Other provinces	-0.020	(0.055)	-0.006	0.420***	(0.053)	0.058	0.405***	(0.053)	0.057

(continued)

Table A7.3. Continued

	(4) 2002			(5) 2013			(6) 2013		
	Estimates	Std. errors	Marginal effects (dy/dx)	Estimates	Std. errors	Marginal effects (dy/dx)	Estimates	Std. errors	Marginal effects (dy/dx)
Proportion of non-agricultural laborers (%)									
Non-agricultural laborers	-0.130***	(0.038)	-0.038	-0.438***	(0.047)	-0.048	-0.420***	(0.047)	-0.048
Non-agricultural business laborers	-0.431***	(0.064)	-0.107	-0.223***	(0.063)	-0.022	-0.207***	(0.064)	-0.022
Household structure									
Proportion of children (%)	0.730***	(0.130)	0.211	0.402**	(0.156)	0.044	0.391**	(0.158)	0.045
Proportion of elderly (%)	0.114	(0.117)	0.033	0.029	(0.098)	0.003	0.045	(0.098)	0.005
Proportion of unhealthy elderly in the household (%)	0.184**	(0.074)	0.056	0.140**	(0.070)	0.017	0.131*	(0.070)	0.016
Proportion of unhealthy children in the household (%)	0.368	(0.251)	0.120	0.233	(0.245)	0.031	0.249	(0.246)	0.035
Others (control variables)									
Brick or mud houses (%)	0.250***	(0.041)	0.070	0.095**	(0.046)	0.011	0.074	(0.046)	0.009
Provinces	Yes			Yes			Yes		
Constant	-1.252***	(0.312)	—	-1.655***	(0.299)	—	-1.642***	(0.305)	—
Obs.	7106		—	8865		—	8865		—

Sources: Authors' calculations based on the rural CHIP data for 2002 and 2013.

8

Unequal Growth

Long-Term Trends in Household Incomes and Poverty in Urban China

Björn Gustafsson and Sai Ding

8.1 Introduction

In 2008 the Great Recession hit most high-income countries. The GDP fell and average household income decreased. Unlike in the countries in the West, in the People's Republic of China (PRC) GDP continued to grow at rates between 7 to 10 percent per annum (World Bank 2016). How did this growth affect trends among Chinese urban residents: that is, people with urban residence permits (*hukou*)? More specifically, we ask, what was the average household income growth and what were the trends in the income distribution? Did income inequality increase, remain constant, or decrease? How and why did poverty grow? How did different income components develop, and how were they related to disposable income?

In this chapter, we report new results based on data from the China Household Income Project (CHIP) for 2007 and 2013. As very similar data were collected for 1988, 1995, and 2002, we use these surveys to put development between 2007 and 2013 in perspective against the background of China's two and one-half decades of rapid economic growth and transition toward a market economy. During this long period, political priorities as well as the political leaders changed several times. Policies under the leadership of Jiang Zemin, from 1989 to 2003, are often described as placing a priority on economic growth, whereas under the leadership of Hu Jintao and Wen Jiabao from 2013 to 2013 there was more of a focus on equality.

We use the CHIP definition of income for all years, which, unlike the National Bureau of Statistics (NBS) definition, includes imputed rents from owner-occupied housing. We add the income for all household members, divide it by the number of household members, and then assign this per

Björn Gustafsson and Sai Ding, *Unequal Growth* In: *Changing Trends in China's Inequality*. Edited by: Terry Sicular, Shi Li, Ximing Yue, and Hiroshi Sato, Oxford University Press (2020). © Oxford University Press.
DOI: 10.1093/oso/9780190077938.003.0008

capita household income to all household members. The motivation for aggregating income to the household is that people typically live with other household members with whom they share income. It is true that in many households earnings are from paid work or self-employment, which are the most important sources of income. However, a household often receives income from various other sources as well. For example, pensions are the most important source of income for the elderly. The levels and inequality of household income are not necessarily the same as the levels of earnings and earning inequality among workers.

Several authors have studied how household income, income inequality, and poverty in urban China have developed since the latter part of the 1980s. Rapid increases in income, accompanied by increases in inequality, are typically reported in studies that analyze the early years after the introduction of the reforms. One example is Meng (2004) who uses data from the CHIP 1988, 1995, and 1999 surveys. Another example is Wang (2008), who focuses on development during the period from 1986 to 2000. A third example is Cai, Chen, and Zhou (2010) who use the Household and Expenditure Data from the NBS to study income as well as expenditure inequality from 1992 to 2003. Appleton, Song, and Xia (2010), who study income poverty during 1988, 1995, 1999, and 2002, report fewer households and fewer persons falling below the poverty line, as expressed as the constant purchasing power during the year under study. However, authors who analyze the annual rounds of the NBS urban household surveys have pointed out that the movement toward fewer persons with incomes below a poverty line expressed as the constant purchasing power has not always been smooth.[1]

In studies of the more recent years, Gustafsson and Ding (2013) use the CHIP data for 1995, 2002, and 2007 to investigate how larger proportions of those who are of active working age were not earning incomes. They find that much of this lack of income was absorbed within the households. Deng and Gustafsson (2013), using the CHIP data, report a rapid increase in urban income between 2002 and 2007 as well as an increase in income inequality. Their study also shows that the previous trend of fewer persons living in households with incomes below the absolute poverty line continued. However, larger proportions of people were living on incomes below a relative poverty line set to a proportion of the contemporary median income. As stated earlier, the period of study in this chapter places the developments since 1988 into perspective. We are not aware of any previous study that has investigated income, income inequality, and poverty in urban China over such a long period.

Looking at the results from 2007 to 2013, we find that real income among Chinese urban residents grew by an average of 7 percent per annum. This means a growth rate only marginally lower than the trend since 1988. However, earnings grew by not more than 3 percent per annum, much lower than that in previous years. In contrast, pensions and imputed rents from owner-occupied housing grew much more rapidly and together they represented slightly more than one-half of the growth in average household income. The trend of fewer persons in urban China having incomes lower than an absolute poverty line expressed as the constant purchasing power (as found in research on previous periods) continued between 2007 and 2013. However, we also report that income growth from 2007 to 2013 was slower at the lower part of the income distribution. The trend of increased income inequality continued, as did the trend toward more people falling below a relative poverty line.

The remainder of this chapter is organized as follows: In the next section we discuss changes in urban China that are particularly relevant to our research questions. In Section 8.3 our data and definitions are presented. Section 8.4 contains the results in terms of the development of household income, income inequality, and income poverty. In Section 8.5 we report how the development of various income components is related to household income, thus providing some insights into those channels by which income inequality increased. Section 8.6 contains an analysis of relative and absolute poverty. Finally, we sum up and present our conclusions in Section 8.7.

8.2 Background

First, we present a brief description of early developments in urban China since the 1980s to place the longer period into perspective.[2] During the 1980s most economic activity in urban China took place in state-owned or collective-owned enterprises. Investment and productive inputs and outputs were allocated administratively. Additionally, workers were administratively allocated to their work units, where they often remained until retirement and they rarely risked losing their jobs. The work units played a key role in workers' lives, as they typically provided housing at a very low cost, various social services, and post-retirement pensions. The compensation package typically included consumer goods and a limited amount of money. Very few economic activities took place outside of the state and collective sectors.

This description has gradually become outdated. Foreign trade has expanded rapidly, as has foreign direct investment (FDI), affecting both urban labor demand and wages. Furthermore, the economy has been growing rapidly. Consumer markets and markets for productive inputs (including for labor) have also been put into place. By the second half of the 1990s tens of millions of workers were facing layoffs, and the proportion of workers employed by state-owned enterprises (SOEs) decreased rapidly. Furthermore, the work unit no longer played such a dominant role in the lives of the workers. For example, housing was privatized and many workers bought their own apartments. Parallel to these changes, self-employment increased, as did employment in privately owned firms and foreign-invested enterprises.

Ever since the early days of the PRC, people who lived in rural and urban China have been treated differently. To a considerable extent, the urban population was and remains a privileged group, whereas the rural population is disadvantaged. A large income gap has prevailed for decades, though recently there have been attempts to close this gap.[3] For decades, very few rural persons could find opportunities to work and live in the cities. This situation has gradually changed. More rural people have moved to the cities, either temporarily or permanently. They often take positions that pay less than those held by urban residents, and they tend to live in inferior housing. In this chapter, as in all writings on income inequality in urban China of which we are aware, the analysis does not include the migrant population. Nevertheless, the increased presence of rural migrants in urban China has had several economic consequences that have affected the incomes of urban residents. For example, the presence of migrants places downward pressures on the wages of less-skilled workers. It is also likely to increase the demand for housing and thus to place upward pressures on housing prices and thereby on the imputed rents from owner-occupied housing enjoyed by urban residents.

Urbanization has been one of the most significant changes in China's population structure. There have also been major changes in other dimensions as well. One is the growth of higher education, whereby the newer cohorts of workers are better educated than the older cohorts. As is well known, high-income countries are rapidly aging. The same situation also applies to China, especially China's urban areas. Our data show that in 1988 children constituted 22 percent of urban residents, but by 2013 this figure had declined to

14 percent. In contrast, between the two years the share of the elderly population increased from 7 percent to 16 percent.

China's aging population is a consequence of two trends. One is the low birth rate, consistent with the strict family planning policy that limited the number of births for most urban couples until the end of 2015. The low birth rate is also consistent with the rapid increase in female education. The other cause of aging is the impressive increase in life expectancy. According to the World Bank, life expectancy at birth in China increased from as low as 43 years in 1960 to as high as 76 years in 2014, or by as much as 33 years. This increase means that the gap in life expectancy between China and, for example, the United States (which was 27 years in 1960) had declined to 3 years by 2014.

By the standards of high-income countries, China today has low retirement ages. The legal retirement age for women is 55 years and for men is 60 years. In fact, the actual retirement age for women is likely lower because by the second half of the 1990s, many enterprises had laid off female workers. To some extent, this finding also reflects a combination of the lack of subsidized public child care in urban China and strong family norms, according to which grandmothers take care of their grandchildren.

In urban China, most elderly people receive pensions, as they were employed for most years of their working lives. Some receive generous pensions, whereas for others the pensions are not so generous and for some there are even no pensions at all. Furthermore, a slowing of the rapid economic growth may cause challenges to funding the growing pension expenditures. Until now, there has not been much discussion of policy measures to increase the age at which one receives a pension. It is conceivable that in the future China will take steps to increase the legal as well as the actual retirement age.

Anyone who has regularly visited China cannot have missed the substantial changes in the housing market. Many new dwellings have been constructed, and others are in the process of construction. A possible fall in the historically high housing prices is not out of the question. Reasons that housing prices have increased so rapidly are numerous. One is the increased migration from the rural areas. Also, rapidly increasing incomes have made it possible for urban households to afford larger apartments. To these reasons can also be added expectations of future increases in income because of recent historical experiences as well as because of increased possibilities to obtain loans. This study includes the value of imputed rents from owner-occupied housing as one component of household income. Like others who have studied income inequality in urban China, we do not include the income from realized capital gains when housing is sold at higher prices than the purchase prices.

In the West, the government assumes responsibility for providing many social services and transfers to the population. For example, most high-income countries except for the United States provide families with regular child allowances. In addition, some countries allocate funds to child-care programs and to programs for parental leave. Much of the funding for these programs comes from taxes. The situation in urban China is somewhat different and has changed over time. In urban China the work units assumed many of the roles that in the West are the responsibilities of local governments, the central government, or social insurance systems. The work units paid for these programs from their sales revenue, so that it was less necessary, as compared to the situation in the West, to fund such programs through taxes. As we will see, in this respect the situation in China has not radically changed since the 1980s. In addition, the retreat of the work units from the lives of urban employees has not been fully matched by increased government commitments.

We now turn to macroeconomic developments in China since 2007.[4] In that year the financial crisis in the United States sent the world economy on a downward spiral. The Chinese economy was adversely affected because of its international ties. Inward direct investments fell rapidly, as did foreign demand for manufactured goods. Consequently, labor demand put downward pressures on earnings, particularly on those earnings that were derived from exports. The possibility of increased unemployment, losses of household income, and resultant mass protests and social instability was most probably the motivation for the Chinese government to take rapid measures. In September 2008, the People's Bank of China (PBC) initiated a monetary easing policy, which resulted in a drastic increase in bank loans. A large fiscal stimulus package was presented in October 2008 when the government announced that RMB 4 trillion would be spent during the following two or three years. Almost one-half of the stimulus package was directed toward improvements in the transportation system, and one-quarter went to reconstruction after the 2008 Wenchuan earthquake (He, Zhang, and Zhang 2009). Most of those investments were financed by bank loans. Most observers agree that the stimulus program had a positive effect on the Chinese economy during a period of a sharp global economic slowdown.[5]

8.3 Data and Definitions

We use the urban survey from the CHIP, in which income information applies to the years 1988, 1995, 2002, 2007, and 2013. On the basis of the five surveys, we can show changes during four different periods covering as much as two and a half decades. The two first subperiods generally correspond to the period when Jiang Zemin held power; the third and fourth periods correspond to the time when Hu Jintao and Wen Jiabao were the top policymakers. Because the five waves of the CHIP surveys do not cover identical provinces, to increase comparability across years, we use in our analysis only observations from those provinces that were included in all five years. The provinces are Beijing, Shanxi, Liaoning, Jiangsu, Anhui, Henan, Hubei, Guangdong, Chongqing, Sichuan, Yunnan, and Gansu.[6] To achieve a better representation of the population in this study we use weights developed by the CHIP project that are based on the regional distribution of the urban population.[7]

Prior to 2013, the CHIP urban surveys are subsamples of the urban household sample used by the NBS to produce China's official statistics. This approach means that the surveys for 1988, 1995, 2002, and 2007 were sampled from a frame that covered areas that were defined as urban during the year of the sample.[8] For our analysis we limit our sample to those households in the CHIP urban survey that had an urban registration (*hukou*). In 2013 the NBS integrated the sample frame so it includes urban as well as rural households independent of registration status. As a consequence, the CHIP 2013 urban household survey contains households with different registration statuses that reside in urban areas. For our analysis, we again limit our sample to those households in the CHIP survey that had urban registrations. This constraint means that people with rural residence permits living in the urban areas are not included in our sample.

Features of the CHIP household surveys are explained in Chapter 1. Here we note that in the CHIP urban survey, as in similar surveys, there are nonresponse and underreporting problems. Such problems are particularly acute for high-income households. To the extent that this lack of data affects our estimates, like all estimates of which we are aware, the "true" income inequality in urban China will probably be underestimated. In cases in which problems of nonresponse and underreporting have increased over the years, then we will have underestimations rather than overestimations of the "true" increase in income inequality.

As noted in Chapter 1, information in the CHIP datasets makes it possible to estimate components such as the value of imputed rents from owner-occupied housing, thus allowing us to use a definition of household income that is more in line with international practice.[9] Household income is defined as including the components of earnings, pensions, property income, in-kind income, imputed rent on owner-occupied housing, housing subsidies, and net transfer income. In-kind income and housing subsidies were rather important for many urban resident households during the planning period, but thereafter they were largely phased out. Net transfers are in some cases positive, such as social assistance (*dibao*), and in other cases negative, such as income taxes. As we will report in more detail in Section 8.5, the relative importance of different income sources has changed dramatically over the years.

Following what is now customary practice in such studies, in the following analysis we add the income of all household members and divide this income by the number of household members to obtain the per capita income. After the per capita household income is assigned to each household member, we can study the income distribution among individuals. Income is measured in constant prices by using the NBS national average urban consumer price index (CPI).

8.4 Overall Development

We start the overall description by presenting the income growth curves (Ravallion and Chen 2003) computed by percentiles, as shown in Figure 8.1 for the four periods—1988–1995, 1995–2002, 2002–2007, and 2007–2013. We find that the overall level of income growth between 2007 and 2013 (6.8 percent per annum on average) was similar to that during the first two subperiods, but lower than that between 2002 and 2007.

These results merit some comments: First, we report a sizable reduction in the growth of median income from 2007 to 2013, compared to the rapid growth of 12.3 percent per annum during the period from 2002 to 2007. On the one hand, Chinese households may have been disappointed as the growth rate slowed to almost one-half that in the previous period, and this slowdown probably led to downward adjustments to expectations regarding future income growth. On the other hand, seen from the perspective of the income growth experienced by households in high-income countries, a median income growth of 6.8 percent was still very impressive. For example, Thervissen et al. (2015) report that on the basis of median household growth

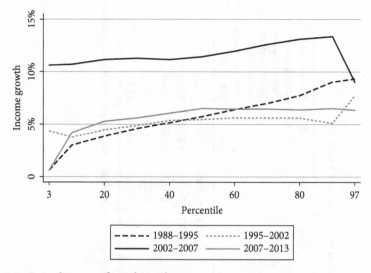

Fig. 8.1 Growth curves for urban China

Note: Income is calculated in constant prices by using the urban Consumer Price Index.

Source: Authors' estimates from the CHIP data for 1988, 1995, 2002, 2007, and 2013.

rates computed for twenty-nine countries over relatively extended periods, only one country, Estonia (2000 to 2010; 6 percent) is reported to have a growth rate similar to that of urban China from 2007 to 2013. The growth rate of urban China at 6.1 percent between 1988 and 2013 can be compared to the second most rapidly growing countries in Thervissen et al. (2015), that is, Ireland, with a growth rate of not more than 3 percent (between 1987 and 2010), or to the median growth rate of 0.3 percent in the United States (1979–2013).

Second, by examining the shape of the growth curves we can make statements about how income inequality developed. There is a tendency for the curves to slope upward, meaning that income inequality increased. This increase is very clear for the period from 1988 to 1995, and relatively clear for the period from 2002 to 2007 and the period from 2007 to 2013. Information on the numerical values of the summary inequality indexes are consistent with this pattern. The Gini coefficient shows an increase of as much as ten units between 1988 and 1995. This is similar to the increase that Atkinson (2015) reports for the United Kingdom between 1980 and the end of the 2000s. Since 1995, however, increases in income inequality in urban China have been modest (Table 8.1 and Figure 8.2). Our estimate of the Gini

Table 8.1. Income and income inequality 1988, 1995, 2002, 2007, and 2013, according to various inequality indexes

	Mean income (in current prices)	Mean income (in 2013 prices)	Median income (in current prices)	Median income (in 2013 prices)	Annual growth at the median in comparison to the previous year studied (percent)	Gini	MLD	Theil index	Proportion having an income above 200 percent of the contemporary median income (percent)
1988	1828	6197	1639	5556	—	0.2313	0.0964	0.0881	5.65
1995	5698	8490	4618	6881	4.6	0.3320	0.1891	0.2407	11.10
2002	8618	11,634	7435	10,037	4.6	0.3113	0.1624	0.1653	9.68
2007	18,186	21,823	15,405	18,486	13.5	0.3350	0.1875	0.1875	14.33
2013	31,524	31,524	25,710	25,710	7.6	0.3522	0.2131	0.2184	12.77

Notes: Mean and median incomes are in RMB. The annual growth at the median for the period from 1988 to 2013 was 6.1 percent. The numerical values of the inequality indexes are calculated from the income per capita in current prices.

We used the NBS consumer price index (CPI) for urban China to convert the income to 2013 prices.

MLD stands for "mean logarithmic deviation."

Source: Authors' estimates from the CHIP data for 1988, 1995, 2002, 2007, and 2013.

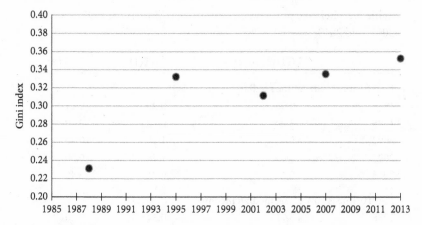

Fig. 8.2 Gini coefficients for urban China, 1988, 1995, 2002, 2007, and 2013
Source: Authors' estimates from the CHIP data for 1988, 1995, 2002, 2007, and 2013.

for urban China in 2013 is 0.35, which is lower than that reported for many high-income countries.[10]

A closer look at the upper segments of the growth curves and the information in Table 8.2 reveals that after the period from 1988 to 1995 there were no obvious signs of increased inequality at the top of the income distribution. For example, the proportion of persons with incomes higher than 200 percent of the median varied irregularly from 1995 to 2013, and they were similar during the two years. As we will see, income inequality in urban China since the beginning of the CHIP surveys in 1988 has been characterized by those at the lower part of the distribution not experiencing the same income growth as those at the higher part of the distribution.

The trend whereby urban residents at the lower part of the income distribution are lagging behind those who are at the higher end of the distribution becomes clear once we examine the movement of relative poverty rates over time. The relative poverty rates reported here are derived from the poverty lines based on the median income observed during the same year. They are based on a poverty line set at 40, 50, 60, and 70 percent of the median per capita income observed in the same year. This measure means that as the living standard at the median has increased, the living standard at the poverty line has increased as well.

This definition of poverty is used today in many situations: One example is the Eurostat assessment of poverty in the member states of the European Union (EU). The most often used alternative in such situations

Table 8.2. Relative poverty rates for urban China, 1988, 1995, 2002, 2007, and 2013

	FGT(0), poverty rate	FGT(1)	FGT(2)
Poverty line is 40% of the median income			
1988	0.86	0.20	0.11
1995	4.20	0.98	0.40
2002	5.52	1.18	0.40
2007	6.60	1.48	0.50
2013	9.17	3.31	2.45
Poverty line is 50% of the median income			
1988	3.11	0.54	0.20
1995	8.21	2.00	0.78
2002	11.58	2.63	0.93
2007	12.63	3.06	1.13
2013	14.76	5.05	3.08
Poverty line is 60% of the median income			
1988	7.37	1.29	0.42
1995	14.75	3.54	1.38
2002	18.78	4.70	1.76
2007	19.07	5.16	2.04
2013	21.42	7.20	4.01
Poverty line is 70% of the median income			
1988	14.74	2.66	0.81
1995	23.29	5.72	2.23
2002	26.99	7.28	2.88
2007	27.13	7.70	3.20
2013	28.63	9.76	5.20

Note: The poverty lines are set at a fixed percentage of the median income, as observed in the sample of the year under investigation.

Source: Authors estimates from the CHIP data for 1988, 1995, 2002, 2007, and 2013.

is to set the poverty line at 60 percent of the equivalent median income.[11] A similar approach is the Organisation for Economic Co-operation and Development (OECD) comparison of poverty across rich countries, which typically places the poverty line at 50 percent of the median income in the country of interest. The same approach is used for the official poverty line in Hong Kong.

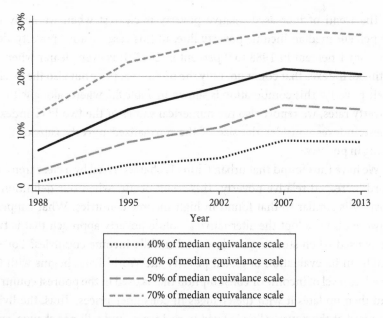

Fig. 8.3 Relative poverty rates for urban China, 1988, 1995, 2002, 2007, and 2013

Note: The poverty lines are defined as a constant percentage of the contemporary median per capita income.

Source: Authors' estimates from the CHIP data for 1988, 1995, 2002, 2007, and 2013.

The relative poverty rates that we report for 1988, 1995, 2002, 2007, and 2013 in Table 8.2 and that we illustrate in Figure 8.3 show a clearly increasing trend.[12] In 1988 7 percent of urban residents lived in a household having an income that was less than 60 percent of the median; in 1995, this proportion increased to 15 percent; in 2002 and 2007 it increased further to 19 percent; and by 2013 it reached 21 percent.

In terms of international comparisons, were the levels of the relative poverty rates in urban China in 2013 considered high or low? One answer is that the 21 percent under the 60 percent median poverty line in urban China is somewhat higher than the 17 percent in the Eurostat report (2016) for the EU 28 during the same year. In the Eurostat report, only Bulgaria, Greece, Romania, and Spain have relative poverty rates that are 20 percent or higher. Another point of reference is Hong Kong, for which it is reported that 15 percent of the residents were living under 50 percent of the median income line, the same proportion we report in Table 8.2 for urban China in the same year.[13]

The trend of increased relative poverty is clearest when we apply the 40 percent median income poverty line. In this case, relative poverty went up from 1 percent in 1988 to 9 percent in 2013. It is even clearer when we estimate indexes that count not only the number of poor but also the level of their poverty. This combination is shown in Table 8.2 where, along with the poverty rates, we report also the numerical values of the two FGT indexes. These indexes consider the size of the normalized poverty gaps of those living in poverty.[14]

We have thus found that urban China is characterized by a clear trend toward increased relative poverty. This result occurs when our definition of poverty is similar to that found in high-income countries. What happens, however, if we adopt the alternative absolute poverty approach that is typically used when studying the low- and middle-income countries? For example, in its evaluation of global poverty the World Bank begins with the absolute level of income or consumption that is used in the poorest countries and then updates it with the changes in consumer prices. Thus, the living standard at the poverty line is fixed in real terms and will not change, even in cases when the general living standard has increased. Such a poverty line is absolute in that it refers to the same living standard during each year. The same idea can also be applied to the updating of the official poverty line in the United States.

At what level should one apply an absolute poverty line in urban China? Unlike the case in rural China, there is no official poverty line to serve as a guide for urban China. However, income thresholds are used in assessing household claims for social assistance (*dibao*), and we use this information related to the year 2013. As the *dibao* lines differ by location, we apply the extreme values found when we average the lines in those provinces represented in our samples. The lowest line is 3384 yuan per person and year; this result is found in Yunnan; the highest is 6960 yuan per person and year and this result is found in Beijing.[15] The *dibao* line in Yunnan 2013 is slightly below the poverty line of US$1.9 per person per day that the World Bank uses to measure global poverty and that we also report in Table 8.3.

In Figure 8.4 we show the cumulative density functions for 1988, 1995, 2002, 2007, and 2013. Comparisons across years show that poverty, measured against the poverty lines representing the same purchasing power, decreased very rapidly during the three periods. The decrease in poverty based on Beijing's *dibao* line in place in 2013 was particularly rapid. As many as 81 percent of the persons living in urban China would have fallen below

Table 8.3. Poverty indexes for urban China computed for different absolute poverty lines, 1988, 1995, 2002, 2007, and 2013

	FGT(0), poverty rate	FGT(1)	FGT(2)
Poverty line is set at 3384 yuan, which corresponds to the *dibao* line in Yunnan in 2013.			
1988	6.20	1.07	0.34
1995	4.39	1.02	0.41
2002	1.43	0.28	0.09
2007	0.08	0.02	0.004
2013	1.00	0.57	0.48
Poverty line is set at 6960 yuan, which corresponds to the *dibao* line in Beijing in 2013.			
1988	81.00	27.52	11.66
1995	48.52	14.39	6.06
2002	24.25	6.42	2.50
2007	5.51	1.19	0.40
2013	3.90	1.54	0.94

Note: Incomes for 1988, 1995, 2002, and 2007 are all adjusted with the urban CPI for 2013 prices. Poverty lines are per person per year.

Source: Authors' estimates from the CHIP data for 1988, 1995, 2002, 2007, and 2013.

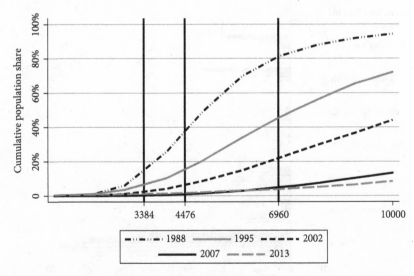

Fig. 8.4 Cumulative density functions for urban China, 1988, 1995, 2002, 2007, and 2013

Note: 3384 yuan per person and per year corresponds to the 2013 *dibao* line in Yunnan; 6960 yuan per person and per year corresponds to the 2013 *dibao* line in Beijing; 4476 yuan is the World Bank poverty line for US$1.9 per day.

Source: Authors' estimates from the CHIP data for 1988, 1995, 2002, 2007, and 2013.

this line in 1988, whereas the proportion decreased to 49 percent in 1995 and it was down to only 4 percent in 2013. In 2013 only 1 percent had incomes lower than the *dibao* line in Yunnan.

8.5 The Changed Role of the Income Components

To better understand how income growth in urban China has come about and what is behind the trend of increased income inequality, in this section we decompose household income per capita by the income components. This process is done for each of the five years—1988, 1995, 2002, 2007, and 2013. Figure 8.5 shows the relative shares of the eight components. Table 8.4 shows the average value in 2013 prices of each component as well as the annual growth rates computed for the subperiods and for the entire period from 1988 to 2013.

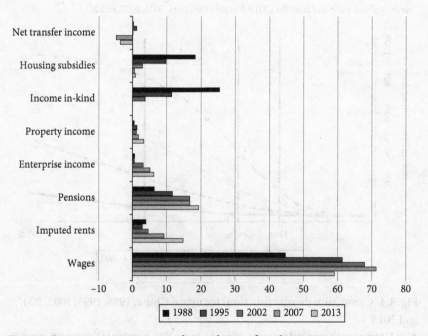

Fig. 8.5 Income components as relative shares of total income, 1988, 1995, 2002, 2007, and 2013 (%)

Source: Authors' estimates from the CHIP data for 1988, 1995, 2002, 2007, and 2013.

Table 8.4. Household income components 1988, 1995, 2002, 2007, and 2013 and their growth for urban residents (mean value)

	Wages	Imputed rents of owner-occupied housing equity	Pensions	Enterprise income	Property income	Income in-kind	Housing subsidies	Net transfer income	Total
1988	2773	243	407	39	31	586	1133	985	6197
1995	5208	969	994	45	108	241	828	97	8490
2002	7897	422	1950	360	132	533	330	10	11,634
2007	15,604	1958	3694	1102	370	2	110	-1016	21,824
2013	18,718	4736	6090	1942	917	0	289	-1168	31,524
Annualized growth rates (%)									
1988–1995	9.4	21.9	13.6	2.1	19.6	-11.9	-4.4	-28.2	4.6
1995–2002	6.1	-11.2	10.1	34.6	2.9	12.0	-12.3	-27.2	4.6
2002–2007	12.0	29.2	11.2	20.5	18.8	-61.7	-16.8	na	11.1
2007–2013	3.1	15.9	8.7	9.9	16.3	-100.0	17.5	-2.3	6.3
1988–2013	7.8	12.5	11.3	16.9	15.0	-100.0	-5.7	na	6.6

Notes: Incomes are in 2013 constant prices (RMB) using the urban CPI as published by the NBS. The mean values for 2007 and 2013 are calculated by using the sample weights, but this is not the case for the mean values for 1988, 1995, and 2002. For calculating the annualized growth rates between 2002 and 2007 and between 1988 and 2013, the mean values for 2007 and 2013 used in the calculations are not weighted. Growth of net transfer income between 2002 and 2007 and between 1998 and 2013 cannot be calculated, because of changed signs. The CPI from 1988 to 2013 is 3.57; the CPI from 1995 to 2013 is 1.54; the CPI from 2002 to 2013 is 1.40; and the CPI from 2007 to 2013 is 1.20.

Source: Authors' estimates from the CHIP data for 1988, 1995, 2002, 2007, and 2013.

Not surprisingly, wages were the single largest component during each year under study. Their relative share increased from 1988 to 2007 as in-kind income and housing subsidies, both of which were of substantial importance in 1988, had diminished. In-kind income was almost totally eradicated by 2002 and the relative share of housing subsidies in total income declined from 16 percent in 1988 to only 1 percent in 2013.

However, between 2007 and 2013 another change also occurred. An increasing number of workers moved into self-employment and the relative share of enterprise income grew, whereas the relative share of wages decreased.[16] There were also other changes to note. Urban China has been, and still is, aging, and for many older people pensions are relatively generous. In consequence, the share of pensions in disposable income rose from 6 percent in 1988 to 18 percent in 2013. Housing reform has meant that many urban households are living in owner-occupied housing. Furthermore, housing prices have increased rapidly. In consequence of both these factors, imputed rents of owner-occupied housing increased, constituting a larger proportion of total income. In 2013 the relative share of imputed rents of owner-occupied housing was not less than 16 percent.[17] The small income sources, property income, grew very rapidly, increasing its relative share of total disposable income to 5 percent in 2013.

Finally, average net transfers changed from positive in 1988 to be rather small in 1995 and 2002 and to become negative in 2007 and 2013.

The various income sources contribute to income inequality and changes in income inequality in several ways. We can decompose the Gini coefficient for household income by income sources as the sum of the various concentration coefficients weighted by their relative shares of income.[18] The concentration coefficient for a specific income source relative to the Gini coefficient for total income indicates whether the component is equalizing or disequalizing. The results of such an exercise for the five years are shown in Figure 8.6 and Table 8.5.

Some comments are in order. Starting with earnings, we see that its concentration coefficient was rather low in 1988, lower than the low Gini coefficient in the same year. Therefore, earnings were equalizing. Thereafter and up until 2007, the concentration coefficient for earnings increased. From this follows that the increased concentration of earnings to high-income households was one force moving the distribution of household income in urban China toward higher inequality. In 2007 as much as three-fourths of urban China's income inequality could be attributed to earnings. However,

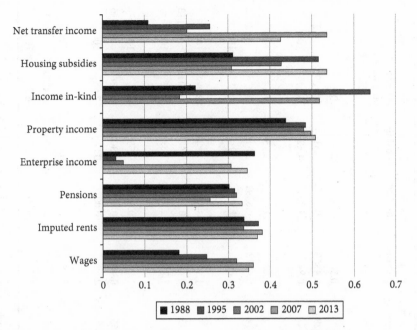

Fig. 8.6 Concentration coefficients for various income components, 1988, 1995, 2002, 2007, and 2013

Source: Authors' estimates from the CHIP data for 1988, 1995, 2002, 2007, and 2013.

because of the decline in its relative share, the corresponding proportion decreased to 58 percent in 2013.

The next largest contributors to income inequality in 2013 were pensions and imputed rents from owner-occupied housing, both of which had concentration coefficients similar to the Gini coefficient for household income. In 2013 the fourth largest contributor to income inequality was self-employment income, with a concentration coefficient of 0.35. In contrast, the concentration coefficient of property income, with a small relative share and rather concentrated in the higher part of the income distribution, was as high as 0.51.

The numerical values of the relative shares and concentration coefficients in 2007 and 2013 allow us to understand how the channels of urban income inequality, as measured by the Gini coefficient for disposable income, became more unequal. One channel is the expansion of the relative share of property income. Other channels are pensions, among which the concentration coefficient increased from 0.26 to 0.33, and enterprise income, which

Table 8.5. Household income per capita and its decomposition for urban residents

	Wages	Imputed rents of owner-occupied housing equity	Pensions	Enterprise income	Property income	Income in-kind	Housing subsidies	Net transfer income	Total
1988									
% of income	44.75	3.92	6.32	0.63	0.50	25.36	18.29	0.24	100
Concentration coefficient	0.1815	0.3372	0.3016	0.3628	0.4368	0.2216	0.3114	0.1090	0.2313
Contribution to inequality (%)	35.12	5.71	8.24	0.99	0.94	24.30	24.62	0.11	100
1995									
% of income	61.35	2.84	11.71	0.53	1.27	11.41	9.75	1.14	100
Concentration coefficient	0.2478	0.3718	0.3154	0.0314	0.4842	0.6391	0.5163	0.2567	0.3320
Contribution to inequality (%)	45.79	3.18	11.12	0.05	1.85	21.96	15.16	0.88	100
2002									
% of income	67.88	4.58	16.76	3.09	1.13	3.63	2.84	0.09	100
Concentration coefficient	0.3192	0.3364	0.3195	0.0495	0.4798	0.1835	0.4267	0.2012	0.3113
Contribution to inequality (%)	69.60	4.95	17.20	0.49	1.74	2.14	3.89	0.06	100
2007									
% of income	71.32	9.26	16.83	5.06	1.74	0.00	0.55	-4.79	100
Concentration coefficient	0.3592	0.3812	0.2560	0.3065	0.4975	0.5186	0.3079	0.5368	0.3350
Contribution to inequality (%)	76.47	10.54	12.86	4.63	2.58	0.00	0.51	-7.68	100
2013									
% of income	59.03	14.84	19.34	6.22	3.28	0	0.85	-3.57	100
Concentration coefficient	0.3482	0.3691	0.3327	0.3453	0.5083	0	.5364	0.4252	0.3522
Contribution to inequality (%)	58.36	15.55	18.27	6.10	4.73	0.00	1.29	-4.31	100

Note: The decomposition of the Gini is based on the sample and is not weighted. Therefore, the income shares reported in this table are not weighted and are not identical to those reported in Table 8.3.

Source: Authors' estimates from the CHIP data for 1988, 1995, 2002, 2007, and 2013.

had a concentration coefficient moving from 0.31 to 0.35. A fourth contributor to the increased urban income inequality between 2007 and 2013 was the decreased negative concentration coefficient of net transfers, i.e., mainly taxes. Taken together, the results from decomposing the Gini of disposable income by the income source indicate that during this period it is not appropriate to refer to one single reason for the increased Gini.

The information presented in the tables and figures in this section also illustrates that the nature of urban income inequality in China was rather different in 1988 than it was in 2013. Much of the income inequality in 1988 was due to in-kind income and housing subsidies; the first components were nonexistent and the second components were almost nonexistent in 2013. Instead, much more of urban China's inequality in 2013 than before can be attributed to (in this order) pensions, imputed rents of owner-occupied housing, enterprise income, and finally property income.

8.6 Conclusions

In this chapter, we present new results on how household income, household inequality, and income poverty among urban residents developed from 2007 to 2013. As very similar data were collected from the CHIP project for 1988, 1995, and 2002, we use these surveys to place this development in perspective. As shown, during a period when many countries in the West experienced stagnating or falling incomes, household income in urban China was growing by an average of 7 percent per annum. On the one hand, Chinese households may have been disappointed because the growth rate slowed down by almost one-half, compared to that during the period from 2002 to 2007. On the other hand, from the perspective of the income growth experienced by households in high-income countries, a median income growth of 7 percent was still very impressive.

Another finding is that during the period from 2007 to 2013 the components of total income grew at rather different speeds. The largest component, consisting of wages, was characterized by slow growth; this should be understood from the perspective that more workers were moving into self-employment or nonemployment. This trend means that most of the growth in the median income came from a combination of other income sources. The most important were pensions as the Chinese population is aging and imputed rents from owner-occupied housing. The latter should be seen against the background of rapidly increased housing prices. Smaller contributions came from rapidly increasing sources of enterprise income and property income.

We have also shown that from 2007 to 2013 real household income grew for all positions on the income distribution. The trend of fewer persons in urban China having incomes below the poverty line, expressed as the constant purchasing power, continued between 2007 and 2013. In 2013, not more than 4 percent of urban residents had incomes lower than the *dibao* line for Beijing and as few as 1 percent had incomes lower than the average of the *dibao* line for Yunnan. However, growth in urban household income was uneven across the distribution. The Gini coefficient jumped by 10 percentage units from 1988 to 1995. Thereafter, development of the Gini was irregular and did not show a clear trend. For 2013 we report a Gini of 0.35, which is higher than that in many high-income countries, but somewhat lower than that in the United States.

The distribution of income among urban residents since 1988 has been characterized by growth at the lower part lagging behind growth at the higher part. This lag means that more urban residents had incomes that are lower than a fixed percentage of the median income; 3 percent of the population had incomes lower than 50 percent of the median in 1988, 8 percent had incomes lower than 50 percent of the median in 1995, 12 percent had income lower than 50 percent of the median in 2002, and 15 percent had incomes lower than 50 percent of the median in 2013. It can also be observed that urban China has become home to large numbers of migrants with a rural *hukou* who earned incomes lower than those of the urban residents we have studied here.

Notes

Note: We thank members of the CHIP research team and particularly Terry Sicular for comments on previous drafts and versions.

1. See Fang, Zhang, and Fan (2002) who analyze 1992 and 1994–1998, and Meng, Gregory, and Wang (2005), who study the period from 1986 to 2000.
2. For more details, see, for example, Naughton (2007).
3. On the former, see, for example, Whyte (2010); on the latter, see, for example, Shi (2012).
4. For more information, see, for example, Lardy (2012).
5. Two concerns about the program have been raised. First, the stimulus program fueled an increased level of local debt in China. Second, it has been argued that the stimulus

program accelerated the advance of the role of the state in the economy. On the latter, see, for example, Johansson and Feng (2016).

6. Chongqing was part of Sichuan province until 1997, when it became a separate province. This history means that the territory of present-day Chongqing was included in the sample frame of Sichuan province during for the first two surveys.

7. This approach differs from Deng and Gustafsson (2013), who did not use sample weights.

8. The territory of China has experienced rapid urbanization as an increasing number of homes have been constructed on formerly agricultural land. When one takes this point into consideration, more areas are now administratively defined as urban. In some cases, local leaders have perceived urban status to be advantageous and thus they have actively pushed for reclassifications.

9. This component was estimated in the CHIP 2007 and 2013 surveys of urban residents by using the market rent approach; although not available in the surveys of urban residents for 1988, 1995, and 2002, in those surveys we estimate imputed rents as 8 percent of the net worth of owner-occupied housing.

10. See http://www.lisdatacenter.org/lis-ikf-webapp/app/search-ikf-figures. Accessed October 28, 2019. Our estimate for urban China is based on a definition of disposable income that includes imputed rents from owner-occupied housing; these are not included in the income definition of the Luxembourg Income Study (LIS). Our estimates of the urban Gini in 2007 and 2013 are very similar to those reported in Chapter 2 of this book.

11. Most studies of poverty in low- and middle-income countries, including China, are based on per capita income. Studies on income inequality and poverty in rich countries typically use equivalence scales. This measure assumes that the expenditure needs of two persons living in a single household are less than the sum of the needs of two single persons living separately. Equivalence scales typically also assume that children require fewer resources than adults.

12. A similar conclusion is drawn by Qi and Wu (2016) in an analysis of child poverty rates from 1989 to 2011, based on the China Health and Nutrition Survey Data (CHNS).

13. The purchasing power of the Hong Kong poverty line is much higher, amounting to 3500 Hong Kong dollars per person and month. With the use of the 2013 exchange rate, this rate corresponds to 3000 yuan per person and month. See Government of Hong Kong (2014).

14. See Chapters 6 and 7 for further explanation of the FGT indexes. Also see Foster, Greer, and Thorbecke (1984). The poverty gap for poor households is defined as the difference between the poverty line and household income. This gap is normalized by dividing it by the poverty line to produce a value in the interval from 0 to 1 (in cases in which the incomes are nonnegative). FGT(1) is the average of the poverty gaps for all poor households; FGT(2) squares each observation's poverty gap before taking the average.

15. When local governments assess *dibao* claims, they do not include the imputed rents of owner-occupied housing in the income test. The 2013 *dibao* line for Beijing is given at http://district.ce.cn/newarea/roll/201212/26/t20121226_23978605.shtml. Accessed

November 19, 2019. For Yunnan, the 2012 year-end urban *dibao* line continued to be used in 2013 (personal communication). The 2012 year-end *dibao* line for Yunnan can be found at https://wenku.baidu.com/view/b0f9f9660b4c2e3f56276333.html. Accessed November 19, 2019.

16. In 2007, among persons between the ages of 16 and 70, 56.3 percent were wage earners, but the proportion decreased to 51.0 percent in 2013. Mirroring these data, the proportion of those who were self-employed increased from 11.9 percent in 2007 to 19.8 percent in 2013. Whereas wages per wage earner continued to grow rapidly from 2007 to 2013, wages per household member increased slowly.

17. This result means that measures of household income that do not include imputed rents from owner-occupied housing will show lower rates of household income growth from 2007 to 2013 than those here applied (results that we consider to be more relevant).

18. See Chapter 2 for an explanation of the decomposition methodology of the Gini coefficient by income sources.

References

Appleton, S., L. Song, and Q. Xia (2010). "Growing out of Poverty: Trends and Patterns of Urban Poverty in China 1988–2002." *World Development*, 38(5), 665–678.

Atkinson, A. B. (2015). *Inequality: What Can Be Done?* Cambridge, MA: Harvard University Press.

Cai, H., Y. Chen, and L.-A. Zhou (2010). "Income and Consumption Inequality in Urban China: 1992–2003." *Economic Development and Cultural Change*, 58(3), 385–413.

Deng, Q. and B. Gustafsson (2013). "A New Episode of Increased Urban Income Inequality in China," in S. Li, H. Sato, and T. Sicular, eds., *Rising Inequality in China: Challenges to a Harmonious Society*, 255–288. Cambridge and New York: Cambridge University Press.

Eurostat (2016). "File: At-Risk-of-Poverty Rate and At-Risk-of-Poverty Threshold (for a Single Person), 2013 and 2014." http://ec.europa.eu/eurostat/statistics-explained/index.php/File:At-risk-of-poverty_rate_and_at-risk-of-poverty_threshold_(for_a_single_person),_2013_and_2014.png. Accessed March 5, 2017.

Fang, C., X. Zhang, and S. Fan (2002). "Emergence of Urban Poverty and Inequality in Urban China: Evidence from Household Surveys." *China Economic Review*, 13(4), 430–443.

Foster, J., J. Greer, and E. Thorbecke (1984). "A Class of Decomposable Poverty Indices." *Econometrica*, 52(3), 761–766.

Government of Hong Kong SAR (2014). *Hong Kong Poverty Situation Report: Report 2013*. http://www.povertyrelief.gov.hk/eng/pdf/poverty_report13_rev2.pdf. Accessed March 5, 2017.

Gustafsson, B. and S. Ding (2013), "Unemployment and the Rising Number of Nonworkers in Urban China: Causes and Distributional Consequences," in S. Li, H. Sato, and T. Sicular, eds., *Rising Inequality in China: Challenges to a Harmonious Society*, 289–331. Cambridge and New York: Cambridge University Press.

He, D., Z. Zhang, and W. Zhang (2009). "How Large Will Be the Effect of China's Fiscal-Stimulus Package on Output and Employment?" Hong Kong Monetary Authority

Working Paper no. 05/2009. http://www.hkma.gov.hk/media/eng/publication-and-research/research/working-papers/HKMAWP09_05_full.pdf.   Accessed   March 5, 2017.

Johansson, A. C. and X. Feng (2016). "The State Advances, the Private Sector Retreats? Firm Effects of China's Great Stimulus Programme." *Cambridge Journal of Economics*, 40(6), 1635–1668.

Lardy, N. R. (2012). *Sustaining China's Economic Growth after the Global Financial Crisis*. Washington, DC: Peterson Institute for International Economics.

Meng, X. (2004). "Economic Restructuring and Income Inequality in Urban China." *Review of Income and Wealth*, 50(3), 357-379.

Meng, X., R. Gregory, and Y. Wang (2005). "Poverty, Inequality and Growth in Urban China, 1986-2000." *Journal of Comparative Economics*, 33(4), 710-729.

Naughton, B. (2007). *The Chinese Economy: Transitions and Growth*. Cambridge, MA: MIT Press.

Qi, D. and Y. Wu (2016). "Child Income Poverty Levels and Trends in Urban China From 1989 to 2011." *Child Indicators Research*, 9(4), 1043–1058.

Ravallion, M. and S. H. Chen (2003). "Measuring Pro-Poor Growth." *Economic Letters*, 78(1), 93-99.

Shi, S.-J. (2012). "Towards Inclusive Social Citizenship? Rethinking China's Social Security in the Trend towards Urban–Rural Harmonisation." *Journal of Social Policy*, 41(4), 789-810.

Thewissen, S., L. Kenworthy, B. Nolan, M. Roser, and T. Smeeding (2015). "Rising Income Inequality and Living Standards in OECD Countries: How Does the Middle Fare?" Luxembourg Income Study Working Paper Series no 656. http://www.lisdatacenter.org/wps/liswps/656.pdf. Accessed March 5, 2017.

Wang, F. (2008). *Boundaries and Categories: Rising Inequality in Post-Socialist Urban China*. Stanford, CA: Stanford University Press.

Whyte, M. K., ed. (2010). *One Country, Two Societies: Rural-Urban Inequality in Contemporary China*. Cambridge, MA: Harvard University Press.

World Bank (2016). *World Development Indicators*. http://databank.worldbank.org/data/reports.aspx?source=2&series=NY.GDP.PCAP.KD.ZG&country=. Accessed March 5, 2017.

9

Consumption Inequality in Urban China

Qingjie Xia, Shi Li, and Lina Song

9.1 Introduction

According to Sen (1995), there are many kinds of external inequalities, such as inequalities of opportunity (education and health care), income, wealth, and so forth. Just like poverty, these external inequalities are multidimensional. For a clear picture, it is necessary to examine every dimension of these inequalities. In this chapter, we study household consumption inequality in urban China by using the urban survey data of the China Household Income Project (CHIP). Like income inequality, consumption inequality is an ex post outcome of a country's political, social, and economic arrangements. The existence of a highly unequal distribution of income or of consumption leads us to focus on ensuring that a country's political, social, and economic institutions are equitable, because these institutions have implications in terms of equality of opportunity for the next generations (Atkinson 2015, p. 10).

Compared to income or wealth, however, consumption is more accurate in revealing people's economic well-being (Deaton 1997, pp. 350–354), more comprehensively reflecting the material resources of individuals and families other than money, such as the level of education, health care housing, private cars, and social security (Meyer and Sullivan 2011, 2012, and 2013). Cutler and Katz (1992) point out that income, which often is subject to fluctuations, is easily affected by temporary shocks and prone to measurement errors. In contrast, consumption is not only more stable than income but it also is more easily measured. According to the life cycle and permanent income hypotheses (Modigliani 1949; Modigliani and Brumberg 1954; Ando and Modigliani 1963; Friedman 1957), under the constraints of the income stream, households will smooth their consumption by saving or borrowing in order to maximize their lifetime utility; in other words, consumption is determined by expected long-term income rather than by temporary income.

Qingjie Xia, Shi Li, and Lina Song, *Consumption Inequality in Urban China* In: *Changing Trends in China's Inequality.*
Edited by: Terry Sicular, Shi Li, Ximing Yue, and Hiroshi Sato, Oxford University Press (2020). © Oxford University Press.
DOI: 10.1093/oso/9780190077938.003.0009

Consumption inequality has been widely researched throughout the world. Attanasio, Battistin, and Ichimura (2007) find that American consumption inequality increased substantially in the 1980s and 1990s. Aguiar and Bils (2011) show that American consumption inequality closely followed income inequality during the period from 1980 to 2007. Hassett and Mathur (2012) find that American consumption inequality has increased only marginally since the 1980s and that consumption inequality has narrowed during periods of recession, such as during the 2007–2009 recession. Norris and Pendakur (2015) demonstrate that Canadian household-level consumption inequality, measured by the Gini coefficient, increased from 0.251 to 0.275 from 1997 to 2006 but then declined to 0.264 in 2009.

In the developing world, Idrees and Ahmad (2010) find that Pakistani inequality, in terms of consumption expenditures, improved slightly between 1992 and 1993 and 2004 and 2005, but the extent of the inequality in food consumption remained substantially lower than the inequality of non-food consumption; household expenditures on education were more unequally distributed than overall consumption expenditures; in recent years healthcare expenditures in urban areas have become relatively more evenly distributed, whereas the level of inequality in terms of rural health-care expenditures has remained consistent, if not somewhat higher. Shanbhogue (2014) shows that among all the major states of India, inequality in rural consumption is less than that of urban consumption and that there was a very insignificant decline in rural consumption inequality from 2004–2005 to 2009–2010. Mukhopadhyay (2014) shows that access to microcredit in India exacerbates consumption inequality both at the slum level and at the household level. Basole and Basu (2015) find that the rise in overall expenditure inequalities in India has been due to the increased weight of non-food spending in household budgets, which tends to be more unequal than food spending; consumption inequality varies widely across broad non-food items: durables, education, health care, and consumer services show the most rapid increases in real expenditures and display the highest levels of inequality.

Since 1978, during the years of China's rapid upgrading from a poor and backward agricultural economy to a global manufacturing hub and the world's second largest economy, the mode of Chinese household consumption has been shifting at a dazzling speed—first from "wristwatches, bicycles, and sewing machines" in the 1970s to "refrigerators, color televisions, and washing machines" in the 1980s, then to "air conditioners, computers, and video recorders" in the 1990s, "apartments, automobiles, and large bank deposits" in the first decade of the 2000s, and finally to "deluxe apartments and automobiles, and study and travel abroad." Nevertheless, it can be observed that while the rich are pursuing luxuries, the poor are still contending with subsistence living, and there remain some 30 million people living in poverty in China (Zhengzhiju 2018).

Uncertainty is one of the main characteristics of a transitional country such as China. There are many kinds of risks and uncertainties for households in urban China (illness, unemployment, retrenchment, unpredictable events, etc.) and a rigidity of needs (home purchases, children's education and marriage, etc.). Since the beginning of the new century, the Chinese government has gradually improved its social security system, extending health care and retirement pensions to all citizens, setting up an effective low-income family allowance system and various employment encouragement schemes, allowing the children of rural/urban migrants to attend urban schools, and so forth. Notwithstanding these changes, the household savings rate in urban China increased from 8.74 percent in 1995 to 18.86 percent in 2002, and further to 22.77 percent in 2013.[1]

Given that the household consumption pattern in urban China is diversified and rapidly changing, closely monitoring consumption inequality should reveal the depth and diversity of inequality in modern China. In this regard, the existing literature provides some clues. Qu and Zhao (2008) find that the lower quantiles are associated with large consumption disparities. Guo and N'Diaye (2010) show that efforts to further raise household income and the share of employment in the services sector, as well as to develop capital markets, including liberalizing interest rates and creating alternative savings instruments, are likely to have the greatest impact on consumption. Gao and Zeng (2010) show that economic development has a negative impact on consumption inequality because of controls on inequality of after-tax income. Cai, Chen, and Zhou (2010) find a steadily rising trend in income and consumption inequality from 1992 to 2003 in urban China, but in general all urban residents remain better off economically. Liu and Li (2011) find that consumption inequality among urban households steadily increased from 1988 to 2007. Qiao (2013) finds that China experienced consumption inequality, with full or partial insurance of consumption against both permanent and transitory income shocks. Ma (2014) finds that after the Chinese economic reforms, inequalities in urban consumption deteriorated, becoming more serious than income inequalities. However, these studies on consumption inequality are rather general. In other words, apart from providing a general picture, household consumption inequalities should be studied in greater detail, in the same way that inequalities of household expenditures on food, clothing, housing, education, health care, and so forth are studied. Thus, household consumption inequalities are the focus of this chapter.

The chapter is arranged as follows. Section 9.2 introduces our data. Section 9.3 examines the results. Section 9.4 presents a concluding summary.

9.2 The Data

We use the CHIP survey data for the years 1995, 2002, and 2013 to investigate inequalities in urban household consumption expenditures. We do not use the 2007 data, because they lack certain variables on urban household consumption. Our analysis extends back to 1995 in order to reveal the marked changes in household consumption during the transition era. As mentioned in Chapter 1, the CHIP datasets are subsamples drawn from the larger annual national household surveys conducted by the National Bureau of Statistics (NBS). The CHIP 1995 survey covers eleven out of thirty-one provinces, the 2002 survey covers twelve provinces, and the 2013 survey covers fifteen provinces. For the cross-sectional analysis, following Khan and Riskin (1998, 2005), we constructed a self-estimated market rental price of owner-occupied housing that was not included in the older NBS official surveys. With respect to adjustments in the price levels, we adjusted total consumption expenditures from all years to 2013 constant prices by using the urban provincial-level CPI as published by the NBS.

The CHIP datasets contain urban household consumption expenditures provided by the NBS from its household survey data. The consumption data are collected by using a diary method. The surveyed households keep records of their daily consumption expenses, which are recorded by the statistical office. Following the NBS practice, consumption expenditures are subdivided into eight categories: food, clothing, housing, household equipment and services, transportation and communications, education and entertainment, health and medical care, and other expenditures. Consumption of housing equipment refers to the purchase of durable home appliances, such as refrigerators, televisions, automobiles, and so forth. The gradual consumption of durable good services is not considered here, because the prices of the durable goods cannot be identified and the value of their annual consumption cannot be calculated.

In the 1995 data, households received a certain amount of income in-kind from their work units; when possible, the value of this in-kind income was computed and included in the wage income. In urban China, universal nine-year compulsory education and a medical insurance system for those working in the state sector was implemented, and by 2013 medical insurance was extended to the entire country. This expansion indicates that to a certain extent those working in the state sector enjoyed medical subsidies.

In 1995, 57 percent of the surveyed urban households lived in houses rented from the state, for which they paid a very small amount of rent. With the marketization of residential housing, the proportion of urban households living in state-owned housing steadily declined. By 2002, only 18 percent of the surveyed urban households lived in state-owned housing, whereas by 2013 the questionnaire no longer asked whether housing was rented from the state. Housing consumption by urban households is calculated as the estimated rental value of owner-occupied housing if they live in their own houses or as the real rent if they live in rented houses. All comparable consumption figures over the years have been adjusted to 2013 constant prices, according to the relevant provincial urban consumer price indices, as reported by the statistical yearbooks collected and published by the NBS.

One issue regarding the 1995 consumption data is that in 1995 the mean of the total household consumption expenditures is much less than the mean of the sum of the previous eight subcategories. The former was *renminbi* (RMB) 8301 yuan and the latter was RMB 10,078 yuan, both including the market rental value of owner-occupied housing or the market rent for rental housing at 2013 constant prices. Yuan, Xia, and Wang (2016) report that the growth rate of household consumption expenditures from 1995 to 2002 was 4.18 percent, whereas the equivalent figure was 1.19 percent if the calculation used the sum of the eight categories of household consumption expenditures. Given that in both the 2002 and the 2013 surveys total household consumption expenditures are equal to the sum of the eight categories, for the 1995 survey we use the sum of the eight categories instead of the overall variable. We use this approach because part of our focus is on changes over time in each of the eight categories of household consumption.

As a two-person household would not consume more heating than a one-person household, there are economies of scale in household consumption. For this reason, we employed the widely used Organisation for Economic Co-operation and Development (OECD) equivalence scale for household consumption expenditures (Jappelli and Pistaferri 2010), under which the first adult of a household is given a weight of 1, each of the other adults in the household is given a weight of 0.7, and each of the children or teenagers (16 years old or younger) in the household is given a weight of 0.5. All consumption variables are adjusted according to this scale.

After this adjustment, equivalized per capita household consumption expenditures are higher than unadjusted per capita household consumption expenditures by 30 percent in 1995, 28 percent in 2002, and 24 percent in 2013, and the Gini coefficient of per capita household consumption is lower by 2.61 percent in 1995, 2.38 percent in 2002, and 3.78 percent in 2013 (see Tables 9.1 and 9.2). The differences between estimates using equivalized and unadjusted per capita values are due to the decrease in household size from

Table 9.1. Summary statistics of per capita household consumption (not using the household equivalence scale) and inequality of per capita household income

	No. of obs. (households)	Consumption					Income
		Gini	Mean	Standard deviation	Minimum	Maximum	Gini
1995	6930	0.3425	10,078	10,052.60	977	391,378	0.3295
2002	6835	0.3254	10,956	7517.52	1048	103,622	0.3078
2013	6742	0.3714	26,230	21,101.66	1631	346,366	0.3501

Note: At 2013 constant prices. Units for the consumption means, standard deviations, minima, and maxima are yuan. Here and elsewhere, we use the CHIP household income definition for household income per capita, as explained by Khan and Riskin (1998, 2005).

Table 9.2. Summary statistics of per capita household consumption (household size adjusted by the equivalence scale)

	No. of obs. (households)	Gini	Mean	Standard deviation	Minimum	Maximum
1995	6930	0.3364	13,092	13,252.01	1397	539,832
2002	6835	0.3262	14,063	9387.34	1431	141,303
2013	6742	0.3580	32,604	24,803.95	2223	346,366

Note: At 2013 constant prices. Units for the consumption means, standard deviations, minima, and maxima are yuan. In this table and all later ones, per capita consumption is calculated by using an equivalence scale (see the main text for an explanation of the equivalence scale adjustments to the household size).

3.13 persons per household in 1995 to 3.02 persons in 2002 and further to 2.97 persons in 2013.

9.3 Results

9.3.1 Inequality of per Capita Urban Household Consumption Expenditures

Table 9.2 presents per capita household consumption expenditures in constant 2013 prices after being adjusted by the equivalence scale. Average annual growth in per capita urban household consumption expenditures was 1.02 percent from 1995 to 2002 and 7.64 percent per annum from 2002 to 2013.[2] In contrast, the corresponding figures were 1.19 percent and 7.94 percent when we were using the per capita household consumption expenditures in constant 2013 prices without the equivalence scale adjustment. This result implies that beginning from 2002 the well-being of Chinese urban residents has been improving in terms of consumption. In contrast, the annual growth rate of per capita household income was 5.62 percent from 1995 to 2002 and 13.61 percent from 2002 to 2013.[3] Therefore, during both periods the growth of household consumption lagged behind that of household income by as much as about 4–6 percentage points.

The ratio of per capita household consumption to per capita household income, or the Engel curve, also changed substantially; it was 108 percent in 1995, 78 percent in 2002, and 71 percent in 2013.[4] It is strange that urban households consumed more than they earned in 1995.

During the period from 1995 to 2002, China implemented a series of unprecedented reforms and encountered numerous hardships. First, it implemented its most radical reform of the urban sector, characterized by a downsizing of the state-owned enterprises (SOE) and resulting in a reduction of nearly 30 million SOE workers by 2002 (Guowuyuan xinwen bangongshi 2004). Following the retrenchment, there were no longer pressures for a rise in urban wage rates and growth in urban wages slowed. However, due to the transition from a planned to a market supply of consumer goods, in the mid-1990s the prices of consumer goods were increasing. As a consequence, after meeting their monthly basic daily expenses, typical urban households with workers in the SOE sector would have nothing left to save. Moreover, those households with workers who had been laid off because of the enterprise reforms would have experienced a fall in their living standards and might have had to use their savings to maintain a certain level of consumption. In all, the hardships caused by the widespread retrenchment of one-half of the SOE labor force during the 1990s might partly explain the slow growth rate of urban household consumption. But this hypothesis does not entirely solve the previous puzzle.

Second, the Asian financial crisis in the late 1990s and the 2001–2002 recession in the developed countries resulted in a reduction in the volume of exports from China and hence a light deflation in urban consumer prices. In addition, the withdrawal of the SOEs from the consumer goods manufacturing sector led to an increase in the supply of such goods by the fledgling private sector. All these factors contributed to the fall in price levels. This drop might also provide some explanation for the low growth rate of urban household consumption during the period from 1995 to 2002.

In contrast, the period from 2002 to 2013 witnessed a high economic growth rate in China. Furthermore, improvements in the social security system, including the expansion of the medical insurance and pension systems, helped reduce the uncertainties faced by urban households. Encouraged by the high growth rate of income and the reduced uncertainties, Chinese urban households exhibited some consumption capacity, which resulted in a modest increase in the consumption growth rate, as compared to the earlier period.

Table 9.3 reports the annual growth rate of per capita household consumption expenditures by decile, which for the period from 1995 to 2002 exhibited an inverse U-shape, with a maximum growth rate of 1.74 percent at the 6th decile. In contrast, for the period from 2002 to 2013 the growth rate steadily increased across the deciles, from 6.15 percent for the lowest decile to 7.83 percent for the highest decile. In other words, during the first period the middle 50 percent of urban households enjoyed relatively high growth consumption, which tended to reduce consumption inequalities. During the second period, however, richer households enjoyed a higher consumption growth rate, implying an increase in consumption inequality.

Indeed, overall inequality of per capita urban household consumption expenditures measured by the Gini coefficient slightly decreased from 0.34 in 1995 to 0.33 in 2002, and then increased to 0.37 in 2013 (see Table 9.1).[5] The change in urban household consumption expenditure inequality followed the same trend as that of urban household income, in which the Gini coefficient first decreased from 0.33 in 1995 to 0.31 in 2002 but then increased

Table 9.3. Urban per capita household consumption by decile, 1995-2013

Decile	1995	2002	2013	1995-2002 Average annual growth	2002-2013 Average annual growth
10th	5493	5873	11,555	0.96%	6.15%
20th	6916	7520	15,377	1.20%	6.50%
30th	8106	8924	19,102	1.37%	6.92%
40th	9333	10,291	22,379	1.39%	7.06%
50th	10,563	11,766	26,272	1.54%	7.30%
60th	11,942	13,489	30,604	1.74%	7.45%
70th	13,839	15,583	36,021	1.70%	7.62%
80th	16,714	18,740	44,366	1.63%	7.83%
90th	22,560	24,462	60,539	1.16%	8.24%

Note: Per capita household consumption expenditure is adjusted by the equivalence scale and is at 2013 constant prices (yuan). The value of per capita household consumption for each decile is the value at exactly that decile point.

to 0.35 in 2013 (Table 9.1; see also Chapter 8 in this volume). These results imply that urban household consumption inequality is increasing a bit more rapidly than urban household income inequality.

In addition to the Gini coefficient, we also describe the inequality of urban household consumption with the 90th/10th, 90th/50th, 50th/10th, and 75th/25th percentile ratios. The percentile ratios are companions to the Gini coefficient in terms of measuring inequality, but these ratios are a more direct measure of inequality. However, the value of some consumption categories at certain percentiles might not match the overall consumption; for example, at a certain percentile point, some of the households might not have medical expenses. To avoid this possibility, we use the mean of household consumption per capita; for example, to represent per capita household consumption at the 90th percentile point we use the mean of the range of the 87.5th percentile point to the 92.5th percentile point (≥ the former, < the latter), to represent the 10th percentile point we use the mean of the range of p7.5th to p12.5th to represent p10th, and so forth. Then we calculate the mean of the values of each subcategory of per capita consumption strictly falling within the given range of overall per capita household consumption. For example, we use the mean of the per capita values of health and medical care expenditures falling in the range of the 87.5th to the 92.5th percentile

Table 9.4. Inequality of overall household consumption expenditures

	(p87.5–p92.5)/ (p7.5–p12.5)	(p87.5–p92.5)/ (p47.5–p52.5)	(p47.5–52.5)/ (p7.5–p12.5)	(p72.5–77.5)/ (p22.5–27.5)	Gini
1995	3.74	2.06	1.82	1.91	0.3364
2002	3.97	2.05	1.93	1.95	0.3262
2013	4.29	2.15	2.00	2.08	0.3580

Note: The per capita household consumption expenditure is adjusted by the equivalence scale and is at 2013 constant prices.

point of the overall per capita household consumption to represent per capita health and medical care expenditures at the 90th percentile point.

All the range ratios presented in Table 9.4 show that consumption inequality is increasing, which is slightly different from the picture provided by the Gini coefficient, as shown previously.[6] The range ratio "(p87.5–p92.5)/(p7.5–p12.5)" increases from 3.74 in 1995 to 3.97 in 2002 and further to 4.29 in 2013, whereas the middle range ratio "(p72.5–77.5)/(p22.5–27.5)" increases only from 1.91 in 1995 to 2.08 in 2013. In addition, consumption inequality is slightly larger in the upper half of the consumption distribution than in the lower half.

9.3.2 Inequality of the Major Components of Urban Household Consumption

Tables 9.5a show estimates of inequality for each of the major components of urban household consumption. The tables report the Gini coefficients and the range ratios for each component. In addition, they report the concentration coefficients. The concentration coefficient of a component is a measure of the inequality of that component relative to the distribution of overall consumption. In comparison, the Gini coefficient of a component measures the inequality of that component relative to its own distribution. Consequently, for example, a consumption component that is mainly consumed by poor households may have a high Gini coefficient but a low concentration coefficient. Note that if the concentration coefficient of a component is lower than the Gini coefficient for overall consumption, then it can be considered to be equalizing; the opposite is the case if the component's concentration coefficient is higher than the Gini for overall consumption. (See Chapter 2 for a fuller discussion of the concentration coefficient.)

Table 9.5a. Inequality of food, cigarettes, and alcohol consumption

	(p87.5–p92.5)/ (p7.5–p12.5)	(p87.5–p92.5)/ (p47.5–p52.5)	(p47.5–52.5)/ (p7.5–p12.5)	(p72.5–77.5)/ (p22.5–27.5)	Concentration coefficient	Gini
1995	2.04	1.41	1.44	1.43	0.2504	0.2505
2002	2.54	1.58	1.61	1.57	0.2735	0.2735
2013	2.39	1.60	1.49	1.55	0.3001	0.3003

Note: The per capita household consumption expenditure is adjusted by the equivalence scale and is at 2013 constant prices. The percentiles used to calculate the range ratios in this table are the percentiles of overall household consumption per capita.

Compared with the inequality of total consumption, the inequality of per capita food consumption is much lower (the concentration coefficients and Gini coefficients increased from 0.25 in 1995 to 0.27 in 2002 and further to 0.30 in 2013), as shown in Table 9.5a. The range ratio "(p87.5–p92.5)/ (p7.5–p12.5)" increased from 2.04 in 1995 to 2.54 in 2002 but then decreased to 2.39 in 2013, whereas all the other range ratios remained at about 1.50 across the period. These results strongly indicate that inequality in basic food consumption is much smaller than overall consumption, almost equal between the upper half and the lower half of the entire distribution and with a decreasing trend.

In contrast to food consumption, inequality of per capita clothing consumption is much larger and it increased sharply over time (the concentration coefficients and the Gini coefficients increased from about 0.41 in 1995 to 0.44 in 2002 and further to almost 0.50 in 2013) (see Table 9.5b). The range ratio "(p87.5–p92.5)/(p7.5–p12.5)" increased from 2.67 in 1995 to 3.20 in 2002 and further to 4.12 in 2013. The middle 50 percent of the distribution and the lower half exhibit almost the same inequality, at about 2.00, increasing only slightly. More interestingly, inequality was larger in the lower half of the distribution than in the upper half.

In general, housing consumption inequality (Table 9.5c) was decreasing (the concentration and Gini coefficients decreased from 0.62 in 1995 to 0.44 in 2002, but then increased slightly to 0.46 in 2013). The range ratio "(p87.5–p92.5)/(p7.5–p12.5)" decreased from 5.98 in 1995 to 4.39 in 2002 but it increased to 4.99 in 2013; the range ratio of the middle 50 percent indicates a similar trend, at about 2.00. Inequality was much larger in the upper half of

Table 9.5b. Inequality of clothing consumption

	(p87.5–p92.5)/ (p7.5–p12.5)	(p87.5–p92.5)/ (p47.5–p52.5)	(p47.5–52.5)/ (p7.5–p12.5)	(p72.5–77.5)/ (p22.5–27.5)	Concentration coefficient	Gini
1995	2.67	1.55	1.73	1.73	0.4165	0.4087
2002	3.20	1.58	2.02	1.85	0.4451	0.4392
2013	4.12	1.99	2.07	2.23	0.4958	0.4886

Note: The per capita household consumption expenditure is adjusted by the equivalence scale and is at 2013 constant prices. The percentiles used to calculate the range ratios in this table are the percentiles of overall household consumption per capita.

Table 9.5c. Inequality of housing consumption

	(p87.5–p92.5)/ (p7.5–p12.5)	(p87.5–p92.5)/ (p47.5–p52.5)	(p47.5–52.5)/ (p7.5–p12.5)	(p72.5–77.5)/ (p22.5–27.5)	Concentration coefficient	Gini
1995	5.98	2.88	2.07	2.17	0.6208	0.6202
2002	4.39	2.49	1.76	1.91	0.4435	0.4433
2013	4.99	2.24	2.22	2.14	0.4646	0.4640

Note: The per capita household consumption expenditure is adjusted by the equivalence scale and is at 2013 constant prices. The percentiles used to calculate the range ratios in this table are the percentiles of overall household consumption per capita.

the distribution than it was in the lower half, and it decreased in the former but it increased in the latter.

Consumption of household equipment and services is much more unequal than overall consumption, but this inequality has been falling sharply (the concentration coefficients and the Gini coefficients increased from about 0.54 in 1995 to 0.64 in 2002 but then decreased to 0.57 in 2013) (see Table 9.5d). The range ratio "(p87.5–p92.5)/(p7.5–p12.5)" decreased from 8.43 in 1995 to 7.26 in 2002 and further to 4.97 in 2013; the range ratio of the middle 50 percent indicated the same trend, at a value of about 3.00. In 1995 inequality was larger in the upper half of the distribution than it was in the lower half, but in the latter two years this phenomenon was reversed.

Inequality of transportation and communications consumption is much larger than that of overall consumption, and this inequality was decreasing during the first period but increasing during the second period (both the

Table 9.5d. Inequality of household equipment and services consumption

	(p87.5–p92.5)/ (p7.5–p12.5)	(p87.5–p92.5)/ (p47.5–p52.5)	(p47.5–52.5)/ (p7.5–p12.5)	(p72.5–77.5)/ (p22.5–27.5)	Concentration coefficient	Gini
1995	8.43	3.18	2.66	3.10	0.5435	0.5427
2002	7.26	2.32	3.13	2.96	0.6413	0.6350
2013	4.97	1.99	2.50	2.45	0.5777	0.5742

Note: The per capita household consumption expenditure is adjusted by the equivalence scale and is at 2013 constant prices. The percentiles used to calculate the range ratios in this table are the percentiles of overall household consumption per capita.

Table 9.5e. Inequality of transportation and communications consumption

	(p87.5–p92.5)/ (p7.5–p12.5)	(p87.5–p92.5)/ (p47.5–p52.5)	(p47.5–52.5)/ (p7.5–p12.5)	(p72.5–77.5)/ (p22.5–27.5)	Concentration coefficient	Gini
1995	7.36	1.91	3.85	2.60	0.6773	0.6096
2002	5.06	2.18	2.32	2.41	0.5183	0.5124
2013	7.07	3.28	2.16	2.67	0.6364	0.6354

Note: The per capita household consumption expenditure is adjusted by the equivalence scale and is at 2013 constant prices. The percentiles used to calculate the range ratios in this table are the percentiles of overall household consumption per capita.

concentration coefficients and the Gini coefficients decreased from 1995 to 2002 and then increased from 2002 to 2013) (see Table 9.5e). The range ratio "(p87.5–p92.5)/(p7.5–p12.5)" decreased from 7.36 in 1995 to 5.06 in 2002 but increased to 7.07 in 2013; the range ratio of the middle 50 percent revealed the same trend, at a value of about 2.50. In 1995 and 2002, the inequality was larger in the lower half of the distribution than it was in the upper half, but in 2013 this phenomenon was reversed. In addition, inequality increased in the upper half of the distribution but decreased in the lower half.

Inequality of education, culture, and entertainment consumption was much larger than that of overall consumption and it was increasing over time (the concentration coefficient initially decreased from 1995 to 2002 but then increased; the Gini coefficient increased throughout these years) (see Table 9.5f). The range ratio "(p87.5–p92.5)/(p7.5–p12.5)" increased from 5.36 in 1995 to 7.62 in 2002 and further to 8.10 in 2013; the range ratio of the middle

Table 9.5f. Inequality of education, culture, and entertainment consumption

	(p87.5–p92.5)/ (p7.5–p12.5)	(p87.5–p92.5)/ (p47.5–p52.5)	(p47.5–52.5)/ (p7.5–p12.5)	(p72.5–77.5)/ (p22.5–27.5)	Concentration coefficient	Gini
1995	5.36	2.15	2.49	2.88	0.6874	0.5736
2002	7.62	2.65	2.88	2.76	0.6005	0.5888
2013	8.10	2.37	3.42	2.93	0.6387	0.6239

Note: The per capita household consumption expenditure is adjusted by the equivalence scale and is at 2013 constant prices. The percentiles used to calculate the range ratios in this table are the percentiles of overall household consumption per capita.

Table 9.5g. Inequality of health and medical care consumption

	(p87.5–p92.5)/ (p7.5–p12.5)	(p87.5–p92.5)/ (p47.5–p52.5)	(p47.5–52.5)/ (p7.5–p12.5)	(p72.5–77.5)/ (p22.5–27.5)	Concentration coefficient	Gini
1995	3.99	2.11	1.89	1.93	0.7068	0.6739
2002	5.74	2.19	2.62	2.26	0.6519	0.6353
2013	4.51	2.41	1.87	2.26	0.7217	0.7050

Note: The per capita household consumption expenditure is adjusted by the equivalence scale and is at 2013 constant prices. The percentiles used to calculate the range ratios in this table are the percentiles of overall household consumption per capita.

50 percent revealed roughly the same trend at a value of about 2.80. This inequality was larger in the lower half of the distribution than it was in the upper half, and both halves exhibited a rising trend.

Inequality of health and medical care consumption was about the same as that of overall consumption in terms of the range ratios (the concentration coefficient and the Gini coefficient decreased from 1995 to 2002 and then increased to 2013) (see Table 9.5g). The range ratio "(p87.5–p92.5)/(p7.5–p12.5)" increased from 3.99 in 1995 to 5.74 in 2002 and decreased to 4.51 in 2013. The range ratio of the middle 50 percent increased during the first period but remained unchanged during the second period, at a value of about 2.00. Inequality was also about 2.00 in both the upper and lower halves of the distribution, but it increased in the upper half and decreased in the lower half during the second period.

9.3.3 Decomposition of Consumption Inequality
by its Components

We employ Rao's (1969) decomposition method to decompose the inequality of urban household consumption expenditures into eight consumption-items categories. The contribution of food to overall consumption inequality remained almost unchanged at 20 percent in 1995 and 2002, but it decreased to 19 percent in 2013 (see Table 9.6a). The contribution of housing also remained the same at 35 percent in the earlier two years, but it increased to 40 percent in 2013. The contribution of clothing remained about the same at about 6.5 percent. The contribution of home equipment and services was about 30 percent in 1995, but it fell to 7 percent in 2002 and further to 6 percent in 2013. The contributions of transportation and communications, education and entertainment, and health and medical care all exhibited an upward trend, in particular, the contributions of transportation and communications increased sharply from less than 2 percent in 1995 to 9 percent in 2002 and further to 13 percent in 2013.

9.3.4 Shares of the Major Consumption Components
in Urban Household Consumption

The contribution of each consumption component to inequality in overall consumption depends not only on how equally or unequally it is distributed but also on how large it is relative to overall consumption, that is, its share of total consumption. Now we will tackle the shares of each consumption category in total consumption (Table 9.6b) and their changes in the entire distribution (Figures 9.1–9.7).

As Chinese urban households were becoming richer, the share of food expenditures was decreasing steadily, from 34 percent in 1995 to 30 percent in 2002 and further to 24 percent in 2013 (see Table 9.6b). In addition, in each of these three years the share of food expenditures was inversely related to the level of overall consumption expenditures. In 1995 the share was 50 percent at the 10th percentile and 28 percent at the 90th percentile (see Figure 9.1). Similarly, in 2002 the shares of food expenditures for the 10th and 90th percentiles were 40 percent and 26 percent, and in 2013 they were 36 percent and 21 percent respectively. According to the National Commission of

Table 9.6a. The relative contributions of each consumption component to the inequality of overall consumption (%)

	1995	2002	2013
Food, cigarettes, and alcohol	18.69	19.40	14.97
Clothing	5.30	6.10	6.44
Housing	34.24	34.93	41.45
Household equipment and services	30.31	6.78	5.68
Transportation and communications	1.63	9.05	13.31
Education, culture, and entertainment	3.22	14.66	9.70
Health and medical care	2.35	5.93	5.47
Others	4.26	3.14	2.98
Total	100	100	100

Table 9.6b. The share in total consumption of each consumption component (%)

	1995	2002	2013
Food, cigarettes, and alcohol	34.26	29.52	23.85
Clothing	8.21	7.56	7.23
Housing	22.78	30.29	37.89
Household equipment and services	22.22	5.09	5.29
Transportation and communications	1.36	7.76	9.54
Education, culture, and entertainment	3.46	11.68	8.71
Health and medical care	2.37	5.50	5.25
Other	5.35	2.60	2.24
Total	100	100	100

Development and Reform of China (Guojia fazhan gaige weiyuanhui 2018), in an affluent society the share of food expenditures in a household's total consumption expenditures is not greater than 30 percent. By this standard, only 15 percent of the Chinese urban households can be considered to be affluent in 1995; the figure climbed to 25 percent in 2002, and then to a much higher 65 percent in 2013 (see Figure 9.1). However, affluence was primarily an urban phenomenon. No rural households reached this standard in 1995 and 2002, and in 2013 they reached only 25 percent.[7]

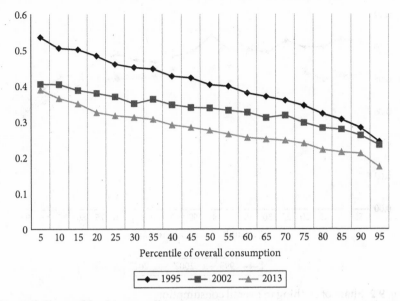

Fig. 9.1 Share of food in overall consumption

For all three years the share of clothing fell slightly over time and across the percentiles of the consumption distribution of the same year. The share of clothing in overall consumption decreased from 8.21 percent in 1995 to 7.56 percent in 2002 and further to 7.23 percent in 2013 (see Table 9.6b). In 1995, the clothing share decreased almost steadily as the level of overall consumption increased from 11 percent at the 10th percentile to 9.8 percent at the median and then sharply to 7.5 percent at the 90th percentile (see Figure 9.2). In 2002 at first the share remained almost unchanged at about 8 percent from the 80th percentile downward, but it then decreased to 6.6 percent at the 90th percentile. In 2013 the share first slowly increased from 6.8 percent at the 10th percentile to 8.4 percent at the 70th percentile, but it then sharply decreased to 7 percent at the 90th percentile.

In contrast with the decline in the food share over time, the share of housing consumption increased sharply, from 23 percent in 1995 to 30 percent in 2002 and further to 38 percent in 2013 (see Table 9.6b). In 1995 the housing share rose steadily across the percentiles of the consumption distribution, from 14 percent at the 10th percentile to 23 percent at the 90th percentile (see Figure 9.3). In 2002 the curve of the share exhibited an inverse U-shape, first decreasing from 28.6 percent at the 10th percentile to

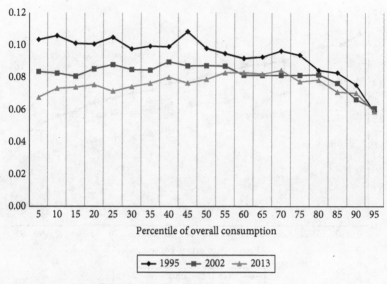

Fig. 9.2 Share of clothing in overall consumption

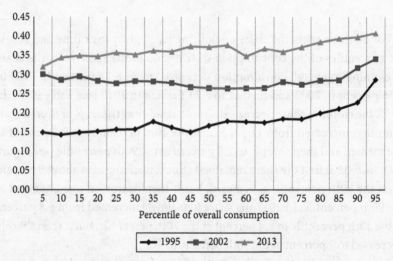

Fig. 9.3 Share of housing in overall consumption

26.5 percent at the median, but then increasing to 31.8 percent at the 90th percentile. In 2013 the share slowly increased from 34.4 percent at the 10th percentile to 39.7 percent at the 90th percentile.

The share of household equipment and services in overall consumption decreased sharply over time, from 22.22 percent in 1995 to 5.09 percent in

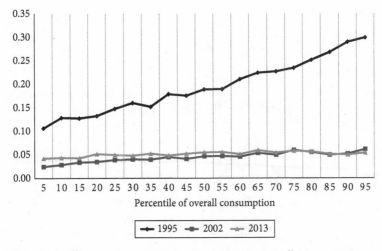

Fig. 9.4 Share of housing equipment and services in overall consumption

2002, but it then increased slightly to 5.29 percent in 2013 (see Table 9.6b). In 1995 the share steadily rose from 12.9 percent at the 10th percentile to 29.0 percent at the 90th percentile (see Figure 9.4). However, the share in 2002 was almost indistinguishable from that in 2013, and it was not much different from the mean over the entire distribution. This result may be because in 1995 the prices of domestic electric and electronic appliances (televisions, video cassettes, washing machines, refrigerators, etc.) were relatively high compared to wages, and these expenditures accounted for a large share of household consumption. The richer households could afford to buy more of such equipment. After the turn of the twenty-first century, these household appliances became much less expensive relative to household incomes and hence expenditures on these items did not make much of a difference among households with different incomes.

The share of transportation and communications in overall consumption increased sharply over time, from 1.36 percent in 1995 to 7.76 percent in 2002 and further to 9.54 percent in 2013 (see Table 9.6). Interestingly, the curves in the first two years are sloping slightly upward, but in 2013 the curve almost coincides with the 2002 curve from the 80th percentile downward (Figure 9.5). This result implies that there was not much difference in terms of consumption of transportation and communications among families at different expenditure levels in the same year. From the 80th percentile upward, the share increased sharply as overall consumption moved to the top

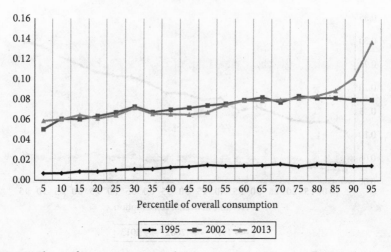

Fig. 9.5 Share of transportation and communications in overall consumption

in 2013. This group of households may also be those households that owned family cars.

The share of education and entertainment in overall consumption expenditures initially sharply increased from 3.5 percent in 1995 to 11.7 percent in 2002, but it then decreased 8.7 percent in 2013 (see Table 9.6b). In general, in all three years the curves are upward-sloping, with the curves in the latter two years much steeper than those in the first year (Figure 9.6). This result indicates that the share of education and entertainment increased with the overall consumption level during the period from 1995 to 2013. Since the establishment of New China, the Chinese government has pursued an expansion of urban education through relatively low tuition fees. This expansion might explain why both the share and the relative contribution of education in overall consumption accounted for only about 10 percent of overall household consumption and its inequality, respectively. Both indicators, moreover, show a decreasing trend since 2002. Interestingly, in 2002 and 2013 the education share increased with overall household consumption expenditures. This increase may reflect the recent emergence of more expensive education alternatives that are pursued by households that have sufficient resources.

The share of health and medical care in overall consumption increased from 2.4 percent in 1995 to 5.5 percent in 2002 but then decreased to 5.3 percent in 2013 (see Table 9.6b). The curves in all three years fluctuate up and down around the mean. This fluctuation means that the share would not be

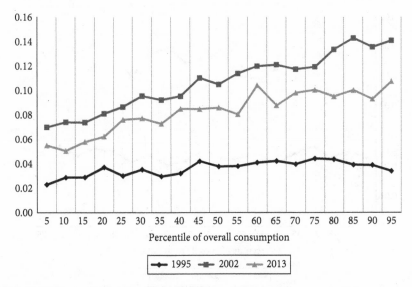

Fig. 9.6 Share of education and entertainment in overall consumption

much different at the different consumption levels (see Figure 9.7). This result implies that health and medical care expenditures differ significantly
from other types of consumption in the sense that the share of health and
medical care expenditures depends not so much on income but rather on
whether any family member is ill.

Although Chinese urban household health and medical care expenditures
exhibit the biggest Gini coefficient and other inequality measures among the
eight household consumption categories, the share of household health and
medical care against overall consumption expenditures was rather stable in
1995 and sloping slightly upward in 2002 and 2013 (see Figure 9.7).

The Chinese medical care system has continually been undergoing changes.
Before the reform, those who worked in the state sector and their direct relatives
with official urban household registrations were covered by the state urban
medical insurance. After the reform, urban medical insurance increasingly
encountered difficulties because of the decline in the number of SOEs. In 1998,
only 44 percent of urban residents were covered by the state medical insurance
(Lei 2018). But in the late 1990s, China gradually began to re-establish a medical insurance system: an urban medical insurance system for those who were
employed in the formal sector, a basic medical insurance system for rural and
low-income urban households in 2005, and a basic medical insurance system

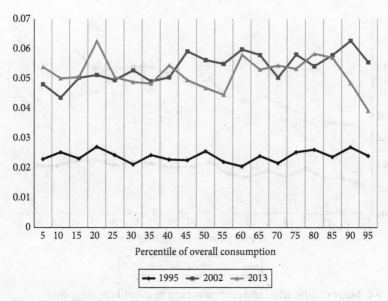

Fig. 9.7 Share of health and medical care in overall consumption

for urban residents in 2007. Since then, nearly all residents have been covered by one of the various medical care insurance systems.[8] It is perhaps because of the re-establishment of the medical insurance system that the share of health and medical care in overall household consumption expenditures and its contribution to overall consumption inequality did not shoot up after 2000 even as Chinese urban households became wealthier.

9.4 Summary

We use the CHIP 1995, 2002, and 2013 data to investigate inequality in urban household consumption expenditures. After adjustments by an equivalence scale, per capita urban household consumption expenditures increased by 1 percent per annum from 1995 to 2002 and by 7.64 percent per annum from 2002 to 2013. This result implies that only beginning from 2002 did the well-being of Chinese urban residents show a rapid improvement in terms of consumption.

The overall inequality of urban household consumption expenditures measured by the Gini coefficient decreased slightly from 0.33 in 1995 to 0.32 in 2002, but it then increased to 0.36 in 2013, following the same trend, but more severely, as that of urban income. However, the percentile ratio of p90/ p10 shows that consumption inequality between the two tails of the distribution increased over the entire period. In addition, consumption inequality was slightly larger in the upper half of the consumption distribution than it was in the lower half.

Inequality of basic food consumption was much smaller than that of overall consumption, almost equal between the upper half and the lower half of the entire distribution, and revealing a decreasing trend. Unlike food, clothing consumption inequality was much larger and it was increasing more sharply over time. Inequality of housing consumption was decreasing, and it was much larger in the upper half of the distribution than it was in the lower half and it was decreasing in the former but increasing in the latter.

The contribution of food to overall consumption inequality remained almost unchanged at 20 percent in 1995 and 2002, but it decreased to 15 percent by 2013. The contribution of housing also remained the same at 35 percent in the first two years, but it increased to 40 percent by 2013. The contribution of clothing remained at about 6.5 percent.

As Chinese urban households were becoming richer, the share of food expenditures was decreasing steadily from one-third in 1995 to one-quarter in 2013. In addition, the food share steadily decreased as the overall consumption level moved up the distribution in each of the three years. The share of clothing in overall consumption remained at about 7 percent over time, but it exhibited a downward slope as overall consumption increased in each of the three years. In contrast with the falling food share over time, the share of housing consumption increased sharply from 23 percent in 1995 to 30 percent in 2002 and further to 38 percent in 2013. Furthermore, it showed an upward sloping trend as overall consumption increased in each of the three years. The share of household equipment and services in overall consumption decreased sharply from 22 percent in 1995 to 5 percent in the latter two years.

These trends in urban household consumption are a reflection of economic and government policy changes over time. In general, for households at the bottom and lower-middle income levels, improvements in China's social programs (retirement pensions, medical insurance, unemployment insurance, disability and subsistence allowances, etc.) and public services (education, health care and public transportation, etc.) encouraged more consumption and to some extent also reduced consumption inequalities. For the unemployed, training or other re-employment schemes helped them find employment and thus increase their consumption capacity.

Yet housing privatization and the rising costs of housing had a different effect. Since 1998, the consumption of the majority of households at the bottom- or lower-middle income levels has been constrained in order to save for housing purchases. The supply of low-cost housing alternatives for low-income households reduced their consumption power. With respect to some of the components of consumption, changes in the level and inequality of consumption reflect the expansion of markets and falling prices. This trend is specifically relevant to consumption of communications and transportation items, such as telephones, Wi-Fi, mobile phones, Internet car services, and online shopping.

Notes

Note: Qingjie Xia's research work for this chapter was supported by the 2015 Beijing Municipal Social Science Foundation's Research Base Project on "A Study of Multidimensional Poverty in Urban Beijing" (Grant No. 15JDJGA071).

1. Calculated from the urban CHIP data by the authors.
2. The growth rate of household consumption is calculated by using exponential growth rate = [natural log of (household income per capita at year-end divided by that of the base year figure)]/(no. of years).
3. Calculated from the CHIP urban household data by the authors, using the exponential growth rate; the household income definition of Khan and Riskin (1998, 2005) is applied here.
4. The figures are calculated by the authors using the CHIP urban household data. We calculated household income per capita by following the definition of Khan and Riskin (1998, 2005), which follows the CHIP income definition.
5. So that the household consumption inequality is comparable to the household income inequality, we use the Gini coefficient of household consumption per capita before the equivalence adjustment.
6. This discrepancy might be explained by the fact that by employing the Gini coefficient, giving an extra yuan to a person a quarter of the way up from the bottom of the income distribution will produce an effect on measured inequality that is three times that of giving an extra yuan to a person a quarter of the way down from the top (Atkinson 2015, p. 17).
7. Calculated by the authors using the rural CHIP survey data.
8. In 2003 the Chinese government re-established its rural medical care system, called the "New Rural Cooperative Medical System" (NRCMS).

References

Aguiar, M. A. and M. Bils (2011). "Has Consumption Inequality Mirrored Income Inequality?" NBER Working Paper, no. 16807.

Ando, A. and F. Modigliani (1963). "The 'Life Cycle' Hypothesis of Saving: Aggregate Implications and Tests." *American Economic Review*, 53(1), 55–84.

Atkinson, A. B. (2015). *Inequality: What Can Be Done?* Cambridge, MA: Harvard University Press.

Attanasio, O., E. Battistin, and H. Ichimura (2007). "What Really Happened to Consumption Inequality in the United States?" in E. R. Berndt and C. R. Hulten, eds., *Hard-to-Measure Goods and Services: Essays in Honor of Zvi Griliches*, 515–543. Chicago: University of Chicago Press.

Basole, A. and D. Basu (2015). "Non-Food Expenditures and Consumption Inequality in India." University of Massachusetts Amherst, Department of Economics, Working Paper, no. 2015-06. https://www.umass.edu/economics/publications/2015-06.pdf. Accessed January 6, 2017.

Cai, H., Y. Chen, and L. Zhou (2010). "Income and Consumption Inequality in Urban China: 1992–2003." *Economic Development and Cultural Change*, 58(3), 385–413.

Cutler, D. and L. Katz (1992). "Rising Inequality? Changes in the Distribution of Income and Consumption in the 1980s." *American Economic Review*, 82(2), 546–551.

Deaton, A. (1997). *The Analysis of Household Surveys: A Microeconometric Approach to Development Policy*. Baltimore: Johns Hopkins University Press.

Friedman, M. (1957). *A Theory of the Consumption Function*. Princeton, NJ: Princeton University Press.

Gao, Z., and Z. Zeng (2010). "Economic Development and Consumption Inequality: Evidence and Theory." http://www.rbnz.govt.nz/-/media/ReserveBank/Files/Publications/Seminars%20and%20workshops/AMW2010/3955105.pdf?la=en. Accessed January 6, 2017.

Guo, K. and P. N'Diaye (2010). "Determinants of China's Private Consumption: An International Perspective." IMF Working Paper, no. WP/10/93.

Guojia fazhan gaige weiyuanhui (National Commission of Development and Reform) (2018). *2017 nian Zhongguo jumin xiaofei fazhan baogao* (Report on the development of consumption among Chinese residents in 2017). Beijing: Renmin chubanshe.

Guowuyuan xinwen bangongshi (News Office of the State Council) (2004). " 'Zhongguo de jiuye zhuangkuang he zhengce' baipishu" (White paper on the situation and policies of employment of China). Beijing. http://www.people.com.cn/BIG5/shizheng/1026/2468764.html. Accessed January 7, 2017.

Hassett, K. A. and A. Mathur (2012). "A New Measure of Consumption Inequality." *American Enterprise Institute Economic Studies*. https://papers.ssrn.com/sol3/papers.cfm?abstract_id=2212998. Accessed October 20, 2019.

Idrees, M. and E. Ahmad (2010). "Measurement and Decomposition of Consumption Inequality in Pakistan." *Lahore Journal of Economics*, 15(2), 97–112.

Jappelli, T. and L. Pistaferri (2010). "Does Consumption Inequality Track Income Inequality in Italy?" *Review of Economic Dynamics*, 13(1), 133–153.

Khan, A. R. and C. Riskin (1998). "Income and Inequality in China: Composition, Distribution and Growth of Household Income, 1988 to 1995." *China Journal*, no. 154, 221–253.

Khan, A. R. and C. Riskin (2005). "China's Household Income and Its Distribution, 1995 and 2002." *China Quarterly*, no. 182, 356–384.

Lei, X. Y. (2018). "Zhongguo yiliao baozhang tixi jianshe de huigu yu zhanwang" (Review and prospects for the formation of a medical care system in China). https://3g.163.com/dy/article_cambrian/DJNMK5KC0519R8II.html#qd=cambrian. Accessed July 23, 2018.

Liu, J. and S. Li (2011). "Changes in Consumption Inequality in China." Centre for Human Capital and Productivity. CHCP Working Paper, 2011-11. London, Canada: Department of Economics, University of Western Ontario.

Ma, F. (2014). "Consumption Inequality in Urban China: 1988–2009." *International Business and Management*, 8(2), 41–44.

Meyer, B. D. and J. X. Sullivan (2011). "Viewpoint: Further Results on Measuring the Well-Being of the Poor Using Income and Consumption." *Canadian Journal of Economics*, 44(1), 52–87.

Meyer, B. D. and J. X. Sullivan (2012). "Identifying the Disadvantaged: Official Poverty, Consumption Poverty, and the New Supplemental Poverty Measure." *Journal of Economic Perspectives*, 26(3), 111–135.

Meyer, B. D. and J. X. Sullivan (2013). "Consumption and Income Inequality and the Great Recession." *American Economic Review*, 103(3), 178–83.

Modigliani F. (1949). "Fluctuations in the Saving-Income Ratio: A Problem in Economic Forecasting," in *Studies in Income and Wealth*, 369–344. New York: National Bureau of Economic Research.

Modigliani, F. and R. H. Brumberg (1954). "Utility Analysis and the Consumption Function: An Interpretation of Cross-Sectional Data," in K. Kunhara, ed., *Post Keynesian Economics*, 388–436. New Brunswick, NJ: Rutgers University Press.

Mukhopadhyay, J. P. (2014). "Does Access to Microfinance Affect Consumption Inequality? Evidence from a Randomized Controlled Trial in Andhra Pradesh, India." Institute for Financial Management and Research (IFMR), Chennai, India. https://editorialexpress.com/cgi-bin/conference/download.cgi?db_name=acged2013 &paper_id=264. Accessed January 7, 2017.

Norris, S. and K. Pendakur (2015). "Consumption Inequality in Canada, 1997 to 2009." *Canadian Journal of Economics*, 48(2), 773–792.

Qiao, K. (2013). "Consumption Inequality in China: Theory and Evidence from the China Health and Nutrition Survey." *Frontiers of Economics in China*, 8(1), 91–112.

Qu, Z. and Z. Zhao (2008). "Urban-Rural Consumption Inequality in China from 1988 to 2002: Evidence from Quantile Regression Decomposition." IZA Discussion Paper, no. 3659.

Rao, V. M. (1969). "Two Decompositions of Concentration Ratio." *Journal of the Royal Statistical Society, Series A*. 132(3), 418–425.

Sen, A. (1995). *Inequality Reexamined*. Cambridge, MA: Harvard University Press.

Shanbhogue, A. (2014). "Consumption Inequality in India." *ZENITH International Journal of Multidisciplinary Research*, 4(4), 281–289.

Yuan, H. L., Q. J. Xia, and Z. W. Wang (2016). "Zhongguo chengzhen jumin xiaofei xuqiu fenxi" (Analysis of consumption demand in urban China). *Jingji kexue*, no. 4, 54-64.

Zhengzhiju (Politburo [of the CCP]) (2018). "Guanyu daying tuopin gongjianzhan sannian xingdong de zhidao yijian" (On the guidelines for winning the battle of poverty alleviation during the next three years). May 31.

10

Income and Poverty Gaps between Han and Ethnic Minorities in Rural China

Xiaomin Liu and Lidan Lyu

10.1 Introduction

As a vast country with many ethnic minorities, China is bound to have social and economic inequalities among different regions and ethnicities. Because of varying natural resources, geographic locations, and historical and cultural factors, Chinese ethnic minorities have often experienced economic underdevelopment to different extents. In general, research has revealed that rural ethnic areas have a higher poverty rate than non-ethnic areas and that ethnic minorities living in rural areas have a higher poverty rate than Han.

On the basis of the rural data from the CHIP 2002 and the CHIP 2013 surveys, we have verified some conclusions from previous research, but we have also come up with some new, different results. Like other studies, our findings are that minorities and ethnic regions face more serious poverty than Han and non-ethnic areas. However, when we control for variables such as household characteristics and region, in 2002 ethnic minority households had a lower risk of poverty than Han households, whereas, unlike the findings in previous research, in 2013 there was no significant difference between ethnic minority and Han households.

This chapter uses data from the CHIP 2002 and the CHIP 2013 surveys to examine poverty patterns and trends for ethnic minorities and Han living in rural areas. Our work does not use the CHIP 2007 survey data, unlike other chapters in this volume, because that survey contains too few minority respondents to support our research aims.[1] To outline the status and changes in poverty for ethnic minorities and Han, we have selected those provinces that are included in both the 2002 and 2013 surveys to estimate, from an income perspective, how the distribution of poverty and its changes over time differ among ethnic minorities.[2]

Xiaomin Liu and Lidan Lyu, *Income and Poverty Gaps between Han and Ethnic Minorities in Rural China* In: *Changing Trends in China's Inequality*. Edited by: Terry Sicular, Shi Li, Ximing Yue, and Hiroshi Sato, Oxford University Press (2020).
© Oxford University Press.
DOI: 10.1093/oso/9780190077938.003.0010

The CHIP survey samples used in our analysis do not cover China's five ethnic autonomous regions. Therefore, in this study we focus on the status of rural ethnic minority households living outside of China's five ethnic autonomous regions. The sample does, however, include designated ethnic prefectures and counties. Our findings thus reflect policies targeted to designated ethnic areas at the subprovincial levels as well as policies targeted to minority households and individuals.

According to most empirical studies of poverty alleviation, income is the main measure for defining poverty. Therefore, an analysis of income inequality, especially inequality between Han and ethnic minorities, will contribute to an understanding of poverty distribution among the various ethnic groups. Björn Gustafsson and Li Shi (2003) use the rural sample from the CHIP 1988 and the CHIP 1995 surveys to analyze the income gap and trends between Han and ethnic minorities. They find that between 1988 and 1995, both Han and ethnic minorities increased their per capita income, but the increase among the Han was 1.4 times that of the increase among the minorities, Because of geographical and historical reasons, the per capita income gap between Han and ethnic minorities has since expanded.

On the basis of the preceding empirical studies, we can say that there are differences in the distribution of poverty and its changes, even when the definition of poverty is based solely on income. Wang Xiaolin (2012) uses rural household survey data from thirteen counties in the Ngawa Tibetan and the Qiang autonomous prefectures to show that the poverty rate among ethnic minorities is 1 percent higher than that among the Han; in this research, the poverty rate shows obvious ethnic patterns. In 2013 Liu Xiaomin used data from the "2011 Economic and Social Development Survey in the Western Ethnic Areas" to examine the differences in poverty and the contributing factors in rural ethnic areas of Hunan, Guizhou, and Guangxi. The study concludes that minority households in these rural areas are more likely to be living in poverty than Han households, and the depth and the intensity of the poverty are also higher.

The mechanism for poverty differentiation among ethnic minorities is a topic that demands serious attention, and the extent to which we become aware of this issue should determine specific antipoverty schemes and measures. Some scholars have begun to study this subject. For example, Wang (2012) finds that ethnic identity, the number of people in the labor market from the same household, the education level of the household head, and ownership of an agricultural vehicle are important determinants of a household's poverty status. Liu (2013) finds that ownership of human capital, social capital, and economic capital either increases or reduces the rate of poverty of ethnic minorities in rural areas of Hunan, Guizhou, and Guangxi. She finds that imbalanced regional development is also a key factor.

In summary, on the basis of empirical studies of variations in the patterns of poverty distribution among Chinese ethnic minorities, scholars have reached varying conclusions. Since implementation of the Western Development Strategy, the Chinese government has strongly supported poverty alleviation for ethnic minorities and ethnic minority areas; however, poverty alleviation policies may have differing impacts, depending on the area.

Because of a limited number of datasets, there are few quantitative studies on the mechanisms of poverty distribution among ethnic minorities and ethnic minority areas after the launch of the Western Development Strategy. Therefore, this chapter seeks to contribute to current research on the basis of the following: 1.) We use the rural sample of the CHIP 2002–2013 surveys and focus on a quantitative study of the status and distribution of poverty among ethnic minorities and in ethnic minority areas. In 2000 the Chinese government launched the Western Development Strategy, which has since brought benefits to the majority of the ethnic minority areas and populations. The analysis in this chapter provides empirical evidence to shed light on the effects of this antipoverty policy. 2.) In our samples, the ethnic minority areas do not include the five autonomous regions, i.e., Xinjiang, Tibet, Ningxia, Guangxi, and Inner Mongolia, which can be considered typical ethnic areas (detailed data sources and definitions of the ethnic minority areas are discussed in Section 10.3). Unlike previous researchers, we analyze the status and distribution of poverty among ethnic minorities in atypical ethnic areas to determine different patterns of ethnic poverty.

The remainder of this chapter includes the following. Section 10.2 reviews the preferential policies that aim to promote economic development and to reduce poverty among ethnic minorities in ethnic areas. This review provides background for understanding how poverty patterns have changed among the various ethnic minorities. Section 10.3 discusses data issues and provides descriptive statistics of important regional, household-level, and individual-level variables. Section 10.4 discusses the level and the composition of the income gap between Han and ethnic minorities as well as the contribution of the ethnic income gap to rural income inequality. Section 10.5, in a discussion of both absolute and relative poverty, analyzes poverty differences between Han and ethnic minorities and the changes over time. Section 10.6 summarizes our findings and evaluates the policy implications.

10.2 Preferential Policies for Ethnic Minorities

China is a large and multiethnic country with significant imbalances in terms of economic development. There are 55 ethnic minorities, with a population of 114 million, according to the 2010 national census, accounting for 8.49 percent of the entire population. China has established 155 ethnic autonomous areas, including 5 autonomous regions/provinces, 30 autonomous prefectures, and 120 autonomous counties; together, these areas cover 6.16 million square kilometers of land, approximately 63.9 percent of the entire land area of the country.

Because of historical, cultural, and other reasons, the specific characteristics of the ethnic minorities and the ethnic minority areas in China include the following: 1.) In general, ethnic minorities reside with Han, but each minority also has its own small settlements. Though all ethnic groups have closely related habitats, they also interact with other groups. Ethnic minorities usually live in places far from the metropolitan areas, located in remote, inaccessible areas, such as drylands or grasslands (Fei 2004, p. 148);[3] 2.) Because of geographic, historical, cultural, and other factors, ethnic minorities and ethnic minority areas are less-developed economically, and ethnic minority areas tend to have the highest poverty rates and highest levels of poverty concentration in the country; 3.) Because of the different histories of the various minorities, their natural resources, locations, and populations differ as well. In addition to the great disparities in the social resources of ethnic minorities in terms of historical evolution, possession of resources, natural habitation, and population size, there are major economic inequalities not only between ethnic and non-ethnic areas but also among ethnic minorities themselves (Guan 2007).

To close these gaps, after the establishment of the People's Republic of China (PRC) in 1949 the State Council adopted preferential policies for the ethnic minorities and the ethnic minority areas. In the Chinese political context, those subject to the preferential policies are the fifty-five ethnic minorities and their natural habitats. All preferential policies operate under the general principle that all ethnicities are equal, and policies should provide preferential treatment to ethnic minorities and ethnic minority areas to support their political, economic, social, cultural, and ecological well-being (Naribilige 2000). There are two major categories of preferential policies: the first is for ethnic minorities; the second is for ethnic minority areas. The former refers to the special benefits that ethnic minorities enjoy in terms of education, employment, fertility, and so on, whereas the latter relates to the special policies promoting social and economic development in ethnic minority areas (Han 2012). The poverty levels of the minority groups are certainly affected by these preferential policies. In the following section, we focus on the specific preferential fiscal and taxation schemes as well as the education, poverty alleviation, and development policies.

10.2.1 Fiscal and Taxation Policies

Given that the ethnic minority areas have specific difficulties in terms of social and economic development, beginning in the 1950s the State Council launched a series of preferential fiscal and taxation policies (see Table 10.1). In addition to providing ethnic minority areas with a certain degree of financial autonomy, the State Council required that only the fiscal surplus should be turned over to the state and the state would pay any deficit. The state also provided production subsidies, health subsidies, social assistance, interest-free loans, and other subsidies.

Beginning in the 1960s, the ethnic autonomous areas could retain and use all the extra income generated from surplus funds from the previous year and from the budget of the current year, thus implementing preferential treatment that was referred to as "appropriate financial care and necessary subsidies." The preferential treatment for ethnic minorities in the 1980s was referred to as "appropriate care": apart from implementing a subsidy system whereby the eight autonomous regions and prefectures could receive a 10 percent annual increase in fixed subsidies, the government also launched other programs, including "ethnic regional subsidies," "development funds for supporting underdeveloped areas," and "subsidies for Chinese border affairs."

Beginning in 2000, China implemented the Western Development Strategy[4] to provide "prosperity to the border [regions] and to enrich the people" and other similar programs. The central government also increased financial support for ethnic minority areas: in addition to general transfer payments, the central government established special transfer payments

Table 10.1. Preferential economic policies in ethnic minority areas

Preferential policy	Period of implementation
National subsidies for ethnic minority residential areas	1955–present
National preferential fiscal policies for ethnic minority residential areas	1964–present
National subsidies for construction in border areas	1977–present
National subsidies and development funds for underdeveloped areas	1980–present
National fiscal transfer payments for ethnic minority residential areas	1995–present
Lower tax rates for agriculture and animal husbandry in ethnic minority residential areas	1953–present
Tax reductions for agriculture in ethnic minority residential areas	1958–present
Income tax exemptions and reductions for "old, small, border[land], and poor" areas	1985–present
Regulated tax reductions for fixed-asset investments in ethnic minority residential areas	1992–present
Three-year income tax exemptions for newly established enterprises in "old, small, border[land], and poor" areas	1994–present
10 percent agricultural product tax for the acquisition of raw tea materials along the borders	1994–present
Periodical reductions or exemptions of enterprise income taxes for local enterprises in the West autonomous regions	2001–2010
Two-year tax exemptions and three-year half income tax exemptions for newly established transportation, electricity, water, post, and broadcasting enterprises in the West regions	2001–2010
Ten-year agricultural product tax exemption for agricultural products in areas where farmland has been converted to forests and grasslands	2001–2010

Sources: Wen 2004; Li 2011; Han 2012.

for agriculture, social security, education, science and technology, health, birth control, planning, culture, and environmental protection. From 2000 to 2013, the transfer payments from the central government to the ethnic minority areas increased from 1 billion yuan to 46.4 billion yuan (Cai 2014), representing a forty-six-fold increase.

The Chinese government has also implemented long-term preferential tax policies for the ethnic minority areas (see Table 10.1). Beginning in the 1950s, the ethnic minority areas were subject to long-term lower agricultural and animal husbandry taxes, and the border areas were subject to lower industrial and commercial tax burdens than the inland areas. At the end of the 1970s, the state implemented tax relief and preferential tax rates for the ethnic minority areas, and enterprises in border areas and autonomous counties were exempt from the industrial and commercial income tax for five years. Enterprises in the eight ethnic provinces and autonomous regions can retain 70 percent of their income after deducting non-operating expenses and extracting cooperative funds; the supply and marketing cooperatives in the three ethnic areas are subject to reduced income taxes, and ethnic handicraft enterprises are subject to periodic reduced income taxes.

After the 1980s, the state expanded the preferential tax policies for the ethnic minority areas and reduced and exempted township enterprises in "old, small, border, and poor" regions from the income tax. Since 2000, the West regions have been subject to more preferential taxation policies; the state now provides diverse levels of tax relief for local-funded enterprises and foreign-invested enterprises in industries that are encouraged by the state. To protect the environment, cropland has been converted to forests and grassland, but at the same time there was a ten-year agricultural product tax exemption for these lands to secure the income of the residents. Newly established transportation, electricity, water, postal and broadcasting enterprises in the western part of the country were also given a two-year tax exemption and a three-year one-half income tax exemption.

Evidence suggests that these preferential financial and taxation policies have played a role in promoting economic development, balancing the distribution of public services, coordinating regional development, and narrowing the income gap between minorities and minority areas. At the same time, economic development contributed to poverty alleviation in the ethnic minority areas.

10.2.2 Population and Education Policies

To improve the human capital of the minority populations, the Chinese government adopted various preferential and education policies in accordance with the various characteristics of the ethnic minorities during different periods (see Table 10.2). In the early years of the PRC, a "Population Prosperity" policy was adopted to increase fertility rates and to reduce mortality rates in order to increase the supply of labor. Meanwhile, the Chinese government adopted policies to improve literacy among the minorities.

Table 10.2. Preferential population and education policies for ethnic minorities

Preferential policy	Period of implementation
"Population Prosperity" policy for ethnic minorities	1951–1980
Family planning and birth control policies for ethnic minorities	1982–present
Family planning and birth control in ethnic minority residential areas	1982–present
Preferential family planning and birth control policies for ethnic minorities	1984–present
Ethnic colleges and universities	1950–present
Special national funds and subsidies for ethnic minority education	1952–present
Launch of a nationwide education administrative organization for ethnic minorities	1952–present
Taking ethnic characteristics into consideration when establishing ethnic minority education	1951–present
National provisions for education expenditures at ethnic colleges and universities	1963–present
Admission of ethnic minority students to colleges and universities on the basis of lower scores	1977–present
Special education benefits for various ethnic minorities	1979–present
National policy for developing ethnic education	1981–present
Preferential policies for vocational and technical education in ethnic minority areas	1992–present
National exemptions of education fees for children from poverty households	1985–present
Corresponding support for schools in West China	2000–present
Comprehensive training programs for primary and secondary school teachers in ethnic poverty areas	2000–2003
Comprehensive training programs for teachers and new curricula for primary and secondary schools in ethnic poverty areas	2004–2008

Source: See Table 10.1.

There were special subsidies for ethnic education and efforts to improve school equipment, teacher benefits, student life, and specific requirements and difficulties for minority students.

In the early 1980s, the state implemented a formal preferential population policy with respect to family planning and birth control for the ethnic minorities (Zhang 1989). Additionally, beginning in the 1970s and especially in the 1980s, the state developed a series of "affirmative action policies" for minority education. For example, ethnic minority students were given priority and allowed lower scores for admission to colleges and universities, and minority students who face financial difficulties were given living allowances. Policies to develop education in the ethnic minority areas included "preferential benefits for teachers who support education in the ethnic minority areas" (Guihua gangyao gongzuo xiaozu 2010).

10.2.3   Poverty Alleviation and Development Policies

Beginning in the late 1980s, the government began to adopt a new set of poverty alleviation policies that focused on preferential funding aimed at designated poor counties. These new policies targeted ethnic minority areas. Among the 592 designated poverty counties identified in the "August 7th Poverty Relief Program" in 1994, 257 were located in ethnic minority areas. This result represented 43 percent of the total number of poverty counties nationwide; furthermore, the designated poverty counties accounted for 39 percent of the total number of counties and cities in the ethnic minority areas. At that time, 40 percent of the nationwide population living in absolute poverty belonged to an ethnic minority, and 35 percent of all ethnic minorities were living in poverty (Kang 1995, pp. 147–150). Table 10.3 presents a list of China's poverty alleviation programs and related policies that have supported the development of ethnic minorities.

10.3   Data and Descriptions of the Sample

10.3.1   Data, Sample Selection, and Weights

For our analysis, we use data from the CHIP 2002 and the CHIP 2013 rural household surveys. The 2002 survey includes twenty-two provinces and the

Table 10.3. Poverty alleviation and development policies in ethnic minority areas

Policy	Period of implementation
Establishment of national poverty standards for counties	1986–present
Poverty ethnic minority areas receive special consideration in terms of the allocation of agricultural materials	1989–present
Poverty ethnic minority areas receive special consideration in terms of funding allocations	1989–present
Ethnic minority enterprises in poor ethnic minority areas are subject to low interest rates on loans, low taxes, and price subsidies from the state	1989–present
Ethnic minority areas are allowed extended periods for loan repayments	1989–present
The state provides financial support for the construction of transportation in poor ethnic minority areas	1991–present
Scientific and technical personnel working in ethnic minority areas may receive state subsidies	1993–present
Nationwide implementation of the "Work-for-Food" program	1984–present
Nationwide implementation of the "Adequate Food and Clothing" program	1989–present
Nationwide implementation of the "August 7th Poverty Relief Program"	1994–2000
Nationwide implementation of poverty alleviation loans	1983–present
Nationwide implementation of subsidized loans for poor pastoral areas	1987–present
Nationwide implementation of special loans for enterprises in poor counties	1988–present
National funding for adequate food and clothing in poor ethnic minority areas	1990–present
Western development in the eleventh five-year plan	2006–2010
Western development in the twelfth five-year plan	2011–2015
Bringing prosperity to the borderlands and enriching the people in the eleventh five-year plan	2006–2010
Bringing prosperity to the borderlands and enriching the people in the twelfth five-year plan	2011–2015
Development plan for support of less populous ethnic minorities	2005–2010
Development plan for support of less populous ethnic minorities	2011–2015
Ethnic minority public affairs in the eleventh five-year plan	2006–2010
Ethnic minority public affairs in the twelfth five-year plan	2011–2015
Outline of Chinese rural poverty alleviation	2001–2010
Outline of Chinese rural poverty alleviation	2011–2020

Source: See Table 10.1.

2013 survey includes fifteen provinces, all of which are included in the 2002 survey. To outline the status and changes in poverty for ethnic minorities and Han, we restrict our sample to those provinces that are included in both surveys, specifically, the fourteen provinces of Beijing, Shanxi, Liaoning, Jiangsu, Anhui, Shandong, Henan, Hubei, Hunan, Guangdong, Chongqing, Sichuan, Yunnan, and Gansu. The CHIP 2007 survey contained only a small number of minority respondents, so we did not include the CHIP 2007 survey in our analysis. Also, we dropped all observations for which information on ethnicity was missing. Our resulting estimation sample contains 22,751 individuals for 2002 and 38,961 individuals for 2013 in the same provinces.

When analyzed with population weights, the CHIP survey data are representative of the national and regional levels Therefore, our analyses use weights that are based on the regional (East/Central/West) rural populations in the country.

10.3.2 Ethnic Minority Regions and Counties

China's ethnic autonomous areas include 5 autonomous regions/provinces, 30 autonomous prefectures, and 120 autonomous counties. The Chinese government refers to the 5 autonomous regions (the Uygur, Ningxia, Guangxi, Inner Mongolian, and Tibetan autonomous regions) plus the 3 multiethnic provinces (Yunnan, Guizhou, and Qinghai) as the "eight ethnic minority provinces." Within this context, the sum number of ethnic minority counties within the 8 ethnic minority provinces and the 30 autonomous prefectures, plus the autonomous counties totaled 836 in 2002 and 792 in 2013. Most of the ethnic minority counties are located in the 8 ethnic minority provinces; about 10 percent are located in autonomous prefectures or counties in the remaining 23 non-ethnic minority provinces (i.e., 48 ethnic autonomous counties are located in non-ethnic minority provinces). All these autonomous areas and provinces, prefectures, and counties are subject to preferential policies.

The CHIP survey data analyzed in this chapter include counties in one of the eight ethnic minority provinces (Yunnan) as well as counties in other provinces that are within ethnic autonomous prefectures or that are designated as ethnic autonomous counties. Because the fourteen provinces in the CHIP 2002 and 2013 rural samples do not include the Uygur, Ningxia,

Table 10.4. Counts of ethnic minority counties in China, CHIP 2002 and CHIP 2013 surveys

	China	CHIP survey
2002		
Total number of ethnic minority counties	836	8
Counties in one of the eight ethnic minority regions/provinces	700	5
Counties in an ethnic autonomous prefecture	88	2
Ethnic autonomous counties	48	1
2013		
Total number of ethnic minority counties	792	12
Counties in one of the eight ethnic minority regions/provinces	664	11
Counties in an ethnic autonomous prefecture	80	0
Ethnic autonomous counties	48	1

Notes: We define ethnic minority counties to include all counties within the eight ethnic minority regions/provinces, counties within an ethnic autonomous prefecture outside of those regions/provinces, and counties that are designated ethnic autonomous counties outside of those regions/provinces and prefectures. The only one of the eight ethnic minority provinces in the CHIP 2002 and 2013 surveys is Yunnan. The counts of the national ethnic minority counties are based on the administrative divisions reported on the official websites of the National Bureau of Statistics of China. http://www.stats.gov.cn/tjsj/tjbz/xzqhdm/. Accessed January 24, 2017.

Guangxi, Inner Mongolian, and Tibetan autonomous regions, but do include Yunnan, we cover very few typical ethnic autonomous areas; as a result, the analysis is mainly based on data from atypical ethnic autonomous areas.

The CHIP 2002 contains eight ethnic minority counties and the CHIP 2013 dataset contains twelve ethnic minority counties, as shown in Table 10.4. Yunnan is the only province among the eight ethnic minority regions/provinces included in our CHIP samples. The CHIP 2002 sample includes five counties, one autonomous county, and two counties under the jurisdiction of an autonomous prefecture, and the CHIP 2013 includes eleven counties and one autonomous county under the jurisdiction of an autonomous prefecture.

On the basis of the distribution of the ethnic minority counties in our sample, ethnic minority respondents in this chapter are from only a small portion of the typical ethnic minority areas; hence, our findings mainly apply to income and poverty differences between Han and ethnic minorities living outside of the typical ethnic minority areas.

10.3.3 Poverty Areas

The CHIP samples include some officially designated poverty counties. This chapter uses two criteria to define whether a county is classified as poor; any county that meets either one or both of the following official criteria is classified as poor. 1.) The county is designated as a poverty county by the State Council. The counties given priority for poverty alleviation are commonly known as state-level poverty-stricken counties. According to the "2006 China Rural Poverty Alleviation and Development Report" of the State Council, there were 592 state-level poverty-stricken counties, of which 341 were ethnic autonomous counties. 2.) The county is in a government-designated impoverished area. On the basis of the guidance of the "Outline of China's Rural Poverty Alleviation and Development Program (2011–2020)" and given the increasing demand for poverty alleviation in the old revolutionary base areas, the ethnic minority areas, and the borderlands, the Chinese government has classified 14 joint impoverished areas that are subject to special policies. They number 676 counties, among which 440 counties have been designated by the state as key counties requiring economic development and poverty alleviation. Those counties, numbering 828 nationwide, that meet both criteria are defined as poverty-stricken counties.

The CHIP 2002 rural survey contains 16 poverty counties among the 74 counties in the dataset: 1 in Shanxi, 3 in Anhui, 1 in Hubei, 2 in Hunan, 1 in Chongqing, 1 in Sichuan, 3 in Yunnan, and 4 in Gansu. There were 4 ethnic minority counties among the 16 poverty counties in 2002. Among the 199 counties in the CHIP 2013 survey, 32 counties were designated as poverty counties: 5 in Shanxi, 2 in Anhui, 3 in Henan, 4 in Hubei, 4 in Hunan, 1 in Chongqing, 1 in Sichuan, 6 in Yunnan, and 6 in Gansu. There were 6 ethnic minority counties among the 32 poverty counties in the 2013 sample (see Table 10.5).

10.3.4 Summary Statistics in the Sample

Table 10.6 reports a summary of the individual- and household-level descriptive statistics based on our rural sample in the fourteen provinces of the CHIP 2002 and the CHIP 2013 surveys. Ethnic minorities constituted 7.2 percent of the 2002 sample, with the Manchu, Yi, and Miao constituting the three main ethnicities and accounting for 1.4 percent, 1.4 percent, and

Table 10.5. Counts of poverty counties in the CHIP 2002 and CHIP 2013 surveys

	Poverty counties		Not poverty counties		
	Ethnic minority county	Non-ethnic minority county	Ethnic minority county	Non-ethnic minority county	Total
2002	4	12	4	54	74
2013	6	26	6	161	199

Notes: There are 8 ethnic minority counties in our selected CHIP 2002 sample, of which 4 are also defined as poverty counties. Of the 76 non-ethnic minority counties in the 2002 selected sample, 12 are defined as poverty counties. There are 12 ethnic minority counties in our selected CHIP 2013 sample, of which 6 are defined as ethnic minority counties. Of the 187 non-ethnic minority counties in the 2013 selected sample, 26 are defined as poverty counties.

0.4 percent respectively. Observations of the Manchu, Yi, and Miao in 2002 total 580, 257, and 92 respectively. Ethnic minorities constituted 8.1 percent of the 2013 sample, with the Yi, Manchu, Zhuang, and Hui representing the main minorities, accounting for 1.8 percent, 0.9 percent, 0.5 percent, and 0.4 percent, respectively. The corresponding observations totaled 666, 327, 179, and 157, respectively.

The share of individuals in the CHIP samples living in poor countries was 25.3 percent in 2013, roughly 5 percentage points higher than that in 2002, meaning that coverage of the 2013 survey might be somewhat more biased toward poor localities. The percentage of individuals living in ethnic counties was 8.4 percent in 2013, slightly lower than that in 2002. Compared with Han, ethnic minorities apparently tended to live in poor counties and ethnic areas in both 2002 and 2013.

Individual and household characteristics in the two surveys are quite different. The proportions of children were lower and the proportions of elderly were higher in 2013, as opposed to 2002. In the 2013 sample there was a slightly larger proportion of those who had finished senior high school or higher-level education, and a larger percentage of the sample was located in the West. Households were smaller in 2013 than they were in 2002. The percentage of households containing village cadres decreased from 34.2 percent in 2002 to 6.4 percent in 2013. The percentage of households with Communist Party members decreased from 21.6 percent in 2002 to 15 percent in 2013.

Table 10.6. Summary statistics for the selected rural sample, 2002 and 2013 (%, persons)

	2002			2013		
	All	Han	Ethnic minorities	All	Han	Ethnic minorities
Panel A: individual level						
Percentage of ethnic minorities	7.2	—	—	—	—	—
Percentage living in poverty areas	20.8	5.0	79.0	25.3	4.2	55.8
Percentage living in ethnic areas	10.9	19.1	40.6	8.4	21.8	64.2
Age structure						
0–14 years	19.7	19.3	24.2	15.3	15.0	18.4
15–59 years	72.1	72.5	66.7	67.7	67.8	66.4
60+ years	8.2	8.2	9.1	17.0	17.1	15.2
Total	100	100	100	100	100	100
Education						
No schooling	9.0	8.6	14.7	10.5	10.4	11.8
Primary school	33.1	32.3	41.2	30.4	29.7	39.2
Middle school	42.4	43.2	34.3	40.8	41.4	34.5
High school+	15.4	15.9	9.8	18.2	18.6	14.4
Total	100	100	100	100	100	100
Region						
East	31.5	32.3	22.4	33.8	35.5	14.1
Central	42.4	44.3	20.8	38.2	38.7	31.8
West	26.2	23.5	56.8	28.1	25.8	54.1
Total	100	100	100	100	100	100
Panel B: household level						
Percentage with a Chinese Communist Party (CCP) member	21.6	21.4	24.4	15.0	14.9	15.5
Percentage with a cadre	34.2	34.4	31.9	6.4	6.5	6.1
Percentage with a laborer who had outmigrated	35.2	36.1	24.7	45.7	46.0	42.2
Household size (persons)	4.0	4.0	4.3	3.7	3.7	4.0

The proportion of households with at least one laborer who had outmigrated increased from 35.2 percent in 2002 to 45.7 percent in 2013.

10.4. Income Inequality and Its Changes

On average, the income of ethnic minorities is lower than that of Han, but the income gap narrowed from 2002 to 2013 in the fourteen provinces in our sample. Table 10.7 reports the annual income per capita for Han and ethnic minorities in the 2002 and 2013 surveys; the income levels are reported in nominal values, but when we compare the differences between 2002 and 2013, the 2002 value is adjusted to 2013 prices so that growth is in constant prices. In this chapter we use the NBS income variable, without adjustments for imputed rents, etc.

As shown in Table 10.7, the average annual income for Han in 2002 was 2694 yuan; for ethnic minorities it was 1934 yuan, or 72 percent that of Han income. The average Han income increased to 7848 yuan in 2013 and the average income for ethnic minorities increased to 6120 yuan in 2013, which was 78 percent of Han income. The annual growth rate of income for ethnic

Table 10.7. Annual household income per capita of Han and ethnic minorities, 2002 and 2013

	All	Han	Ethnic minorities
2002			
Mean (yuan)	2633	2694	1934
Median (yuan)	2152	2203	1561
2013			
Mean (yuan)	9883	10,040	8109
Median (yuan)	7676	7848	6120
2002–2013 change (% average annual growth)			
Mean	9.2	9.1	10.3
Median	8.7	8.7	9.6

Note: We used the NBS income definition in this chapter. We used constant prices when computing the rate of the increase in income between 2002 and 2013. We converted to constant prices by using the national average rural consumer price index (CPI). According to the National Bureau of Statistics (2015), with 1985 as the base year the 2002 rural CPI was 315.2 and the 2013 rural CPI was 449.9. Therefore, from 2002 to 2013 rural consumer prices increased 43 percent.

minorities was 10.3 percent from 2002 to 2013, higher than the increase in Han income (9.1 percent). Although the income of ethnic minorities was lower than that of Han, its growth was faster, and therefore the income gap narrowed between 2002 and 2013.

The income composition among Han and ethnic minorities was very different (see Table 10.8). The leading source of income was agricultural for both Han and ethnic minorities in 2002, but it was especially important for ethnic minorities, accounting for about 70 percent of the ethnic minority income in 2002. Wage income accounted 37.7 percent of Han income in 2002, whereas the corresponding rate for ethnic minorities was 17.9 percent— much less than that for Han. In 2013, wage income became the most important income source for both Han and ethnic minorities. Meanwhile, the annual growth rate of wage income for ethnic minorities was 17.7 percent from 2002 to 2013, and it was 16.9 percent for net non-agricultural income during the same period. Moreover, the shares of property income, net transfer income, and pension income became more important in 2013, as compared to 2002.

In addition, it is worth noting that the shares of net transfer and pension income for ethnic minorities were lower than the shares for Han in 2013. The literature indicates that redistributive policies, such as public transfers, play a key role in reducing inequality and poverty created by market forces. The two kinds of income sources mentioned previously accounted for only 5.5 percent of the total income of ethnic minorities, whereas the corresponding number for Han was 10.7 percent. The mean amount of net transfer income for ethnic minorities was roughly 260 yuan, which was only 43 percent of the corresponding amount for Han. The mean pension income for ethnic minorities was 170 yuan, which was only 38 percent of that for Han.

Table 10.9 displays the income inequality indicators and their decomposition by ethnic group in our selected samples of the fourteen provinces for 2002 and 2013. Compared to 2002, the Gini coefficient in 2013 increased by 14.8 percent for the entire sample. But the inequality of ethnic minorities increased more rapidly, with its Gini coefficient increasing by 24.3 percent, higher than the change for Han (14.8 percent). Inequality was a bit lower among minorities than among Han in 2002, but the opposite was the case in 2013. Inequality in ethnic minority areas also increased more rapidly than that in non-ethnic minority areas. This increase implies that inequality among ethnic minorities deteriorated during this period in atypical ethnic areas.

Table 10.8. Composition of household income per capita for Han and ethnic minorities

Income composition (%)	2002			2013			Annual growth rate, 2002–2013 (%)		
	Total	Han	Ethnic minorities	Total	Han	Ethnic minorities	Total	Han	Ethnic minorities
Wage income	36.5	37.7	17.9	47.1	47.8	36.7	11.7	11.5	17.7
Net agricultural income	44.3	42.7	70.5	22.1	21.3	33.7	2.5	2.4	3.1
Net non-agricultural business income	13.7	14.0	7.7	13.0	12.8	14.7	8.6	8.2	16.9
Property income	4.7	4.8	3.7	7.5	7.3	9.3	13.9	13.3	19.9
Net transfer income	0.8	0.8	0.1	5.9	6.1	3.3	30.9	31.2	51.5
Pension income	—	—	—	4.4	4.6	2.2			
Total	100.0	100.0	100.0	100.0	100.0	100.0	9.2	9.1	10.3

Note: Data on pension income were not collected in the 2002 survey, but because of the absence of a rural pension plan at that time it was probably zero.

Table 10.9. Decomposition of income inequality by Han and ethnic minorities based on our selected sample

	2002		2013	
	MLD	Theil	MLD	Theil
Theil index	0.204	0.215	0.279	0.276
Within group	0.200	0.212	0.278	0.275
Between group	0.004	0.003	0.001	0.001
% of between group	1.96	1.40	0.36	0.36
Gini coefficient		0.345		0.396
Gini coefficient of Han		0.343		0.394
Gini coefficient of ethnic minorities		0.325		0.404

Note: Our estimates of the rural Gini coefficient are slightly lower than those reported in Chapters 2 and 6 mainly because those chapters calculate the Gini for all provinces in the CHIP surveys, but we exclude Xinjiang because of its missing information on ethnicity and we restrict our sample to the fourteen provinces that are common to the 2002 and 2013 CHIP surveys (see the main text).

Regardless, the income gap between Han and ethnic minorities contributes little to the overall inequality in the rural areas of the fourteen provinces. Using a standard decomposition of inequality by population subgroup, we decomposed the inequality index of the rural areas by Han and ethnic areas.[5] According to the results, the contribution of between-group ethnic inequality to inequality was less than 2 percent in 2002 and less than 1 percent in 2013.

10.5 Empirical Analysis of the Distribution of Poverty Households and Contributing Factors

10.5.1 Poverty Rate

Table 10.10 reports our estimates of the poverty rates and their changes from 2002 to 2013 in the rural areas of the fourteen CHIP provinces.[6] We report estimates of absolute and relative poverty, with the Foster-Greer-Thorbecke (FGT) poverty indexes, and of the head-count ratio (FGT[0]), poverty gap (FGT[1]), and squared poverty gap (FGT[2]).[7] No matter whether we consider absolute poverty or relative poverty, ethnic minorities had a higher

Table 10.10. Rural head-count ratios and their changes for Han and ethnic minorities and for ethnic and non-ethnic areas, 2002 and 2013 (%)

| | 2002 | | | | | | 2013 | | | | | | Change from 2002 to 2013 | |
| | Absolute | | | Relative | | | Absolute | | | Relative | | | Absolute | Relative |
	FGT (0)	FGT (1)	FGT (2)	FGT (0)	FGT (1)	FGT (2)	FGT (0)	FGT (1)	FGT (2)	FGT (0)	FGT (1)	FGT (2)	FGT (0)	FGT (0)
All	27.2	7.7	3.3	10.8	2.7	1.1	8.8	3.1	1.1	21.3	7.4	4.3	−18.4	10.5
Han	25.5	7.1	3.0	10.0	2.6	1.1	8.4	3.0	1.1	20.6	7.1	3.7	−17.1	10.6
Ethnic minorities	49.2	14.9	6.2	21.2	5.1	1.9	13.1	5.1	1.9	29.6	11.0	11.7	−36.1	8.3
Non-ethnic areas	23.8	6.3	2.6	8.7	2.1	0.8	8.8	3.1	0.8	21.0	7.3	3.9	−15.0	12.3
Ethnic areas	57.5	19.9	9.3	29.4	8.5	3.6	8.8	3.5	3.6	25.1	8.2	9.7	−48.7	−4.3

Notes: We use the same absolute and relative poverty standards that are used in Chapter 7 of this volume. The absolute poverty line is equivalent to 2300 yuan in 2010 and the relative level is equivalent to 50 percent of the median income in 2010. The absolute poverty level and the relative poverty levels in 2002 were 1522 yuan and 1045 yuan, respectively. The corresponding levels in 2013 were 2736 yuan and 4308 yuan, respectively. FGT(0) is the poverty head-count ratio, FGT(1) is the poverty gap index (a measure of the depth of poverty), and FGT(2) is the squared poverty gap (a measure of the severity of poverty). See Chapters 6 and 7 for a fuller explanation of the FGT indexes.

head-count ratio, poverty gap, and squared poverty gap than Han in both 2002 and 2013. In addition, the ethnic minority areas had a higher head-count ratio, poverty gap index, and squared poverty gap index than the non-ethnic minority areas.

From the perspective of absolute poverty, the head-count ratio for the entire sample was 27.2 percent in 2002, but it declined to 8.8 percent at 2013, amounting to an 18 percentage point reduction; during the same period, the average poverty gap index declined from 7.7 percent to 3.1 percent and the squared poverty gap index decreased from 3.3 to 3.0 percent. The preceding reductions all show that the absolute poverty level narrowed from 2002 to 2013.

From the perspective of relative poverty, the head-count ratio, poverty gap index, and the squared poverty gap index increased 10.5 percentage points, 4.6 percentage points, and 3.2 percentage points respectively from 2002 to 2013. Thus, in terms of relative poverty, the level of poverty increased. In sum, from 2002 to 2013 the income of people living in poverty increased, but two-thirds of the poor escaped absolute poverty. However, the income growth of people living in poverty was less than the growth in the median income, thus exacerbating relative poverty.

On the basis of a comparison between Han and ethnic minorities, from 2002 to 2013 there was a large decrease in absolute poverty among ethnic minorities. The poverty head-count ratio declined from 49.2 percent in 2002 to 13.1 percent in 2013, representing a decrease of 36 percentage points. The absolute poverty head-count ratio among Han dropped from 25.5 percent in 2002 to 8.4 percent in 2013, representing a decrease of 17 percentage points. However, both Han and ethnic minorities experienced an increase in their relative head-count ratio; there was an increase of 10.6 percentage points for Han and an increase of 8.3 percentage points for ethnic minorities. The relative head-count ratio for Han and ethnic minorities in 2013 were 20.6 percent and 29.6 percent respectively.

Ethnic minority regions and areas witnessed significant decreases in absolute poverty head-count ratios. In 2002 the absolute head-count ratio in ethnic minority areas was twice that in non-ethnic minority areas, whereas in 2013 the absolute head-count ratio in ethnic minority regions had decreased by 49 percentage points. In 2013 the absolute head-count ratio in both ethnic minority areas and non-ethnic minority areas was 8.8 percent.

But ethnic and non-ethnic minority areas showed different patterns in terms of their relative head-count ratio. In non-ethnic minority areas, the relative head-count ratio increased from 8.7 percent in 2002 to 21.0 percent in 2013, representing a 12.3 percentage point increase; the relative head-count ratio in ethnic minority areas declined from 29.4 percent in 2002 to 25.1 percent in 2013. From 2002 to 2013 income growth for people living in poverty in ethnic minority areas helped 83.3 percent of the poor escape absolute poverty, exceeding the median income growth and alleviating their relative poverty levels.

10.5.2 Poverty: Regression Analysis

In this section, we discuss those factors that are associated with poverty as revealed in a regression analysis. Table 10.11 shows selected results of our probit regressions on absolute and relative poverty of households in 2002 and 2013. The table reports the marginal effect of the ethnic minority dummy variable

Table 10.11. Marginal effect of the ethnic dummy variable (Han = 0, ethnic minority = 1) on the probability of poverty

	2002	2013
Panel A: dependent variable = absolute poverty		
Marginal effect, no controls	0.146*	0.042***
Marginal effect, with household characteristics controls	0.104	0.032**
Marginal effect, with province, ethnic area, and poverty area dummy controls	−0.050*	0.024
Marginal effect, with household characteristics, province, ethnic area, and poverty area controls	−0.061**	0.021
Panel B: dependent variable = relative poverty		
Marginal effect, no controls	0.067	0.092***
Marginal effect, with household characteristics controls	0.040	0.067**
Marginal effect, with province, ethnic area, and poverty area dummy controls	−0.041***	0.036
Marginal effect, with household characteristics, province, ethnic area, and poverty area dummy controls	−0.049***	0.031

Notes: 1.) The preceding estimates are from probit regressions with the poverty dummy variable as the dependent variable, estimated by using the pooled Han and ethnic minority household-level dataset. Education corresponds to the maximum level of education attained in the household. Other household characteristics include the number of household members, the dependency ratio, if there are any cadres in the household, and if there are any CCP members in the household. Ethnic area corresponds to the ethnic county dummy and poverty area corresponds to the poverty county dummy. (2) *** $p < 0.01$, ** $p < 0.05$, and * $p < 0.1$.

on the probability of a household being poor estimated from regressions that include various other control variables.

When we do not include any other control variables, in 2002 ethnic minorities had a 14.6 percent higher probability than Han to fall into absolute poverty, with the difference significant at the 10 percent level. This marginal effect declined slightly and became statistically insignificant when we added household characteristics as controls. We note that many of the control variables of household characteristics in our regressions may in fact be affected by ethnic status; for example, the household size and the dependency ratios are different for the minorities and for the Han because of different family planning policies. In addition, education levels may be lower for ethnic minorities than for Han because of discrimination, language barriers, curricula design, and cultural differences. Thus, even though including the household characteristics as control variables reduces the marginal effect of ethnicity as measured by the ethnicity dummy variable, it is still possible that ethnicity indirectly contributes to the difference in average head-count ratios because of differences in household characteristics.

Further, when we add controls for regional characteristics, such as a provincial dummy, an ethnic minority county dummy, and a poverty county dummy, there are dramatic changes in the marginal effect. In the regressions with controls for these regional effects, the estimated coefficient on the minority dummy variable becomes significantly negative in 2002, implying that the Han have a 6.1 percent higher probability than the ethnic minorities to fall into absolute poverty. The estimates are similar when controls for household characteristics and regional effects are included. The results of regressions for relative poverty with regional effects are similar to those for absolute poverty. In the relative poverty regressions that include the ethnic area and poverty area dummies, the Han had a 4.9 percent higher probability than the ethnic minorities to fall into relative poverty.

The findings based on the 2013 dataset reveal a substantial narrowing of the difference between the Han and the ethnic minorities. In the regressions without regional controls, the probability of poverty remained 3 to 4 percent higher for ethnic minorities than it was for Han and it was statistically significant. When regional controls are added, however, there was no significant difference between Han and ethnic minorities.

Although our descriptive statistics show that a higher proportion of ethnic minorities than of Han were poor in both 2002 and 2013 (see Table 10.10), the preceding regression analysis suggests that this result may be attributed to the fact that ethnic minorities are mainly located in less-developed regions. This finding implies that the income differential may not be due to ethnicity per se.

10.6. Conclusions and Discussion

The central government has implemented a series of major policies to boost the economy and income of the ethnic minority population and ethnic minority regions during the past several decades. The amount of investment has been very large, especially after implementation of the Western Development Strategy in 2000. Concurrently, the income gap and the poverty differences between Han and ethnic minorities changed dramatically. The literature has generally discussed patterns within the West ethnic minority regions, and we know very little about patterns in atypical ethnic regions, such as those in the Central or East regions, or even in non-ethnic minority areas in the West region. In this chapter, using a selected rural sample from the CHIP 2002 and the CHIP 2013 surveys in fourteen provinces, we have focused on the ethnic differentiation of income and poverty and its changes over time in atypical ethnic regions.

The income of ethnic minorities has always been lower than that of Han, as shown by our analysis as well as in other literature, but the income gap between ethnic minorities and Han narrowed from 2002 to 2013 in the atypical ethnic areas covered in the CHIP data. At the same time, it is worth noting that inequality among ethnic minorities increased more when compared to inequality among Han during the same period. Our decomposition of the inequality index shows that the income gap between Han and ethnic minorities is mainly correlated with household characteristics and location of residence rather than to their ethnic status. In addition, although public transfers have been proved to be an effective way to reduce income inequality, the share of net transfer income and pension income in the total income for ethnic minorities has been significantly less than the share for Han.

Poverty patterns have changed for both Han and ethnic minorities. But the changes in absolute poverty and relative poverty have proceeded in the opposite directions. The head-count ratio, poverty gap index, and squared poverty gap index have narrowed for absolute poverty. But the head-count ratio, poverty gap index, and squared poverty gap index have increased for relative poverty. From the perspective of ethnic differences, in terms of both absolute poverty and relative poverty ethnic minorities experienced higher head-count ratios, average poverty gaps, and squared poverty gaps than Han in both 2002 and 2013. The descriptive analysis shows that the ethnic differentiation of poverty narrowed during the 2002–2013 period. The regression analysis suggests that this narrowing may be attributed to the fact that ethnic minorities are mainly located in less-developed regions rather than being attributed to their ethnic identity. The poverty level among Han is even more serious than that among ethnic minorities when we control for all the regional variables.

The conclusions from this research provide some policy suggestions to alleviate poverty and improve income equality among minorities: 1.) In dealings with the increase in income inequality, income redistribution policies should be tilted more toward the minority population. 2.) Ethnic identity is not a major factor when one is considering antipoverty strategies among minorities who live in atypical ethnic areas. Since the location of residence is a key factor determining the level of poverty, two kinds of policy will contribute to alleviating poverty among minorities: either helping them migrate to more developed areas or providing those minorities living in underdeveloped regions with more resources. (3) The development of education is an effective way to alleviate poverty among minorities.

Notes

1. The CHIP 2007 survey includes only about 400 ethnic minority respondents, which is about 1.2 percent of the entire rural sample.
2. We do not include Xinjiang in our analysis, because the 2013 Xinjiang sample does not provide ethnic information about the respondents.
3. According to Fei Xiaotong (2004, p. 148), "the habitations of ethnic minorities are mostly places to which the Han cannot become accustomed, i.e., plateaus, prairies, ravines, arid areas, and remote locations. That is to say, ethnic minorities live in the places where the 'agriculture-based' Han cannot display their advantage."
4. The State Council implemented the Western Development Strategy to cover all 5 autonomous regions, 30 autonomous prefectures, and most of the 120 autonomous counties. Autonomous counties that are not included in the Western Development Strategy receive similar policy support.
5. For a fuller discussion of the methodology for the inequality decomposition by subgroup, see Chapter 2.
6. Our estimates of poverty are very similar to those in Chapter 7. As the authors of Chapter 7 do, we use the NBS definition of income. We also use the same absolute

and relative poverty standards as those in Chapter 7, but with a different provincial coverage. Chapter 7 includes all provinces in the CHIP surveys; here we restrict our sample to the fourteen provinces that are present in both the CHIP 2002 survey and the CHIP 2013 survey.

7. See Chapters 6 and 7 for fuller explanations of these poverty measures.

References

Cai, M. (2014). "Push for New Developments in China's Human Rights." *China Daily*, December 24. http://europe.chinadaily.com.cn/opinion/2014-12/24/content_19153653.htm. Accessed January 25, 2017.

Fei, X. (2004). *Lun renleixue yu wenhua zijue* (Anthropology and cultural consciousness). Beijing: Huaxia chubanshe.

Guan, K. (2007). *Zuqun zhengzhi* (Ethnic politics). Beijing: Zhongyang minzu daxue chubanshe.

Guihua gangyao gongzuo xiaozu (Working Group on the Planning Outline) (2010). "Guojia zhongchangqi jiaoyu gaige fazhan guihua gangyao (2010–2020)" (National long- and medium-term education reform and development planning [2010-2020]), Xinhuashe, February 23. http://news.xinhuanet.com/politics/2010-02/28/content_13069032.htm. Accessed January 25, 2015.

Gustafsson, B. G. and S. Li (2003). "The Ethnic Minority-Majority Income Gap in Rural China during Transition." *Economic Development and Cultural Change*, 51(4), 805–822.

Han, G. (2012). "Zhongguo minzu youhui zhengce yanjiu" (Research on Chinese ethnic preferential policies). Ph.D diss., Nankai University.

Kang, X. (1995). *Zhongguo pinkun yu fanpinkun lilun* (Chinese poverty and anti-poverty theory). Nanning: Guangxi renmin chubanshe.

Li, N. (2011),. "Zhongguo minzu diqu jingji fuchi zhengce yu jingji zengzhang yanjiu" (Economic support policy and economic growth in China's ethnic areas). Ph.D diss., Jilin University.

Liu, X. (2013). "Minzu shijiaoxia de nongcun jumin pinkun wenti bijiao yanjiu: Yi Guangxi, Guizhou, Hunan wei li" (Comparative studies of the poverty problems of rural residents from an ethnic point of view: Taking Guangxi, Guizhou, and Hunan as examples). *Minzu yanjiu*, no. 4, 37–49.

Naribilige (2000). *Xiandai beijingxia de zuqun jiangou* (Ethnic construction against a modern background). Kunming: Yunnan jiaoyu chubanshe.

National Bureau of Statistics (various years). *Zhongguo tongji nianjian* (China statistical yearbook). Beijing: Zhongguo tongji chubanshe.

Wang, X. (2012). *Pinkun celiang: Lilun yu fangfa* (The measurement of poverty: Theories and methods). Beijing: Shehui kexue wenxian chubanshe.

Wen, J. (2004). *Minzu yu fazhan: Xinde xiandaihua zhuigan zhanlüe.* (New strategy to pursue modernization). Beijing: Qinghua daxue chubanshe.

Zhang, T. (1989). "Zhongguo shaoshu minzu renkou zhengce jiqi bianhua" (Chinese minority population policy and its change). *Renkou yu jingji*, no. 5, 27–31, 34.

11

China's Urban Gender Wage Gap

A New Direction?

Jin Song, Terry Sicular, and Björn Gustafsson

11.1 Introduction

As discussed elsewhere in this volume, urban income inequality in China has experienced a long-term increase, including during the latest period from 2007 to 2013. An important factor underlying this upward trend has been wage earnings, the largest component of urban incomes. Indeed, in 2007 as much as three-fourths of urban China's income inequality could be attributed to wage earnings (see Chapter 9). From 2007 to 2013, however, the upward trend in the concentration of wage earnings finally reversed, and their contribution to urban inequality declined to 58 percent, although urban inequality continued to rise because of growth in other, more unequal income sources (see Chapter 9).

In this chapter we analyze an important facet of urban earnings inequality—the gender wage gap. Past studies of the gender wage gap in urban China have found that since the 1980s the gap between female and male wage earnings has progressively widened. This widening gender wage gap is consistent with the increase in overall urban earnings inequality and reflects that during this period China was undergoing the transition from a planned economy with an egalitarian wage structure to a predominately market-driven system with considerable wage differentiation. Using new data from 2013 China Household Income Project (CHIP) survey, we find a reversal in this trend. As measured by the ratio between mean female and mean male wages, the gender wage gap declined from 29 percent in 2007 to 25 percent in 2013. After controlling for age, education, marital status, ownership of work unit, occupation, production sector, and other characteristics, we find that the size of the gap is smaller, but the decline persists. Although the extent of the decline in the gender wage gap is modest, it represents a

Jin Song, Terry Sicular, and Björn Gustafsson, *China's Urban Gender Wage Gap* In: *Changing Trends in China's Inequality.* Edited by: Terry Sicular, Shi Li, Ximing Yue, and Hiroshi Sato, Oxford University Press (2020). © Oxford University Press. DOI: 10.1093/oso/9780190077938.003.0011 change from the past and hints at possible future trends in the gender wage differential as well as in urban inequality more generally.

In theory, systematic differences in wage earnings, such as those observed in urban China, should reflect differences in labor productivity. Productivity is related to individual characteristics, such as education, experience, and age. Productivity can also vary across regions, types of employers, sectors, and jobs or occupations. Life events such as marriage, children, and aging may have different effects on the perceived and actual productivity of women and men. Parental leave and retirement policies, which differ between female and male employees, influence the costs to employers. Consequently, life events can affect expectations, behavior, and productivity in ways that are likely to influence the gender wage gap.

Empirical studies of the gender wage gap typically find that controlling for such productivity-related characteristics reduces, but does not eliminate, the gender wage gap. The gender gap that remains after controlling for such characteristics is "unexplained" and is often attributed to discrimination. Discrimination can occur in the form of preferential hiring of men over women, and at higher starting salaries, as well as more promotions and wage increases for men than women over time. The unexplained portion of the gender wage gap may also be due to factors other than discrimination that are not captured in an empirical analysis. In addition, questions exist about why women and men differ in their observed characteristics.

In this chapter, we document and discuss long-term trends in the urban gender wage gap in China from 1995 through 2013, with a focus on the most recent years when, according to our estimates, the gap narrowed. Our analysis of long-term trends sheds light on the changing factors driving women's versus men's wage earnings and provides a useful context for understanding the new decline in the gender wage gap from 2007 to 2013. For reasons of comparability over time and consistency with the literature, we restrict our analysis to formal urban residents. Using data from the CHIP urban household surveys for the years 1995, 2002, 2007, and 2013, we estimate the size of the gender wage gap with and without controls for observable characteristics such as age, education, marital status, and sector. We find that controlling for observable characteristics reduces but does not eliminate the gender wage gap. An Oaxaca-Blinder decomposition identifies the extent to which the gap is explained by differences in the characteristics of women and men. The results show that by 2013 the gap was largely unexplained, reflecting that the characteristics of urban women have converged with those of urban men over time.

Wage regressions provide some insights into the recent narrowing of the gender wage gap. The estimates for 2007 reveal a larger gender wage gap between women and men with lower levels of education. In 2007 the gap was also larger between married women and married men (with and without children) than it was for those who were unmarried. Estimates for 2013 indicate that the narrowing of the overall gender wage gap from 2007 to 2013 was driven by improvements for particular subgroups. Specifically, the gender wage gaps narrowed for young, less-educated, and married workers.

Our work builds on a large literature on the gender wage gap in urban China. Recent studies include Li and Song (2013); Liu (2011); and Xiu and Gunderson (2013). We contribute to this literature in several ways. First, we provide in one place a set of consistent estimates of the gender wage gap from 1995 through 2013, therefore providing a long-term perspective. Second, using the CHIP 2013 data we update the literature and identify the recent narrowing of the gap. Third, we provide new evidence on factors underlying the changes in the gender wage gap, including life events such as marriage and children, that have been the subject of interesting recent research (Jia and Dong 2013; Qi and Dong 2016; Zhang and Hannum 2015).[1]

Although differences in labor force participation are not the focus of this chapter, we recognize that the gender wage gap cannot be entirely disentangled from the question of who chooses to work (see Chi and Li [2014] for a discussion in the Chinese context). To some extent, we sidestep this selection problem by restricting our estimation sample to workers between the ages of 25 and 49, thus removing those younger and older individuals who are choosing when to enter and when to leave the labor force. Nevertheless, we present some background statistics on female and male labor force participation for a broader age range (ages 16 to 60). During the prime working age range from 25 to 49, which is the focus of our gender wage gap analysis, labor force participation is high for both women and men, although it is higher for men. More in-depth discussion of labor force participation, using the CHIP data from 2013 and earlier years, is provided by Xu and Li (2016), and additional analysis is available elsewhere in the literature (e.g., Hare 2016).

The wages of women and men are, of course, related to broad shifts in China's urban labor market and to changes in government policies. We therefore begin with an overview of recent developments in urban China's labor market and discuss some major policy measures relevant to gender wage differences. In Section 11.3 we introduce the data, present the descriptive statistics, and discuss the broad patterns of employment and the raw gender wage gap. Section 11.4 explains our empirical methods. Sections 11.5 and 11.6 report on our findings from the wage regressions and the Oaxaca decompositions. We conclude in Section 11.7 with a discussion of our key findings and their implications.

11.2 Background: Developments in China's Urban Labor Market and Relevant Policies

11.2.1 Developments in China's Urban Labor Market

As discussed in other chapters, since the 1980s labor allocations in China have undergone a transition from planning to markets. This transition has influenced wage determination and a variety of labor market practices, e.g., the procedures governing the hiring and firing of workers. Here we highlight some aspects of the transition that are relevant to the gender wage gap.

Under the planned economy the gender wage gap was relatively small. Liberalization of the setting of wages and the hiring of personnel led to the emergence of wage differentials, including those between men and women. Economic structural shifts due to market reforms also influenced the gender wage gap. For example, non-state and foreign-owned sectors have increased since 2000, whereas state and collective sectors have declined. The gender wage differential is smaller in the state sector than in other ownership sectors, so the declining share of employment in the state sector has contributed to the widening of the average gender wage differential.

A significant change in recent years, especially since 2000, has been rural/urban migration. The entry of large numbers of relatively unskilled rural workers into the urban labor markets is thought to have widened the gap in pay between unskilled and skilled laborers. Higher proportions of women than men in urban China work in unskilled jobs. Increased competition from migrants for these unskilled jobs therefore may have influenced the gender wage gap.

Another notable development has been the dramatic expansion of higher education in China. The number of new graduates from regular institutions of higher education rose from 850,000 in 1999 to 4.5 million in 2007 and further to 6.4 million in 2013.[2] Women, who historically were less likely to continue to post-secondary education, have benefited disproportionately from this expansion of education. Education among urban women has been catching up with that of urban men, with positive implications for their relative earnings.

During the global financial crisis, overall economic growth in China slowed down. The economy weathered the crisis well, in part due to a large stimulus package, but it is possible that the crisis had an impact on the urban gender wage gap. Our data are for one year before (2007) and one year after (2013) the peak years of the crisis. By 2013 China's economic recovery was well underway. Compared with 2007, in 2013 national GDP had increased 68 percent and urban employment had increased 24 percent.[3] We therefore consider our findings to be indications of long-term trends rather than of the short-term effects of the crisis.

11.2.2 Policies

In this section, we discuss selected recent policies relevant to the urban gender wage gap, specifically, minimum-wage, parental-leave, and retirement policies.

Minimum wages can unevenly increase workers' wages and influence the gender wage gap. Minimum-wage regulations were introduced in China in 1993. During the early years, implementation of the policy was uneven and minimum-wage levels remained low. Starting in 2004, however, steps were taken to strengthen implementation and expand coverage, especially with the implementation of China's Labor Contract Law in 2008.[4] Thereafter, the minimum-wage standard was significantly increased.

Adopting minimum-wage regulations can increase the wages of low-paid workers and may also have spillover effects for workers higher up on the pay scale. Using Chinese data, Li and Ma (2015) find such an effect for low-income workers during the period from 2002 to 2009. Since women are disproportionately represented in the lower rungs of the wage distribution, minimum-wage policies potentially can reduce the gender wage gap. It is thus possible that China's minimum-wage increases have contributed to the recent narrowing of the gender wage gap, especially among low-wage workers.

Child care and parental leave can influence women's labor force participation and wages. A study by Du and Dong (2013) reports that the decline in urban female labor force participation in China in the late 1990s and the early 2000s was associated with the loss of affordable, convenient child care accompanying the restructuring of public-sector enterprises. Du and Dong also find that the presence of day care services in the community and the cost of child care affect urban women's labor participation and work hours.

Parental-leave legislation tends to increase women's labor force participation, but it is associated with lower relative wages for women (e.g., Ruhm 1998). China's parental-leave policies have evolved since 2012 as provisions have become more generous and coverage has widened to cover more workers in more sectors. National policy allows fathers one week of parental leave with compensation. It also includes provisions for mothers' extended maternity leave with compensation as well as coverage for medical expenses. In the past, employers shouldered most of the costs associated with parental leave, costs that discouraged employers from hiring young women. Since 2012, however, the government has reduced the burden on employers by establishing and expanding a maternity insurance program that pays many of the costs associated with the national parental-leave regulations. Maternity insurance is funded by mandatory employer contributions equal to a small percentage of the wage bill.

Two recent national policies affecting parental leave are the Social Insurance Law (2011) and the Special Provisions on Labor Protection for Female Employees (2012). Together these policies specify national standards for parental leave, including the length of maternity leave, which was extended from 90 to 98 days in 2011, compensation levels during maternity leave, and employer contributions to maternity insurance. The Special Provisions also reinforce employment protection for women who become pregnant and take maternity leave. Local governments have adopted additional regulations and policies, so that benefits vary regionally.

In recent years the number of people covered by maternity insurance has grown substantially. From 2007 to 2013 coverage grew from 78 million employees to 164 million employees; as a share of employees in urban work units, coverage rose from 65 percent to 91 percent (NBS Department of Population and Employment Statistics 2014, pp. 11, 390–393). The number of beneficiaries has also increased but remains relatively low, at 1.1 million in 2007 and 5.2 million in 2013 (NBS Department of Population and Employment Statistics 2014, pp. 390–393). The small number of beneficiaries, which has been noted in several reports, is attributed to ongoing problems and uneven policy implementation (see, for example, China

Labour Bulletin 2016; Lin 2011; Liu and Sun 2015). Reportedly, employers have been slow to join the maternity insurance program and to register all eligible employees. Employers have also been reluctant to hire young women who do not yet have children because of the "high risk" that they will become pregnant and take maternity leave. Moreover, when female employees become pregnant, employers have been known to try to "persuade" them, through semi-coercive measures, to resign. Such practices can affect the employment and wage earnings of women through their life cycles.

Since the 1950s the statutory retirement age has remained at age 60 for men, age 55 for women who are civil servants and employees of the state sector, and age 50 for all other women. In recent years the government has considered changing the statutory retirement age, and in 2016 it announced its intention to gradually increase the retirement age, with the specifics to be announced in the future. Some reports hint that the plan may include reducing the difference in retirement ages for women and men.

Regardless of possible future changes in the retirement age, for the period under analysis the retirement age for women remained five to ten years earlier than that for men. Women's earlier retirement age has implications for the gender wage gap. For both women and men, the age-earnings profile tends to flatten among older workers as they approach retirement age. Wages increase with age from entrance into the labor market through middle age, when they reach a peak, and then they flatten or even decline for workers as they approach retirement. As will be seen from the CHIP data, this is the case in urban China. Moreover, the age-earnings profile flattens at an earlier age for women than it does for men, a reflection of the earlier retirement age, thus creating a widening of the gender wage gap among older workers.

11.3 Data and Descriptive Statistics

11.3.1 Data

For our analysis, we use data from the CHIP 1995, 2002, 2007, and 2013 urban household surveys. To obtain consistent samples over time, we restrict the sample to the twelve provinces that are present in all four waves of the survey. In all cases, the sample provinces cover the East, Central and West regions of China.[5] Except where noted otherwise, we employ two-level province times region (East/Central/West) population weights in all calculations and regressions so that the estimates are nationally representative.

Because of labor market segmentation between formal urban residents and rural/urban migrants as well as the non-comparability of some data between these two groups, we do not incorporate migrant households in our analysis. In other words, the sample is confined to formal urban residents, i.e., individuals with an urban household registration (*hukou*).

For the descriptive analysis of labor force participation our sample includes individuals between the ages of 16 and 59. For analysis of the wage gap, including the wage regressions and the Oaxaca decompositions, we restrict the sample to individuals of prime employment age, that is, between ages 25 and 49 inclusive. We use the narrower age range for analysis of the wage gap to reduce the impact on our wage estimates of selection because of choices regarding labor market participation, which are concentrated among the young who are choosing when to transition from school to work and among older workers who are choosing when to retire.

The wage data in the CHIP datasets were collected by the National Bureau of Statistics (NBS) for its household survey and then provided to the CHIP. In 2013 the NBS changed its definition of wage earnings. Consequently, the wage data for 2013 are not entirely comparable to those in earlier years. The new definition adds several new components of wages that were not included previously (see Table 11.1). Using available information in the 2013 data on the components of wages, we have adjusted the NBS 2013 wage data to be as consistent as possible with the NBS 2007 wage definition. A full correction is not possible, due to a lack of information on some components of employer-paid contributions to benefits and social insurance. In our judgment, the remaining inconsistencies are minor and unlikely to significantly affect our findings.

11.3.2 Descriptive Statistics: Labor Force Participation and Employment

Table 11.2 summarizes information in the CHIP 1995, 2002, 2007, and 2013 surveys about the employment status of working-age adults (ages 16–59). In all years, most working-age adults worked; however, work participation

Table 11.1. Definition of wage earnings before and after 2013

	NBS definition of wage earnings before 2013	NBS definition of wage earnings, 2013	Adjusted wage earnings, 2013
Wage and salary income (including bonuses and allowances)	√	√	√
In-kind payments from employer	×	√	×
Contributions to social insurance deducted by employer from employee earnings	√	√	√
Employer contributions to social insurance	×	√	√
Retirement payments and reimbursed medical expenses received by employees of administrative organizations that make no social insurance contributions	×	√	√
Severance payments	×	√	×

rates were consistently lower for women than for men. Work participation was highest in 1995, at 85 percent for men and 75 percent for women, but in 2002 it dropped to 76 percent for men and 59 percent for women, a reflection of the enterprise restructuring and layoffs that took place in the late 1990s. By 2007 work participation rates for men had recovered, and they remained stable through 2013 at about 80 percent. However, work participation rates for women never fully recovered, leading to the emergence of a gender gap in work participation. In 2007 and 2013 women's participation in work was at a rate of 62–63 percent, only modestly higher than that in 2002.

The persistent gender gap in work participation since 2002 is due largely to a gender gap in wage employment. In 1995 wage employment participation was 10 percentage points higher for men than for women. The gap widened to about 15 percentage points in 2002 and thereafter remained at this level through 2013. This gap would have been even larger had it not been that more males than females moved into self-employment.[6]

Aside from wage employment, the largest gender differences in Table 11.2 are in the categories of retirement, homemaker, and "other." Women are

Table 11.2. Employment status of working-age adults, 1995, 2002, 2007, and 2013 (%)

	1995		2002		2007		2013	
	Male	Female	Male	Female	Male	Female	Male	Female
Working, total	85.2	75.3	75.9	59.1	80.4	62.3	81.0	62.8
Of which: wage jobs	83.7	73.7	72.0	56.4	74.4	58.4	72.1	54.9
Of which: self-employed	1.5	1.2	3.9	2.8	6.0	3.9	7.8	5.8
Unemployed	2.8	2.6	7.2	9.3	4.3	6.4	2.8	3.6
Retired	3.6	11.4	5.7	16.9	4.3	17.4	3.3	11.3
Student	7.8	7.5	10.1	9.8	10.3	8.8	9.4	9.3
Homemaker	0.1	2.3	0.2	3.7	0.2	3.7	0.8	8.7
Other	0.6	0.9	0.9	1.2	0.5	1.3	2.8	4.2
Total	100.0	100.0	100.0	100.0	100.0	100.0	100.0	100.0
Sample size (unweighted)	7440	7817	7417	7755	7919	8370	5741	5990

Notes: Working age is 16-59 years, inclusive. Calculated by using the CHIP urban data, with weights. The sample is restricted to formal urban residents (with an urban *hukou*) in the twelve common provinces. Note that because of missing values and rounding in some years the percentage with wage jobs plus the percentage of self-employed does not equal the total percentage of those working.

disproportionately represented in these three categories. In all years only 4 to 7 percent of men belonged to these three categories, as compared to 15 percent of women in 1995 and rising to more than 20 percent in later years.

Interestingly, although the share of women in these three categories combined was virtually identical in 2007 and 2013, the allocation of women among the three categories changed markedly. The proportion of women who reported being retired declined from 17 percent in 2007 to 11 percent in 2013, whereas those who reported being homemakers rose from 4 percent to 9 percent, and those belonging to the "other" category rose from 1 percent to 4 percent. These shifts may reflect changing attitudes about these categories that affected the self-reporting in the survey. Individuals often fall into more than one of these categories, e.g., a retired person may also be a homemaker. We speculate that over time retired women became more willing to identify themselves as homemakers or as "other"; therefore, we consider the three categories together as a single group.

Figure 11.1 shows the shares of women and men with wage employment by age for the most recent two years of the CHIP data. For both women and

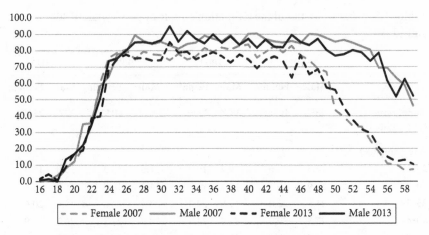

Fig. 11.1 Shares of women and men with wage employment, by age (%)
Note: Calculated by using the CHIP urban data, ages 16–59, with weights.

men, wage employment is low for the youngest age group but it increases rapidly, reaching over 75 percent for women and over 80 percent for men by the age of 25. After age 25 wage employment participation remains stable for women until their late 40s and for men until about age 50, after which it declines. Our choice of ages 25 through 49 as the cut-offs for the gender wage gap analysis is based on this age-employment pattern.

Comparing 2007 to 2013, we find that between these two years the gender gap in job participation rates remained stable for ages 16 through 35. For those between the ages of 35 and 49 the gender gap in job participation widened somewhat because of a decline in female participation. For older ages, the gap in wage job participation narrowed slightly as men hastened and women delayed their departure from the wage labor force.

11.3.3 Descriptive Statistics: Characteristics of Female and Male Wage Employment

Table 11.3 provides descriptive statistics for the restricted estimation sample of individuals between the ages of 25 and 49 with wage employment. Here we note several patterns of interest. First, for both genders the age structure of wage workers shifted somewhat over time. In 1995 the dominant age groups were 35–39 and 40–44, with relatively few younger and older workers.

Table 11.3. Characteristics of the estimation sample by gender, CHIP 2007 and 2013

	1995		2002		2007		2013	
	Male	Female	Male	Female	Male	Female	Male	Female
Sample size (unweighted)	4588	4686	3876	3549	4062	4033	2773	2510
Age group (%)								
25–29	11.3	11.6	9.4	10.7	11.5	13.3	15.0	16.3
30–34	17.9	19.4	15.8	18.7	14.3	16.8	16.9	18.1
35–39	21.5	22.8	21.8	22.3	23.4	24.8	18.6	20.6
40–44	27.8	29.0	22.8	24.2	28.9	27.3	24.7	23.9
45–49	21.5	17.2	30.2	24.1	21.8	17.9	24.8	21.1
Ethnicity (%)								
Han	95.6	95.4	97.3	97.0	97.3	97.1	97.4	97.5
Ethnic minority	4.4	4.6	2.7	3.0	2.7	2.9	2.6	2.5
Marital status (%)								
Single	5.9	2.9	8.2	5.4	9.5	6.9	9.0	7.8
Married	93.3	95.5	90.8	92.0	89.7	89.8	88.4	88.4
Others	0.8	1.6	1.0	2.6	0.8	3.3	2.6	3.8
Educational attainment (%)								
Primary school or less	5.6	8.8	2.6	2.9	0.9	1.4	2.8	4.3
Middle school	34.0	38.2	24.7	25.7	14.8	15.3	24.3	23.6
High school	18.8	21.8	26.1	29.2	25.5	29.6	15.8	16.7
Vocational secondary school (*zhongzhuan, jixiao*)	13.6	14.2	8.5	12.5	10.1	11.5	12.7	11.7
Vocational post-secondary school (*dazhuan*)	19.6	12.7	24.2	21.9	27.2	29.1	20.6	22.0
College and beyond	8.4	4.3	14.0	7.8	21.5	13.1	23.7	21.7
Number of children under the age of 16 in the household (%)								
0	30.4	32.6	43.9	45.4	45.8	48.8	47.4	50.9
1	65.7	64.1	53.9	53.2	51.7	48.9	46.9	44.9
2 or more	3.9	3.3	2.2	1.5	2.5	2.2	5.7	4.2

Table 11.3. Continued

	1995		2002		2007		2013	
	Male	Female	Male	Female	Male	Female	Male	Female
Ownership of work unit (%)								
Public unit or SOE	85.0	76.9	69.2	64.3	58.8	50.6	45.0	39.7
Collective sector	12.3	20.3	5.7	10.1	5.5	7.8	4.3	5.0
Private firm, self-employed, joint-venture. or foreign firm	2.2	2.0	13.7	11.7	31.4	31.8	44.6	47.5
Other ownership	0.5	0.7	11.4	13.9	4.3	9.7	6.1	7.8
Occupation (%)								
Manual worker	38.6	40.8	35.3	26.8	23.9	12.7	27.3	15.0
Commercial or service worker	—	—	7.9	17.7	10.0	23.5	20.9	33.9
Office worker	20.9	22.7	19.3	25.1	33.1	38.3	19.8	20.2
Manager or official	15.8	5.3	14.1	4.8	7.3	2.5	5.9	4.5
Professional or technician	21.7	24.3	21.3	23.1	20.9	17.5	19.8	21.8
Agricultural and related	—	—	—	—	0.6	1.2	0.9	0.7
Other	2.9	6.9	2.1	2.5	4.2	4.3	5.3	3.9
Sector of employment (%)								
Primary	1.9	1.5	1.2	1.2	1.0	0.7	1.4	0.9
Secondary	48.5	48.3	35.5	31.6	27.9	19.1	30.8	19.8
Tertiary	49.6	50.3	63.3	67.2	71.1	80.2	67.7	79.3

Notes:

1.) Calculated by using the CHIP urban data with weights. The sample is restricted to formal urban residents (with an urban *hukou*) between the ages of 25 and 49 with wage employment in the twelve provinces common to all four years of the data.

2.) Marital status "other" includes widowers/widows, divorcees, and cohabitation.

3.) Primary industry is agriculture; secondary industry is mining, manufacturing, public utilities, and construction; and tertiary industry is all other sectors. These definitions are from the NBS national accounts classifications. See http://www.stats.gov.cn/english/ClassificationsMethods/Definitions/200204/t20020419_72392.html. Accessed April 28, 2016.

4.) In the CHIP 1995 survey the questionnaire did not include the occupation categories "commercial or service worker" or "agricultural and related." The reason is that in the 1990s the tertiary sector was quite underdeveloped and employment within commercial and service departments was small. Also, *hukou* restrictions in the 1990s were strict, preventing rural residents from living in the cities. Consequently, workers holding "agricultural and related" occupations were basically nonexistent.

By 2013 the age distributions had evened out, with some increases in the shares of younger (ages 25–29) and older (ages 45–49) workers. These shifts in age patterns reflect the combined effects of changes over time in the demographics of the urban population and in work participation by different age groups.

Second, the composition of the sample with respect to marital status also changed over time. The share of singles for both women and men increased and the share of married women and married men declined. Also, over time the differences in marital status between women and men narrowed. In 1995 a larger proportion of men than of women were single and a higher proportion of women than of men were married; by 2013 these proportions were basically the same for both women and men. Note that the proportion reporting an "other" marital status, which includes divorced or widowed, increased slightly but remained very small.

Third, education levels rose for both women and men. In 2013 more than 40 percent of both women and men had a post-secondary education, and fewer than 5 percent had only a primary education or less. Over time, the share of individuals with a post-secondary education or higher rose and those with less education—junior high school or below—fell. From 2007 to 2013 the share of women with a post-secondary education or above increased markedly so that by 2013 it was almost the same as that for men.

Changes in the employment structure in the sample are consistent with the structural changes in the labor market. The share of individuals working in public and state-owned work units declined markedly, whereas the share of individuals working in private, joint-venture, and foreign-owned units increased. Similarly, the structure of employment by occupation shifted away from manual work toward commerce and services. With respect to production sectors, there was a substantial shift from the secondary sector to the tertiary sector.

Table 11.3 reveals some changes over time in gender differences. In 1995 the sectoral pattern of employment for women and men was similar, but in 2013 gender differences in the production sector of employment were substantial; in particular, in 2013 a much higher proportion of women than men were employed in the tertiary sector and a much lower proportion of women were employed in the secondary sector. With respect to most other characteristics, however, differences between men and women narrowed between 1995 and 2013. Notably, between 1995 and 2007 the education levels of women converged with those of men. Additionally, in 2013 the ownership of work units for women and men was more similar than it was in earlier years. As will be discussed later, the convergence of women's and men's characteristics has contributed to the trends over time in the gender wage gap.

11.3.4 Descriptive Statistics: The Raw Gender Wage Ratio

The gender wage ratio, calculated as the average female wage divided by the average male wage, provides a raw measure of the gender wage gap. This measure is "raw" in the sense that it is not adjusted for differences in the characteristics of women and men. A gender wage ratio of 100 percent indicates no gender wage gap; a ratio below 100 percent indicates that on average women earn less than men.

Table 11.4 shows the raw gender wage ratio: that is, the ratio of the average woman's wage earnings to the average man's wage earnings, overall and by subgroups. The overall ratio declined progressively from 87 percent in 1995 to 83 percent in 2002, and then further to 71 percent in 2007. Between 2007 and 2013 the downward trend reversed and the gender wage ratio increased to 74 percent.

The gender wage ratio varies by age and education. Figures 11.2 and 11.3 show the ratios by age and education subgroups respectively. With respect to age, in all years the wage ratio was higher for young workers and lower for older subgroups (Figure 11.2). Moreover, from 1995 to 2007 the gender wage ratio declined for all age groups, but especially for older workers. Notably, from 2007 to 2013 the gender wage ratio improved for middle-aged and older workers, but it changed little for younger age groups. As age is correlated with other variables such as education and marital status, we later report on the gender wage ratios by age, based on multivariate regressions that also control for other characteristics.

The decline in the gender wage ratio with age is also evident if one follows birth cohorts in the CHIP sample over time. For example, consider individuals born in the years 1968 through 1972. This five-year birth cohort entered the labor force in 1995, at which time its members were between the ages of 23 and 27. In that year the average gender wage ratio for this cohort was 101 percent, that is, on average women and men in this age group received the same wages. Seven years later (2002) when this cohort reached the ages of 30 to 34, its gender wage ratio had fallen to 84 percent. Five years later (2007) at ages between 35 and 39, its gender wage ratio had fallen

Table 11.4. The raw gender wage ratio in the overall CHIP estimation sample and by subgroup (%)

	1995	2002	2007	2013
Overall average	86.7	82.7	70.6	74.2
Ethnicity				
Han	86.7	82.4	70.5	74.3
Ethnic minority	86.2	92.0	75.7	74.3
Marital status				
Single	95.5	98.3	96.5	100.6
Married	85.7	81.4	68.5	72.0
Other	112.5	96.4	119.4	91.4
Number of children under the age of 16 in the household				
0	88.5	85.6	72.4	77.5
1	86.3	80.6	69.5	71.9
2 or more	81.2	73.6	68.2	68.7
Ownership				
Public unit or SOE	89.6	87.6	74.9	78.9
Collective sector	81.5	79.4	76.9	70.9
Private firm, self-employed, joint-venture, or foreign firm	93.3	69.7	70.7	72.7
Other ownership	76.6	76.4	65.6	85.2
Sector				
Secondary	84.3	85.3	68.5	71.3
Tertiary	88.7	80.9	70.0	74.8

Notes:

1.) Here and elsewhere, the CHIP 2013 wage data have been adjusted to be consistent with the wage data for the earlier years.

2.) Calculated by using the CHIP urban data, with weights. Restricted to formal urban residents between the ages of 25 and 49 in the twelve common provinces.

3.) The primary sector is not shown because of the very small number of observations.

4.) Marital status "other" includes widowers/widows, divorcees, and cohabitation.

further to 68 percent. In 2013 at ages between 41 and 45 the ratio remained at 69 percent.

The next five-year birth cohort, born in the years 1973 through 1977, had not yet entered the labor force in 1995. Seven years later (in 2002) at ages 25–29, its gender wage ratio was 90 percent. Five years later (in 2007) at ages

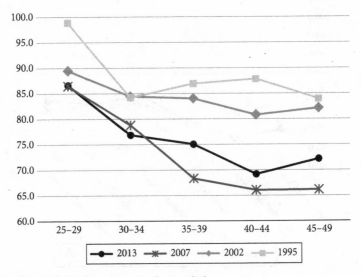

Fig. 11.2 Female/male wage ratio, by age (%)

Notes:

1.) 2013 wages are adjusted to be consistent with the 2007 NBS income definition of wage earnings.

2.) Calculated by using the CHIP urban data for the twelve provinces common to all four waves of the survey, with weights.

3.) The sample is restricted to individuals with wage employment between the ages of 25 and 49 who are formal urban residents (with urban *hukou*).

30-34, the gender wage ratio of this birth cohort had declined to 79 percent, where it remained in 2013, at ages 36-40. These cohort-based patterns confirm that the gender wage gap is small when women enter the labor force but widens over time spent in the labor force.

With respect to education, the gender wage ratio has followed a two-step pattern that is lower for education levels up through high school and higher for vocational secondary school, vocational post-secondary school, college, and above (see Figure 11.3). The gender wage ratio shifted downward for the least educated from 1995 to 2002 and shifted downward again for all education groups from 2002 to 2007. From 2007 to 2013 the curve remained unchanged except for the least-educated subgroup, primary school and lower, for which the gender ratio improved. As of 2013, the gender wage ratios for primary education or less, middle school, and general high school were roughly 70 percent, and for higher levels of education they were 77-79 percent. These differences in the gender wage ratio across education levels to some extent are correlated with age, as older cohorts tend to have less education. Later we examine the relationship between education and the gender

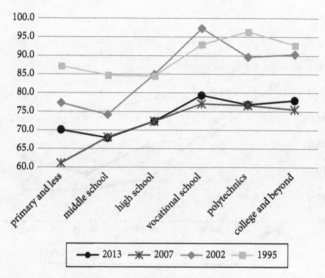

Fig. 11.3 Female/male wage ratio, by education (%)

Notes:

1.) 2013 wages are adjusted to be consistent with the 2007 NBS income definition of wage earnings.

2.) Calculated by using the CHIP urban data for the twelve provinces common to all four waves of the survey, with weights

3.) The sample is restricted to individuals with wage employment between the ages of 25 and 49 who are formal urban residents (urban *hukou*).

wage ratio by using a multivariate regression that controls for correlated characteristics.

Table 11.4 reports the wage ratios for additional subgroups of interest. The gender wage ratio was close to 100 percent for single individuals in all years, indicating little or no gender wage gap. For married individuals the wage ratio was lower, declining markedly to 70 percent in 2007, and then remaining basically unchanged at 72 percent in 2013. This pattern by marital status is consistent with that found in other countries. Married women typically earn less than married men.

The gender wage ratio also varies by the number of children. In all years the gender wage ratio is lower for individuals with children than for individuals without children. Among all such subgroups the gender wage ratio deteriorated between 1995 and 2007. From 2007 to 2013 the increase in the wage ratio was most noticeable for women without children.

The gender wage ratio varies by ownership of the work unit and sector of employment. In most years the gender wage ratio was highest in public

and state-owned work units. These subgroups include more highly educated workers, so their higher wages may reflect differences in education.
With respect to sectors, increasingly few urban workers were employed in
the primary sector. For the secondary and tertiary sectors, we do not see a
clear pattern, except that for both sectors the gender wage ratios declined to
about 70 percent in 2007 and then recovered between 2007 and 2013. Such
differences in the gender wage ratios across ownership and occupation suggest that structural changes in the urban economy may be associated with
trends in the gender wage gap.

11.4 Empirical Methodology

Our empirical analysis is mainly based on an estimation of Mincer wage
earnings equations using ordinary least squares (OLS), with standard errors
adjusted to reflect the clustering arising from the survey sampling design.
First, we estimate regressions pooling women and men together by using the
regression equation:

$$lnY_i = \alpha + \beta Female_i + \sum_j \gamma_j X_{ji} + \mu_i, \tag{11.1}$$

where for each individual i the ln of wage earnings lnY_i is a function of
whether the individual is female (the dummy variable $Female$ equals one if
female, zero otherwise), plus j other characteristics X_{ji} and the residual μ_i.
The coefficient of interest is β, which if less than one indicates the presence of
a gender wage gap after controlling for other characteristics.

Using the results from the estimation of Equation (11.1) we calculate the
gender wage gap in percentage terms after controlling for other characteristics. As discussed in Giles (2011), in a semi-log regression the estimator of the
percentage effect p of a dummy variable on the outcome variable is given by

$$p = \frac{e^c}{e^{(0.5 * V_c)}} - 1, \tag{11.2}$$

where c is the OLS estimate of the coefficient on the dummy variable and
V_c is the estimated variance of that coefficient (see also Halvorsen and
Palmqvist 1980).

To explore more fully the impact of marriage and children on the gender wage gap, we also estimate the pooled wage equations with added interactions between the gender dummy variable and the dummy variables for marital status and the number of children under the age of 16. The estimation equation becomes

$$
\begin{aligned}
lnY_i = {} & \alpha + \beta_0 Female_i + \beta_1 (Female_i * Single_i) \\
& + \beta_2 \left(Female_i * OtherMarital_i \right) \\
& + \beta_3 \left(Female_i * Onechild_i \right) \\
& + \beta_4 \left(Female_i * Morechildren_i \right) \\
& + \gamma_1 Single + \gamma_2 OtherMarital_i \\
& + \gamma_3 Onechild_i + \gamma_4 Morechildren_i \\
& + \sum_{j=5} \gamma_j X_{ji} + \mu_i.
\end{aligned} \tag{11.3}
$$

The omitted reference group is male, married, with no children. Using estimates from this equation and the formula for the percentage effect (Equation [11.2]), we calculate the percentage gender wage gaps for each of the following subgroups: single with no children (the sum of the percentage effects of β_0 and β_1); married with no children (the percentage effect of β_0); married with one child (the sum of the percentage effects of β_0 and β_3); and married with more than one child (the sum of the percentage effects of β_0 and β_4).

Second, we estimate wage equations for women and men separately. For each of the female and male samples we estimate Equation (11.1), but without the dummy variable *Female*. The estimated coefficients from the separate wage equations are used to carry out a decomposition of the gender wage gap. According to the Oaxaca-Blinder decomposition (Blinder 1973; Oaxaca 1973), the difference between average ln male and average ln female wages can be written as

$$
\overline{lnY_m} - \overline{lnY_f} = \left(\hat{\alpha}_m + \sum_j \hat{\gamma}_{j,m} \overline{X_{j,m}} \right) - \left(\hat{\alpha}_f + \sum_j \hat{\gamma}_{j,f} \overline{X_{j,f}} \right), \tag{11.4}
$$

where the bars indicate the mean values for males m and females f. The difference in average ln wages can then be divided into two components:

$$
\overline{lnY_m} - \overline{lnY_f} = \left[(\hat{\alpha}_m - \hat{\alpha}_f) + \sum_j \left(\hat{\gamma}_{j,m} - \hat{\gamma}_{j,f} \right) \overline{X_{j,m}} \right] + \left[\sum_j \hat{\gamma}_{j,f} \left(\overline{X_{j,m}} - \overline{X_{j,f}} \right) \right]. \tag{11.5}
$$

The first term on the right-hand side of Equation (11.5) is that portion of the wage difference that can be attributed to differences between the coefficients of the two regressions, including the constant terms (the "unexplained" portion). The second term is the portion of the wage difference that can be attributed to differences between male and female characteristics (the "explained" portion).

In all wage regressions, the dependent variable is the ln of monthly wage earnings. For 1995, 2002, and 2007 we use the NBS wage variable in the CHIP dataset; for 2013, we use the adjusted 2013 wage variable. Individual characteristics include dummy variables for marital status, number of children, ethnicity, age group, and education level. Dummy variables for province of residence control for provincial fixed effects. In some specifications, we include dummy variables for the ownership of the individual's work unit, the occupation, and the employment sector. All variables are from the CHIP datasets, and all estimates are carried out by using two-level weights.

11.5 Pooled Wage Equations: Results

11.5.1 Results of the Basic Specification

Estimates of the β coefficient are reported in Table 11.5. The first row gives estimates from wage equations estimated without, and the second row with, controls for sector of ownership, occupation, and sector of production. The estimates are uniformly negative and significant, indicating an urban gender wage gap that is robust to specification and that persists over time. The coefficients are smaller with than without the additional controls, reflecting that women tend to work in lower-wage sectors and occupations than men.

Changes in the magnitude of the coefficient over time confirm that the gender wage gap widened from 1995 to 2007 but narrowed from 2007 to 2013. Without controls for sector and occupation, the gender wage gap increased from 12 percent in 1995 to 18 percent in 2002 to 27 percent in 2007, and then decreased to 24 percent in 2013. With controls for sector and occupation, the gap increased from 10 percent in 1995 to 15 percent in 2002 to 22 percent in 2007, and then decreased to 19 percent in 2013.

Our regression-based estimates of the urban gender wage gap are similar to those in the literature, which indicate a widening trend in the gap

Table 11.5. Estimated coefficient on the female dummy variable and the % gender wage gap

	1995	2002	2007	2013
Coefficient, without sector and occupation controls	−0.132***	−0.200***	−0.319***	−0.270***
Coefficient, with sector and occupation controls	−0.106***	−0.162***	−0.252***	−0.213***
% wage gap, without sector and occupation controls	−12.4%	−18.1%	−27.3%	−23.7%
% wage gap, with sector and occupation controls	−10.1%	−15.0%	−22.3%	−19.2%

Notes:

1.) Estimates of $\hat{\beta}$ from the pooled female and male wage regressions by using the CHIP urban data, with weights. The sample is restricted to formal urban residents, between the ages of 25 and 49, with wage employment in the twelve common provinces. These regressions do not include interactions between the female dummy variable and the other characteristics. Refer to the tables in the Appendix of our working paper for the full results (see ftn. 8).

2.) Estimates of the % gender wage gap are calculated as $p = [exp(\hat{\beta})/exp(0.5V(\hat{\beta}))]-1$, where $V(\hat{\beta})$ is the estimated variance of the coefficient $\hat{\beta}$. See Giles (2011) and Halvorsen and Palmqvist (1980).

3.) *** $p < 0.01$, ** $p < 0.05$, and * $p < 0.1$

during years prior to 2010. Li and Song (2013) report coefficients for the gender dummy variable estimated with the urban CHIP data without controls for sector/occupation of 0.12, 0.20, and 0.27 in 1995, 2002, and 2007 respectively. Liu (2011) reports coefficients estimated with the China Health and Nutrition Survey data of about 0.15 for the late 1990s and early 2000s.

Full results from the pooled wage equations can be found in the tables in the Appendix of the working paper for this chapter;[7] here we note selected findings of interest. The coefficient on single marital status in all cases is negative and significant, ranging from -0.17 to -0.24 (married is the omitted reference category), with no clear trend over time. This result indicates that after the study controls for other characteristics such as age and education, single individuals have lower wages, thus suggesting the presence of a marriage wage premium. The coefficients on the dummy variable for one child are largely insignificant, but the coefficients on the dummy variable for two or more children are significant and negative in 2002, 2007, and 2013 in the regressions that do not include controls for sector/ownership. These results indicate no wage penalty for the first child but a wage penalty for two or more children, as compared to no children. The fact that the coefficients on two or more children are mostly not significant when controls for occupation/sector are included in the regression suggests that people with two or more children may sort into lower-wage occupations and sectors.

The coefficients on the age variables indicate that in general wages rise with age up through the early 40s and then they level out. The estimated coefficients on education are mostly significant and consistent with expectations, with higher levels of education producing higher returns. Moreover, the additional returns to higher levels of education compared to lower levels of education increased substantially over time, especially from 1995 to 2007. The steepening of the education-earnings relationship implies that differences in education increasingly generate wage inequality.

We see the expected patterns for ownership of work unit, occupation, and sector of employment. Estimates of the relevant coefficients are shown in Table 11.6. With respect to sector of ownership, in all years except for 1995 the coefficients are negative and significant, indicating that wages are highest in the reference category, i.e., the state sector. Moreover, the magnitude of the wage difference is large. In 2013, for example, the log point difference in wages between the state sector and the non-state sector was 0.23–0.24. Since proportionately fewer women than men are employed in the state sector, these wage differentials are relevant to the gender wage gap.

With respect to production sector, the reference category is manufacturing. As shown in Table 11.6, the coefficients for construction and mining are either positive and significant or not significant, which implies that wages in construction and mining have been similar to or higher than wages in manufacturing. As of 2013, wages in construction and mining were not significantly different from those in manufacturing.

How do wages in the tertiary sector, which employs a high proportion of women, compare? The coefficients differ among the tertiary sectors and across the years, but as of 2013 none of the tertiary sector industries had positive, significant coefficients, and four had negative, significant coefficients. In other words, as of 2013 no tertiary sectors paid wages higher than the secondary sector, and some paid significantly less. These wage differences across production sectors contribute to the raw gender wage gap.

Table 11.6. Estimated coefficients on the sector of the employment dummy variables

	1995	2002	2007	2013
Sector of ownership (reference category: state ownership)				
Collective sector	−0.246***	−0.250***	−0.225***	−0.242***
Foreign/joint venture/private	0.142*	−0.241***	−0.162***	−0.229***
Other ownership	−0.107	−0.134***	−0.399***	−0.335***
Sector of production (reference category is secondary: manufacturing)				
Primary: agriculture	−0.054	0.038	0.016	−0.131
Secondary: mining	0.127***	−0.048	0.330***	0.100
Secondary: public utilities	−0.014	0.006	0.171***	−0.065
Secondary: construction	0.084**	−0.024	0.015	−0.008
Tertiary: transportation and communication	0.060*	0.124***	0.068***	0.059
Tertiary: commerce and trade	−0.109***	−0.025	−0.027	−0.149***
Tertiary: finance and insurance	0.229***	0.121***	−0.066**	−0.200***
Tertiary: education and culture	−0.003	0.090***	0.048*	−0.230***
Tertiary: health and social welfare	0.038	0.171***	0.177***	−0.093
Tertiary: scientific research and technology	0.110***	0.187***	0.200***	0.009
Tertiary: government and social organizations	0.002	0.068**	0.018	−0.180***

Note: Based on the pooled female and male wage regressions estimated by using the CHIP urban data, with weights. The sample is restricted to formal urban residents, between the ages of 25 and 49, with wage employment in the twelve common provinces. These regressions do not include interactions between the female dummy variable and other characteristics. Refer to the tables in the Appendix to our working paper for the full results (see ftn.8).

*** $p < 0.01$, ** $p < 0.05$, and * $p < 0.1$

11.5.2 With Interactions between Gender, Marital Status, and Children

Table 11.7 reports the estimated β coefficients from the pooled regression with interactions between the gender dummy variable and dummy variables for life events (Equation [11.2]). Figure 11.4 shows the gender wage ratio in percentage terms for each life-event group, calculated by using the estimated coefficients. These coefficients and ratios control for other characteristics such as age, education, and location, and thus they provide a clearer picture

Table 11.7. Estimated coefficients on the female dummy variable and its interactions with life-event dummy variables

	Without sector controls				With sector controls			
	1995	2002	2007	2013	1995	2002	2007	2013
	(1)	(2)	(3)	(4)	(5)	(6)	(7)	(8)
b0 Female	-0.167***	-0.234***	-0.358***	-0.248***	-0.140***	-0.176***	-0.289***	-0.191***
b1 Female*single	0.071	0.175***	0.210***	0.182**	0.059	0.130*	0.178***	0.151
b3 Female*1 minor children	0.047*	0.044	0.036	-0.078*	0.045	0.016	0.036	-0.079*
b4 Female*2 plus minor children	-0.030	-0.046	-0.000	-0.114	-0.032	-0.142	0.024	-0.077

Notes:

1.) Based on pooled female and male wage regressions estimated by using the CHIP urban data, with weights. The sample is restricted to formal urban residents between the ages of 25 and 49, with wage employment in the twelve common provinces. These regressions are the same as the pooled wage regressions in Part A of Section 11.5.1, except that they include interactions between the female dummy variable and marital status and between the female dummy variable and the children dummy variables.

2.) Earnings are the predicted wages by age group, which are calculated by using the estimated coefficients from the separate female and male wage regressions without sector and occupation controls. All characteristics except education are set at the respective female and male means. Estimates with sector/occupation controls yield similar results. 2007 wages are expressed in 2013 prices based on the NBS national urban consumer price index (NBS, various years).

3.) *** $p < 0.01$, ** $p < 0.05$, and * $p < 0.1$

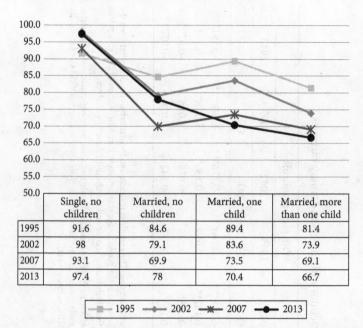

	Single, no children	Married, no children	Married, one child	Married, more than one child
1995	91.6	84.6	89.4	81.4
2002	98	79.1	83.6	73.9
2007	93.1	69.9	73.5	69.1
2013	97.4	78	70.4	66.7

────■──── 1995 ────◆──── 2002 ──✳── 2007 ──●── 2013

Fig. 11.4 Regression-based female/male wage ratio, by life-event groups (%)

Notes: This figure shows the regression-based gender wage ratios within life-event groups, e.g., the ratio of the wages of married women with no children to those of married men with no children. Calculated by using the Giles (2011) formula for the percentage effects of dummy variables in semi-log regression equations, using estimates from pooled wage regressions without sector/occupation controls that include the interaction female * life-event dummy variables. The results with sector/occupation controls are similar. See Table 11.7.

of the relationship between life events and wages than the raw gender wage ratios reported earlier.

As shown in Figure 11.4, in 1995 when wages were largely determined administratively, differences in the gender coefficient across life-event groups were modest. However, the differences widened in later years. In all years the gender wage ratios for singles remained high, fluctuating but always above 90 percent. In other words, for single women and men the wage gap was nonexistent or small. For married groups, however, the wage ratio deteriorated. Regardless of the number of children, the wage ratio for married women declined markedly from 80–90 percent in 1995 to below 75 percent in 2007. Between 2007 and 2013 the gender wage ratios for those married without children recovered substantially, but for those married with one or more children the ratios declined slightly.

Thus, as of 2013 and after the study controlled for other characteristics such as education, ethnicity, and location, the gender wage gap was smallest for individuals who were single with no children. The gap widened progressively from being single, to being married, to being married with one child, and to being married with more than one child. In 2013 single women without children earned only 3 percent less than single men without children. Married women without children earned 22 percent less than married men without children. Married women with children earned 30 to 33 percent less than married men with the same number of children.

These estimates indicate that the life event with the greatest impact on the gender wage gap is marriage. As will be seen in the separate female and male regressions, the impact of marriage on earnings differs for women and men.

11.6 Separate Wage Equations for Women and Men and Oaxaca-Blinder Decompositions

11.6.1 Results of Separate Wage Equations for Women and Men

In this section, we report and discuss selected results of interest from separate wage equations for women and men—specifically the results related to age, education, and life events. The estimates without and with controls for ownership sector, occupation, and production sector are similar, so here we discuss only the results from the regressions without these controls. We mainly focus on the estimates for 2007 and 2013.

Figure 11.5 plots the age-earnings profiles of women and men for 2007 and 2013, based on the predicted wages from the separate female and male wage equations, expressed in constant 2013 prices. All characteristics except age are held constant and set equal to their respective means for each gender. As expected, in both years men's wages are on average higher than women's wages at all ages. In both years and for both women and men, the age-earnings relationship is steeper at younger ages and it flattens or turns down at older ages. Consistent with the younger statutory retirement age for women, the flattening of the age-earnings curve begins earlier for women. In 2013, for example, the wages of women rise with age through age 35–39, after which they remain flat for the two oldest age groups. For men, wages

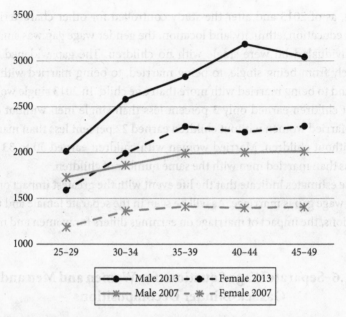

Fig. 11.5 Regression-based age-earnings profiles, 2007 and 2013 (constant 2013 prices)

Notes: Earnings are the predicted wages by age group, which are calculated by using the estimated coefficients from the separate female and male wage regressions without sector and occupation controls. All characteristics except age are set at the respective female and male means. Estimates with sector/occupation controls yield similar results. 2007 wages are expressed in 2013 prices based on the NBS national urban consumer price index.

rise with age through ages 40–44, after which they decline for the oldest age group.

The implications of these age-earnings curves for gender wage ratios are shown in Figure 11.6, which plots the gender wage ratios by using the predicted wages in Figure 11.5. In 2007 the gender wage ratios do not change much with age. From 2007 to 2013, however, the wages of women in younger age groups catch up with the wages of men, so that the gender wage ratios improve for these subgroups. For older age groups, however, the catch-up is either smaller or nonexistent. Consequently, in 2013 the gender wage gap is two tiered, at 20 percent for younger age groups and at 25–30 percent for older age groups.

More education is associated with higher earnings for both women and men. Figure 11.7 plots the education-earnings profiles for women and men in 2007 and 2013, based on the predicted wages. Earnings for both women

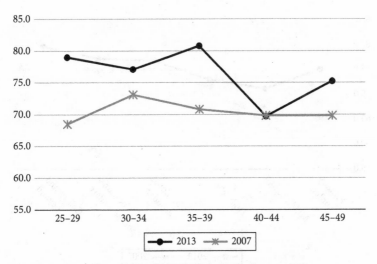

Fig. 11.6 Regression-based female/male wage ratio, by age (%)

Note: Calculated by using the predicted wages shown in Figure 11.5. See the note to Figure 11.5.

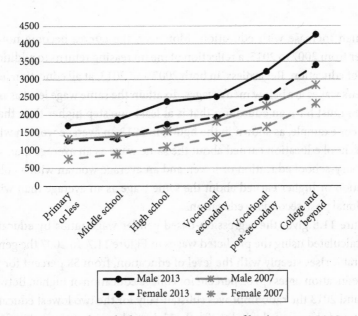

Fig. 11.7 Regression-based education-earnings profiles (constant 2013 prices)

Notes: Earnings are the predicted wages by age group, which are calculated by using the estimated coefficients from the separate female and male wage regressions without sector and occupation controls. All characteristics except education are set at the respective female and male means. Estimates with sector/occupation controls yield similar results. 2007 wages are expressed in 2013 prices based on the NBS national urban consumer price index.

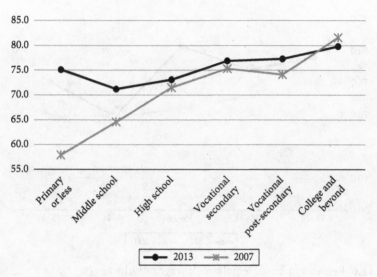

Fig. 11.8 Regression-based female/male wage ratio, by level of education (%)
Notes: Calculated by using the predicted wages shown in Figure 11.7. See the note to Figure 11.7.

and men increase with education. Moreover, the curves become notably steeper from 2007 to 2013, a reflection of the increasing returns to additional years of education. Regardless, in both 2007 and 2013, at all education levels women's wages are below men's wages. To attain the same wage level as men, women must have an education that is at least one step higher than that of men. For example, as shown in the figure, in 2013 an average woman with a high-school education earned about the same wage as an average man with a primary-school education or lower, and an average woman with a college education or higher earned about the same wage as an average man with a vocational post-secondary education.

Figure 11.8 gives the regression-based gender wage ratios by education level calculated using the predicted wages in Figure 11.7. In 2007 the gender wage ratio rises steeply with the level of education, from 58 percent for primary education or less to 82 percent for college education or higher. Between 2007 and 2013 the ratio improves substantially for the two lowest education groups and changes only slightly for the higher education groups. As of 2013 an average woman with a primary education or less earned 75 percent that of an average man with the same level of education. For those with a middle-school education the ratio was 70 percent, and for those with a college education or higher it was 80 percent.

The separate female and male regressions provide information about the differential impact of marriage and children on the earnings of both women and men. Studies in other countries have found that after controlling for other characteristics, married men earn more than single men, thus enjoying a "marriage premium." For women, the opposite is the case, that is, women experience a "marriage penalty." Furthermore, men with children tend to earn more than men without children, whereas the opposite is true for women. There is some debate regarding the explanations for such differentials, e.g., whether this is due to time out of the labor force or differences in productivity. Such premiums and penalties can underlie the gender wage gaps within life-event groups, as discussed earlier.[8]

Our estimates indeed reveal differences between women and men in the estimated coefficients on marital status and children, as reported in Table 11.8. The patterns, however, are somewhat different from those found in

Table 11.8. Estimated coefficients on marital status and children for women and men, 2007 and 2013, from separate wage equations for women and men

	2007	2013
Marriage		
Men	0.318***	0.253***
Women	0.153***	0.151**
One child		
Men	−0.039	0.062
Women	−0.036	−0.064
Two or more children		
Men	−0.146	−0.018
Women	−0.156*	−0.137*

Notes:

1.) The coefficients on marriage are a measure of the wage premium relative to being single, after controlling for all other characteristics.

2.) The coefficients on the children variables are a measure of the wage penalty of having one child, age 16 or less, in the household, relative to having no children, or having two or more children, age 16 or less, in the household relative to no children.

3.) Estimates are from separate female and male wage regressions, weighted, without controls for sector/occupation. The samples are restricted to formal urban residents between the ages of 25 and 49 in the twelve common provinces.

other countries. The coefficients on the marital status dummy variables are significant for both women and men and indicate that both women and men enjoy a marriage premium, although the premium for women is smaller than that for men. From 2007 to 2013 the male marriage premium declined, so the gender difference narrowed. As of 2013, the log point difference between married men and single men was 0.25 and that between married women and single women was 0.15.

With respect to children, the estimates indicate that, overall, having children has little effect on men's earnings: for men, the coefficients on the children dummy variables are all insignificant. For women, the coefficients on the dummy variable for having a single child are insignificant but the coefficients for having two or more children are (weakly) significant and negative, suggesting the presence of a wage penalty for women with more than one child.[9]

11.6.2 Decomposition Results

The results of the Oaxaca-Blinder decompositions based on the separate ln wage equations for women and men are shown in Table 11.9. The "explained" component of the decomposition is the share of the difference in ln wages

Table 11.9. Decomposition of the ln gender wage gap

	Without ownership, occupation, and sector controls				With ownership, occupation, and sector controls			
	1995	2002	2007	2013	1995	2002	2007	2013
Total differential ($T = E + C$)	15.5	23.9	35.6	28.2	15.2	23.6	35.4	27.0
Amount attributable to								
Endowments (E)	2.0	2.9	3.6	0.9	4.2	5.9	9.4	7.0
Coefficients + constant term (C)	13.5	21.0	32.0	27.3	11.0	17.7	26.0	20.0
% of total explained by endowments (E/T)	12.9%	12.1%	10.1%	3.2%	27.6%	25.0%	26.6%	25.9%
% of total unexplained (C/T)	87.1%	87.9%	89.9%	96.8%	72.4%	75.0%	73.4%	74.1%

Note: Calculated by using estimates from the separate wage equations for women and men.

between men and women that can be attributed to differences in the average endowments of women and men, that is, differences in the means of characteristics such as age and education. The remainder, or "unexplained," component of the difference can be attributed to differences in the estimated coefficients and constant terms for women and men, and it may reflect discrimination as well as unobserved factors that are not captured by the regressions.

As shown in the table, a large majority of the difference in ln wages between men and women is unexplained. Without controls for sector/ownership, the unexplained portion is 87–90 percent of the gender gap in 1995, 2002, and 2007, and it rises to 97 percent in 2013. Differences in endowments contribute the remainder, roughly 10–13 percent of the gender gap in 1995, 2002, and 2007, and only 3 percent of the gender gap in 2013.

With sector/occupation controls, the explained contribution is larger, no less than 25 percent in all years and the unexplained contribution accordingly is smaller. Here, the ownerships of the work unit, occupation, and sector of employment are included in the regressions and so are treated as endowments. Consequently, the fact that women tend to work in lower-wage sectors and occupations increases the explained component of the gender wage gap. Regardless, with or without the controls, most of the gender wage gap is unexplained. In other words, differences between women and men in terms of their observed characteristics are not the major source of the gender wage gap. Rather, the gender wage gap is largely unexplained.

To what extent are changes over time in the gender wage gap the result of changes in the contributions of endowments versus the contributions of the coefficients? From 1995 to 2007 the total differential between men and women in the ln wage (T) increases, but from 2007 to 2013 it declines. The decomposition results reveal that the increase in the differential from 1995 to 2007 is associated with increases in both the difference due to endowments (E) and to the difference due to the coefficients, including the constant terms (C). Similarly, the decline from 2007 to 2013 is associated with declines in both these components. In all years, however, the contribution of endowments is relatively small. In other words, changes over time in the gender wage gap, including the decline in the gender wage gap from 2007 to 2013, reflect changes in both the explained and unexplained components of the gap, but especially changes in the unexplained component.

11.7 Conclusions

In this chapter, we provide consistent estimates of the gender wage gap in urban China from 1995 to 2013 and investigate factors contributing to this gap. From 1995 to 2007 we find a substantial and progressive widening of the gap. From 2007 to 2013 we find that the gender wage gap narrows.

Changes in China's gender wage gap are related to changes in the urban economy as well as to changes in government policies that have different effects on women and men. Employment of both women and men has been shifting from the higher-paid to the lower-paid sectors, specifically from the state-owned sector to the non-state-owned sector and from the secondary sector to the tertiary sector. Women continue to be disproportionately employed in the lower-paid sectors. These sectoral patterns contribute to the persistent gender wage differential.

Policies relevant to the gender wage gap include the minimum-wage policy, the expansion of higher education, parental-leave regulations, and retirement policies. Our findings indicate that recent changes in these policies in China have very likely contributed to the narrowing of the gender wage gap after 2007. Retirement age policies, however, remain unchanged and continue to mandate earlier retirement by women, thus depressing the earnings of older women relative to those of older men.

Changes in China's gender wage gap are also related to life-cycle events. In our data, the proportion of single individuals gradually increases for both women and men, but more so for women. Concurrently, the number of children slowly declines for both women and men. These trends in life-cycle events tend to moderate the gender wage gap because the gender wage differentials are smaller for single people than they are for married people and for people with no children or one child compared to those with more than one child.

What factors underlie the recent narrowing of the gender wage gap? Our decomposition analysis shows that to some extent the narrowing is due to the convergence of characteristics between women and men, that is, a reduction in the "explained" component of the gap. In this regard, the main change is in terms of education. Between 2007 and 2013 differences in the education levels of women and men narrows. Notably, the proportion of women with college education or higher catches up with that of men.

The recent narrowing of the gender wage gap also reflects a reduction in the differences in the estimated coefficients or returns to the characteristics of women and men: that is, a reduction in the "unexplained" component of the gap. Our estimates from the separate female and male regressions indicate that the reduction in this unexplained component of the wage gap between 2007 and 2013 is mainly driven by changes in the returns to several specific characteristics: being young (ages 25–39), having less education (middle school or less), being unmarried, and being married without children.

Recent changes in the coefficients on young ages and lower levels of education might reflect increases in minimum-wage levels and strengthened enforcement of the minimum wage. Minimum-wage policies compress wage differentials, including the gender wage gap, for low-paid groups, which are mainly composed of young and unskilled workers. At the other end of the age spectrum, our estimates show that older workers continue to experience a larger gender wage gap. This finding is not surprising, given the lack of any change in the statutory retirement ages for women and men. If the proposed changes to the statutory retirement age include a reduction in the retirement age differential between women and men, it is possible that in the future the gender wage gap for older age groups will shrink.

Reductions in the gender wage gap for those who are single and have no children or who are married with only one child may be related to improvements in parental-leave regulations and maternity insurance. In principle, these policy changes should lower the costs of maternity leave for employers, so employers would have less of an incentive to discriminate against women who are at "risk" of having children.

Is the new direction in China's urban gender wage gap a short-term or a long-term phenomenon? Prediction is a difficult business, but our analysis provides some basis for speculation. First, we suggest that the trend in the gender wage gap from 2007 to 2013 is not due to the short-term economic impact of the global financial crisis. The global financial crisis began a year after 2007 and the recovery was well underway by 2013. Second, many of the underlying changes in the gender wage differences from 2007 to 2013 are related to secular changes in the economic structure; long-term trends in individual characteristics, such as education, marriage, and children; and policy changes that are ongoing and that are likely to continue.

Yet it is possible that some recent developments, in particular, the relaxation of the one-child policy, might offset these trends. Our analysis identifies a significant, positive relationship between having multiple children and the gender wage gap. This relationship reflects the heavier child-care burden on women, indicating the lack of well-funded child-care options (Guo and Xiao

2013; Du and Dong 2013; Qi and Dong 2013, 2016). Moreover, in a setting where the government mandates generous parental leaves for women but not for men and in which some of the costs of those leaves are still borne by the employers, the relaxation of the one-child policy will exacerbate the negative incentives for employers and will have future consequences for the gender wage gap.[10]

Although we discuss the relationship between patterns in the gender wage gap and concurrent structural changes and policy measures, we do not formally analyze these relationships. In addition, our estimates of the gender wage gap are not corrected for selection, that is, we do not employ estimation methods that consider the possibility that the differences in the wages of women and men are affected by gender differences in wage job participation. Nevertheless, our findings provide a starting point for further research in these areas.

Notes

1. Li and Song (2013) analyze the gender wage gap by using CHIP data for 1995, 2002, and 2007. The analysis in this chapter differs not only by adding year 2013 but also by using a different data sample. First, we restrict our sample to the provinces that are present in all four waves of the survey. Second, since the main focus here is on the period from 2007 to 2013, we use earnings data collected from NBS records, whereas Li and Song (2013) worked with data collected in the 2007 survey. Third, here we emphasize the importance of the life cycle. Finally, in our regression analyses we include as controls dummy variables indicating whether the worker has minor children and we restrict the sample to an age range that is different from that in Li and Song (2013).

2. National Bureau of Statistics data available in *Zhongguo tongji nianjian 2015* (China statistical yearbook 2015), Table 21-9. http://www.stats.gov.cn/tjsj/ndsj/2015/indexeh.htm. Accessed August 9, 2016.

3. GDP growth is in constant prices. Urban employment is for registered urban work units. National Bureau of Statistics data are from *Zhongguo tongji nianjian 2014* (China statistical yearbook 2014), Tables 3-5 and 4-2. http://www.stats.gov.cn/tjsj/ndsj/2015/indexeh.htm. Accessed January 15, 2017.

4. For a fuller discussion of minimum-wage policies in China, see Ye, Li, and Gindling (2015) and Chapter 12 of this volume.

5. The twelve provinces common to all four waves of the survey are Guangdong, Beijing, Shanxi, Liaoning, Jiangsu, Anhui, Henan, Hubei, Chongqing, Sichuan, Yunnan, and Gansu. Note that in 1995 Chongqing was part of Sichuan province (and thus was included in the Sichuan sample of the CHIP survey for that year).

6. For an analysis of gender differences in terms of movement into self-employment in urban China based on data for 1978 to 1996, see Zhang and Pan (2012).
7. The working paper is available at: https://ir.lib.uwo.ca/economicscibc/137/. Accessed April 30, 2019.
8. See Ribar (2004); Rodgers and Stratton (2010); and Schoeni (1995) for reviews of the literature on wage premiums and penalties associated with marital status and children.
9. Note that in some years the number of women with two or more children in the dataset is small, a point that might lead to imprecise estimates and thus the weak significance of this coefficient. The number of women with two or more children in 1995 is 196, in 2002 it is 46, in 2007 it is 93, and in 2013 it is 96.
10. See *The Economist*, "China's Two-Child Policy Is Having Unintended Consequences," July 26, 2018. https://www.economist.com/china/2018/07/26/chinas-two-child-policy-is-having-unintended-consequences. Accessed July 31, 2018.

References

Blinder, A. S. (1973). "Wage Discrimination: Reduced Form and Structural Estimates." *Journal of Human Resources*, 8(4), 436-455.
Chi, W. and B. Li (2014). "Trends in China's Gender Employment and Pay Gap: Estimating Gender Pay Gaps with Employment Selection." *Journal of Comparative Economics*, 42(3), 708-725.
China Labour Bulletin (2016). "China's Social Security System." http://www.clb.org.hk/content/china%E2%80%99s-social-security-system. Accessed August 10, 2016.
Du, F. and X. Y. Dong (2013). "Women's Employment and Child Care Choices in Urban China during the Economic Transition." *Economic Development and Cultural Change*, 62(1), 131-158.
Giles, D. E. (2011). "Interpreting Dummy Variables in Semi-logarithmic Regression Models: Exact Distributional Results." University of Victoria, Department of Economics, Econometrics Working Paper, no. 1101.
Guo, J. and S. Xiao (2013). "Through the Gender Lens: A Comparison of Family Policy in Sweden and China." *China Journal of Social Work*, 6(3), 228-243.
Halvorsen, R. and R. Palmqvist (1980). "The Interpretation of Dummy Variables in Semilogarithmic Equations." *American Economic Review*, 70(3), 474-475.
Hare, D. (2016). "What Accounts for the Decline in Labor Force Participation among Married Women in Urban China, 1991–2011?" *China Economic Review*, 38, 251-266.
Jia, N. and X. Y. Dong (2013). "Economic Transition and the Motherhood Wage Penalty in Urban China: Investigation Using Panel Data." *Cambridge Journal of Economics*, 37(4), 819-843.
Li, S. and X. Ma (2015). "Impact of Minimum Wage on Gender Wage Gaps in Urban China." *IZA Journal of Labor and Development*, 4(1), 1-22.
Li, S. and J. Song (2013). "Changes in the Gender-Wage Gap in Urban China, 1995-2007," in S. Li, H. Sato, and T. Sicular, eds., *Rising Inequality in China: Challenges to a Harmonious Society*, 384–413. Cambridge and New York: Cambridge University Press.

Lin, Y. (2011). "Nü zhigong teshu laodong baohu zhidu de kunjing ji duice yanjiu" (Research about the plight of the protection system for special labor of female workers and countermeasures). *Faxue zazhi* (Law Science magazine), no. 11, 59-63.

Liu, H. (2011). "Economic Reforms and Gender Inequality in Urban China." *Economic Development and Cultural Change*, 59(4), 839-876.

Liu, T. and L. Sun (2015). "Maternity Insurance in China: Global Standards and Local Responses." *Asian Women*, 31(4), 23-51.

NBS (various years), *Zhongguo tongji nianjian* (China statistical yearbook). Beijing: Zhongguo tongji chubanshe.

NBS Department of Population and Employment Statistics (2014). *Zhongguo laodong tongji nianjian 2014* (China labour statistical yearbook 2014). Beijing: Zhongguo tongji chubanshe.

Oaxaca, R. (1973). "Male-Female Wage Differentials in Urban Labor Markets." *International Economic Review*, 14(13), 693-709.

Qi, L. and X. Y. Dong (2013). "Housework Burdens, Quality of Market Work Time, and Men's and Women's Earnings in China." University of Winnipeg, Department of Economics, Departmental Working Paper, no. 2013-01.

Qi, L. and X. Y. Dong (2016). "Unpaid Care Work's Interference with Paid Work and the Gender Earnings Gap in China." *Feminist Economics*, 22(2), 143-167.

Ribar, D. C. (2004). "What Do Social Scientists Know about the Benefits of Marriage? A Review of Quantitative Methodologies." IZA Discussion Paper, no. 998.

Rodgers, W. M. and L. S. Stratton (2010). "Male Marital Wage Differentials: Training, Personal Characteristics, and Fixed Effects." *Economic Inquiry*, 48(3), 722-742.

Ruhm, C. J. (1998). "The Economic Consequences of Parental Leave Mandates: Lessons from Europe." *Quarterly Journal of Economics*, 113(1), 285-317.

Schoeni, R. F. (1995). "Marital Status and Earnings in Developed Countries." *Journal of Population Economics*, 8(4), 351-359.

Xiu, L. and M. Gunderson (2013). "Gender Earnings Differences in China: Base Pay, Performance Pay, and Total Pay." *Contemporary Economic Policy*, 31(1), 235-254.

Xu, M. and S. Li (2016). "Female Labor Force Participation in China, 1998 to 2013." Unpublished manuscript.

Ye, L., T. H. Gindling, and S. Li (2015). "Compliance with Legal Minimum Wages and Overtime Pay Regulations in China." *IZA Journal of Labor and Development*, 4(1), 1-35.

Zhang, Q. F. and Z. Pan (2012). "Women's Entry into Self-employment in Urban China: The Role of Family in Creating Gendered Mobility Patterns." *World Development*, 40(6), 1201-1212.

Zhang, Y. and E. Hannum (2015). "Diverging Fortunes: The Evolution of Gender Wage Gaps for Singles, Couples, and Parents in China, 1989-2009." *Chinese Journal of Sociology*, 1(1), 15-55.

12

The Effects of the Minimum-Wage Policy on the Wage Distribution in Urban China

Evidence from the CHIP Data

Xinxin Ma and Shi Li

12.1 Introduction

In China, income inequality increased during the period of economic transition (Li, Sicular, and Gustafsson 2008; Li, Sato, Sicular et al. 2013). Because wage earnings are the main component in household income, particularly for urban and migrant households, wage inequality may greatly influence household income inequality. To reduce income inequality, the government has implemented social security systems (see Chapter 5) and adopted a set of labor policies, one of which is a minimum wage (MW) policy. The rationale behind a MW policy is to increase wage levels for low-income groups, a change that is expected to reduce poverty and moderate inequality between high-wage groups and low-wage groups. A MW policy is an important approach to address poverty and income inequality in both the developing and developed countries.

There have been some empirical studies on the effects of the MW on employment, wage gaps, and income inequality in the developed countries, but few empirical studies attempt to understand the effects of the MW on wage distribution in China. In this chapter, we utilize data from the Chinese Household Income Project (CHIP) to provide empirical evidence. Specifically, we attempt to answer the following questions. First, does the MW level affect wage levels? In particular, does the MW level affect the mean wage level, and how does the effect of the MW differ among different groups in the wage distribution? Second, do changes in the MW levels cause changes in the wage distribution? Third, after controlling for heterogeneity among

Xinxin Ma and Shi Li, *The Effects of the Minimum-Wage Policy on the Wage Distribution in Urban China* In: *Changing Trends in China's Inequality.* Edited by: Terry Sicular, Shi Li, Ximing Yue, and Hiroshi Sato, Oxford University Press (2020).
© Oxford University Press.
DOI: 10.1093/oso/9780190077938.003.0012

groups in the wage distribution,[1] does the MW policy still affect the wage distribution?

This study uses the CHIP survey data from the years 1995, 2002, 2007, and 2013. Although we focus on the latest period from 2007 to 2013, we analyze the effect of the MW for a longer time span. The main reason is that use of these rounds of the CHIP survey allows us to investigate the effects of MW policies during three distinct periods—the period during promulgation of the MW (1993–1995), the period during implementation of the MW (1998–2002), and the period during enforcement of the MW (2007–2013). Therefore, we can compare the effects of the MW policy among the three periods to gain a better understanding of the situation from 2007 to 2013.

Because the MW primarily affects low-wage groups, we analyze both average wages and the different wage percentiles. In addition, because both the CHIP 1995 and the CHIP 2002 contain retrospective data, income information for the previous five years can be extracted. We utilized this information to build panel datasets and to perform a detailed analysis. Because we attempt to analyze the long-term effects of the MW on wage distribution, we therefore utilize the 1995 CHIP data. Since migrants are not included in the 1995 CHIP survey, urban workers with local urban registrations are the focus of the analysis.

This chapter is structured as follows. Section 12.2 introduces the reform of the MW in China. Section 12.3 presents a review of the literature on the effects of MWs on wage distribution and points out the main contributions of this study. Section 12.4 describes the analytical methods, including an introduction to the models (the ordinary least squares [OLS] model, the quantile regression [QR] model, the Neumark model, and the difference in differences [DID] model), the survey data, utilization of national MW data, and the setting of the variables, particularly the definition of wages and the treatment group. Section 12.5 presents and interprets the results, compares the results obtained from the different empirical analytical methods, and provides an explanation for the results. The concluding section presents our main conclusions and suggests some policy implications.

12.2 Background: MW Policy in China

Accompanying the progress in the market reforms, the Chinese government promulgated its first MW law in 1993—the Enterprise Minimum Wage

Regulations. In principle, the MW level was to be determined by the local governments (the provincial-level municipalities or the city governments within a province) in consultation with union and company representatives. In reality, the influence of the provincial governments was dominant. Moreover, the MW levels varied across regions.

The MW applies to two kinds of wages, monthly wages and hourly wages. Minimum monthly wage standards are applied to regular workers, whereas minimum hourly wage standards are applied to non-regular workers. The wage as defined by the policy is the basic wage, with the exception of overtime work payments and some allowances.

In 2004 the central government published a new MW policy to enforce implementation throughout the country; thereafter, there was a substantial increase in MW levels. On the basis of the 2004 MW policy, which has remained in place to the present, the MW level is adjusted once every one or two years. The many factors to be considered in setting the MW levels include local living costs, the consumer price index, social insurance (e.g., pensions and health-care insurance), the housing provident fund for which individual workers are responsible, the average wage level, the level of economic development, and the employment situation in the local labor market. The MW level is adjusted by the local governments; as a result, regional disparities continue to exist (Xing and Xu 2016). For example, the MW level is higher in the East region than it is in the West and Central regions, and the rise within the bands of the MW levels differs among regions. Such regional disparities allow us to utilize a quasi-natural experiment model to estimate the effects of the MW policy on wage distribution.

12.3 Literature Review

There have been some empirical studies on the effects of a MW on employment, wage gaps, and income inequality in the developed counties,[2] but empirical studies on the effects of a MW on the wage distribution in China are less common.[3] Studies of the effects of a MW on the wage distribution generally use three types of analyses that are conducted with individual-level survey data.

The first type of analysis uses OLS and QR models to investigate the effects of the MW on the average wage level and on the wage levels of different wage percentile groups (Card and Krueger 1995a; Neumark 2001; Gindling and Terrell 2005; Neumark, Cunningham, and Siga 2006; Hohberg and Lay 2015).

The second type of analysis, similar to that conducted by Neumark, Schweitzer, and Wascher (2004) (referred hereafter to the "Neumark model") analyzes the effects of changes in the MW levels on changes in the wage levels. This analysis is done by comparing the rate of change in the MW and the wage level over time $\left(\dfrac{W_{it} - W_{it\_1}}{W_{it\_1}}, \dfrac{MW_{it} - MW_{it\_1}}{MW_{it\_1}} \right)$, in addition to comparing the ratio of the wage level to the MW level in the prior year (w_{t_1} / MW_{t_1}). These variables and their interactions are utilized in the analysis.

The third type of analysis is a DID method, which is used to evaluate the effects of the MW policy and to address heterogeneity problems caused by unobservable factors, which may influence whether the MW policy plays a role in the various regions (Neumark, Cunningham, and Siga 2006; Dinkelman and Ranchhod 2012; Bhorat, Kanbur, and Stanwix 2014).

How do MWs affect the wage distribution? Past studies have highlighted the spike and spillover effects. First, the spike effect appears when the MW affects a group whose wages are below the MW level or a group whose wages are slightly above the MW (called "the group with wages around the minimum wage"). If there are no compliance problems, the spike effect should be visible when a MW is implemented. Neumark and Wascher (1992); Card and Krueger (1995a, 1995b); Baker, Benjamin, and Stanger (1999); and Lee (1999) all find that the spike effect of the MW is visible in both the United States and the United Kingdom.

Second, a MW may also affect groups with wages above the MW level, which is referred to as the "spillover effect of the minimum wage" (Grossman 1983; Card and Krueger 1995a; Lee, 1999; Neumark, Schweitzer, and Wascher 2004). The results of such empirical studies have not been consistent. For example, Lee (1999) finds that a spillover effect does in fact exist, whereas Autor, Manning, and Smith (2010) find that a spillover effect is not noticeable.

Various theories can explain the spillover effect of the MW. For example, on the basis of neoclassical economic theory, the skill substitution hypothesis proposes that because implementation of a MW policy increases labor costs for low-skilled workers, firms therefore might employ high-skilled workers rather than low-skilled workers. This substitution will result in an increase in the wages of high-skilled workers because of the increased demand. However, the substitution effect is greater for workers closer to the low-skilled group (e.g., the middle-wage group) (Pettengill 1981). In addition, the monopoly model reveals that when a monopoly firm increases the wage level for the low-wage group, the wage gap between the low-wage group and the middle- or high-wage group should decrease. Furthermore, the efficiency wage hypothesis provides an explanation for why firms increase the wage levels for groups that are not covered by MW regulations. A firm might increase wage levels for groups that are not affected by the MW in order to increase motivation. However, the labor cost constraint hypothesis proposes that when labor costs are constant and a MW is implemented, the increase in labor costs for the low-wage group might result in a decline in firm profits over the short term, in which case firms will not increase wage levels for groups that are not covered by the MW. If the effects of the labor cost constraint hypothesis outweigh the effects of the skill substitution hypothesis, the monopoly hypothesis, and the efficiency wage hypothesis, the spillover effect does not appear. This issue requires an empirical examination because of the complex factors that in theory may affect the spillover effect.

In considering the empirical studies with respect to China, Jia and Zhang (2013) utilize the Neumark model to analyze the MW spillover effects in China by using 1997–2009 data from the CHNS (Chinese Health and Nutrition Survey). They find that the spillover effect of an increase in the MW can reach 1.00~1.25 times the MW level for the male and female wage distributions. Di and Han (2015), utilizing the OLS, QR, and DID models to analyze the effects of the MW on the income of Chinese urban residents using 1996–2010 data from the CHNS, reveal that when the MW level increases by 1 percent, the average wage will increase by 0.281~0.899 percent, and this effect will be mainly concentrated in the low-income group. Moreover, on the basis of the results of a DID analysis, they point out that a MW provides protection, especially for the elderly and low-skilled laborers. Wang and Tan (2014) utilize the 2003–2006 Migrant Household Survey conducted by the Research Center of Rural Economy (RCRE) to analyze the effect of the MW on the wage distribution on the basis of the Neumark model. They find that an increase in the MW has a positive lagged effect on the increase in the wage level of the group with the lowest income, but this effect is not significant for the group with wages near the MW level. In addition, on the basis of the OLS model, Ma, Zhang, and Zhu (2012) utilize Chinese manufacturing firm-level data and city-level MW data from 1997 to 2007 to analyze the effects of the MW on average firm wages. They find that if the MW increases by 10 percent, the average wages in firms will increase by 0.4–0.5 percent.

The main contributions of this study are as follows: First, previous studies utilized only one or two types of analytical methods. Here we utilize three such methods, as summarized previously. These methods allowed us to analyze the effect of the MW on the wage distribution from different perspectives and to provide more detailed evidence for the China case. Second, although Wang and Tan (2014) utilize the Neumark model to investigate the MW effect on wage distribution among migrants, the approach has not been used for local urban residents. This study is intended to compensate for this gap. Third, this is the first time that CHIP 1995–2013 data have been employed for an empirical study on this issue. We can compare these results with the previous studies that use the CHNS data and the RCRE data. Moreover, analysis using the latest survey data—CHIP 2013—provides us with the most up-to-date information on the effects of the MW on wage distribution. Fourth, we analyze the effects of the MW policy for three different periods—the MW promulgation period (1993–1995), the MW implementation period (1998–2002), and the MW enforcement period (2007–2013). This analysis reveals the disparities in the MW effects on wage distribution, disparities that may be due to differences in government enforcement behavior.

12.4 Methodology and Data

12.4.1 Models

12.4.1.1 The OLS and QR Models of the Effects of the MW on Average Wages and on Different Percentile Wage Groups

The first analysis involves using the OLS and QR models to determine the effects of the MW on average wages and on different percentile wage groups. The wage function using the OLS model is represented by Equation (12.1).

$$\ln W_{ijt} = a_t + \beta_1 \ln MW_{jt} + \beta_2 X_{ijt} + \varepsilon_{ijt} \qquad (12.1)$$

In Equation (12.1), i represents individual workers, t represents periods, and j represents provinces or municipalities. $\ln W$ is the logarithm value of the annual wage, $\ln MW$ is the logarithm value of the MW level, X represents the other variables affecting wages (such as education and work experience as a proxy for human capital, gender, occupation, industry, and public-sector dummies), a is a constant, ε is an error term, and β_1, β_2 represent the estimated coefficients of the variables. The estimated coefficient on ln MW (β_1) reveals the effects of the MW level on the average wage.

To determine the effects of the MW on wages throughout the wage distributions, we use the QR model (Koenker and Bassett 1978), which can be expressed as

$$\min\left[\sum_{h_1:\,\ln W_{ijt}\,\geq\,\beta H_{ijt}} \theta\left|\ln W_{ijt}-\beta H_{ijt}\right| + \sum_{h_0:\,\ln W_{ijt}\,<\,\beta H_{ijt}} (1-\theta)\left|\ln W_{ijt}-\beta(\theta)H_{ijt}\right|\right] \quad (12.2)$$

$$\rho_\theta \in (0,1)$$

In Equation (12.2), θ represents the wage distribution position, which is more than 0 percentage points and less than 100 percentage points.[4] H includes ln MW and X as presented in Equation (12.1). The equation's other variables are the same as those in Equation (12.1). So, for example, when θ is 0.01, the coefficients of ln MW reveal the effect of the MW on the group at the 1 percentage wage distribution position, which is a low-wage group.

12.4.1.2 The Neumark Model of the Effects of Changes in the MW on Wage-Level Changes throughout the Wage Distribution

Although the effect of the MW on the wage distribution can be estimated by the OLS and QR models, it is also useful to provide evidence about whether changes in the MW affect changes in the wage level for different groups: e.g., the group with wages lower than the MW, the group with wages equal to the MW, and the group with wages higher than the MW. Specifically, if the MW level increases 1 percent from the prior year (year t_1) to the survey year (year t), how much does the wage level increase for the group with wages lower than the MW or for the group with wages higher than the MW?

Neumark, Schweitzer, and Wascher (2004) established an econometric model to analyze this question. This model is primarily used to show the effects of the change in the MW level on changes in the wage level throughout the wage distribution (called the "contemporaneous effects") in the United States. This model is expressed as follows:

$$\frac{W_{it} - W_{it\_1}}{W_{it\_1}} = a + \sum_{j} \beta_{1j} \frac{MW_t - MW_{t\_1}}{MW_{t\_1}} * R(W_{it\_1}, MW_t)$$

$$+ \sum_{j} \beta_{2j} R(W_{it\_1}, MW_t)$$

$$+ \sum_{j} \beta_{3j} R(W_{it\_1}, MW_t) * \frac{W_{it\_1}}{MW_{t\_1}}$$

$$+ \beta_{4j} X_{ijt} + \beta_5 District_{it} + \beta_6 Year_{ij} * District_i + v_{ijt} \quad (12.3)$$

In Equation (12.3), i represents individual workers, j denotes the provinces or municipalities, t and t_1 denote the policy-enforced year and the prior year (e.g., 2013 and 2007). $District$ is the district dummy variable (East, Central, or West). $District$ and $Year$ control for some omitted variables, including the effects of the region-specific business cycle and macroeconomic circumstances on the local labor market. Also, v is a random error term. R denotes a set of dummy variables that describe the relations between the wage level in year t_1 and the MW level in year t; for example, there is a point at which the wage in 2007 is lower (equal or higher) than the MW level in 2013. We will provide more detailed explanations in the following sections. Panel data will be utilized for the analysis.

12.4.1.3 The DID Model of the Effects of the MW on Wages

It is difficult to show the influence of a MW on wages because the direction of causality goes in both directions. For example, the policy mandates that each locality's MW should be set with reference to the average local wage level; in other words, the local MW is a function of the local average wage. Although the effects of the MW on wages can be estimated by the OLS model, the QR model, and the Neumark models, these analyses show only that the two variables are correlated and they cannot tell us if the MW in fact affects wages or vice versa. To address this problem and identify the "real" effect of a MW on wages, a DID method, which is frequently used in policy impact evaluations, can be applied. It is represented as follows:

$$\ln W_{ij} = a + \gamma_1 Year_{ij} + \gamma_2 Treat_{ij} + \gamma_3 DID_{ij} + \gamma_4 X_{ij} + u_{ij} \quad (12.4)$$

Table 12.1. DID items

	Estimation 1		Estimation 2	
	T	C	T	C
1993–1994	Beijing	Shanxi	Beijing	Liaoning
1999–2000	Beijing	Shanxi	Gansu	Yunnan
2000–2001	Beijing	Shanxi	Anhui	Hubei
2001–2002	Hubei	Henan	Sichuan	Gansu
2007–2013	Henan	Hubei	Henan	Jiangsu

Notes:

1.) *T* represents the treatment group. The treatment group is the group in which the MW level has increased from year t_1 to year t.

2.) *C* represents the control group. The control group is the group in which the MW level has not changed from year t_1 to year t (or has increased only a little) and that is closest to the target group's province or municipality.

Sources: Based on the questionnaires in CHIP 1995, CHIP 2002, CHIP 2007, and CHIP 2013.

In Equation (12.4), i stands for the individual, j represents the municipality, *Year* represents the MW level adjustment years, and *Treat* is a dummy variable that identifies the treatment group (Table 12.1). The treatment group is the group that is influenced by the MW policy, for example, the group with wages lower than the MW level. *DID* is the interaction of *Year* and *Treat*. The coefficients of *DID* indicate the "real" policy effect by capturing two differences: i.) the difference between the pre-policy period and the post-policy period, and ii.) the difference between the treatment group and the control group that is not influenced by the policy. X represents other variables affecting wages, a is the constant term, v is the error term, and y represents the estimated coefficient for each variable. If y_3 is statistically significant, then implementation of a MW affects the wage level. If y_3 has a positive value, then if the level of the MW increases, the wage level will increase, and vice versa.

12.4.2 Data

The CHIP 1995, 2002, 2007, and 2013 survey datasets are utilized for our analysis. Even though it is thought that the MW may influence the wages of migrants, because CHIP 1995 does not include a migrant survey and the migrant survey in CHIP 2002 does not include retrospective income data, the Neumark, Schweitzer, and Wascher (2004) model shown in Equation (12.3) cannot be utilized for the migrant group. Therefore, this study focuses only on the MW effect on the wage distribution for urban residents with an urban *hukou*. Using retrospective survey data on individual incomes in CHIP 1995 and CHIP 2002, and survey data in CHIP 2007 and CHIP 2013 for urban residents, we can differentiate the years before and after the MW adjustment to construct the treatment and control groups and to utilize standard econometric analysis methods to investigate the MW effects.

Because there are design similarities in the questionnaire, we can use the same information in the analysis for all three periods—the MW promulgation period (1993–1995), the MW performance period (1998–2002), and the MW enforcement period (2007–2013).

The CHIP urban surveys cover representative provinces and provincial-level municipalities in China.[5] For our analysis we merge the provincial-level MW information from the Chinese National Minimum Wage Databases (CNMWD) with the CHIP survey data to construct a new dataset that contains individual-level data and provincial-level MW data. Because the city governments set their MW levels on the basis of the MW levels in the province, MW levels within a province may vary among cities. The CNMWD includes a set of city MW levels in a province; in our analyses, we select the highest MW level in a province or municipality.[6]

We utilize data only from the provinces that appear in all four years of the CHIP, that is, Beijing, Shanxi, Liaoning, Jiangsu, Anhui, Guangdong, Henan, Hubei, Sichuan, Yunnan, and Gansu. Three regional dummy variables (the East, Central, and West regions) are constructed to control for regional disparities.[7]

The wage is defined as the total earnings from work (called "the total wage").[8] It comprises the basic wage, bonus, cash subsidies, and in-kind (goods) subsidies. The retrospective data on incomes in CHIP 1995 and CHIP 2002, and wages in CHIP 2007 and CHIP 2013 are utilized. The unit of analysis is the individual wage or income. The 1995 CPI[9] is utilized as a standard to deflate the nominal monthly wage or income and the nominal monthly MW in every year.[10]

The unit of observations in the analyses is the individual employee; the self-employed and the unemployed are not included. In light of the retirement system in the state-owned sector, the sample is restricted to those between the ages of 16 and 60.

In the wage function, the explained variable is the logarithm of the monthly wage, and the explanatory variables are the variables very likely to affect the wage, such as years of schooling years, years of experience,[11] a public-sector dummy,[12] an occupation dummy,[13] an industrial dummy,[14] a region dummy (the East, Central, and West regions), and the year dummy variables.

The analysis based on the DID model requires construction of the appropriate DID items (see Equation [12.4]). As described previously, we obtained the regional maximum values of the MW levels on the basis of the CNMWD. We utilized information about the MW levels in the policy-enforced year (year t) and in the year prior to year t (year t_1) to create the control and treatment groups. Specifically, the treatment group is the group in which the MW level has increased from year t_1 to year t; the control group is the group in which the MW level has not changed from year t_1 to year t (or has increased only a little from year t_1 to year t), and it is closest to the target group's province or municipality.[15] The smallest geographic distance can provide a nearly similar macroeconomic and labor-market situation for the treatment and control groups, which is necessary for a quasi-natural experiment analysis. We construct the DID items on the basis of the information for the regions, as shown in Table 12.1.

12.5. Descriptive Statistics

12.5.1 Variable Distributions during the Three Periods

Table 12.2 shows sample descriptive statistics for the three periods. Because the potential groups that will be greatly influenced by the MW are those whose wage levels were lower than the MW level in the pre-policy period, the table reports comparisons between the wage in the pre-policy period (year t_1) and the MW level in the policy-enforced period (year t). First, the proportion of workers with wages below the MW level in year t_1 is greater for Panel A (1993–1995) than for Panel B (1998–2002). For example, the proportion of workers with wages in year t below half of the MW level in year t_1 ($0 < w/MW \leq 0.5$) is 2.2 percent for 1993–1995 and 1.5 percent for 1998–2002; the proportion of workers with wages between half of the MW level and one times the MW level ($0.5 < w/MW \leq 1$) is 11.2 percent for 1993–1995 and 6.2 percent for 1998–2002.

Table 12.2. Descriptive statistics

	Panel A: 1993–1995		Panel B: 1998–2002		Panel C: 2007–2013	
	Means	S.D.	Means	S.D.	Means	S.D.
W/MW dummies						
R1: $0.00 < w/WM \leq 0.50$	2.2%	14.6%	1.5%	12.1%	—	—
R2: $0.50 < w/WM \leq 1.00$	11.2%	31.5%	6.2%	24.1%	—	—
R3: $1.00 < w/WM \leq 1.01$	0.3%	5.4%	0.3%	5.5%	—	—
R4: $1.01 < w/WM \leq 1.05$	1.6%	12.5%	0.9%	9.3%	—	—
R5: $1.05 < w/WM \leq 1.10$	2.4%	15.4%	1.1%	10.6%	—	—
R6: $1.10 < w/WM \leq 1.20$	2.8%	16.4%	2.4%	15.3%	—	—
R7: $1.20 < w/WM \leq 1.30$	3.8%	19.2%	2.4%	15.5%	—	—
R8: $1.30 < w/WM \leq 1.50$	6.2%	24.1%	6.1%	24.0%	—	—
R9: $1.50 < w/WM \leq 2.00$	21.2%	40.9%	15.7%	36.3%	—	—
R10: $2.00 < w/WM \leq 3.00$	27.7%	44.7%	29.4%	45.6%	—	—
R11: $3.00 < w/WM \leq 4.00$	13.1%	33.8%	17.4%	37.9%	—	—
R12: $4.00 < w/WM \leq 5.00$	4.3%	20.2%	8.1%	27.3%	—	—
R13: $5.00 < w/WM \leq 6.00$	1.7%	12.7%	3.9%	19.4%	—	—
R14: $6.00 < w/WM \leq 8.00$	1.2%	10.8%	2.8%	16.5%	—	—
R15: $w/WM > 8.00$	0.4%	6.6%	1.7%	12.9%	—	—
Total ranges	100.0%		100.0%		—	—
DD	0.226	0.418	0.173	0.378	0.307	0.461
Male	0.502	0.500	0.564	0.496	0.544	0.498
Years of schooling	11	3	11	3	12	3
Experience years	28	10	29	9	29	11
Sectors: public sector	0.805	0.397	0.675	0.468	0.183	0.387
Non-skilled job	0.388	0.487	0.291	0.454	0.165	0.371
Industries: manufacturing	0.396	0.489	0.261	0.439	0.497	0.500
Regions						
West	0.470	0.499	0.468	0.499	0.480	0.500
Central	0.263	0.441	0.264	0.441	0.283	0.450
East	0.267	0.442	0.269	0.443	0.238	0.426
Observations	40012		37,597		24,438	—

Table 12.2. Continued

Notes:

1.) R1~R15 are the groups divided by the wage level in year t_1 (pre-policy period) compared to the MW level in year t (policy implementation period). w/MW is the ratio of the wage level in year t_1 to the MW level in year t. $0.00 < w/MW \leq 0.50$ is the group with a wage level in year t_1 that is more than 0 and less than one-half of the MW level in year t, $0.50 < w/MW \leq 1.00$ is the group with a wage level in year t_1 that is more than one-half and less than the MW level in year t. These two groups are greatly influenced by the MW policy enforced in year t. The total of the ranges from R1 to R15 is 100%.

2.) DD is a DID item that is the interaction of the treatment group and the MW policy implementation year. The treatment group is the group that is greatly influenced by the MW policy. The treatment group is the group in which the MW level has increased from year t_1 to year t; the control group is the group in which the MW level has not changed from year t_1 to year t (or has increased only a little), and it is closest to the target group's province or municipality (see Table 12.1)

3.) Experience years is calculated by "age—6 years of schooling"; public sector is equal to 1 if the individual is working in a government organization, public organization (*shiye danwei*), or a state-owned enterprise; otherwise it is equal to 0. The East region includes Beijing, Liaoning, Jiangsu, Guangdong; the Central region includes Shanxi, Liaoning, Anhui, Henan, Hubei; the West region includes Sichuan, Yunnan, and Gansu.

Sources: Calculations based on CHIP 1995, 2002, 2007, and 2013.

Second, the proportion of workers with wages around or not much higher than the MW level ($1.05 < w/MW \leq 1.1$, $1.1 < w/MW \leq 1.2$, $1.2 < w/MW \leq 1.3$, $1.3 < w/MW \leq 1.5$) is greater in Panel A (1993–1995) than in Panel B (1998–2002). For example, the proportion of workers with wages between 1.01 and 1.05 times the MW level ($1.01 < w/MW \leq 1.05$) is 1.6 percent for the 1993–1995 period and 0.9 percent for the 1998–2002 period.

Third, the proportion of workers with wages much higher than the MW level (more than two times the MW level) is smaller for the 1993–1995 period than for 1998–2002. For example, the proportion of workers with wages between three and four times the MW level ($3 < w/MW \leq 4$) is 13.1 percent for the 1993–1995 period and 17.4 percent for the 1998–2002 period.

These results show that the proportion of workers with wages below the MW level was greater when the Chinese government first imposed the MW system. However, the proportion became smaller from the 1993–1995 period to the 1998–2002 period. These results indicate that the effects of the MW on wages may have differed, depending on the period.

12.5.2 The Distributions of the Ratios of the Wages to the MW (w/MW) by Groups

The characteristics of individuals may differ among the different wage distributions, so we calculated the distribution of the ratios of the wages in year t_1 to the MW in year t by gender, age, occupation, low and high skills (blue-collar or white-collar worker groups), and industry (manufacturing or non-manufacturing) groups. The results are shown in Table 12.3, where w represents the wage in the pre-policy period (year t_1) and MW represents the highest MW level in the year t. The main results of the proportions for the low-wage group (the group with wages in year t_1 below the MW level in year t and the high-wage group (the group with wages in year t_1 more than three times the MW level in year t) are as the follows.

First, with regard to gender differences, the proportion of workers with wages below the MW level ($0 < w/MW \leq 0.05$, $0.5 < w/MW \leq 1$) is greater for females than for males in both the 1993–1995 and the 1998–2002 periods. For example, the proportion of workers with wages below one-half of the MW level ($0 < w/MW \leq 0.05$) is larger for females than for males in the 1993–1995 period and the 1998–2002 period (the gender gap is 1.7 percent in the 1993–1995 period, 0.8 percent in the 1998–2002 period). Similarly, the proportion of workers with wages between one-half and one times the MW level ($0.5 < w/MW \leq 1$) is greater for females than for males in the 1993–1995 and the 1998–2002 periods (9.3 percent and 5.8 percent, respectively). The proportion of workers with wages more than five times the MW level is greater for males than for females. For example, the proportion of workers with wages between five and six times the MW level ($5 < w/MW \leq 6$) is greater for males than for females in the 1993–1995 and the 1998–2002 periods (2.1 percent and 2.3 percent, respectively).

Second, comparing the younger group (the group between the ages of 16 and 24), the middle-aged group (between the ages of 25 and 29), and the elderly group (between the ages of 50 and 60), the proportion of workers with wages below the MW level ($0 < w/MW \leq 0.05$, $0.5 < w/MW \leq 1$) is greater for the younger group than for the middle-aged and elderly groups during the two periods. For example, the proportion of workers with wages below one-half the MW level ($0 < w/MW \leq 0.05$) is 9.0 percent for the 16–24 age group, 1.8 percent for the 25–40 age group, and 2.2 percent for the 50–60 age group during the 1993–1995 period. Similarly, the proportion of workers with wages between one-half and one time the MW level ($0.5 < w/MW \leq 1$) is 6.8 percent for the 16–24 age group and 1.2 percent for the 25–40 and the 50–60 age groups during the 1998–2002 period. However, the proportion of workers with wages more than five times the MW level is greater for the 16–24 age group than for the 25–49 and the 50–60 age groups during both periods.

Table 12.3 (1) The distribution of the ratios of wages to the MW (w/MW) by gender, age and skill group (%)

	Male	Female	Age 16–24	Age 25–49	Age 50–60	Low-skilled	High-skilled
	(1)	(2)	(3)	(4)	(5)	(6)	(7)
Panel A: 1993–1995							
R1: $0.00 < w/WM \leq 0.50$	1.6	3.4	9.0	1.8	2.2	3.1	1.3
R2: $0.50 < w/WM \leq 1.00$	6.7	16.0	18.9	9.1	15.8	18.0	3.2
R3: $1.00 < w/WM \leq 1.01$	0.2	0.4	0.4	0.3	0.3	0.5	0.0
R4: $1.01 < w/WM \leq 1.05$	0.9	2.1	2.9	1.3	1.9	2.0	0.8
R5: $1.05 < w/WM \leq 1.10$	1.8	3.0	4.1	2.4	1.8	2.8	0.8
R6: $1.10 < w/WM \leq 1.20$	2.3	3.2	6.2	2.1	3.5	3.1	1.3
R7: $1.20 < w/WM \leq 1.30$	4.0	3.7	4.9	3.7	3.5	4.1	2.4
R8: $1.30 < w/WM \leq 1.50$	5.4	6.9	4.5	5.8	7.8	8.0	3.4
R9: $1.50 < w/WM \leq 2.00$	20.4	21.4	14.8	22.8	17.4	21.3	15.2
R10: $2.00 < w/WM \leq 3.00$	29.9	25.6	19.7	29.7	24.3	23.4	34.7
R11: $3.00 < w/WM \leq 4.00$	16.3	10.0	12.7	13.2	13.1	8.7	21.8
R12: $4.00 < w/WM \leq 5.00$	5.9	2.5	2.1	4.4	4.5	3.3	7.4
R13: $5.00 < w/WM \leq 6.00$	2.7	0.6	0.0	1.8	1.9	1.2	2.4
R14: $6.00 < w/WM \leq 8.00$	1.5	0.8	0.0	1.2	1.4	0.2	3.9
R15: $w/WM > 8.00$	0.6	0.3	0.0	0.6	0.3	0.4	1.3
Total (%)	100.0	100.0	100.0	100.0	100.0	100.0	100.0
Panel B: 1998–2002							
R1: $0.00 < w/WM \leq 0.50$	1.1	2.0	6.8	1.2	1.2	2.2	0.9
R2: $0.50 < w/WM \leq 1.00$	3.8	9.6	13.7	6.2	4.1	10.7	2.5
R3: $1.00 < w/WM \leq 1.01$	0.2	0.5	0.4	0.3	0.1	0.5	0.2
R4: $1.01 < w/WM \leq 1.05$	0.6	1.3	1.8	0.9	0.7	1.5	0.4
R5: $1.05 < w/WM \leq 1.10$	0.8	1.7	1.8	1.2	0.7	1.7	0.6
R6: $1.10 < w/WM \leq 1.20$	1.8	3.3	4.4	2.5	1.3	3.4	1.2
R7: $1.20 < w/WM \leq 1.30$	1.9	3.2	4.2	2.5	1.8	3.8	1.1
R8: $1.30 < w/WM \leq 1.50$	5.3	7.4	10.0	6.2	4.3	8.6	3.3
R9: $1.50 < w/WM \leq 2.00$	14.7	16.8	19.1	15.7	13.6	19.6	10.9
R10: $2.00 < w/WM \leq 3.00$	30.1	28.2	24.5	29.9	27.1	26.6	30.4
R11: $3.00 < w/WM \leq 4.00$	19.7	14.4	7.3	17.3	21.7	12.0	23.3
R12: $4.00 < w/WM \leq 5.00$	9.6	6.3	3.3	7.9	11.8	4.9	11.6
R13: $5.00 < w/WM \leq 6.00$	4.9	2.6	1.6	3.8	5.6	2.2	6.2

(continued)

Table 12.3 (1) Continued

	Male	Female	Age 16–24	Age 25–49	Age 50–60	Low-skilled	High-skilled
	(1)	(2)	(3)	(4)	(5)	(6)	(7)
R14: $6.00 < w/WM \le 8.00$	3.5	1.8	0.8	2.7	3.9	1.2	4.8
R15: $w/WM > 8.00$	2.2	1.0	0.4	1.7	2.2	1.3	2.7
Total (%)	100.0	100.0	100.0	100.0	100.0	100.0	100.0

Notes:

1.) *MW* is the minimum-wage level in year t (the policy enforced year); w is the wage in year t_1 (the year prior to year t or the pre-policy year).

2.) R1~R15 are the groups divided by the wage level in year t_1 compared to the MW level in year t. w/MW is the ratio of the wage level in year t_1 to the MW level in year t. For example, $0.00 < w/MW \le 0.50$ is the group with a wage level in year t_1 that is greater than 0 but less than one-half of the MW level in year t, $0.50 < w/M \le 1.00$ is the group with a wage level in year t_1 that is more than one-half but less than the MW level in year t. These two groups are greatly influenced by the MW policy enforced in year t. The total of the ranges from R1 to R15 is 100%.

3.) The low-skilled group includes those with a low level of education (the education level is no greater than senior high school) and unskilled manufacturing workers; the high-skilled group includes highly educated workers (whose education level is higher than senior high school), managerial and professional workers, and skilled manufacturing workers.

Sources: Calculations based on CHIP 1995 and 2002.

Table 12.3 (2) The distribution of the ratios of wages to the MW (w/MW) by type of job and sector (%)

	Public	Non-public	Blue-collar worker	White-collar worker	Manu-facturing	Non-manufacturing
	(8)	(9)	(10)	(11)	(12)	(13)
Panel A: 1993–1995						
R1: $0.00 < w/WM \le 0.50$	1.7	3.5	2.8	2.3	1.2	3.2
R2: $0.50 < w/WM \le 1.00$	9.4	16.3	15.9	8.8	12.7	10.7
R3: $1.00 < w/WM \le 1.01$	0.2	0.7	0.5	0.2	0.3	0.3
R4: $1.01 < w/WM \le 1.05$	1.4	2.2	1.9	1.3	2.2	1.2
R5: $1.05 < w/WM \le 1.10$	2.1	3.4	2.8	2.2	2.8	2.2
R6: $1.10 < w/WM \le 1.20$	2.8	2.6	3.1	2.5	2.6	2.8
R7: $1.20 < w/WM \le 1.30$	3.6	4.6	4.3	3.5	5.1	3.1
R8: $1.30 < w/WM \le 1.50$	5.4	8.4	7.6	5.3	7.1	5.6
R9: $1.50 < w/WM \le 2.00$	20.4	23.3	23.3	19.5	23.8	19.4
R10: $2.00 < w/WM \le 3.00$	30.9	19.0	24.6	29.5	25.0	29.2
R11: $3.00 < w/WM \le 4.00$	14.4	9.8	9.0	15.5	12.2	13.6
R12: $4.00 < w/WM \le 5.00$	4.6	3.4	2.8	5.0	3.0	4.9

Table 12.3 (2) Continued

	Public	Non-public	Blue-collar worker	White-collar worker	Manu-facturing	Non-manufacturing
	(8)	(9)	(10)	(11)	(12)	(13)
R13: $5.00 < w/WM \leq 6.00$	1.8	1.2	1.0	2.0	0.9	2.0
R14: $6.00 < w/WM \leq 8.00$	1.3	1.0	0.1	1.8	0.6	1.4
R15: $w/WM > 8.00$	0.3	0.7	0.3	0.6	0.7	0.4
Total (%)	100.0	100.0	100.0	100.0	100.0	100.0
Panel B: 1998–2002						
R1: $0.00 < w/WM \leq 0.50$	1.2	2.1	1.6	1.5	1.1	1.7
R2: $0.50 < w/WM \leq 1.00$	4.2	10.3	7.6	5.8	6.1	6.4
R3: $1.00 < w/WM \leq 1.01$	0.2	0.5	0.4	0.3	0.3	0.3
R4: $1.01 < w/WM \leq 1.05$	0.6	1.4	1.1	0.8	1.1	0.8
R5: $1.05 < w/WM \leq 1.10$	0.8	2.0	1.3	1.1	1.2	1.1
R6: $1.10 < w/WM \leq 1.20$	1.8	3.7	3.2	2.2	3.0	2.2
R7: $1.20 < w/WM \leq 1.30$	1.8	3.9	3.3	2.1	3.3	2.2
R8: $1.30 < w/WM \leq 1.50$	4.9	8.7	7.9	5.5	8.2	5.5
R9: $1.50 < w/WM \leq 2.00$	13.9	19.4	19.5	14.0	21.2	13.7
R10: $2.00 < w/WM \leq 3.00$	31.5	25.2	30.1	28.9	30.6	28.8
R11: $3.00 < w/WM \leq 4.00$	20.5	11.0	13.5	18.9	13.6	18.7
R12: $4.00 < w/WM \leq 5.00$	9.5	5.3	5.9	9.1	5.6	9.1
R13: $5.00 < w/WM \leq 6.00$	4.5	2.7	2.5	4.4	2.4	4.4
R14: $6.00 < w/WM \leq 8.00$	3.2	2.1	1.3	3.4	1.3	3.3
R15: $w/WM > 8.00$	1.6	1.8	1.0	2.0	1.0	1.9
Total (%)	100.0	100.0	100.0	100.0	100.0	100.0

Notes:

1.) MW is the MW level in year t (the policy enforced year); w is the wage in the year t_1 (the year prior to year t or the pre-policy year).

2.) R1~R15 are the groups divided by the wage level in year t_1 compared to the MW level in year t. w/MW is the ratio of the wage level in year t_1 to the MW level in year t. For example, $0.00 < w/MW \leq 0.50$ is the group with a wage level in year t_1 greater than 0 and less than one-half of the MW level in year t; $0.50 < w/M \leq 1.00$ is the group with a wage level in year t_1 more than one-half and less than the MW level in year t. These two groups are greatly influenced by the MW policy enforced in year t. The total of ranges from R1 to R15 is 100%.

3.) Public sector includes government organizations, public organizations (*shiye danwei*), and state-owned enterprises; non-public sector includes all others.

4.) Blue-collar worker includes the skilled manufacturing workers, unskilled manufacturing workers, clerk staff, service workers; white-collar worker includes managers and professional workers (e.g., engineers, doctors, lawyers).

5.) Manu. refers to manufacturing workers; non-manu. refers to non-manufacturing workers (e.g., a worker in the tertiary industry).

Sources: Calculations based on CHIP 1995 and 2002.

Third, regarding skill levels,[16] the proportion of workers with wages below the MW level ($0 < w/MW \leq 0.05$, $0.5 < w/MW \leq 1$) is greater for the low-skilled group than for the high-skilled group during the two periods. For example, the proportion of workers with wages below one-half the MW level ($0 < w/MW \leq 0.05$) is 3.1 percent for the low-skilled group and 1.3 percent for the high-skilled group during the 1993–1995 period. Similarly, it is 2.2 percent for the low-skilled group and 0.9 percent for the high-skilled group during the 1998–2002 period. The proportion of workers with wages between one-half and one time the MW level ($0.5 < w/MW \leq 1$) is 18.0 percent for the low-skilled group and 3.2 percent for the high-skilled group during the 1993–1995 period; it is 10.7 percent for the low-skilled group and 2.5 percent for the high-skilled group during the 1998–2002 period.

Fourth, regarding segmentation among sectors, the proportion of workers with wages below the MW level is smaller for the public-sector group than for the non-public-sector group during the two periods.[17] For example, the proportion of workers with wages below one-half of the MW level ($0 < w/MW \leq 0.05$) is 1.7 percent for the public-sector group and 3.5 percent for the private-sector group during the 1993–1995 period. Similarly, it is 1.2 percent for the public-sector group and 2.1 percent for the private-sector group during the 1998–2002 period. The proportion of workers in the public-sector group with wages between one-half and one times the MW level ($0.5 < w/MW \leq 1$) is 9.4 percent for the public-sector group and 16.3 percent for the private-sector group during the 1993–1995 period; it is 4.2 percent for the public-sector group and 10.3 percent for the private-sector group during the 1998–2002 period. However, the proportion of workers with wages more than two times the MW level is greater for the public-sector group than for the private-sector group during both periods.

Fifth, the proportion of workers with wages below the MW level is smaller for the blue-collar-worker group than for the white-collar-worker group during the two periods.[18] For example, the proportion of workers with wages between one-half and one time the MW level ($0.5 < w/MW \leq 1$) is 15.9 percent for the blue-collar-worker group and 8.8 percent for the white-collar-worker group during the 1993–1995 period; it is 7.6 percent for the blue-collar-worker group and 5.8 percent for the white-collar-worker group during the 1998–2002 period. The proportion of workers with wages more than two times the MW level is greater for the blue-collar-worker group than for the white-collar-worker group during both periods.

Sixth, the proportion of workers with wages below the MW level and greatly higher than the MW level is smaller for the manufacturing-worker group than for the non-manufacturing-worker group during the two periods. For example, the proportion of workers with wages below one-half the MW level ($0 < w/MW \leq 0.05$) is 1.2 percent for the manufacturing-worker group and 3.2 percent for the non-manufacturing-worker group during the 1993–1995 period; it is 1.1 percent for the manufacturing-worker group and 1.7 percent for the non-manufacturing-worker group during the 1998–2002 period. In addition, the proportion of workers with wages more than four times the MW level is smaller for the non-manufacturing-worker group during both periods. For example, the proportion of workers with wages between four and five times the MW level is 3.0 percent for the manufacturing-worker group and 4.9 percent for the non-manufacturing-worker group during the 1993–1995 period; it is 5.6 percent for the manufacturing-worker group and 9.1 percent for the non-manufacturing-worker group during the 1998–2002 period.

The results show that the proportion of workers with wages below or around the MW levels is greater for female, younger, low-skilled, and blue-collar-worker groups, and for workers in the private sector and in the non-manufacturing industries. Thus, it can be assumed that the effect of a MW should be greater for these groups.

12.5.3   MW Levels and Estimates of the Wage Distributions

With respect to the effect of the MW on the wage distribution, previous studies have found a spike effect for the group with wages below or around the MW level. Does such a spike effect exist in China? We calculated the monthly wage distributions for the three periods. The distributions are kernel density estimates (see the notes to the figures).[19] The results are shown in Figure 12.1.

The proportion of groups around the maximum values of the MW level, particularly the group with wages just a little more than the maximum values of the MW level shows relatively greater convexity on the curves in 1994, 1998, and 2013. These estimated results suggest that such spike effects exist in China.

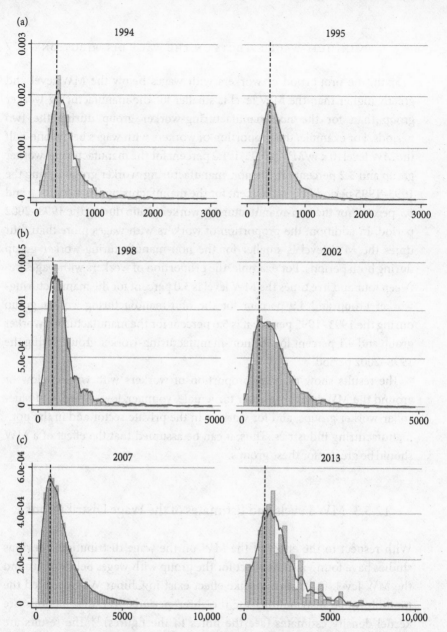

Fig. 12.1 Minimum-wage levels and estimates of the wage distributions. Panel A: 1993–1994 (MW policy promulgation period). Panel B: 1998–2002 (MW policy implementation period). Panel C: 2007–2013 (MW policy enforcement period)

Notes:

1.) Because the city government sets the MW level on the basis of the provincial MW level, the MW levels vary within a province. The Chinese National Minimum Wage Databases (CNMWD) includes a set of city MW levels in a province; here we select the highest monthly MW level in a province or municipality. The dotted line shows the mean value of the monthly MW levels in all surveyed provinces or municipalities. The mean values are the arithmetic average values.

2.) Wages in 1994 and 1998 are retrospective survey data in CHIP 1995 and CHIP 2002. Monthly wages are utilized in these calculations.

3.) The bar heights are histograms for the wage density frequency distribution and the curves show the smoothed density distribution based on Kernel density estimates (KDEs). In statistics, a KDE is a nonparametric way to estimate the probability density function of a random variable.

Sources: Calculations based on CHIP 1995, 2002, 2007, and 2013.

12.6 Results of the Econometric Analysis

12.6.1 Estimated Results of the MW Effects on Wages by Using the OLS and QR Models

Table 12.4 and Figure 12.2 show the results of the wage function by using the OLS and QR models. The effect of the MW on wages is given by the estimated coefficient on the MW variable in the regression (the log of the MW).

First, the estimated coefficients on the MW variable based on the OLS model are positive and statistically significant at the 1 percent level during each period. These coefficients imply that when the MW level increases by 1 percent, the average wage will increase by 0.759 percent, 0.883 percent, and 0.882 percent respectively during each period. These results are consistent with those of Di and Han (2015), who use 1996~2010 data from the CHNS.

Second, the estimated coefficient on the MW for the lowest wage group (the 1st percentile wage group) is higher than that for the middle- and high-wage groups during the 1993–1995 period; the estimated coefficients on the MW for the low-wage group (the 1st, 5th, and 10th percentile wage groups) are higher than those for the middle-wage group during the 1998–2002 period and the 2007–2013 period. Moreover, comparing the coefficients on the MW variables for the low-, middle-, and high-wage groups during each period shows that the effect of the MW on the low-wage group is greater during the 2007–2013 period than during the 1993–1995 or the 1998–2002 periods (see Figure 12.2). Comparing the MW policy during the promulgation and the implementation periods reveals that the effects of the MW on the low-wage group are increasing, perhaps the result of stronger government enforcement of the MW since 2004.

Third, the estimated coefficients on the MW variables are also higher for the high-wage group (the 80th and 90th percentile wage groups) than for the middle-wage groups during the 1993–1995 and 1998–2002 periods. These results are consistent with the findings by Di and Han (2015). However, these results might not indicate a causal relation of the MW effect on the high-wage group. For example, it is possible that in a high MW region (e.g., the East region), the wage levels for the high-wage group increased more than those for the middle-wage group because of unobservable factors or factors that cannot be estimated (e.g., regional unobservable factors that might affect the

Table 12.4 Estimates of the effects of the MW on wages by using the OLS model

	Panel A: 1993–1995		Panel B: 1998–2002		Panel C: 2007–2013	
	Coeff.	t-value	Coeff.	t-value	Coeff.	t-value
ln MW	0.759***	28.90	0.883***	65.82	0.882***	55.23
Male	0.155***	15.86	0.188***	34.93	0.371***	34.90
Years of schooling	0.041***	21.16	0.064***	55.81	0.096***	42.82
Years of experience	0.059***	24.43	0.040***	26.60	0.067***	27.90
Years of experience squared	−0.001***	−18.56	0.000***	−17.62	−0.001***	−26.45
Non-skilled job	−0.133***	−11.60	−0.063***	−9.41	−0.027*	−1.76
Manufacturing industry	−0.013	−1.27	−0.071***	−10.87	0.074***	4.76
Public sector	0.174***	13.73	0.160***	27.25	0.085***	7.54
Regions (East is the omitted category)						
Central	−0.078***	−5.46	−0.065***	−8.97	0.038***	2.96
West	0.081***	5.08	0.075***	9.70	−0.040***	−2.99
Year	Yes		Yes		Yes	
Constants	0.573***	3.38	−0.129	−1.56	−0.914***	−7.51
Observations	13,410		46,740		24,428	
Adj. R-squared	0.322		0.254		0.245	

Notes:

1.) *, **, ***: statistically significant at the 10%, 5%, and 1% levels.

2.) OLS models are utilized in these calculations. The dependent variables are the logarithm values of the monthly wages; ln MW is the logarithm value of the MW level; years of experience is calculated as age minus years of schooling; public sector is equal to 1 if the individual is working in a government organization, public organization (*shiye danwei*), or a state-owned enterprise; otherwise it is equal to 0. The East region includes Beijing, Liaoning, Jiangsu, Guangdong; the Central region includes Shanxi, Liaoning, Anhui, Henan, Hubei; the West region includes Sichuan, Yunnan, and Gansu. Year dummy variables: 1994 and 1995 dummy variables in Panel A; 1999, 2000, 2001, and 2002 dummy variables in Panel B; 2013 dummy variables in Panel C are also estimated, but these results are not shown in Table 12.4.

Sources: Calculations based on CHIP 1995, 2002, 2007, and 2013.

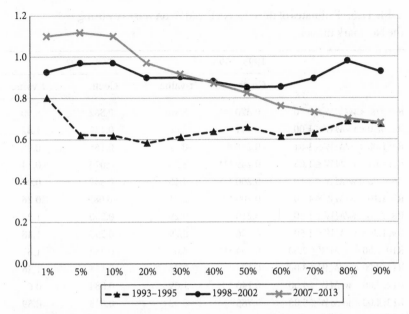

Fig. 12.2 Estimates of the effects of the MW on wages by using the QR model

Notes:

1.) The results are estimated by using quantile regressions. Each point on the graph is an estimate of the effect of the MW on wages at the percentile of the wage distribution shown on the horizontal axis.

2.) The other variables (years of schooling, years of experience, occupation, industry, region dummy, year dummy variables) are also controlled in these models.

Sources: Calculations based on CHIP 1995, 2002, 2007, and 2013.

design of the MW level). We analyze the regional heterogeneity problem in Section 12.6.3.

12.6.2 Estimated Results of the Effects of the MW on Wages by Using the Neumark Model

Next, the Neumark model is utilized to analyze the effects of the change in the MW level on the change in the wage level throughout the wage distributions compared to the MW level. The results of our estimates of Equation (12.2) are shown in Table 12.5.

First, when other conditions (gender, education, work experience, occupation, industry, work sector, district, and year special effects) are held constant, the estimated change coefficients on the MW variables are all

Table 12.5. Estimates of the effect of the MW on wages by using the Neumark model

	1993–1995		1998–2002	
	Coeff.	t-value	Coeff.	t-value
R1: 0.00 < w/MW ≤ 0.50	0.670 ***	8.90	0.562 ***	5.90
R2: 0.50 < w/MW ≤ 1.00	0.441 ***	7.06	0.137	1.62
R4: 1.00 < w/MW ≤ 1.01	−0.248	−0.72	0.165	0.08
R5: 1.01 < w/MW ≤ 1.05	0.249 ***	3.55	0.075	0.14
R6: 1.05 < w/MW ≤ 1.10	0.200 ***	4.15	0.349	0.07
R7: 1.10 < w/MW ≤ 1.20	0.209 **	2.21	−0.089	0.36
R8: 1.20 < w/MW ≤ 1.30	0.218	0.29	0.200	1.22
R9: 1.30 < w/MW ≤ 1.50	0.136	0.79	0.293	1.48
R10: 1.50 < w/MW ≤ 2.00	0.194 ***	4.08	0.232	1.61
R11: 2.00 < w/MW ≤ 3.00	0.136 **	2.48	0.154	1.26
R12: 3.00 < w/MW ≤ 4.00	0.140 *	1.69	0.084	0.64
R13: 4.00 < w/MW ≤ 5.00	0.788	−0.32	0.033	0.39
R14: 5.00 < w/MW ≤ 6.00	0.153	0.45	0.056	0.26
R15: 6.00 < w/MW ≤ 8.00	0.778	−0.19	−0.009	0.09
R16: w/w/MW > 8.00	3.438	0.28	−0.054	−0.05
Observations	2446		36,998	—
Adj. R-squared	0.500		0.263	—

Notes:

1.) *, **, ***; statistically significant at the 10%, 5%, 1% levels.

2.) The Neumark model (Neumark, Schweitzer, and Wascher 2004) expressed by Equation (12.3) is used in the analyses.

3.) The dependent variables are the rate of change in the wage level between year t (policy enforced year) and year t_1 (pre-policy year, that is the year prior to year t).

4.) MW is the MW level in year t, w is the wage in year t_1. R1~R16 are the groups divided by the wage level in year t_1 (pre-policy period) compared to the MW level in year t (policy enforced period). w/MW is the proportion of the wage level in year t_1 to the MW level in year t. The group in which the wage level in year t_1 is more than 0 and less than one-half of the MW level in year t is $0.00 < w/MW \leq 0.50$. The reference group is the group whose wage in year t_1 is equal to the MW level in year t ($w/MW = 1.00$).

4.) Other independent variables included in the regression equations are a male dummy variable, years of schooling, years of experience, an occupation dummy variable, an industry dummy variable, a public-sector dummy variable, a regional dummy, a year dummy, the interactions of the regional dummy and the year dummy, the interactions of R1~16 and the w/MW dummy variables, and the interactions of R1~16 and the rate of change in the MW.

Sources: Calculations based on CHIP 1995, 2002, 2007, and 2013.

statistically significant for the lowest wage groups ($0 < w/MW \leq 0.05$) during the 1993–1995 and the 1998–2002 periods and for the low-wage groups ($0.5 < w/MW \leq 1$) during the 1993–1995 period. Moreover, the coefficient values are higher for the 1993–1995 period, indicating that the MW effect on the low-wage group is greater during the MW promulgation period than during the rest of the implementation period. These results are consistent with the results in Figure 12.2, based on the QR model.

Second, the estimated change coefficients on the MW variables are also statistically significant for groups with wages around the MW during 1993–1995. However, the estimated coefficients are not statistically significant for the middle- and high-wage groups (e.g., the groups with wages more than three times the MW in both the 1993–1995 and the 1998–2002 periods). These results demonstrate the existence of spillover effects for groups with wages around the MW during 1993–1995. However, the spillover effects are not visible for the middle-wage groups during 1998–2002.

12.6.3 Estimated Results of the Effects of the MW on the Wage Distribution by Using the DID Method

Although the estimation results in Tables 12.4 and Table 12.5 show the effects of the MW level and the MW level changes on the wage distributions, they do not control for heterogeneity between districts implementing the MW and districts not implementing the MW. Therefore, we utilize the DID method to evaluate the effects of the MW on the wage distribution after addressing the heterogeneity problems. The estimated coefficients of the DID variables are summarized in Table 12.6 (1), Table 12.6 (2), and Table 12.6 (3). The estimations use the two types of treatment-control groups shown in Table 12.6 (1)~(3) and expressed as Estimation 1 and Estimation 2.

First, from the use of information for two years (1994 and 1995), the results show that the coefficients for the DID variables are statistically significant for all percentile wage groups; however, in both estimations the values for the low-wage groups (the first and fifth percentiles in the wage distribution) are highest. This finding indicates that even though the MW affects the entire wage distribution, the MW effect is greatest for the low-wage groups during the promulgation period (1993–1995).

Table 12.6 (1). DID analysis results of the effects of the MW on the wage by percentile in the wage distributions (1993–1994)

Panel A: 1993–1994

	Estimation 1 (Beijing vs. Shanxi)		Estimation 2 (Beijing vs. Liaoning)	
	Coeff.	t-value	Coeff.	t-value
DID variables				
1%	0.462 *	1.74	1.000 ***	3.08
5%	0.392 **	2.53	0.422 ***	3.11
10%	0.249 ***	5.19	0.321 ***	3.72
20%	0.302 ***	8.35	0.286 ***	7.13
30%	0.312 ***	10.43	0.282 ***	9.70
40%	0.306 ***	11.83	0.280 ***	9.95
50%	0.309 ***	11.83	0.267 ***	10.68
60%	0.318 ***	11.83	0.266 ***	10.56
70%	0.323 ***	11.75	0.280 ***	11.27
80%	0.328 ***	10.98	0.287 ***	8.98
90%	0.358 ***	10.97	0.292 ***	8.20

Notes:

1.) The t-value measures the size of the difference relative to the variation in the sample data.

2.) The symbols *, **, and *** denote statistical significance at the 10%, 5%, and 1% levels.

3.) The results for the 1%~90 % percentiles in the wage distribution are estimated by using a quantile regression model.

4.) Other independent variables included in the regression equations are a male dummy variable, years of schooling, years of experience, an occupation dummy variable, an industry dummy variable, a public-sector dummy variable, a regional dummy, and a year dummy.

5.) DID items are the interactions of the year and the treatment-group dummy variables. The treatment group is the group in which the MW level has increased from year t_1 to year t; the control group is the group in which the MW level has not changed from year t_1 to year t (or has increased only a little) and that is closest to the target group's province or municipality (see Table 12.1).

Source: Calculations are based on CHIP 1995.

Table 12.6 (2). DID analysis results of the effects of the MW on the wage by percentile in the wage distributions (1999–2002)

Panel B (1): 1999–2000

	Estimation 1 (Beijing vs. Shanxi)		Estimation 2 (Gansu vs. Yunnan)	
	Coeff.	t-value	Coeff.	t-value
DID variables				
1%	0.011*	2.03	0.011	0.03
5%	0.029	0.25	0.029	0.25
10%	0.014	0.23	0.014	0.23
20%	0.006	0.12	0.006	0.12
30%	0.041	0.92	0.041	0.92
40%	−0.002	−0.04	−0.002	−0.04
50%	0.005	0.13	0.005	0.13
60%	0.021	0.58	0.021	0.58
70%	0.012	0.29	0.012	0.29
80%	0.025	0.55	0.025	0.55
90%	0.023	0.41	0.023	0.41

Panel B (2): 2000–2001

	Estimation 1 (Beijing vs. Shanxi)		Estimation 2 (Anhui vs. Hubei)	
	Coeff.	t-value	Coeff.	t-value
DID variables				
1%	0.453	1.34	0.258*	2.84
5%	0.022	0.20	0.059	0.55
10%	−0.036	−0.53	0.017	0.29
20%	0.001	0.02	0.007	0.15
30%	−0.023	−0.56	0.016	0.29
40%	−0.013	−0.30	0.043	0.85
50%	0.029	0.74	−0.001	−0.02
60%	0.008	0.20	−0.015	−0.42
70%	0.042	1.03	−0.008	−0.22
80%	0.011	0.25	0.008	0.17
90%	−0.002	−0.03	0.035	0.58

Panel B (3): 2001–2002

	Estimation 1 (Hubei vs. Henan)		Estimation 2 (Sichuan vs. Gansu)	
	Coeff.	t-value	Coeff.	t-value
DID variables				
1%	0.283*	2.69	0.077	0.27
5%	0.091	−0.08	0.029	0.32
10%	0.008	0.14	0.047	0.54
20%	0.032	0.70	−0.050	−0.70
30%	0.012	0.26	0.015	0.26
40%	0.015	0.39	0.009	0.17
50%	−0.007	−0.20	0.019	0.37
60%	0.025	0.72	−0.001	−0.02
70%	−0.023	−0.59	0.006	0.12
80%	−0.050	−1.33	0.034	0.69
90%	−0.045	−0.83	−0.026	−0.42

Notes: See Table 12.6 (1).

Sources: Calculations based on CHIP 2002.

Table 12.6 (3). DID analysis results of the effects of the MW on the wage by percentile in the wage distributions (2007–2013)

Panel C: 2007–2013

	Estimation 1 (Henan vs. Hubei)		Estimation 2 (Henan vs. Jiangsu)	
	Coeff.	t-value	Coeff.	t-value
DID variables				
1%	0.589	1.31	0.065	0.16
5%	0.343	1.34	0.689**	2.18
10%	0.180	1.45	0.550**	4.84
20%	−0.174**	−2.52	−0.536***	−9.66
30%	−0.145***	−2.71	−0.433***	−8.45
40%	−0.069	−1.34	−0.396***	−9.05
50%	−0.014	−0.30	−0.393***	−8.94
60%	0.022	0.44	−0.383***	−9.17
70%	0.084	1.66	−0.403***	−9.54
80%	0.050	0.99	−0.447***	−9.51
90%	0.040	0.56	−0.385***	−6.42

Notes: See Table 12.6 (1).

Sources: Calculations based on CHIP 2007 and 2013.

Second, for 1998–2002 the results are as follows: 1.) From the use of information for 1999 and 2000, the results show that although the coefficients for the DID variables are not statistically significant for groups with wages above the 5th percentile, they are positive and statistically significant at the 10 percent level for the lowest-wage group (the first percentile) in Estimation 1. The estimated coefficients of the DID variables are not statistically significant for any of the percentile wage groups in Estimation 2. 2.) For 2000 and 2001, the DID coefficients are not statistically significant for any percentile wage groups in Estimation 1. Although they are also not statistically significant for groups with wages above the 5th percentile, they are statistically significant at the 10 percent level for the lowest wage group (the 1st percentile) in Estimation 2. 3.) For 2001 and 2002, the results are similar to those for 1999–2000; the DID coefficients are positive and statistically significant at the 10 percent level for the lowest wage group (the 1st percentile). These results indicate that the effect of the MW on the lowest wage group was visible during the MW implementation period (1998–2002), consistent with the results from the Neumark model (see Table 12.5). However, there was no spillover effect during the implementation period.

Third, for 2007 and 2013 the results show positive and significant DID coefficients for the low-wage groups (the 5th and 10th percentiles) at the 5 percent level in Estimation 2. Moreover, the DID coefficients are negative and statistically significant for the 20th and 30th wage percentile groups at the 5 percent level in Estimation 1. These negatively affect the wage levels for all groups with wages above the 30th percentile at the 1 percent level in Estimation 2. When the heterogeneity problem is addressed for 2007–2013, the MW increases the wage levels for the low-wage groups and it decreases the wage levels for the middle- and high-wage groups during the enforcement period. These results indicate that over the long term, there may be a substitution effect between the low-wage group and the other groups, possibly because in a competitive market, if the wage levels for the low-wage group increase due to MW regulations, a firm will decrease the wages for the middle- and high-wage groups, employ fewer workers, or increase the work hours to maximize profits.

Fourth, in terms of the coefficients of the DID variables for the low-wage group during each period, the effect of the MW on the low-wage group is greater in 1993–1995 and 2007–2013 than it is in 1998–2002. It appears that government enforcement of the MW policy since 2004 has increased the effect of the MW on low-wage groups.

There are several possible reasons for these results. Specifically, during the 1993–1995 period the MW level changed from "0"—the change ranges are greater than those for the 1998–2002 period—therefore, the MW effect was greater in 1993–1995. Two reasons can explain the results for 2007–2013. First, on the basis of the 2004 MW regulations, the government enforced penalties for firms that violated the regulations. By improving MW compliance via penalties, the proportion of workers with wages below the MW level decreased and thus the effect of the MW on the low-wage group became significant. Second, the magnitude of the increase in MW levels has been larger since 2004, a factor that might have increased the effect of the MW on the low-wage groups.

Finally, several reasons may explain why the spillover effect of the MW is highest in the 1993–1995 period. As described previously, when the effect of the labor cost constraint hypothesis is less than that of the skill substitution hypothesis, the monopoly hypothesis, and the efficient wage hypothesis, the spillover effect will be visible. Compared to 1998–2002 and 2007–2013, in 1993–1995 the government had not yet carried out ownership reform of the public sector (e.g., the SOEs); therefore, the public sector constituted a greater proportion of the economy and thus had a relatively higher influence on the wage determination system. It is thought that the public sector is a monopoly sector in China; since the monopoly hypothesis had a larger effect than the labor cost constraint hypothesis during 1993–1995, the spillover effect appeared during this period. However, at the end of the 1990s the government carried out the SOE reforms, after which the influence of market mechanisms became greater, a factor that might have resulted in the influence of the labor cost constraint hypothesis to become greater than the other hypotheses, and therefore the spillover effect disappeared for 1998–2002 and 2007–2013. Moreover, the results indicate that in 2007–2013 most firms decreased the wage levels for the middle-wage-level groups to respond to increases in labor costs from the increase in the level of the MW in the higher ranges since 2004.

12.7 Conclusions

The Chinese government has been officially implementing a MW policy since 1993 and has enforced a nationwide MW policy since 2004. In theory, a MW policy is expected to contribute to increased incomes of the low-wage groups. Has implementation of the MW policy in China affected the wage distribution? Has the MW affected the wages of the low-wage groups? Is there a spillover effect from the MW in China?

To answer these questions, this study uses cross-sectional survey data from CHIP 1995, 2002, 2007, and 2013 and employs estimations of the OLS and QR models. We also construct panel datasets based on CHIP 1995 and CHIP 2002 to utilize the Neumark model and construct regional panel datasets to utilize the DID method. Several major conclusions emerge.

First, the effect of the MW on wages of the low-wage groups are as follows: 1.) The results of the OLS and QR models show that the MW affected both the average wage and the wages of the low-wage groups in 1993–1995, 1998–2002, and 2007–2013, with the greatest effect on the low-wage group in 1993–1995. 2.) The results from the use of the Neumark model indicate that the change in the MW level affected the wage-level changes for the low-wage group during 1993–1995 and 1998–2002, with the greatest effect during 1993–1995. 3.) The DID model results indicate that when the heterogeneity problems are addressed, the MW considerably affects the wage levels of the low-wage group during all three periods.

Second, the estimation results for the spillover effects of the MW on the wage distribution are as follows: 1.) The results of the OLS and QR models show that the MW levels positively affected the average wages and the middle- and high-wage groups during each period. 2.) The results from the use of the Neumark model show that the change in the MW also affected the wage-level changes for groups with wages above the MW level during 1993–1995. 3.) The DID results indicate that when the heterogeneity problems are addressed, the MW also affected the middle- and high-wage groups during 1993–1995, though the effect was higher for the high-wage group. All the estimation results indicate the presence of a spillover effect in 1993–1995, but no spillover was observed for 1998–2002 and 2007–2013.

On the basis of these empirical analyses, although we can conclude that implementation of the MW affected the increase in the wage level for the low-wage groups during the three periods, and the spillover effect existed during the MW promulgation period (1993–1995), three points are worthy of attention.

First, the results reveal that because the MW levels rose greatly at the beginning of 2004, the MW positively affected the wages for the low-wage group. Hence, an increase in the range of the MW level can be used as a method to reduce poverty problems among the working poor in urban

China. Of course, when assessing the total effects of the MW, one should simultaneously consider the effects of the MW on unemployment.

Second, the spillover effect was visible only during the promulgation period, and when the heterogeneity problems were addressed, the substitution effect occurred during the 2007–2013 period. These results indicate that the effects of a MW policy on reducing income inequalities is complex. The MW seems likely to increase the incomes of low-wage groups, while also hurting the incomes of middle-wage groups over the long term. It is thought that a firm may decrease the wage level of the middle-level wage group (particularly, the group with wages slightly more than the MW) to address the labor cost problem caused by the increase in the MW level. Even though the wage gap between the low-wage group and the middle-level wage group remains, the gap between the low-wage group and the high-wage group may become smaller due to implementation of the MW policy. When the wage gap between the middle-level wage group and the high-level wage group is expanded, income inequality may not become greater. To consider the various effects of the MW policy on the wage levels of the various wage groups, future detailed empirical studies on the effects of the MW policy by groups (for example, skilled and unskilled worker groups, high-, middle-, and low-education groups) should be undertaken.

Third, it may be that MW compliance affects how the MW influences the wage distribution. Because the MW compliance problem in the public sector differs from that in the private sector and a labor market exists in both these two sectors, future studies should conduct an analysis including sector segmentation. Finally, although some hypotheses from neoclassical economics can explain the spillover effect of the MW, we have not analyzed the influence of these hypotheses in this study. This issue can be addressed in future research.

Notes

Note: This research was supported by JSPS (Japan Society for the Promotion of Science) KAKENHI Grant Number JP16K03611 and the Joint Usage and Research Center Project, Institute of Economic Research, Hitotsubashi University. We are very grateful to Professor J. Knight, Professor T. Sicular, and Professor J. Yang for their helpful comments at the international workshop, "CHIP 2013 Workshop on the Income Distribution of China," May 7–8, 2016, Beijing Normal University.

1. It is generally accepted that a heterogeneity problem can occur in empirical studies, in which the estimated results may be different among various individuals or groups because of individual or group disparities. For example, the low-wage groups and the high-wage groups have distinctive characteristics (e.g., education or skill levels are lower among low-wage workers than among high-wage workers), and the effect of the MW on wage levels may therefore vary among the different wage-level groups.

2. For surveys on the effects of a MW on employment and wages, see Brown (1999); Card and Krueger (1995a); Machin and Manning (1997); Neumark and Wascher (2008); and Boeri and van Ours (2013). There is no consensus on the effects of a MW on employment. With respect to the employment effects of a MW, Brown, Curtis, and Andrew (1982) find a negative, significant but modest effect (from −1 percent to −3 percent). Using cross-section data, Deere, Murphy, and Welch (1995); Currie and Fallick (1996); Burkhauser, Couch, and Wittenburg (2000); and Neumark and Wascher (1992, 2000, 2004) produce results that are consistent with the standard model prediction of a negative employment effect. However, using panel data to conduct quasi-natural experiment studies, Card (1992a, 1992b); Katz and Krueger (1992); and Card and Krueger (1995a) reveal that there are no employment effects. For empirical studies on the effects of a MW on wage gaps and income inequality, see Card and Krueger (1995a) and DiNardo, Fortin, and Lemieux (1996) for the United States, and Robinson (2002, 2005) for the United Kingdom.

3. For an empirical study on the effects of a MW on gender wage gaps in urban China, see Li and Ma (2015).

4. $\rho_\theta(.)$ is a probability function for the different wage percentiles. When the wage is higher than θ percentage, ρ_θ is equal to 1; when the wage is lower than θ percentage, ρ_θ is equal to 0. The QR model is designed for an estimation using the optimal method, which minimizes the error terms in these two probability functions.

5. Specifically, CHIP 1995–2013 includes Beijing, Shanxi, Liaoning, Jiangsu, Anhui, Guangdong, Henan, Hubei, Sichuan, Yunnan, and Gansu in CHIP 1995; Beijing, Shanxi, Liaoning, Jiangsu, Anhui, Guangdong, Henan, Hubei, Sichuan, Chongqing, Yunnan, and Gansu in CHIP 2002; Beijing, Shanxi, Liaoning, Jiangsu, Anhui, Guangdong, Henan, Hubei, Sichuan, Chongqing, Yunnan, Gansu, Shanghai, Zhejiang, Fujian, and Hunan in CHIP 2007; and Beijing, Shanxi, Liaoning, Jiangsu, Anhui, Guangdong, Henan, Hubei, Sichuan, Chongqing, Yunnan, Gansu, Shandong, and Hunan in CHIP 2013.

6. We also utilized the mean values and the lowest values of the MW levels in a province or municipality to carry out these analyses, and the results are similar with those utilized with the highest MW levels. In this chapter we report only the estimated results by using the highest MW levels. The authors can be contacted for the other results.

7. The East region includes Beijing, Liaoning, Jiangsu, and Guangdong. The Central region includes Shanxi, Liaoning, Anhui, Henan, and Hubei; the West region includes Sichuan, Yunnan, and Gansu.

8. According to the Enterprise Minimum Wage Regulations published in 1993, the main content of the MW consists of total earnings from work (except for overtime subsidies, any job risk subsidies, and social security subsidies). We cannot distinguish

the detailed subsidy items in the CHIP survey data. We also conducted an analysis by using the basic wage. The results are similar to the results from using the total wage. Therefore, in this chapter we show the results from using the total wages.

9. We use the time-series nationwide urban consumer price index (CPI) data published by the NBS to convert to constant prices. Because we estimate the effects of the provincial MW level on the wage in a province and because the provincial-level CPI may influence both the MW level and the wages in a province, we did not apply the provincial-level urban CPIs for the various provinces,

10. We use the logarithm of the monthly wage as the explanatory variable for two reasons. First, the CHIP 2007 has only monthly wage information; therefore, we calculated the monthly wage by using the CHIP 1995, the CHIP 2002, and the CHIP 2013. Second, the MW level for a regular worker in each region is based on the monthly wage. The sample of workers who are urban residents in the CHIP is dominated by regular workers, so we use the corresponding logarithm of the monthly wage as the explanatory variable in the wage function.

11. Experience years = age−6−years of schooling.

12. It is equal to 1 if the individual is working in a government organization, a public organization (shiye danwei), or a state-owned enterprise; otherwise it is equal to 0.

13. It is equal to 1 if the individual is a blue-collar worker (such as a manual worker); otherwise it is equal to 0.

14. It is equal to 1 if the individual is working in the manufacturing industry; otherwise it is equal to 0.

15. For example, in the 2007–2013 dataset, because there are no provinces in which the MW level was not adjusted from 2007 to 2013, the treatment group is the group in which the increase rate of the MW $((MW_t - MW_{t-1})/MW_{t-1})$ is greatest from 2007 to 2013; the control group is the group in which the increase rate of the MW is smaller from 2007 to 2013 and for which the location is relatively close to the treatment group. Specifically, the increase rate of the MW is 2.99 in Henan (the control group), 0.58 in Hubei (treatment group 1), and 0.45 in Jiangsu (treatment group 2).

16. The low-skilled group includes those with a low level of education (the education level is no greater than senior high school) and unskilled manufacturing workers; the high-skilled group includes those with a high level of education, i.e., higher than senior high school, and managers, professional workers, and skilled manufacturing workers.

17. The public sector includes government organizations, public organizations (shiye danwei), and state-owned enterprises; the non-public sector includes all others.

18. Blue-collar workers include skilled manufacturing workers, unskilled manufacturing workers, clerk staff, and service workers; white-collar workers include managerial and professional workers (e.g., engineers, doctors, and lawyers).

19. In statistics, a kernel density estimation (KDE) is a nonparametric way to estimate the probability density function of a random variable. Let $(x, x_2, \ldots, x_n)$ be a univariate independent and identically distributed sample drawn from some distribution with an unknown density f. The shape of this function f is estimated. Its kernel density estimator is

$$\hat{f}_h(x) = \frac{1}{n}\sum_{i=1}^{n} K_h(x - x_i) = \frac{1}{nh}\sum_{i=1}^{n} K\left(\frac{x - x_i}{h}\right)$$

where K is the kernel—a non-negative function that integrates to one—and $h > 0$ is a smoothing parameter called the bandwidth. A kernel with subscript h is called the scaled kernel and is defined as $K_h(x) = \frac{1}{h}K(\frac{x}{h})$. Intuitively, one wants to choose as small an h that the data will allow.

References

Autor, D., A. Manning, and C. Smith (2010). "The Contribution of the Minimum Wage to U. S. Wage Inequality over Three Decades: A Reassessment." NBER Working Paper, no.16533.

Baker, M., D. Benjamin, and S. Stanger (1999). "The Highs and Lows of the Minimum Wage Effect: A Time-Series Cross-Section Study of the Canadian Law." *Journal of Labor Economics*, 17(2), 318–350.

Bhorat, H., R. Kanbur, and B. Stanwix (2014). "Estimating the Impact of Minimum Wages on Employment, Wage, and Non-Wage Benefits: The Case of Agriculture in South Africa." *American Journal of Agricultural Economics*, 96(5), 1402–1419.

Boeri, T. B. and J. C. van Ours (2013). "Minimum Wages," in T. B. Boeri and J. C. van Ours, eds., *The Economics of Imperfect Labor Markets*, 35–62. 2nd ed. Princeton, NJ: Princeton University Press.

Brown, C. (1999). "Minimum Wages, Employment, and the Distribution of Income," in O. C. Ashenfelder and D. Card, eds., *Handbook of Labor Economics, Vol. 3*, 2101-2163. Amsterdam: Elsevier.

Brown, C., G. Curtis, and K. Andrew (1982). "The Effect of the Minimum Wage on Employment and Unemployment." *Journal of Economic Literature*, 20(2), 487–528.

Burkhauser, R. V., K. A. Couch, and D. C. Wittenburg (2000). "A Reassessment of the New Economics of the Minimum Wage Literature with Monthly Data from the Current Population Survey." *Journal of Labor Economics*, 18(4), 653–681.

Card, D. (1992a). "Do Minimum Wages Reduce Employment? A Case Study of California, 1987-89." *Industrial and Labor Relations Review*, 46(1), 38–54.

Card, D. (1992b). "Using Regional Variation in Wages to Measure the Effects of the Federal Minimum Wage." *Industrial and Labor Relations Review*, 46(1), 22–37.

Card, D. and A. B. Krueger (1995a). *Myth and Measurement: The New Economics of the Minimum Wage*. Princeton, NJ: Princeton University Press.

Card, D. and A. B. Krueger (1995b). "Time-Series Minimum-Wage Studies: A Meta-analysis." *American Economic Review*, 85(2), 238–243.

Currie, J. and B. Fallick (1996). "The Minimum Wage and the Employment of Youth: Evidence from the NLSY (National Longitudinal Study of Youth)." *Journal of Human Resources*, 31(2), 404–428.

Deere, D., K. M. Murphy, and F. Welch (1995). "Employment and the 1990-1991 Minimum-Wage Hike." *American Economic Review*, 85(2), 232–237.

Di, J. and Q. Han (2015). "Zuidi gongzi biaozhun tisheng de shouru xiaoying yanjiu" (The income effects of a minimum wage increase). *Shuliang jingji jishu jingji yanjiu*, 32(7), 90–103.

DiNardo, J., N. M. Fortin, and T. Lemieux (1996). "Labor Market Institutions and the Distribution of Wages, 1973–1992: A Semiparametric Approach." *Econometrica*, 64(5), 1001–1044.

Dinkelman, T. and V. Ranchhod (2012). "Evidence on the Impact of Minimum Wage Laws in an Informal Sector: Domestic Workers in South Africa." *Journal of Development Economics*, 99(1), 27–45.

Gindling, T. H. and K. Terrell (2005). "The Effect of Minimum Wages on Actual Wages in Formal and Informal Sectors in Costa Rica." *World Development*, 33(11), 1905–1921.

Grossman, J. B. (1983). "The Impact of the Minimum Wage on Other Wages." *Journal of Human Resources*, 18(3), 359–378.

Hohberg, M. and J. Lay (2015). "The Impact of Minimum Wages on Informal and Formal Labor Market Outcomes: Evidence from Indonesia." *IZA Journal of Labor & Development*, 4(1), 1–25.

Jia, P. and S. Zhang (2013). "Zuidi gongzi biaozhun tisheng de yichu xiaoying" (Spillover effects of a minimum wage increase). *Tongji yanjiu*, 30(4), 37–41.

Katz, L. F. and A. B. Krueger (1992). "The Effect of the Minimum Wage on the Fast Food Industry." *Industrial and Labor Relations Review*, 46(1), 6–21.

Koenker, R. W. and G. J. Bassett (1978). "Regression Quantile." *Econometrica*, 46(1), 33–50.

Lee, D. S. (1999). "Wage Inequality in the United States during the 1980s: Rising Dispersion or Falling Minimum Wage?" *Quarterly Journal of Economics*, 114(3), 977–1023.

Li, S. and X. Ma (2015). "Impact of Minimum Wage on Gender Wage Gaps in Urban China." *IZA Journal of Labor and Development*, 4(1), 1–22.

Li, S., H. Sato, T. Sicular, eds. (2013). *Zhongguo shouru chaju biandong fenxi—Zhongguo shouru fenpei yanjiu IV* (Analysis of income inequality change in China— Research on income distribution in China IV). Beijing: Renmin chubanshe.

Li, S., T. Sicular, and B. Gustafsson, eds. (2008). *Zhongguo jumin shouru fenpei yanjiu III* (Research on income distribution in China III). Beijing: Beijing shifan daxue chubanshe.

Li, S. and J. Song (2013). "The Change of Gender Wage Gaps in Urban China," in S. Li, H. Sato, and T. Sicular, eds., *Zhongguo shouru chaju biandong fenxi—Zhongguo shouru fenpei yanjiu IV* (Analysis of income inequality change in China—Research on income distribution in China IV). Beijing: Renmin chubanshe.

Ma, S., J. Zhang, and X. Zhu (2012). "Zuidi gongzi dui Zhongguo jiuye he gongzi shuiping de yingxiang" (The effect of the minimum wage on average wage and employment). *Jingji yanjiu*, no. 5, 132–146.

Machin, S. and A. Manning (1997). "Minimum Wages and Economic Outcomes in Europe." *European Economic Review*, 41(3–5), 733–742.

Neumark, D. (2001). "The Employment Effects of Minimum Wages: Evidence from a Prespecified Research Design; The Employment Effects of Minimum Wages." *Industrial Relations*, 40(1), 121–144.

Neumark, D., W. Cunningham, and L. Siga (2006). "The Effects of the Minimum Wage in Brazil on the Distribution of Family Incomes: 1996-2001." *Journal of Development Economics*, 80(1), 136–159.

Neumark, D., M. Schweitzer, and W. Wascher (2004). "Minimum Wage Effects throughout the Wage Distribution." *Journal of Human Resources*, 39(2), 425–450.

Neumark, D. and W. Wascher (1992). "Employment Effects of Minimum and Subminimum Wages: Panel Data on State Minimum Wage Laws." *Industrial and Labor Relations Review*, 46(1), 55–81.

Neumark, D. and W. Wascher (2000). "Minimum Wages and Employment: A Case Study of the Fast-Food Industry in New Jersey and Pennsylvania; Comment." *American Economic Review,* 90(5), 1362–1396.

Neumark, D. and W. Wascher (2004). "Minimum Wages, Labor Market Institutions, and Youth Employment: A Cross-National Analysis." *Industrial and Labor Relations Review,* 57(2), 223–248.

Neumark, D. and W. L. Wascher (2008). *Minimum Wages.* Cambridge, MA: MIT Press.

Pettengill, J. S. (1981). "The Long-Run Impact of a Minimum Wage on Employment and the Wage Structure," in Minimum Wage Study Commission, ed., *Report of the Minimum Wage Study Commission, Vol. 6,* 63–104. Washington, DC: U.S. Government Printing Office.

Robinson, H. (2002). "Wrong Side of the Track? The Impact of the Minimum Wage on Gender Pay Gaps in Britain." *Oxford Bulletin of Economics and Statistics,* 64(5), 417–448.

Robinson, H. (2005). "Regional Evidence on the Effect of the National Minimum Wage on the Gender Pay Gap." *Regional Studies,* 39(7), 855–872.

Wang, X. and X. Tan (2014). "Minimum Wage Impact on Wages, Work Time, and Income Distribution of Migrant Workers." Presentation at the Workshop on "Reforming Minimum Wage and Labor Regulation Policy in Developing and Transition Economies." China Institute for Income Distribution, Beijing Normal University Business School, October 18–19, Beijing.

Xing, C. and J. Xu (2016). "Regional Variation of the Minimum Wages in China." *IZA Journal of Labor & Development,* 5 (1), 1-22.

Index